WHO IS A TRUE CHRISTIAN?

"No true Christian could vote for Donald Trump." "Real Christians are pro-life." "You can't be a Christian and support gay marriage." Assertive statements like these not only reflect growing religious polarization but also express the anxiety over religious identity that pervades modern American Christianity. To address this disquiet, conservative Christians have sought security and stability: whether by retrieving "historic Christian" doctrines, reconceptualizing their faith as a distinct culture, or reinforcing a political vision of what it means to be a follower of God in a corrupt world. The result is a concerted effort to "Make Christianity Great Again": a religious project predating the corresponding political effort to "Make America Great Again." Part intellectual history, part nuanced argument for change, this timely book explores why the question of what defines Christianity has become, over the last century, so damaging and vexatious – and how believers might conceive of it differently in the future.

David W. Congdon is Senior Editor at the University Press of Kansas and an instructor at the University of Dubuque Theological Seminary. He is the author of three previous books, including *The Mission of Demythologizing: Rudolf Bultmann's Dialectical Theology* (2015), which won the Rudolf Bultmann Prize in Hermeneutics from the Philipps University of Marburg, and the editor most recently of *Varieties of Christian Universalism: Exploring Four Views* (2023).

"In this work of exceptional erudition, David W. Congdon shows that Christian apologists from ancient times to the present have failed to acknowledge the historicity of their own constructions of Christianity. Although *Who Is a True Christian?* is primarily a work of intellectual history, it is also a vigorous critique of recent and contemporary Protestant and Catholic efforts to clarify the essence of the faith. Written in the grand tradition of Harvey Cox, Peter Berger, and Charles Taylor, this capacious and contentious book promises to enliven and instruct a generation's debates about the destiny of the Christian faith in the United States and beyond."

—David A. Hollinger, Preston Hotchkis Professor Emeritus, University of California, Berkeley

"In this ambitious intervention in the contemporary culture wars, David Congdon situates current debates in the context of a much longer contestation over the boundaries of orthodoxy. Disruptive and thought-provoking, *Who Is a True Christian?* offers an incisive critique of attempts to define what is true, 'historical,' and 'traditional' and calls instead for a transgressive Christianity—a dynamic conception of faith that is compatible with a commitment to pluralism."

—Kristin Kobes Du Mez, author of the *New York Times* bestselling *Jesus and John Wayne: How White Evangelicals Corrupted a Faith and Fractured a Nation*

"In this compelling challenge to any final answers, political or religious, David Congdon breathes life into a transgressive Christianity: the creativity of his relational, pluralist theology delivers a tour de force of prophetic polydoxy!"

—Catherine Keller, George T. Cobb Professor of Constructive Theology, Drew Theological School, author of *Facing Apocalypse: Climate, Democracy and Other Last Chances*

"Congdon's deeply erudite book is far more than merely another contribution to the debate over the meaning of Christianity that has raged particularly hot in the United States the last ten years. Rather than simply more heat, Congdon brings light. Rather than resolving the debate, Congdon grounds it historically and philosophically, sorting through prescriptivists and descriptivists, revealing what is at stake for all sorts of claimants to the term. And finally, rather than throwing up his hands at the intractability of the problem, Congdon offers a solution that both honors the concept of orthodoxy and preserves the vitality of heterodoxy. I hope it is read, and widely."

—Matthew Bowman, author of *Christian: The Politics of a Word in America*

"Combining learned historical insight with thoughtful ethical critique, Congdon has written a much-needed book for our time, as contests over the past and struggles for any future of "real" Christianity demand careful attention. Congdon offers a necessary and provocative history that historicizes debates about who gets to define the essence of "true" Christianity and reflects on the stakes involved."

—Jill Hicks-Keeton, Associate Professor of Religious Studies,
University of Oklahoma

"I welcome David Congdon's thoughtful, historically informed, and theologically astute reflections on the definition of Christianity. What the author calls the "militant nostalgia" of contemporary evangelicals is a construct devoted not merely to a redefinition of Christianity but rather to the imposition of a thoroughly modern vision of the faith. He identifies the myth of immutability and argues that the real divide in Christianity is not between liberalism and conservativism but between pluralism and fascism. *Who Is a True Christian?* calls, finally, for a "polydox" Christianity that eschews uniformity, one that "is constantly transgressing boundaries precisely as an expression of its internal norms." This is a very important and timely book."

—Randall Balmer, author of *Saving Faith: How American Christianity Can Reclaim Its Prophetic Voice*

"We are living through a time of historic disaffiliation from religious institutions and yet the battle to demarcate the boundaries of Christianity rages on as fiercely as ever. With characteristic insight and wide-ranging analytical breadth Congdon tackles the thorny questions of how we got here and how we might best move forward."

— Heath W. Carter, Associate Professor of American Christianity,
Princeton Theological Seminary

"Congdon's *Who Is a True Christian?* is both engaging and erudite. I applaud Congdon for bringing theology into the history of ideas in the compelling, historical narrative he spends much of the book crafting, and I am aware of very few scholars who are so adept at interdisciplinary work. As a survivor of authoritarian evangelicalism, I am especially impressed by Congdon's full-throated rejection of the notion that "pure" Christianity is innocent of harm and his well-reasoned argument that orthodoxy is inherently authoritarian and can only be maintained with the threat (and sometimes execution) of violence."

—Chrissy Stroop, Senior Correspondent, *Religion Dispatches*, and columnist, *openDemocracy*

"In *Who Is a True Christian?*, David Congdon tells the story of how twentieth-century American Christians have repeatedly sought and failed to define and defend a pristine "orthodox" or "historic" or "biblical" Christianity. In contrast to such efforts, Congdon offers his own challenging and inspiring vision of a supple Christianity consciously constructed around an inclusive norm of polydoxy."

—Matthew Thiessen, Associate Professor of Religious Studies, McMaster University

Nietzsche famously quipped, "There was only one true Christian, and he died at the cross." David Congdon's monumental investigation into the inventions and negotiations of "true Christianity" in the US draws out this indictment with great material force. Uncovering the antimodern anxieties, power plays, and polarizing effects that have animated historical and contemporary investments in the essence, identity, and boundaries of Christian faith, Congdon also gestures toward the deeper hope on the other side of Nietzsche's sentiment, as he opens the door toward a diverse and pluriform, "normatively transgressive Christianity."

—Hanna Reichel, Associate Professor of Reformed Theology, Princeton Theological Seminary

WHO IS A TRUE CHRISTIAN?

Contesting Religious Identity in American Culture

David W. Congdon

University Press of Kansas

CAMBRIDGE
UNIVERSITY PRESS

Shaftesbury Road, Cambridge CB2 8EA, United Kingdom

One Liberty Plaza, 20th Floor, New York, NY 10006, USA

477 Williamstown Road, Port Melbourne, VIC 3207, Australia

314–321, 3rd Floor, Plot 3, Splendor Forum, Jasola District Centre,
New Delhi – 110025, India

103 Penang Road, #05–06/07, Visioncrest Commercial, Singapore 238467

Cambridge University Press is part of Cambridge University Press & Assessment,
a department of the University of Cambridge.

We share the University's mission to contribute to society through the pursuit of
education, learning and research at the highest international levels of excellence.

www.cambridge.org
Information on this title: www.cambridge.org/9781009428996

DOI: 10.1017/9781009429047

© David W. Congdon 2024

First published 2024

Printed in the United Kingdom by TJ Books Limited, Padstow Cornwall

A catalogue record for this publication is available from the British Library

A Cataloging-in-Publication data record for this book is available from the Library of Congress

ISBN 978-1-009-42899-6 Hardback

For Lindsay

Do not say, "Why were the former days better than these?"
 For it is not from wisdom that you ask this.

Ecclesiastes 7:10

To prize traditionalism above all else in a church that began in revolution is to do a great violence to it. . . . Revolution, too, is a tradition that must be upheld.

Patricia Lockwood

What counts as "Christian" is always achieved, never given.

David A. Hollinger

For this reason, there is no need to persuade yourselves that Christ, who is neither here nor there, is more with us than with you, since he is in all of us, since we are all the church of Christ. . . . In sum, pray to God neither here nor there, neither with this nor with that sect, but instead, neglecting all ceremonies, pray to the Lord where he is, here in the temple of your heart, in the innermost depths of your soul and truth; for he is to be found there and not elsewhere.

Sebastian Franck

Contents

Contents

Preface

"Any real, true believer is going to be on your side in this election," Grace Community Church Pastor John MacArthur told President Donald Trump in 2020. According to MacArthur, the two also "talked a little bit about why, certainly from a biblical standpoint, Christians could not vote Democratic."[1] Statements such as these proliferate in our hyper-polarized, social media–driven society, but they are hardly new sentiments. However ill-informed and motivated by crass power politics MacArthur's claim may be, the attempt to define the boundaries of "true Christianity" and "authentic faith" in self-serving ways is one of the oldest practices in Christian history, though it took on a dramatic new significance in the modern era when individuals were increasingly empowered to define these boundaries for themselves in the absence of any church authority.

This book – part intellectual history, part theoretical proposal – analyzes the way traditionalist Christians (though what they mean by "tradition" is part of the story here) have sought to define more rigidly the boundaries of what counts as authentic Christian faith in reaction to what they perceive as the heterodox threats to the faith that characterize modernity.[2] Much like Michael Kammen's classic work *Mystic Chords of Memory: The Transformation of Tradition in American Culture*, this book "traces a longstanding dialogue, of sorts, between traditionalists and modernists," albeit in the context of the Christian tradition rather than the American tradition.[3] This work arose out of a threefold observation. First, the topic of how to define true Christianity has become increasingly important in recent decades as the major denominations and religious communities have declined in both membership and cultural power, while alternative beliefs and practices have proliferated with the rise of digital technology, social media, and the atomization of society. As American society became less institutionally and normatively Christian, it became more important for parachurch networks, local churches, and individuals to clarify what they took to be essential to the faith. Since the major denominations were too slow or too divided to respond to the changing religious landscape in the United States, theological declarations and statements of faith began to multiply in the second half of the twentieth century, as ad hoc alliances formed to oppose new cultural developments and advocate for specific religious beliefs and practices. The topic became especially potent with the dominance of the evangelical Christian Right over the Republican Party – a dominance that Donald Trump's candidacy for president only solidified while simultaneously forcing many to ask what defined a true evangelical, which was a question that was even more vexing in 2016 than it was in 1976, the so-called Year of the Evangelical.

Second, it became apparent to me that there had been an increasing shift among American Christians, and especially Protestants, toward defining Christianity in terms of the past. While Christianity has always fostered a traditionalism that looks backward, this tendency was amplified in reaction to the modern orientation toward the future with its relentless push for progress. Both Catholics and Protestants had their ways of shoring up the tradition in the face of modernity – the doctrines of "papal infallibility" (1870) and "biblical infallibility" (1881) being the two most prominent. But the interest in the ancient creeds and classical tradition had never been strong among Protestants, who associated these with Rome and pursued a biblical primitivism precisely to circumvent the historical development of Christianity. All of this changed in the twentieth century. The full story of how and why that happened is too complex to tell here, but the world wars, the ecumenical movement, and especially the Second Vatican Council all played decisive roles. Less well known is the way many American evangelicals, those typically most insistent on having the "Bible alone" as their norm, have also embraced this interest in "historic Christianity." Key early figures included Robert Webber and Thomas Oden, who laid the foundation in the 1970s. But the interest became widespread in the early twenty-first century. One of many reasons for this is due to the political coalition that evangelicals had formed with Roman Catholics in their joint struggle in the culture wars, as well as the reluctant recognition, especially in the wake of *Obergefell v. Hodges* (2015) – the Supreme Court decision that legalized same-gender marriage – that the Bible alone was insufficient as a political weapon in their apologetic efforts. Much more persuasive, at least superficially, was the Catholic argument that "traditional marriage" was the position of the church throughout history. For evangelical Protestants to embrace this argument required rethinking what grounded their account of normative, true Christianity.

Third, and particularly important for this book, I observed that the conservative efforts to respond to modernity with new (or renewed) accounts of authentic Christianity were part of a much longer effort that began with liberal Christians – referring to the diverse group of thinkers who sought to understand, beginning in the eighteenth century, what it might mean to be Christian under the conditions of modernity. Liberal theologians were on a quest for what they called the "essence of Christianity" – a term that had its origins in the work of traditionalists like Richard Hooker but later became so closely identified with liberal theology that conservatives tended to avoid it, even using it as a foil for their own projects. Much more fashionable for traditionalist Christians was the ancient term "rule of faith," which had a long pedigree that could be traced back to the second century. Other terms, like "historic Christianity" or the "historic, biblical faith," are often used as well. In each case, there is an effort to lay claim to history and tradition as the source of Christianity's norms. But to do so in modernity – and in response to modernity – is a fundamentally different appeal to the tradition than the same use of the rule of faith in, say, the medieval period. In modernity, both liberal and conservative Christians are engaged in a quest for the meaning of true Christianity, and recognizing each *as a quest* is important in understanding the source and significance of religious norms today.

While I only started writing this book toward the very end of 2020, amid the political turmoil that followed the presidential election, the book's origins lie much earlier – arguably at the very beginning of my academic career. My first two books were studies of Rudolf Bultmann, and the driving question that motivated me to pursue those studies in the first place was how to understand what holds Christianity together, if anything, across time.[4] Bultmann's entire project of demythologizing was an effort to address this question. He argued that Christianity is always in a process of being translated from one historical context to another. While he was dismissed as a liberal for doing so, my work showed that conservative Christians contradicted themselves on this point: they rejected translation across *history* as liberalism but embraced translation across *culture* as mission. Framed this way, I argued that those theologians who insist on a rigid adherence to tradition are effectively engaged in cultural imperialism – an imperialism of the past upon the present. Here, in a nutshell, was the germinal insight for the present study. My third book, *The God Who Saves*, got me in professional trouble for criticizing orthodoxy and arguing for what I called at that time "orthoheterodoxy," a paradoxical term that sought to make pluralism and difference internal to the meaning of orthodoxy – not simply in the historically banal sense in which we passively accept that all things change over time but in the normative sense that sees difference as an end in itself.

As I was moving toward ever greater pluralism, the theological academy around me was moving toward ever greater interest in the "tradition," though precisely what people meant by this tradition was a matter of some confusion and concern. After many high-profile theologians and Christian scholars abandoned Protestantism for the Roman Catholic Church and Eastern Orthodoxy, many theologians who remained Protestant often defended their decision by trying to demonstrate their adherence to the tradition, as if this was self-evidently the norm for true Christianity. The working assumption seemed to be that ecumenical agreement on "Nicene Christianity" ought to be the goal of all theological work. I was left uneasy by the entire discourse. Why is tradition normative? Whose tradition do we have in mind? What elements constitute the tradition and according to which interpretation? Over the course of several years, I engaged in a back-and-forth exchange with the biblical scholar R. W. L. Moberly in the pages of the *Journal of Theological Interpretation*, which I treat in detail in Chapter 5. The exchange, which revolved around the role that "the church" (which meaning of church?) ought to play in biblical interpretation, helped clarify my developing critique of the orthodox tradition.

While I often felt alone in my skepticism, that has changed in recent years. John Flett's book, *Apostolicity: The Ecumenical Question in World Christian Perspective*, for which I had the privilege of serving as the acquiring editor, posed a similar set of questions from a missiological perspective.[5] David Bentley Hart's book, *Tradition and Apocalypse: An Essay on the Future of Christian Belief*, came on the heels of his defense of Christian universalism and offered a withering rejoinder to those who appeal in facile fashion to the "tradition," as if this were a stable and self-evident concept.[6] Hart's book is the most sophisticated and historically honest attempt to clarify the essence of Christianity – he talks of the "essence" throughout, despite being a classically minded Eastern Orthodox theologian – since Stephen Sykes in 1984, and arguably since Ernst Troeltsch in 1903, offering an eschatological, even apophatic, interpretation that coheres well in many respects with my own approach, notwithstanding other differences.

I was finally compelled to write this book in the wake of the debates over whether those who voted for Trump were #FakeChristians, as they were called on social media. While the question of whether supporting a racist authoritarian regime disqualified one from being Christian was intriguing in itself (especially given the history of Christianity), it became more complex when ex-Christians and "exvangelicals"[7] criticized the #FakeChristian meme for trying to preserve Christian purity and supremacy by erasing the way Christians have been involved in many atrocities throughout history, often committing them in the name of Christ. This spawned a debate over whether Christianity is a theological category defined by normative principles or whether Christianity is a sociological category defined by what people who identify as Christian have done. The debate was complicated further still by the recognition that political conservatives have long been using the #FakeChristian label (or ones like it) against those who support the Democratic Party or abortion rights, as evidenced by MacArthur's quote above.

A more personal stimulus toward writing this book was the experience of seeing friends and colleagues fired from evangelical institutions of higher education for beliefs (e.g., affirming same-gender marriage or universal salvation) or practices (e.g., wearing a hijab in solidarity with Muslim women) that were deemed outside the bounds of true Christianity. Indeed, I experienced some of this myself, as I navigated my way out of American evangelicalism. The culture wars were a turning point in the quest for the rule of faith because they posed questions about the boundaries of Christian identity that had not been asked before and were not codified in any traditional doctrinal statement. The definition of evangelicalism used by the National Association of Evangelicals was intentionally broad, in part because evangelicalism had tended to be doctrinally minimalist in favor of a simple biblicism. The cultural and moral debates of the late twentieth century, and the growing awareness that conservatives were losing the culture war, prompted many to react by promulgating new statements of faith – everything from the Hartford Appeal for Theological Affirmation (1975) to the Manhattan Declaration (2009) to the Nashville Statement (2017), as well as many others that were required of local communities and organizations.

In 2003 (while I was a student there), Wheaton College replaced its 1979 Pledge, notable for its antiquated restrictions on dancing and faculty drinking, with a Community Covenant that defined "a distinctly Christian way of life" as involving "the sanctity of marriage between a man and woman" and "the God-given worth of human beings, from conception to death," statements that were not in previous versions of the code of conduct.[8] While the Pledge adopted "prudential rules" because "the Scriptures do not provide specific teaching regarding all social practices," the Community Covenant connected every line to a passage from scripture, making it clear that everything in it was essential to the true faith.[9] The Pledge was adopted before evangelicalism had consolidated around a commitment to antiabortion politics, which began to occur during the 1980 presidential campaign and only after the Religious Right mobilized in response to the Internal Revenue Service threatening the tax-exempt status of Bob Jones University for racial discrimination.[10] And it was long before conservatives in the late 1980s pushed for the legislation that became the Defense of Marriage Act, signed by President Clinton in 1996. The Community Covenant included both in 2003 as part of its vision of true Christianity – a vision that the college went to the Supreme Court to defend, achieving initial victory in *Wheaton College v. Burwell* (2014) and a lasting victory in *Wheaton College v. Azar* (2018).

My experience in American evangelicalism was the crucial impetus for pursuing this study of Christian identity formation – all scholarship is autobiography, as they say – but the story is not limited to the evangelicals. After leaving Wheaton College, I attended Princeton Theological Seminary, which remains the flagship institution for the mainline Presbyterian church. Much of the history of the Protestant quest for the rule of faith ends up running through the halls of Princeton Seminary, where many of the leading Protestant theologians engaged in an anxious effort to establish, preserve, or extend Christian influence on American society. The quest for the rule of faith was not merely an interest of the Old Princeton school of Charles Hodge and B. B. Warfield; it was also, and even more so, a driving concern of the so-called modernists who secured leadership of the seminary after the fundamentalist split in 1929 and who subsequently began to disavow modernism in favor of an ecumenical Christian (inter)nationalism. It was the modernists above all who set in motion the rise of interest in historic Christianity. Their efforts to reinforce the doctrinal, cultural, and political boundaries of authentic Christian faith laid a key part of the foundation on which the evangelicals later built their movement for societal dominance.

By and large, the story I tell takes place among the intellectual elite, and that is by design. For one thing, I am not equipped as a scholar to examine whether and how the modern quest for the essence filtered down into local communities and influenced the everyday lives of Christians. As interesting as that might be, it is irrelevant to my argument, since I am not telling a causal narrative. The purpose of this book is to map the quest, to trace the key movements, concepts, and discourses that have shaped both modern and antimodern Christianity. And much of this trendsetting and discourse-shaping activity has occurred primarily in the texts written by academic scholars and church leaders.

I called this work not only an intellectual history but also a theoretical proposal. There is no sense hiding my conviction that the conservative quest to establish the norms of Christian identity has been a disaster, one whose violent consequences we continue to see around us in frightening new forms. Historians are sometimes (baselessly) criticized for only telling us what people have done wrong in the past and not charting an alternative for the future. In an effort to forestall such responses, I have attempted, however unwisely, to do both. My proposal will likely not fall on receptive ears; the institutions of Christianity have too much invested in the idea of orthodoxy to abandon it now, especially as they face shrinking budgets and declining membership. But if anxious times could lead many to tighten the boundaries in the reckless, imprudent belief that this would protect them from future change, perhaps they can still unlearn these exclusionary habits and adopt a different way of being Christian in the world.

One can at least hope. That, at any rate, is an essential Christian value.

Acknowledgments

This book was written over the course of eighteen months in the middle of the COVID-19 pandemic. While the devastating loss of life and health remains a tragedy, the pandemic forced a remote work policy at the University of Kansas (KU) that made a regular writing schedule possible for me. My work as an acquisitions editor in the fields of political science, constitutional law, and religious studies provided some of the initial stimulus for this book. Jared Goldstein's *Real Americans: National Identity, Violence, and the Constitution* (Kansas, 2021) was particularly important in shaping my views. My thanks also to John Colman, Chelsea Ebin, Mark Graber, Nathaniel Green, Dana Lloyd, Ellen Messer-Davidow, Emily Pears, and Tisa Wenger for sharing their work and insights with me on questions of politics, religion, and identity.

I am forever grateful to the University of Kansas Libraries for sending me countless books, articles, and book chapters. My kids would joke about how often packages of books would arrive at our front door. I could not have written this book without the easy access to research materials that KU made possible.

I am grateful to Kait Dugan, the Director of the Center for Barth Studies, for her help with my research on Karl Barth. My thanks as well to the Wheaton College Special Collections for their assistance with the papers related to the Chicago Call. Andrew Chignell graciously responded to my questions regarding Wheaton College.

Throughout the writing of this book, I have had several dialogue partners who have read many or all of the chapters and offered invaluable feedback. James F. Kay has gone above and beyond in the years since he served on my dissertation committee. He was the first person I sent the materials that became this book, and his detailed feedback has been a gift to me. Annette Bourland Huizenga read the chapters and encouraged me to finish it quickly so we could use the book in the DMin course we have been coteaching at the University of Dubuque Theological Seminary. Having this goal in view from the start gave me an audience to target. Jason Bruner read most of the manuscript and gave me excellent notes and suggestions for improvement. His book, *Imagining Persecution: Why American Christians Believe There Is a Global War against Their Faith* (Rutgers, 2021), was an essential source and inspiration for Chapter 4. David Roberts read my chapters and even tested out some of my early material with people at his church. He helped keep me mindful of the constructive implications of my argument when I was tempted to focus only on the historical narrative. I am grateful also to Brach Jennings for reading my manuscript but even more so for hours of stimulating conversation over Zoom.

As with all of my work, W. Travis McMaken has been a constant dialogue partner, and many of the ideas developed here were first worked out in conversation with him.

Additional thanks and appreciation to Collin Cornell, Jacob L. Goodson, J. R. Daniel Kirk, Steven Nemes, Samuel L. Perry, Jonathan Rowlands, Isaac B. Sharp, Austin Steelman, Logan Williams, Stephen L. Young – for sharing your work, time, or ideas with me.

My thanks to Beatrice Rehl, my editor at Cambridge University Press, who has been exceptional in her handling of my project. I am thankful as well to the two anonymous readers of the manuscript, whose encouraging and thoughtful suggestions were very helpful in the revision process.

Finally, my mother, Harriet Congdon, read through my entire manuscript as I wrote it, and offered incisive thoughts in response. Many of the ideas in the conclusion were developed in long phone conversations with her, and I am eternally grateful for her support. Having her eyes on the work helped keep my writing from veering into overly academic territory.

I am thankful to Amy Fong and my two children for keeping me grounded and reminding me there is more to life than books.

My deepest appreciation to Lindsay Wegener for her loving partnership and support throughout the writing of this book. In gratitude I dedicate it to her.

Introduction

The Rule of Faith in an Age of Anxiety

"**S**HAME, SHAME ON THE TEN REPUBLICANS who joined with Speaker Nancy Pelosi and the Democrats in impeaching President Trump yesterday," wrote evangelist Franklin Graham in a post on Facebook a week after the January 6 insurrectionist storming of the United States Capitol. For Graham, breaking faith with Trump was to break faith with God. "It makes you wonder what the thirty pieces of silver were that Speaker Pelosi promised for this betrayal."[1] A year later, former Southern Baptist leader Russell Moore wrote a very different reflection on the insurrection attempt for *Christianity Today*. He commented on the juxtaposition of "a makeshift gallows constructed to threaten the murder of the vice president of the United States" and "a sign, held above that angry crowd, that read, 'Jesus Saves.'" The coexistence of these two images in the same riotous mob, he pointed out, was not an anomalous occurrence but reflective of a larger dynamic in American evangelicalism, and thus the images were "the sign not of a post-Christian culture but of a post-Christian Christianity, not of a secularizing society but of a paganizing church."[2]

These divergent evangelical interpretations of the religious politics surrounding the events of January 6 represent two sides of an ongoing contest over the boundaries of Christianity. For Graham, allegiance to the policies and values of the Trump administration represents a true faith committed to the tenets of the gospel as he understands it. For Moore, the same allegiance represents a "post-Christian Christianity," a Christianity that is paradoxically no longer Christian. Moore here uses the term "Christianity" as a sociological category referring to those who identify as Christian, while the adjective "Christian" is a normative category referring to those who are genuinely within the boundaries of the faith. What those precise boundaries are, however, and who gets to determine them, remains unclear, and that ambiguity is at the heart of the matter.

The situation of January 6 is only the starkest example of an increasingly acute problem – namely, how to clarify who is *truly* Christian in an age where differences proliferate at an even faster rate than (Gordon) Moore's law. The Trump presidency accelerated and exacerbated these differences. In 2015, for instance, Russell Moore wrote a piece in response to the Supreme Court's *Obergefell v. Hodges* decision to legalize same-gender marriage in which he defined true Christianity in terms of those who hold to "thousands of years of definition of the most foundational unit of society," which assumes that it makes sense to think of marriage as a transhistorical norm across vastly different historical periods and cultural contexts. In case readers might miss his point, Moore stated that marriage is "bound up with the gospel itself," so that one's position on this issue determines whether a person is inside or outside the circle of authentic faith. Christians, he claimed, "must embody a gospel marriage culture," here joining "gospel" and "marriage" into a single theological agglomerate that one either accepts or rejects *in toto*. Because American society has rejected this "gospel marriage culture," true Christians are "strangers and exiles in American culture."[3]

At the time Moore wrote this piece, the cultural battle lines were relatively clear: conservative Christians, primarily evangelicals, marched in relative lockstep in support of a cultural agenda defined at least publicly by abortion and marriage. A little more than a year later, however, Trump was in control of the party and new lines were being drawn, with new definitions of who was truly Christian and who was now apostate. While the rapidity with which these boundaries change may reflect our cultural moment, the questions themselves are very old – long predating the rise of the Christian Right.

Eighty years before the apocalyptic fervor of January 6, amid the global apocalyptic anxieties of the Second World War, C. S. Lewis delivered a series of broadcasts on the BBC on what he called "mere Christianity," a term he used to describe the ecumenical hallway connecting the various rooms that represent the different ecclesial traditions. For Lewis this "mereness" was fundamentally doctrinal in nature; it consisted in a set of beliefs to which all Christians must assent. This set of essential beliefs included the triune nature of God, the creation of human beings with free will, the human need for redemption, the incarnation of God's Son in Jesus Christ, and the universal moral law that God has established. Lewis's answer, however, was just one among many proposed during his generation. At the same time Lewis was giving these wartime broadcasts that eventually became *Mere Christianity*, Germans were beginning to debate Rudolf Bultmann's program of demythologizing, first proposed in 1941, which represented a starkly different approach to the essence of Christianity. Whereas Lewis emphasized doctrine, Bultmann emphasized the existential relationship between the individual and God that precedes not only doctrine but all rational and linguistic formulation. Instead of "mere Christianity" – a term that denotes an established religious community – Bultmann spoke of the "kerygma," which refers to something that is both historically and experientially prior to the explicit emergence of the Christian religion.

Lewis and Bultmann were such galvanizing and polarizing figures that they were often treated as virtuosos isolated from their larger historical context, but like today's scholars and preachers proclaiming what is or is not genuinely Christian, both were participating in a very old tradition in Christian theology: the tradition of defining the core of Christianity, the essence of the faith. In a way, this tradition is older than Christianity itself, going back to when the Jerusalem Council decided what status gentiles had within the nascent Jesus movement and what gentiles had to do in order to be included within the family of Abraham. Since then, every creed and confessional document, every reform movement, every church schism has been an effort to clarify precisely what is essential to Christian faith – though the rise of modernity, as future chapters will show, has irrevocably transformed this tradition.

In the early centuries of Christianity, the rule of faith (*regula fidei*) arose as a way of codifying the key points of belief that differentiated Christians from pagans, and over time theological elaboration on these points, combined with political factionalism, resulted in councils and creeds that differentiated the "orthodox" from those who were anathematized as heretics. While the definition of orthodoxy became increasingly complex over the centuries, resulting in more and more fractures and the suppression of movements that demurred from the dominant interpretation, the core tenets of the *regula fidei* remained intact as a fairly reliable summary of what we might call "basic Christianity."

All of that changed with the modern period (especially by the late seventeenth century), as new understandings of the world and new views about human knowing resulted in disputes about Christianity's normative doctrines and texts – indeed about the very notion of normativity itself. Philosophers and theologians across the spectrum embarked on a quest for the essence of Christianity. The result was the proliferation of diverse accounts of what defines a Christian. For some, this gave license to depart from the traditional *regula fidei*, or at least to interpret the rule in unprecedented ways. For others, modernity was a crisis that had to be managed. The rise of skeptical philosophies, scientific discoveries, and historical criticism led to a conservative reaction, a doubling down on the tradition in an effort to protect the faith from change.

Moments of social crisis – whether a divisive political crisis in the case of Graham and Moore, or a war in the case of Lewis and Bultmann, or the rise of Enlightenment science in the case of modern theology more generally – have a way of posing existential questions of identity. Who belongs? Who does not? Who is an ally and who is an enemy? What is truly important to me, and what is inessential?

The crisis of the COVID-19 pandemic is a case in point. As Trump and the Republican base made masks and vaccines a partisan issue, *First Things* editor R. R. Reno made the response to the pandemic a mark of religious identity. People concerned with following mask mandates and social distancing guidelines are those who follow the "false god" of trying to prolong "physical life," while the "true Christians" are those who manifest a calm indifference to illness and death. Reno writes, according to Jason Vickers, as if he is among the shrinking remnant, the "last Christians in America."[4] Similarly, Colorado Republican Congressional representative Lauren Boebert claimed in June 2022 that "the enemy" (meaning Satan) used the pandemic to get Christians to meet virtually rather than in-person, suggesting that true believers are those who resist public health mandates.[5]

While questions about religious identity have been a staple feature of religion in modernity, the explosion of this problem in the public consciousness has occurred at the same time that traditional narratives (e.g., Christian salvation history, American exceptionalism), categories (e.g., gender and sexual binaries), and organizations (e.g., mainline denominations, labor unions, political parties, public universities, arts and culture groups) have been weakened or come under attack, opening space for new understandings of individual and group identity. Questions about identity (who are we? what do we believe?) and boundaries (who belongs?) have become pressing for many people, especially as the institutions that used to provide the answers are increasingly no longer in a position to do so. If we use Avner Greif's definition of an institution as "a system of rules, beliefs, norms, and organizations that together generate a regularity of (social) behavior," then it makes sense that our current situation of institutional crisis would lead to a quest for clarifying and reinforcing the norms and beliefs that people perceive as being under threat or in need of recovery.[6]

The conservative movement, in both its religious and political manifestations, can be understood as the attempt to (re)construct the system of rules that represent its imagined institutional ideal.[7] The increased use of religious statements or declarations in recent decades may be seen in part as a response to the weakening of churches and other institutions as the source of religious identity and social norms. Conservative statements – such as the Hartford Appeal for Theological Affirmation (1975), the Manhattan Declaration (2009), and the Nashville Statement (2017) – are notable for the way they attempt to stake out new boundary markers of orthodoxy around issues about which traditional sources of religious identity, such as the classic confessions of faith, have little or nothing to say, including secularism, abortion, gender roles, sexual identity, and same-gender marriage. These declarations, and the myriad theological and political writings that support them, are efforts to graft such cultural issues onto the traditional rule of faith, in effect jury-rigging an expanded account of Christian orthodoxy in order to leverage the weight of Christian tradition against those deemed outside the bounds of authentic faith.

Operating within these efforts to renegotiate and reinforce the boundaries of Christian orthodoxy is the logic of whiteness and the theopolitics of purity that it demands. Of all the institutions facing crisis, white supremacy is arguably the fundamental institution within Western society, the glue holding the others together – but it is also the one that has come under most sustained attack. A key reason why abortion, gender, and sexuality are the center of conversation today is that, except for isolated pockets, religious leaders across the board acknowledge that white supremacy is morally indefensible as a narrative binding a community together. The philosopher Michael Monahan points out that "whiteness, as a category, demands clear boundaries and distinctions, and when those boundaries and distinctions become fuzzy or indeterminate, something is bound to give way. Either the boundary will shift or the challenge to that boundary will be removed."[8] To be sure, there have been and continue to be efforts to remove the challenges to white supremacy, but by and large religious communities have instead shifted the boundary to accommodate the public rejection of whiteness as an explicit governing norm. This shift does not mean that whiteness is not still integral to the entire structure. Whiteness functions precisely as an invisible norm, so that a person ends up "thinking whitely" while thinking, for instance, about the need to evangelize one's community in order to stem the tide of secularism and restore Christian America.[9] The constant anxiety over protecting true Christianity – along with related purities, such as true Americanism, true masculinity, and the like – makes sense once it is seen as a manifestation of the anxiety over racial purity, intellectually laundered through whatever new boundary is deemed culturally acceptable and institutionally usable for the purpose of defining authentic religious identity.

Rather than attempt to demonstrate that racial boundary-making is at play in each battleground over true Christianity, this study instead focuses on the underlying logic of orthodoxy itself: the idea that religious identity is true when it strictly upholds a tradition in unbroken continuity with the past. To be sure, Christian orthodoxy was bound up with racial purity from its origins in antisemitism, as John Gager, J. Kameron Carter, Jonathan Boyarin, Magda Teter, and others have documented.[10] That story, however important, is beyond the scope of the one I tell here. The aim of this work is to make sense of today's disputes over Protestant Christian identity by examining how the boundaries of Christianity have shifted in modernity, especially in recent decades, as conservatives have latched on to new or redefined marks of orthodoxy in an effort to counter modernity and protect their understanding of the truth.

The story of American Protestantism's right-wing turn – a story that is not limited to American evangelicalism but includes large swaths of mainline Protestantism as well – is one that still needs telling, and this book aims to fulfill part of that need. The primary purpose of this work is to redescribe our current disputes as a contest over the rule, essence, or identity (any term will suffice) of Christianity. Doing so enables us to see how popular religious discourse today regarding what "true Christians" should (or should not) believe and do is a continuation of a much older conversation about what constitutes the genuine rule of faith. Placing today's disputes in the context of that long history shows that Christianity, especially Protestant Christianity, has been struggling for centuries with an identity crisis. While it has roots in the Reformation, the crisis began in earnest with liberal theologians seeking to adjust to the challenges of the Enlightenment, continued with mainline Protestants grappling with modern historical research and new political institutions, and has reached a fever pitch in today's fractured and rapidly changing society.

The analysis of this crisis has been its own academic cottage industry for a long time. We can divide the conversation along three lines. The first line focuses on the normative question of how to define the group identity of Christianity, what theologians used to call the essence of Christianity. While theologians have been wrestling with this since the second century, Christians since the early Enlightenment have faced the problem under very different historical circumstances, in which choosing what to believe became a real possibility for the masses. The development of liberal democracy drove theologians to ask whether and how orthodoxy was compatible with a democratic society.[11] The normative problem became especially acute in the twentieth century, not only because of increasing divisions in the church but also because the world shrank through imperial conquest and technological advancements, forcing global religious diversity to become a pressing concern to those in the West. Responding to Adolf von Harnack's landmark lectures in 1899–1900 on the essence of Christianity, Ernst Troeltsch wrote a groundbreaking essay in 1903 on the idea of the Christian essence, showing the complexity and ambiguity of the concept. In what may seem self-evident today, Troeltsch recognized that what "for one person belongs in the development of the essence is for another a disruption of the continuity," and thus every conception of Christianity is "very strongly conditioned by personal attitudes to it in the present and by the consequent conception of its future."[12] Later scholars, like Hans Wagenhammer and Stephen Sykes, surveyed the history of how monastics, ministers, and theologians have developed their divergent views on the identity of Christianity, showing how disagreement is basic to elite discourse about Christianity, thus raising difficult questions about what it could mean to speak about Christian unity or continuity.[13] The concept of "identity" itself, as it is used today, is of recent vintage, originating in the postwar psychology of Erik Erikson, as Gerald Izenberg has documented.[14] "Identity" now does most of the work that "essence" did for earlier, mostly European generations of thinkers, and whereas essence-talk was largely restricted to the academic elite, identity-talk has become culturally ubiquitous in the West.

The second line of thought regarding the Christian identity crisis focuses on the broad historical conditions of this question and tends to be carried out by historians, philosophers, and theorists intent on understanding how we got into this position. Much of this literature is concerned with the question of modernity and how the Enlightenment has transformed what it means to have a religious identity. Critical theorists like Talal Asad, Saba Mahmood, and Gil Anidjar have argued that the rise of the nation-state in modernity has brought about a secularism that is not the absence of religion but rather the state's sovereign power to regulate what it considers true religion, a power governed by what Mahmood calls "the fundamental centrality of Christian norms, values, and sensibilities."[15] More recently, Jocelyne Cesari has shown that the adoption of the nation-state outside of the West brought with it the secular/religious distinction, but that the relation between religion and nation-state is much more complex than theorists have allowed.[16] Catholic and Anglo-Catholic scholars, such as Alasdair C. MacIntyre, John Milbank, and Brad S. Gregory, have constructed a very different declension narrative, in which modernity – whether the fault of pre-Reformation, Reformation, or later Enlightenment thinkers – brings about the loss of something considered essential, such as medieval metaphysics, natural law ethics, or a vision of society not defined by relativism and secularism.[17] Charles Taylor has left an especially imposing literature on this topic in *Sources of the Self* and *A Secular Age*, books that provide a genealogy of modernity's "immanent frame," characterized by what he calls the interior self's "buffered identity," referring to the boundary between the self and the other (including anything supernatural) that makes autonomous life possible.[18] Like Taylor, but in a way less prone to a declension narrative, Ethan Shagan explains in *The Birth of Modern Belief* how the very idea of belief changed in the wake of the Reformation, as Protestants transformed belief into something arduous and unbearable, in which "true believers … battle their unbelief and ultimately persevere against it."[19] By burdening people with the weight of belief, the authoritarian project of the Reformation eventually collapsed in on itself, giving rise to the modern account of belief as personal judgment or subjective opinion.

The third line of thought focuses on more recent historical developments in North America, especially mainline Protestantism and American evangelicalism. The literature here is too vast to summarize, but a central question animating much of the work in recent decades is to what extent amorphous movements like evangelicalism can be given a clear definition that demarcates in advance who does and does not belong. Complicating this question is the "observer-participant dilemma," referring to the danger that comes when historians of evangelicalism are also practicing evangelicals themselves.[20] The result has been a tendency toward definitions of evangelicalism that highlight what some want evangelicalism to be – an offshoot of orthodox Protestant Christianity defined by traditional doctrines and practices – as opposed to what it actually is, namely, an apocalyptic offshoot of American culture defined by networks of corporate influence and political power.[21] Compared to evangelicalism, mainline ecumenical Protestants have attracted far less attention, in part because they have been less ostentatious and were easily overlooked compared to the much more interesting and scandalous story of evangelicalism's meteoric rise. This has changed in recent years, as historians have begun to examine the role mainline, ecumenical Christians played in the transformation of American culture and politics.[22] Most notably for the purposes of this book, David Hollinger, in his recent work on *Christianity's American Fate*, explores the often parasitic relationship between the ecumenicals (his term for mainline Protestants) and evangelicals. He points out that evangelicalism "gained standing as a point-by-point response to the modernizing initiatives of ecumenicals," while mainline liberals "struggled to maintain and clarify their Christian identity," thus paving the way for liberalism's decline and conservatism's ascendancy.[23]

These three literatures tend not to talk to one another. One reason for this is that the modern evangelical and liberal Protestant movements have typically not been understood as *theological* efforts to propose novel definitions of the rule of faith or essence of Christianity. The historical literature certainly examines their theologies, but these theologies are treated in relative isolation from the longer history of modern theology in which they are embedded – a history that requires understanding how the social and philosophical conditions of modernity posed a challenge to Christianity. As different as the likes of Ernst Troeltsch, Charles Taylor, and Kristin Kobes Du Mez are, the present work integrates these literatures by looking at the Christian Right as *a reactionary contribution to the theological quest for the identity of Christianity*, one that defines this identity in terms of historic Christian culture.[24] In other words, the increasing efforts to establish a normative "historic Christianity" in the late twentieth century are not simply continuations of some unchanged Christian identity, but instead they are constructions of a Christian essence no less modern than the liberal counterparts against which they are reacting. Through its project of "militant nostalgia," the Christian Right anxiously seeks to make Christianity great again – and thereby make *America* great again – by enforcing a vision of church and society that reflects its imagined version of what Christianity was and so ought to be today.[25]

To better understand this dynamic, and the difficult questions regarding identity and boundary-making that they raise, I want to (re-) turn to the clearest example of this dilemma in recent years: the fallout from the evangelical support for Donald Trump in the 2016 US presidential election and the subsequent debate over whether we can call someone a "fake Christian."

THE PROBLEM OF EVANGELICAL GERRYMANDERING

"It's an overwhelming number," observed historian and activist Jemar Tisby, referring to what has become the most cited statistic in recent discussions of religion and politics.[26] According to exit polls analyzed by the Pew Research Center, 81 percent of self-identified white evangelicals voted for Donald Trump in the 2016 US presidential election – and again in 2020.[27] This partisan alignment of American evangelicals was right in line with, and even higher than, previous elections. Compared to the estimated 68 percent of evangelicals who voted for George W. Bush in 2000, the 78 percent for Bush in 2004, the 74 percent for John McCain in 2008, and the 78 percent for Mitt Romney in 2012, the numbers in 2016 reveal that Trump strengthened rather than disrupted the alliance between evangelicals and the Republican Party.[28]

The 2016 election numbers elicited a collective outcry for explanation. Trump of course had his gaggle of court evangelicals who flocked to his defense at every turn and championed his cause – witness Franklin Graham, Jerry Falwell Jr., and Eric Metaxas. But there were also prominent figures who criticized him, and the court evangelicals themselves demanded an explanation. How was it possible for the same voting bloc that claimed to represent "values voters," the "moral majority," and people who were purportedly "pro-life" – how could those same people vote en masse for a man who bragged about sexual assault and was openly and unapologetically racist and xenophobic? The hypocrisy was hardly new, but Trump's behavior was no longer cloaked in civil religious pieties and democratic rhetoric about American unity and progress. There was no disguising the dissonance. The evangelical allegiance to Trump revealed a stark double-standard and demanded a reckoning.

For those who identified as evangelical but were appalled by the support for Trump, the instinctive reaction was to deny that Trump supporters were true evangelicals. They were "fake Christians." Numerous posts on social media claimed that supporting Trump disqualified a person from being a Christian. The two were incompatible, like oil and water. The hashtag #FakeChristians was and remains a popular way to denounce evangelical Trump supporters by excluding them from the ranks of Christianity.[29] In December 2017, people pointed to a LifeWay Research poll that differentiated between evangel-ical self-identification and evangelical beliefs. According to their analysis, a quarter of Americans consider themselves evangelical, but less than half (45 percent) of those who self-identify as evangelical strongly agree with "core evangelical beliefs."[30] (More on those beliefs later.) The survey provided ample ammunition for those looking for a way to protect the evangelical label. Who are these Trump-supporting evangelicals? They must be those with weak or unorthodox beliefs, those who have diluted their faith in compromise with the secular world. One problem with that interpretation, however, were the survey data showing that the white evangelicals who were most supportive of Trump also attended church most regularly.[31]

Others took a slightly different tack. Recognizing that Trump sup-porters were sincere Christians supported by churches led by respected Christian ministers, they did not argue that these people were fake evangelicals but instead that they belonged to a fake evangelicalism. The movement as a whole, rather than individual actors, had gone astray. Evangelicalism had been hijacked by politics. The historian Thomas Kidd is the prime example of this tendency among public evangelical scholars. In his book, *Who Is an Evangelical? The History of a Movement in Crisis*, Kidd acknowledges that he is "a #NeverTrump evangelical" who believes "something has gone terribly wrong in much of white evangel-ical culture," though he remains "as committed as ever to historic evan-gelical beliefs and practices."[32] The contemporary "crisis of evangelicalism," he argues, began in the 1950s when white evangelicals began to align themselves with the Republican Party, beginning with Dwight Eisenhower. Evangelicalism was politicized, thus leading it astray toward the raw pursuit of political power. But this argument alone is not enough for Kidd, because taken at face value it would still call into question anyone's enduring commitment to evangelicalism today. Kidd does not merely want to call for a renewal of evangelicalism; he also seeks to defend people (like himself) who identify as evangelical. In addition to his historical argument, therefore, Kidd claims "there is a major gap between what much of evangelicalism entails in everyday practice and what evangelicalism appears to be in media coverage," and he criticizes pollsters and media outlets for ignoring this gap. Even if the public

image of evangelicalism has been conflated with white Republican politics, Kidd argues that "evangelicalism in practice remains an ethnically
and politically diverse movement" defined by its historic beliefs and
practices.[33]

But what are these "historic evangelical beliefs and practices"? Kidd
defines evangelicalism primarily in terms of the conversion experience
of being "born again," supported by ancillary beliefs in the authority of
the Bible as the Word of God and the significance of a personal relationship with Jesus Christ through the Holy Spirit.[34] Kidd's description thus
overlaps with David Bebbington's well-known four-point definition of
evangelicalism, often referred to as the Bebbington Quadrilateral: (1)
biblicism (the Bible as the infallible Word of God), (2) crucicentrism
(the atoning work of Christ on the cross); (3) conversionism (human
beings need to be born again to receive salvation); and (4) activism (faith
expresses itself in mission and service).[35] Kidd grants greater importance
to conversion than Bebbington, but overall there is a lot of similarity. The
National Association of Evangelicals uses the Quadrilateral to define
what makes someone an evangelical, and it forms the basis for the
LifeWay Research survey's "core evangelical beliefs."[36] Alan Jacobs, formerly Kidd's colleague at Baylor University before Kidd went to
Midwestern Baptist Theological Seminary in 2022, wrote an article on
the latter's book, elaborating on the historical analysis and offering his
own reflections. While acknowledging that "it would be difficult to do
much better" than Kidd's definition, Jacobs also points to Timothy
Larsen's five-point definition of evangelicalism, which Larsen says his
colleagues have dubbed the "Larsen Pentagon."[37] Larsen retains
Bebbington's points but adds theological orthodoxy and a historical
connection to the Great Awakenings as additional marks of
evangelicalism.

Appealing to "historic evangelical beliefs" isolated from the sociocultural context of those beliefs – what we might call *prescriptive*
evangelicalism – ends up doing a lot of rhetorical work. By defining
evangelicalism in terms of a handful of core doctrines, Kidd and others
can disavow those evangelicals they find distasteful by claiming their
beliefs and practices do not line up with "true evangelicalism."[38] The
prescribed theological beliefs articulated by the Bebbington

Quadrilateral and Larsen Pentagon are abstract, immeasurable qualities that one can redefine at a moment's notice in response to whatever or whoever the person wielding them finds problematic today. These definitions are "normative, not descriptive," and thus take historically contested concepts and render them "eternal and ahistorical," resulting in something "very useful for theological partisans who want to adjudicate who is or is not a 'real evangelical,'" but useless to anyone seeking to understand historical figures.[39] For instance, Larsen's first point in his definition states that an evangelical is an "orthodox Protestant," but orthodoxy is one of the most contested terms in Christian history. Even for those who accept that orthodoxy is definable and achievable within history – and I will dispute this in a later chapter – the term has no universally accepted meaning. Like the term "fundamentalist," which tends to mean, as Alvin Plantinga points out, that "stupid sumbitch whose theological opinions are considerably to the right of mine,"[40] the word "orthodox" generally means "a person whose theological opinions are admirable and correct." As the historian Timothy Gloege points out, the goalpost-shifting flexibility of these categories allows #NeverTrump evangelicals "to state (or strongly infer) that only unconverted, 'nominal,' evangelicals supported Trump," while Trump-supporting evangelicals use the same categories to argue that their #NeverTrump rivals were not truly converted to the faith, lacking in genuine faithfulness. Claiming that something as broad as holding the Bible to be authoritative counts as evangelical is like "a political scientist defining Republicans as 'those who take the Constitution seriously.'" Gloege insightfully names this practice of (re)defining formal theological labels to suit one's purposes "evangelical gerrymandering."[41]

But Kidd and other evangelical apologists are also able to claim that those who share those beliefs and practices, even if they have little to no voice within American evangelicalism, represent the diversity of the movement. By virtue of theological affinity alone, Black, Latinx, Asian (and Asian American), and Majority World Christians – all of whom tend to hold more conservative theological positions – are lumped under the label of "evangelical," so that evangelicalism now appears to be a global, multiethnic body of Christians who have far less connection to white American culture and Republican politics. Kristin Kobes Du Mez points out that defining evangelicalism in terms of theological convictions means that "racism necessarily diminishes as a defining feature of the movement" and "the significance of American nationalism to evangelical identity diminishes as well."[42] Theology allows evangelicals to "defin[e] away their embarrassing spiritual kin," while at the same time giving the evangelical brand an instant Diversity, Equity, and Inclusion makeover.[43] But just because white evangelicals want to include their BIPOC theological kin does not mean the feeling is mutual. As a 2015 LifeWay Research survey found, only 25 percent of African Americans who held all four points of evangelical belief identified themselves as evangelicals.[44]

As both tendencies (i.e., exclusion of the bad and inclusion of the good) attest, the biggest problem with theological definitions of evangelicalism – as well as Christianity more generally, or any other religious community – is the way they render the religion or movement under consideration essentially benign and inherently good. No Christian claims to believe a doctrine that is intrinsically and self-evidently harmful, and therefore any reference to toxic Christian behavior must be "fake Christianity," a departure from the goodness that characterizes "real religion." The reflexive association of "Christian" with "good" only serves to reinforce what Chrissy Stroop calls "Christian supremacism," which views Christianity as morally superior and perpetuates Christian privilege – the way white supremacism views white people as superior and perpetuates white privilege.[45] Given the way all text-based religions involve competing interpretations and often contradictory claims, Stroop rightly argues that "there is no such thing as a singular, timeless 'pure' form of any religion," and thus "we must accept that there are a wide variety of Christian communities with competing theological claims."[46] There is no Christianity; there are only *Christianities.*

Given the many problems with prescriptive accounts of evangelicalism, like those proposed by Bebbington, Kidd, and Larsen, scholars in the fields of history and sociology have sought alternative definitions of evangelicalism that are historically grounded and, in some cases, empirically testable. They are more interested in *descriptive*, rather than prescriptive, evangelicalism. As a rule, scholars begin from the conviction that "Christianity is what Christians do in the world," which shifts the discourse away from what adherents think Christianity *ought* to be and toward what Christianity *actually is* in the world.[47] A definition of a religious community must therefore attend to its cultural formation and historical development, as opposed to a purportedly timeless set of principles. Gloege identifies four criteria for such a definition, applicable to any movement:

1. It should indicate a historical starting point.
2. It should give some idea of why the movement emerged when and where it did.
3. It should identify some recognizable point of continuity.
4. It should accommodate change over time.[48]

By and large, theological definitions fail at all four, including even the third criterion, given the many disagreements over how to define basic theological terms. To his credit, Larsen addresses the first criterion in the second point of his Pentagon when he says that an evangelical "stands in the tradition of the global Christian networks arising from the eighteenth-century revival movements associated with John Wesley and George Whitefield."[49] But on its own this statement is a bit like defining a word in terms of its etymology. Locating the meaning of something in its point of origin alone falls prey to the genetic fallacy and gives very little guidance for understanding that term or movement today.

Gloege alternatively proposes defining evangelicalism as "the application of enlightenment ideas about self and society to Protestantism," which has the virtue of encompassing Larsen's point about the revivals, while also giving scholars a fixed point that makes sense of origin, continuity, and development.[50] Gloege's definition does not dismiss theology entirely, but he refocuses the attention away from the formal doctrinal categories and onto the material content of these doctrines and the sociohistorical context for their formation. Instead of a set of contested theological terms, he identifies a set of historically situated ideas about self and society shaped by the Enlightenment that Protestants embraced in their efforts to reform Christianity and influence society. Du Mez likewise argues that "evangelicalism must be seen as a cultural and political movement rather than as a community defined chiefly by its theology. Evangelical views on any given issue are facets of this larger cultural identity, and no number of Bible verses will dislodge the greater truths at the heart of it." Du Mez does not set culture and theology against each other but instead advises readers to "treat the interplay between the two as what ultimately defines evangelicalism."[51] Such nuanced historical claims may lack the checkbox-simplicity that pollsters and journalists crave, but they have the benefit of accuracy and the capacity to explain religious phenomena. Daniel Silliman takes a simple, empirical approach when he argues that evangelicalism should be understood as a discourse community defined by networks of trust and communication. In short, evangelicalism can be understood best by asking, "Who liked Billy Graham?"[52] Likewise, Anthea Butler puts the matter much more bluntly when she forcefully counters "the evangelical historians who claim that the 81 percent of evangelicals who voted for Donald Trump in 2016 aren't really evangelicals. THEY ARE. The historians just wish fervently that they weren't."[53]

PRESCRIPTIVISM AND DESCRIPTIVISM

The so-called crisis in American evangelicalism exposed by Donald Trump's presidency was in fact a crisis in our understanding of Christianity as such, one that is hardly unique to this moment in history. The controversy belongs to a much longer conversation regarding who is or is not a "true Christian," a conversation that arguably goes back to the very origins of the religion but took on special significance in the wake of the Protestant Reformation. Over the past 200 years, the issue has exploded as new faiths and new interpretations have proliferated, especially on the soil of the United States. The revivals mentioned by Larsen set in motion an unprecedented religious diversification that continues to reverberate. Today this religious pluralism, including Christian pluralism, is further complicated by stark binary and partisan divisions between liberal and conservative, similar to the way sectional divisions cleaved Christian denominations in the nineteenth-century lead-up to the Civil War. Can one be an evangelical and a social justice warrior? Can one be a Democrat and Roman Catholic? Can one follow Jesus and join the American military? Is a Mormon a Christian? Is Protestantism compatible with Pentecostalism? Questions like these have become part of the daily discourse as people wrestle with questions about identity, norms, and boundaries.

Two camps emerged in the evangelical crisis – one concerned with protecting the normative tradition and another concerned with respecting historical diversity and complexity. Borrowing from the "language wars" over English usage, we can describe these camps as prescriptivism and descriptivism. "A prescriptivist," according to Henry Hitchings, "dictates how people should speak and write, whereas a descriptivist avoids passing judgements and provides explanation and analysis."[54] Translated from linguistics to religion, the labels mean something like the following: a religious prescriptivist decides how people should believe and practice their faith, whereas a religious descriptivist explains and analyzes why people believe and practice what they do. Put another way, a religious prescriptivist defines *normative* religion, while a religious descriptivist examines *lived* religion. Ultimately, as David Foster Wallace explored in his essay on the "Usage Wars," the distinction between the two sides is a political one, reflecting the vexed relationship "between Authority and Democracy," between tradition and egalitarianism.[55] Just as democracy, as the will of the people, changes in its policy outcomes as the people change in their political views, so too descriptivism, whether linguistic or religious, means that the language or religion in question changes as the people who use that language alter their practices. In contrast to this, linguistic and religious prescriptivism seeks to preserve the authority and tradition of the "right" way to speak and believe, regardless of what the people are doing.

We can unpack these two positions further. The descriptivist camp argues that "Christianity" is whatever people who describe themselves as Christian do. This camp tends to be populated by journalists and historians, those who understand their role as faithfully recording the behavior of humans in all their peculiarity. Descriptivists may be practicing Christians themselves, but this fact is irrelevant to their work. Indeed, in many cases it would be detrimental to their work if their personal beliefs entered the picture in some way that obviously biased the analysis. In this sense, the descriptivist camp includes those scholars of religion or biblical studies who see themselves primarily as disinterested historians who parse the details of the texts and communities under investigation without regard for their authority and significance to people today. The early Christianity scholar Paula Fredriksen gave classic expression to this descriptive neutrality when she asked whether "a historically constituted Jesus or Paul – or Moses or David or Isaiah or Rabbi Akiva; or Mohammed, for that matter – [is] theologically usable for current communities." To which she replied: "I do not know. That is up to Christian, Jewish, and Muslim theologians. I speak here, again, only as a historian – and as only a historian."[56]

The prescriptivist camp argues instead that "Christianity" is defined by a set of norms regarding what constitutes authentic Christian faith. Christianity is not whatever Christians do but is instead a tradition of belief and practice that has norms and boundaries. A person can deviate from those norms and step outside those boundaries, in which case that person is no longer recognized as participating in the tradition. There are various ways of understanding this relationship between the individual believer and the normative tradition. Kevin Hector speaks of tradition as a process of mutual recognition, in which each person is recognized by others in a community as "going on in the same way" as those before, a phrase he takes from Robert Brandom.[57] Communal recognition aims to prevent the problem of assuming that one particular interpretation of the tradition is inherently normative, despite the fact there are other equally valid contenders – something Brandom calls the "gerrymandering problem."[58] This mutual recognition can develop over time as the tradition is mediated through successive generations and responds to new developments, but it is always possible for someone no longer to be recognizable as "going on in the same way," in which case such a person is outside the community and outside the tradition. Hector's is thus a sociohistorical account of prescriptivism that understands the norms as socially mediated and communally determined, rather than as hierarchically imposed from on top, or as given once and for all in some timelessly valid text.

However we understand these norms, and I will come back to these matters later, the point is that prescriptivism can take a variety of forms, and the purpose of this work is to critique some forms in favor of others. What all forms of prescriptivism hold in common is an interest not merely in what Christians *have* done but in what they *should* do. The focus of prescriptivists is on normative, rather than purely historical, Christianity. If descriptivists, to borrow Bruce Lincoln's terminology, analyze "truth-claims" and "regimes of truth," then prescriptivists speak of "truths" themselves, as understood by their religious community.[59] Prescriptivists tend to be theologians, philosophers, and religious leaders, those who see themselves tasked with the responsibility of clarifying the norms and boundaries of the tradition and, if necessary, guarding the tradition from distortion, corruption, or misunderstanding.

The divide between the two camps is not only political but also moral. The descriptivist objection to the prescriptivists is that the latter's normative definitions provide an easy way out of dealing with the violent, abusive, and unjust history of Christian practice. The prescriptivist, as I described above with respect to white evangelicalism, can simply point to the defining norms and claim, "Those people are not true Christians," or somewhat less fallaciously, "True Christianity does not support those actions." As Gloege put it so aptly, prescriptivism too often means "never having to say you're sorry."[60] Prescriptivists who use the norms in this way not only avoid any moral responsibility for the tradition, but they also effectively erase the experiences of those they do not like who believe themselves to be authentic representatives of the tradition. The #NeverTrump evangelical may call evangelical participants at a Trump rally "fake Christians," but those participants certainly think they are Christian, and they more than likely belong to a community that recognizes them as authentically embodying the faith. Denying their experience may be cathartic for the Trump critic, but such a move tries to solve a theological dilemma by committing a moral transgression – not unlike the way a researcher tries to reconcile contradictory data by simply falsifying the results.

The descriptivist challenge to prescriptivism has far-reaching consequences. Many Christians have used (and continue to use) prescriptivism to avoid the hard work of listening to those who have been marginalized and abused by Christians, only to have their stories dismissed because people can explain away what happened as the work of "bad apples" who apparently no longer represent what the religion stands for, as if what a religion "stands for" is so clear cut and self-evident. And the issue is not limited to infractions caused by individuals. History is littered with the radioactive waste of systemic injustices instigated, sustained, and defended by religious piety, including among other things the enslavement and genocide of nonwhite, non-European people, the subjugation of women, and the suppression of LGBTQ persons and experiences. It is impossible to construe such actions as the work of "fake Christians," as if only the abolitionists were really Christian. (Moreover, this alone would hardly get Christianity out of trouble, since those same abolitionists were often misogynistic or opposed to desegregation and miscegenation.) The attempt to justify those harmful and violent actions by appealing to the change in Christian consensus later, as if future progress retroactively absolves the past of any complicity, is yet another effort to escape reckoning with the damage caused by the Christian tradition – not merely in its misuse but precisely in its proper, intended use.[61] The prescriptivists have much to answer for, and the work to be done is vast in scope.

It is important to note that the descriptivists have also not escaped critique. Some academics have focused their critical perspective on descriptivist scholars of religion, arguing that their purportedly neutral categories smuggle in prescriptivist norms of their own. Anthropologist Susan Harding points out that the modern concept of religion "is as much prescriptive as it is descriptive" in the way it centers theological beliefs and views politics as secular and therefore external to religious practice. According to Harding, this notion of religion is a "gerrymandered concept" that "polices the boundary of what counts as legitimate religion," viewing certain kinds of religious politicking as authentic and acceptable, while rejecting others as unacceptable.[62] In other words, gerrymandering is not a problem only for evangelical prescriptivists. L. Benjamin Rolsky goes further and criticizes the way journalists, historians, and sociologists of American religion have analyzed conservative Protestantism through the narrative of the "rise of the Christian Right," a narrative that says more about the interpreters than it does about the people being interpreted. In talking about conservative Protestants in essentialist terms as a unified "New Christian Right," scholars and journalists "have been responsible for producing the very subjects that they are seeking to understand and in some ways discredit." Rolsky implies that a more genuinely descriptive approach would drop the label of "new" and recognize that people are less ideologically unified than journalists would have us believe.[63] The lesson for prescriptivists is to be forthright about one's norms and not assume any account of prescriptive faith to be self-evident or universally held, much less hide norms under the veneer of descriptive objectivity. Scholars who are also practicing Christians have to be rigorous in carefully delineating when they are speaking descriptively and when they are speaking prescriptively, lest they accidentally confuse the two and run the risk of unwittingly promoting Christian supremacy.[64]

Despite the dangers associated with it, we cannot abandon prescriptivism – nor should we want to. If all we had was descriptivism we would have no grounds for hope, no means by which to steer religion in a more just and peaceful direction. Without prescriptivism, Frederick Douglass would be unable to declare his condemnation of "slaveholding religion" in the appendix to his 1845 *Narrative of the Life of Frederick Douglass*: "Between the Christianity of this land, and the Christianity of Christ, I recognize the widest possible difference – so wide, that to receive the one as good, pure, and holy, is of necessity to reject the other as bad, corrupt, and wicked. ... Indeed, I can see no reason, but the most deceitful one, for calling the religion of this land Christianity." If Douglass were speaking descriptively, his statement would be both false and dangerous. His talk about "the pure, peaceable, and impartial Christianity of Christ" could be used to ignore how Christianity, particularly in the United States, became an enslaving religion. But Douglass is speaking prescriptively, in terms of what is *normative* in Christian faith, and these norms allow him to condemn the "Christianity of this land" as a fraudulent misnomer.[65] We need norms if we are going to create a liberating future. Boundaries are already implied when we speak about injustice. We can neither belong to a tradition nor modify the tradition in emancipatory ways without having some account of what is prescribed. The question is not whether to have a normative Christianity but rather what these norms ought to be and how to interpret them. Articulating those norms – what we might call the rule of faith or the essence of Christianity – does not have to mean believing that they and they alone represent "true Christianity." By expressing the norms and making them public, we open up a discursive space to discuss, analyze, and interrogate them – and perhaps to discard them altogether in search for new norms that hold more promise for the future.

We also need to think differently about norms themselves. For prescriptive Christianity to avoid causing further damage, it must relinquish the assumption that any norms worthy of the name must be held universally and remain immutable over time. Much of the defensiveness associated with prescriptive Christianity stems from this presupposition. If the norms are seen as timelessly valid, then Christianity is directly identical with its present norms and any attack on those norms is an attack on Christianity itself. It becomes necessary for many at that point to deflect criticism about the harmful consequences of Christianity, or else risk having the entire faith collapse like a house of cards. An extreme example of this is the Protestant evangelical who identifies Christianity with the norm of biblical inerrancy and finds their faith in ruins after encountering historical-critical scholarship. Those who have abandoned evangelicalism often speak about "deconstructing" their faith – a metaphor that indicates how tightly connected the faith was to the set of norms that were prescribed for them. But the need to rethink what normativity means in Christianity is hardly unique to those leaving evangelicalism; it is a task for any Christian who seeks to make their norms accountable to the weight of historical trauma.

Many Christians, however, including many evangelicals, have not felt the moral weight of the past or the need to rethink what it means to adhere to a normative, prescriptive Christianity. Indeed, they have felt just the opposite. For them, the very cultural changes that have, among other things, brought these historical injustices and inequities to light pose a threat to Christianity and demand the fortification of its norms. Prescriptivism has become more than a way to ensure the continuity of tradition; now it often serves to recover and reinforce a lost cultural identity. Prescriptivism, for many, has become a way to *make Christianity great again*.

CHRISTIAN PRESCRIPTIVISM IN AN AGE OF ANXIETY

The Anglo-American poet W. H. Auden (1907–1973) is known for his Pulitzer Prize–winning long poem, *The Age of Anxiety*. Written in the waning months of the Second World War, the work is a drama starring four characters dealing with the anxieties of wartime and a rapidly changing world. Over the course of a long night of drinking and sex, they wrestle with these anxieties – the horror of necessity and the boredom of freedom – before being "reclaimed by the actual world" and forced to face "another long day of servitude to wilful authority and blind accident."[66] This was hardly the first or the last time Auden explored the anxieties provoked by the modern world. He concluded his earlier Christmas oratorio, "For the Time Being," with a chorus to the Christ child that tells the audience: "Seek Him in the Kingdom of Anxiety."[67] An earlier chorus in the same poem hymned Caesar as the great conqueror of seven kingdoms, those being the kingdoms of Abstract Idea, Natural Cause, Infinite Number, Credit Exchange, Inorganic Giants, Organic Dwarfs, and Popular Soul – these referring, respectively, to philosophy, natural science, mathematics, economics, industry, pharmaceuticals, and propaganda. Christ is here praised as the one who overcomes the ills of modernity and brings us "to a great city that has expected your return for years."[68]

Arguably Auden's most powerful articulation of the relation between religion and modern society is the 1954 poem, "Horae Canonicae," structured around the canonical hours of the divine office. The section on "Vespers" is a prose poem exploring the tension between two impulses in modernity: the one seeking a return to Eden, the other pining for New Jerusalem. This is the conflict between arcadia and utopia, between restoration and advancement, between conservatism and progressivism. The speaker, who expresses nostalgia for an Edenic past, eventually comes to realize that both he and his utopian counterpart have a shared point of contact. Both visions of society depend on a "victim," a blood sacrifice "on whose immolation (call him Abel, Remus, whom you will, it is one Sin Offering) arcadias, utopias, our dear old bag of a democracy are alike founded: / For without a cement of blood (it must be human, it must be innocent) no secular wall will safely stand."[69]

Auden gives voice here to those – encompassing everyone from sophisticated Christian humanists to the most authoritarian Christian theonomists, including evangelical Reconstructionists and Catholic integralists – who believe that society, at least any society worthy of the name, depends on the foundation of religion. Like most Euro-Americans,

Auden has been so thoroughly shaped by the idea and practice of Christian culture that he cannot imagine a society that does not have its basis in religion, and central to the anxiety he diagnoses in his poetry stems from the apparent loss of this religious ground. The war is symbolic and illustrative of the ideological and cultural conflict between modern secularity and the premodern synthesis of church and empire. It is this cultural war between secularism and what we might call cultural theocracy – whether in the soft form that privileges religious liberty over civil rights or in the hard form of religious dominionism and religious nationalism – that come to expression in Auden's poetry. Secularism brings with it the "Kingdom of Anxiety," along with the other kingdoms of science, technology, and mass media propaganda (i.e., "fake news") – kingdoms that cannot safely stand because they lack the religious "cement" to hold them together. For those who share Auden's anxiety about modernity, the only solution is to make religion normative for society.

Apparently, any religion is better than no religion at all. While "Horae Canonicae," like Auden's other work, is suffused with Christian symbolism and references, the specific line in question suggests that any mythic act of redemptive violence will suffice, whether Abel at the hands of Cain or Remus at the hands of Romulus, though the qualification "it must be human" evokes Anselm of Canterbury's argument in *Cur Deus homo* for why God had to become human in Christ. The indifference to which myth or religion people adhere brings into relief the importance of violence – the belief that a "cement of blood" from an innocent person is what society requires. Nature is "red in tooth and claw," as Alfred Lord Tennyson put it, and apparently only a shared scapegoat can assuage humanity's bloodthirsty tendencies and provide the ground for human coexistence. With chilling candor, Auden articulates the underlying conviction of those who lament the loss of Christian civilization and the end of medieval Christendom. Given the violent logic at the heart of Christendom, it is no surprise that cultural theocratists would not blanch at imposing the normativity of religion upon modern society, no matter how at odds with democratic pluralism that may be.

Auden is just one voice among many, albeit an especially eloquent one. Like many of his wartime contemporaries, including C. S. Lewis, Owen

Barfield, Jacques Maritain, and T. S. Eliot, Auden was deeply concerned about the loss of the mythical imagination and its replacement by a cold, modern, technocratic liberalism. More conservative voices in the early twentieth century, like J. Gresham Machen (1881–1937), who taught at Princeton Theological Seminary before founding Westminster Theological Seminary, were less culturally omnivorous and mythically universalist in their thinking. For them, a mythopoeic classical theism was woefully inadequate; it was either their sectarian brand of Christian orthodoxy or the highway – specifically the highway to hell and damnation. Machen and other fundamentalist culture warriors were not willing to embrace Abel or Remus as effective blood sacrifices. It had to be Jesus, and it had to be interpreted according to the dictates of Westminster Calvinism. But while the content of the religion in question was quite different, the overall atmosphere of conflict between religion and modernity remained consistent across these theological and ecclesial divides. Machen and the fundamentalist Presbyterians who announced their five "essential doctrines" in 1910 – as well as those associated with the publication of *The Fundamentals: A Testimony to the Truth* (1910–1915) – have attracted a significant amount of attention from historians for laying the groundwork for postwar evangelicalism and the fusionist political alliance that formed what is often called the New Christian Right. But their "revolt against modernity," as historian Richard Hofstadter famously described the anti-intellectualism of Machen, Billy Sunday, Carl McIntire, and William Jennings Bryan, was only one piece of a much larger revolt that involved even those so-called modernists that Machen rejected as godless liberals.[70]

The wartime anxiety experienced by Auden and others of his generation was part of a long cycle of reactions to the changes wrought by the scientific, philosophical, and industrial revolutions that characterized the modern period. In the generations before Auden, similar anxieties produced analogous reactions and feverish attempts to restore order and security both to the body and body politic. As the literature scholar Justine Murison has argued in her work on anxiety in the nineteenth century, "nervousness characterized the basic psychological assumption of the century." People at the time understood both body and mind to be "shaped by the social and physical environment" and thus "vulnerable to the political climate and the social world." Anxiety was both "somatic and cultural, or, more accurately, somatic *because* cultural." The cultural changes creating this anxiety, according to Murison, included growing urbanization, new technology, Jacksonian democracy, and the increasingly tense relations between genders, races, and classes. People were anxious to protect the soul from social disease, and that meant restoring the cultural order that they considered to be healthy.[71]

In addition to (and closely connected with) the sociopolitical sources of anxiety, Christian ministers and theologians were concerned about the threats posed by historical challenges to the trustworthiness of the Bible and church doctrine. Princeton Theological Seminary professors Archibald A. Hodge (1823–1886) and Benjamin B. Warfield (1851–1921) articulated the modern doctrine of biblical infallibility in an 1881 issue of the *Presbyterian Review*, in which they defended infallibility against "modern criticism" in light of apparent conflicts "with the present teachings of science, with facts of history, or with other statements of the sacred books themselves."[72] But it was more than an effort to secure the Bible in the face of new scientific discoveries. They also understood biblical revelation to include moral and spiritual truths that have held sway "over the noblest men, and over nations and races for centuries," suggesting that the loss of biblical authority would result in moral anarchy.[73]

Indeed, the immediately following article in the *Presbyterian Review* was titled, "The Prevalent Confusion; and, the Attitude of Christian Faith," written by Ransom Bethune Welch (1824–1890), a professor of theology at Auburn Theological Seminary and previously professor at Union College in New York.[74] After reviewing the tenets of orthodoxy, including the "paramount and essential doctrine of Scripture," Welch launched into the following list of the manifest social disorders and anxieties of the time: "anarchy, which reigns supreme in Church and State and social life"; "a tidal wave" of social changes; "widely diffused infidelity"; "a chaos of plans, nostrums, and watch-cries" in the political world; "strife between labor and capital" leading to "open and bitter hostility"; and a general "restlessness." All of this "social, civil, and moral" confusion, Welch says, raises the question "whether Christian Faith has lost or is losing its regulative power."[75] Welch then diagnoses the causes of this confusion. These include immigration and the growing "inter-communication" among culturally diverse people, the advancements of natural science (what he calls "physicalism"), the "emasculation" of morality due to the rise of unbelief and secularism, rapidly growing skepticism, and the spread of socialism and communism. This loss of social harmony and civil order "teems with Communism and Socialism, and matures at last in Nihilism."[76] If any of this sounds familiar, it is because these same anxieties and their proposed sources were repeated constantly in subsequent decades by conservative Christians nervous about cultural changes.

Welch's solution to this social confusion is also familiar – namely, the restoration of the infallible scriptures as the basis not only for true religion, but also for a properly ordered society. In an impassioned appeal for what we might call hyper-prescriptivism, Welch argues that the world needs "the true, true Christian faith, true science, reason, conscience, true religion. These will prove regulative. Thus shall we move toward order, instead of confusion."[77] He goes on to explain that this "true, true Christian faith" ought to have social dominance. True Christianity, he claims, will "win and conquer" society through "its overcoming power" and by demonstrating "its right to supremacy." Christian supremacy, according to Welch, goes hand in hand with "the progress of civilization" and brings about "law and order." Making the case for more missionary activity, Welch says that the Christian faith invites people to observe "the steady conquests of Christianity" and to observe Christianity's "permanent hold upon the civilized world, the more vigorous as the more civilized." With triumphalist optimism, he declares that "Christian civilization is everywhere advancing."[78] The theocratic imperialism evinced in this essay was not an accident. In a piece written in 1873, Welch declared that God's word establishes the "theocracy of mind," referring to morality and social order, corresponding to the "theocracy of matter" that God already has over the cosmos.[79] For Welch it was incumbent upon committed Christians to take control of the wider culture and conquer the world in the name of Christ. It would be hard to conceive a more brazen call for Christian nationalism and Christian supremacy.

Welch's piece, and its juxtaposition with the famous article on biblical inspiration, is instructive for the way it highlights the connection between theological prescriptivism and social prescriptivism: true Christianity is often wed to a vision of the proper society. As Welch put it so clearly, the more Christian a society is, the more civilized. Welch was hardly unique for his time. In 1899, the Moderator of the General Assembly of the Presbyterian Church, Wallace Radcliffe (1842–1930), published a piece in *The Assembly Herald*, the mouthpiece of the General Assembly to the whole denomination, entitled "Presbyterian Imperialism." Radcliffe was here writing in response to the imperial conquest of the Philippines by the United States, an event that he saw as a great opportunity for the church. According to Radcliffe, "imperialism is in the air" but now has "better intentions," because under American leadership "it is imperialism, not for domination, but for civilization." Radcliffe is anxious about the waning power and energy of the church. He is concerned that Christians have become lax in their missionary endeavors. He criticizes Presbyterians for not being more imperialistic, even though "Presbyterianism is imperial in its history and spirit," and suggests that the church ought to imitate the nation "if Presbyterianism is to enter into its imperial inheritance." The nation, he claims, is fulfilling God's mission more faithfully than the church. For this reason, "the Church must go where America goes." If it does, then it will fulfill its commission by God to bring freedom to humanity, for "the imperialism of the Gospel is the emancipation of humanity."[80]

Examples like that of Welch and Radcliffe could be multiplied over and over. These were not fringe positions. Welch was a celebrated professor and had a book of remembrances published upon his death. Radcliffe was not only the Moderator of the Presbyterian General Assembly, but for twenty-seven years he was also the pastor of New York Avenue Presbyterian Church in Washington, DC, where Abraham Lincoln faithfully attended during the years he was in the White House.[81] If these were the mainstream Christian positions proclaimed in mainline Protestant pulpits and classrooms, one can only imagine what this means for the wider population. And it is no surprise that the rapid and wholesale transformation of society brought about by the world wars would inflame these anxieties. Each generation has had its anxieties, its reasons for lamenting the loss of tradition and the need to recover a purportedly more authentic account of prescriptive faith. For the purposes of this book, which focuses on the postliberal conservative turn in the late twentieth century, I am concerned especially with the anxieties inflamed by the cultural upheavals of the 1960s, as the feminist and gay liberation movements, along with the entire sexual revolution, posed a direct threat to the gender and sexual norms of religious conservatives.[82] The civil rights movement and the civil rights legislation passed by the Johnson administration posed a threat to the white supremacy and racial purity that many saw as divinely ordained. For those already primed to see a conflict between religion and modernity, the transformations of society in the 1960s and beyond – with its challenge to the hegemony of white cisheteronormative patriarchy – only confirmed their deepest fears. This was the apparent fruit of abandoning religion as the foundation of civilization. Auden's "secular wall" was no longer standing; it was now openly crumbling, according to Christian culture warriors. Something had to be done.

Much of the blame was placed on those who seemed to undermine the authority of the Bible and the supremacy of Christianity. On the moderate side, the dialectical theology of Karl Barth (at the time often called "neoorthodoxy") started to make inroads into American Protestant seminaries in the mid-twentieth century. Princeton Theological Seminary, once the home of Protestant fundamentalism, began openly espousing Barth's approach to Reformed theology in the 1930s, and Geoffrey Bromiley, one of the cotranslators of Barth's *Church Dogmatics*, began teaching at the evangelical Fuller Theological Seminary in 1958. Conservative mainline Protestants and moderate evangelicals were initially some of the most receptive to Barth's theology, since mainline seminaries were influenced more by the likes of Paul Tillich and Reinhold Niebuhr, and as I show in Chapters 2 and 3, Barth's influence in the United States also laid a key foundation for the postliberal reaction that empowered the conservative movement. More radical elements began to form in the postwar years. The 1950s saw the arrival of Rudolf Bultmann's program of demythologizing to the shores of the United States, beginning with Bultmann's visit in 1951 and followed by the publication in 1953 and 1962, respectively, of the two volumes of *Kerygma and Myth* – the English translations of the main essays from the German debate over demythologizing.[83] By 1964, *Time* could claim that "Dr. Rudolf Bultmann's Marburg Disciples ... dominate German theology the way the Russians rule chess."[84] At the same time, there was growing interest throughout the 1960s in secular, religionless, and even atheist Christianity, marked by the popularity of books by Dietrich Bonhoeffer, Gabriel Vahanian, Paul van Buren, Bishop John A. T. Robinson, Harvey Cox, and Thomas Altizer.[85] It was only to be expected that the forces of conservative reaction would connect these challenges to biblical authority and Christian tradition with the cultural changes in society at large.

The frantic attempts to restore order that followed were predictable. The solution on all sides was a more robust prescriptivism. For evangelicals, the answer lay in the Bible. In 1976, while he was editor of *Christianity Today*, Harold Lindsell (1913–1998) published his broadside, *The Battle for the Bible*, which warned of a coming confrontation between "true Christians" who held to the complete inerrancy of the Bible in all matters and those Christians In Name Only who had been influenced by what he considered liberal and neoorthodox views about the Bible as a fallible human witness to revelation.[86] Lindsell leveled a direct attack on evangelical institutions, such as Fuller Seminary, that he believed were slipping into heresy, due to the presence of the likes of Bromiley. The following year, inspired by Lindsell's call to arms, evangelical leaders such as Francis Schaeffer, R. C. Sproul, J. I. Packer, and Norman Geisler formed the International Council on Biblical Inerrancy. This led to the widely publicized Chicago Statement on Biblical Inerrancy in October 1978.

Evangelicals were not the only ones who were interested in the Bible. Mainline Protestant theologians were also invested in the topic, with Hans Frei publishing his landmark *Eclipse of Biblical Narrative* in 1974 and David Kelsey's *The Uses of Scripture in Recent Theology* appearing in 1975.[87] The signal difference between the evangelicals and what would come to be known as the postliberals – referring to the group of mainline Protestants who publicly disavowed liberalism, both theological and political, in favor of what they considered a more traditional, antimodern Christianity – came down to the question of interpretation.[88] The evangelicals were convinced the Bible's true meaning was self-evidently clear to any individual who read it plainly and faithfully. The postliberals, by contrast, believed that interpretation required participating in a community and tradition of biblical exegesis. This led the postliberals to engage in ecumenical conversation across denominational barriers, and it also led them to situate the question of prescriptivism within the doctrine of the church.

The interest of the postliberals in ecumenical dialogue illuminated a fundamental insight: exegesis alone was not the reason for theological divisions between traditions and denominations, nor would exegesis be able to bring people together. Differences in doctrine were not a matter of disagreements about the biblical anthology but rather reflected the different cultural contexts for reading these texts. In other words, culture, not the Bible, was the solution. George Lindbeck's landmark 1984 book, *The Nature of Doctrine: Religion and Theology in a Postliberal Age*, reshaped the conversation about normativity by viewing religious norms as *cultural* norms.[89] Writing against both conservatives who viewed doctrines as propositional statements corresponding to an objective, metaphysical reality and liberals who viewed doctrines as expressive statements articulating subjective experience, Lindbeck argued that doctrines are cultural statements that regulate the practices of a community. Doctrines are the grammar of religious performance, and like any grammar, doctrines can only be understood by those within the cultural community who "speak" the religious language. Lindbeck rejected the effort to engage in apologetics and instead advised people to focus on their own internal cultural norms. Framed as an intervention in ecumenical and interreligious dialogue, the book's argument aimed to prevent proselytism and increase respect for different traditions.

Lindbeck's key innovation, the one that would have long-term implications for Christian prescriptivism, was to relocate the normativity of Christianity from a set of theological propositions – the traditional creedal rule of faith – to a cultural framework, something more like a language. Whereas the old *regula fidei* meant that Christian norms could, in theory, inhabit any cultural context once the creedal propositions were translated from one linguistic culture to another, the new postliberal model ruled out any translation from the start. You can translate German words into English words, but you cannot translate the German language into the English language without losing the German language.

A language ceases to exist when people stop speaking it. But this was where Lindbeck's own anxieties began to quickly manifest themselves. Once Christianity becomes a culture, in which its norms are identical with its cultural identity, anything that threatens this cultural-linguistic framework becomes a threat to Christianity itself, and the principal threat, as he saw it, was "anti-religious secularism." His work respected the diversity of religious traditions, but he had no respect for those who rejected religion altogether. In his later work he described Christianity as an untranslatable worldview (*Weltanschauung*) that "purports to provide a totally comprehensive framework, a universal perspective," and for this reason is caught in a struggle with secularism, which likewise claims universality. "No reconciliation is possible between the secular and biblical outlooks thus understood," he argued. Both are "untranslatable and competitive," caught in a battle for supremacy.[90]

In an autobiographical piece published in 1990, Lindbeck acknowledged that his experience growing up in China "laid the groundwork for a disenchantment with Christendom that led me 30 years later to hope for the end of cultural Christianity."[91] But later in this article he notes that his mind has changed: "I once welcomed the passing of Christendom ... but now ... I am having uncomfortable second thoughts." The reason he gives is that "traditionally Christian lands when stripped of their historic faith are worse than others. They become unworkable or demonic." He claims that "the Christianization of culture" may be "the churches' major contribution."[92] While expressed in a more sophisticated way, Lindbeck's claim that Christianity makes a society better than non-Christian societies is essentially identical with Welch's claim that "the more Christian, the more civilized," or Radcliffe's notion that Christianity's imperialism is beneficial and civilizing. If a Christian society is superior, then the Christian has a moral obligation to bring the rest of the world under the benevolent rule of Christian norms. Lindbeck articulated the logic behind this imperialistic move in his account of biblical interpretation, articulated most clearly in a lecture given in 1995 at the annual Wheaton Theology Conference held at Wheaton College, the self-styled "Harvard of evangelicalism."[93] If Christian norms are cultural, then the interpretation of scripture, according to Lindbeck, involves the "social construction of reality."[94] And since the Bible provides a "totally comprehensive framework," any interpretation of the Bible ought to be a universal culture, one that encompasses all people within its totalizing worldview. Put simply, "the biblical world absorbs all other worlds," and once we realize that the biblical world is the cultural framework of the church, it follows that biblical interpretation is properly the construction of an ecclesial society – namely, Christendom.[95]

If an actual Christian society is no longer possible, then the answer lies in retreating into sectarian communities where Christians can nurture the virtues and practices that characterize their distinct culture. Christians, according to Lindbeck, "must become, sociologically speaking, sectarian."[96] Such a message was quite at odds with mainline liberal Protestantism, and those who championed this countercultural message attracted significant media attention. Stanley Hauerwas became, for a time, the most famous theologian in the United States by denouncing modern secular society and calling people to form intentional Christian communities. More recently, Rod Dreher has assumed that mantle in his proposal for a so-called Benedict Option. For many mainline Protestants attracted to Lindbeck's way of thinking, the more straightforward response was to join the Roman Catholic Church, or in the case of Radical Orthodoxy, to argue for a renewed Anglican Communion that could engage in a similar effort at totalizing social construction.

The message landed somewhat differently for Lindbeck's evangelical audience. By the mid-1990s, American evangelicals, who had already developed their own subculture, were in retreat from the wider society. Evangelicals already imagined themselves as a sectarian community, a persecuted countercultural minority, even if their actual lives did not look much different from their neighbors.[97] The efforts by the Moral Majority, Christian Coalition, and other groups in the late 1970s and 1980s had brought Ronald Reagan into the presidency, but the results were often disappointing in terms of the hot-button culture-war issues, and with the election of Bill Clinton it seemed like their best days were in the past. Moreover, it had become clear in the wake of the "battle for the Bible" that inerrancy solved nothing, much to the chagrin of evangelical leaders who assumed the meaning of the text would be obvious to all who read it faithfully. Merely holding to biblical authority and infallibility gave no guidance to interpretation.[98] After years of scorning the field of hermeneutics as "liberal," evangelicals rushed to catch up to the wider scholarly world. If merely reading the plain text of scripture was insufficient, what tools were available to guide interpretation in what they considered to be the right direction?

The answer, according to Lindbeck and the postliberals, was the church. This message arrived at just the right time. The 1980s had seen the rise of corporate, megachurch evangelicalism with its emphasis on parachurch organizations. As David Wells observes, "evangelicals began to think of the whole of evangelical faith in *para* terms," and thus "evangelicalism began to think of itself apart from the church."[99] Lindbeck, by contrast, gave evangelicals a way to connect the Bible to the culture wars in a more theologically nuanced and academically respectable way via the sectarian, culturally distinct church. Instead of naively assuming that Billy Graham-style evangelism would change the culture, on the assumption that all born-again Christians would weaponize the handful of verses in the same political way, evangelicals came to understand that they first had to convert the culture. Cultural absorption and political power, rather than classic apologetics and evangelical crusades, became the solution to the problem of modern Christian anxiety. Lindbeck spoke more truly than he knew when, at the Wheaton Theology Conference, he commented in a closing panel discussion that, "if the sort of research program represented by postliberalism has a real future as a communal enterprise for the church, it's more likely to be carried on by evangelicals than anyone else."[100] The statement was prophetic. Whether consciously or not, evangelicals embraced the postliberal emphasis on the church as a distinct culture, a sectarian *polis* whose alternative way of life would be the starting point for widespread social transformation. Evangelicals began to embrace ecclesiology in a way they never had. Books and articles on the evangelical doctrine of the church began to appear. In 2004, the Wheaton Theology Conference held its conference on "evangelical ecclesiology." And in 2015, just before the "crisis" that emerged the following year, Kevin J. Vanhoozer and Daniel J. Treier, two leading evangelical theologians, blamed the fractures in evangelical identity on "the evangelical failure to address ecclesiology" and proposed to solve these fractures by establishing scripture and "the catholic tradition" (along with "ecclesial authority") as the twin principles of evangelical theology, something that would have been unthinkable even a generation earlier.[101]

Lindbeck's turn to the church – a distinctively cultural account of the church – was only part of the answer, but Lindbeck and his postliberal allies also pointed the way toward the second key piece of the prescriptivist puzzle. As evangelicals became convinced that merely believing in Jesus and trusting the Bible were inadequate, they became increasingly open to the idea that understanding church history, and not merely biblical studies, was essential to informing their newly cultural view of Christian faith. For a long time, evangelicals reveled in their status as "Bible-only" believers and disparaged creeds and confessions as the mark of Roman Catholics and liberal Protestants, both of whom, they claimed, made human traditions authoritative over or alongside the Bible. Now that *sola scriptura* was understood to be inadequate, these same traditions took on a more positive significance precisely because they were no longer merely human but were instead part of the cultural framework that defined what they regarded as the orthodox worldview. Despite being children of the modern world, evangelicals increasingly came to see modernity as the source of all the cultural anxieties they had previously sought to oppose on strictly biblicist grounds. The idea of grounding Christian normativity in a *premodern* cultural framework looked like the answer for which they had been searching.

The idea was not wholly novel. In May 1977, the year before the Chicago Statement on Biblical Inerrancy, a group of evangelicals issued "The Chicago Call: An Appeal to Evangelicals." In this document, wholly overshadowed by the publicity surrounding the "battle for the Bible," a group of evangelicals called fellow evangelicals to recover "historic Christianity," a term used five times in the document.[102] The group of forty-five who crafted the statement, including the likes of Robert Webber and Peter Gillchrist, were a distinct minority at the time. This was not long after *Newsweek* had declared 1976 the "Year of the Evangelical," and there was little felt need at the time for such a drastic rethinking of evangelicalism. The situation was very different, however, near the turn of the millennium.[103] The need for a more nuanced and historically grounded identity was apparent to many. And once evangelicals made the turn to the cultural church along with the postliberals, all barriers to ancient Christianity fell away. In place of the "Bible alone," evangelicals began to champion the rule of faith as the guide to Christian prescriptivism. By 2008, *Christianity Today*'s cover story read: "The Future Lies in the Past."[104]

The rule of faith within this new postliberal framework was more than simply the ancient protoorthodox beliefs that formed the basis for ancient liturgical practices and creedal statements. Now it represented the ecclesial grammar of the Christian language, the cultural norms that constitute Christianity and determine its social embodiment. R. R. Reno – who considers Lindbeck "the most significant influence on my intellectual life"[105] and began graduate work at Yale the year Lindbeck published *The Nature of Doctrine* – connects the *regula fidei* to "the Nicene tradition," "the Niceno-Constantinopolitan Creed," "ancient baptismal affirmations of faith," "the Chalcedonian definition," and "the creeds and canons of other church councils." But as if in response to the objection that these do not provide us with a clear definitive list of doctrinal rules, Reno responds in a classic Lindbeckian way that this is precisely the point. The rule of faith is not "limited to a specific set of words, sentences, and creeds. It is instead a pervasive habit of thought, the *animating culture of the church* in its intellectual aspect."[106] Such ideas would have seemed threatening to evangelicals a generation ago, but in a time of deep uneasiness with the prevailing culture, the idea of returning to some premodern golden age – making Christianity great again – was and still is deeply attractive.

My aim here is not to provide a history of evangelicalism or to further explain how evangelicals could have voted in such overwhelming numbers for Trump, though their agitated responses to the age of anxiety no doubt contributed significantly to this result. My interest in this book is not with evangelicals as such but with the question of Christian identity. Evangelicals happen to make a useful case study because of the persistent sense of identity crisis that pervades evangelical-ism in the United States. Chris Armstrong has claimed that "the 1970s marked the beginning – or at least intensification – of an evangelical identity crisis from which we have yet to emerge."[107] To be sure, it was only the intensification. The likes of Welch and Radcliffe laid the foun-dation for the fundamentalist movement in the twentieth century out of which contemporary evangelicalism arose. And there were many others before them.

Every generation has had its age of anxiety, and every generation has had its prescriptivist reactionaries seeking to define "true Christianity" in response to some new threat, whether threats from within (e.g., nominal Christianity, creeping heterodoxy, political and ethical deterioration) or threats from without (e.g., modern liberalism, communism, anti-religious secularism). Every such effort has involved clarifying, implicitly or explicitly, what constitutes Christian normativity and thus who counts as Christian. The term "rule of faith," as I use it here, refers to this prescriptivist rubric for shoring up Christian identity. While it has a certain historical definition connected to the first and second centuries of Christianity, it has become something more than that – a symbol for whatever will address the current sources of anxiety. In this book I examine the history of this quest for a normative, ruled Christianity, the problems with many of the accounts of this rule, and some ways we might rethink the rule so as to avoid the pitfalls that bedevil so much prescriptivism. We cannot abandon prescriptivism, but we might, just possibly, be able to redeem it.

RETHINKING THE RULE OF FAITH

In this book I wrestle with questions concerning who and what counts as Christian and why. If we strip away everything unnecessary to Christianity, what are we left with? What is the enduring core, the permanent essence at the heart of the faith? Is it even possible to strip away the inessentials to find an essence of Christianity at all, or is Christianity simply the irreducible complexity of the forms in which it occurs throughout history? Is there a normative Christianity, or is Christianity merely whatever self-described Christians say and do? And if there is a normative Christianity, how should we understand the norms in a way that will not reproduce the protectionism and imperialism that have characterized so much of Christian prescriptivism?

As we have already seen, these questions have been asked anew by many generations of Christians, and they will continue to arise in the future, as new anxieties confront us. Those who champion the *regula fidei* as the solution to these religious anxieties often see themselves as recovering what they call "historic Christianity" or "consensual Christianity," by which they mean an ancient, ecumenical account of Christian faith that transcends the various divisions between traditions and denominations, including the separations between East and West as well as Catholic and Protestant. Proponents of this "historic Christianity" place it over against the developments that came with modernity. The history of modern theology, according to this view, is a declension narrative, and true Christianity lies in the past – a past that one can recover by adhering to the rule of faith.

The problem with this narrative is that we can only ask these questions *as modern Christians*, as those shaped by the social, political, and ideological changes brought by modernity. There is no recovering a premodern culture, no matter how earnestly one tries. Moreover, *the very posing of this question presupposes precisely the modern changes that one claims to be resisting.* Premodern Christianity had no concept of being able to choose an alternative account of Christian faith and identity. The idea that we can posit a rule or essence or "mere Christianity" in opposition to inessential accretions or undesirable changes is itself a modern notion.

For this reason I begin in Chapter 1 by exploring the history of the modern quest for the essence of Christianity, tracing the developments in defining the normative faith from the Reformation to the mid-twentieth century. I pay special attention to Martin Luther, John Locke, Friedrich Schleiermacher, Albrecht Ritschl, Adolf von Harnack, and Karl Barth – all key figures who contributed to the formation of modern Christianity. They show that the essence of Christianity is inherently flexible, constantly adapting to new conditions and new discoveries. Precisely in response to such flexibility, the rule of faith functions in modernity as the supposedly unchanging antidote to the essence.

Since my focus in this study is on the antimodern reaction to liberal Christianity, I turn in Chapters 2, 3, and 4 to the story of the conservative quest for authentic faith, organized around the three categories of religion identified by Schleiermacher: thinking (doctrine), feeling (culture), and doing (politics). Chapter 2 examines the search for the doctrinal rule of faith, expressed as the retrieval of "historic Christianity." I look at three key figures in modern Christian history who have been instrumental in the rise of theological retrievalism among Protestants: John Henry Newman, Karl Barth (or rather the American neoorthodox theologians who appropriated Barth's work for their agenda), and C. S. Lewis. Chapter 3 then tells the story of how mainline Protestants, responding to the precarious state of Christianity in an increasingly diverse America, advanced the idea of Christianity as a culture. I trace this development from the biblical theology movement in the postwar years to the rise of postliberalism in the 1970s into the theological interpretation of scripture movement in the early twenty-first century, which is an effort to revitalize biblical theology but on the other side of the cultural turn that postliberalism inaugurated. I argue that the cultural rule of faith laid the groundwork for expanding and refining the culture war waged by conservative Christians in the late twentieth and early twenty-first centuries.[108] This leads to Chapter 4, which documents how the quest for true Christian doctrine and culture ultimately led to, and was bound up with, the quest for a truly Christian politics. In addition to examining the question of religion's place in a liberal democratic society, this chapter explores two examples of how the quest for a normative Christian identity has been weaponized for political ends. The first example looks at the construction of global Christian identity that redefines true Christianity in terms of persecution – a definition easily manipulated by the global right-wing in its denunciation of "cancel culture" and alleged infringements on religious liberty. The second example looks at the construction of historic Christian identity through attacks on the supposed gnosticism that pervades modern society. These three chapters demonstrate that talk of the *regula fidei* is thoroughly modern in character. It is an exercise in modern cultural construction more than any retrieval of the past.

The last chapter then lays out the argument against the recent retrieval of the rule of faith and its quest for a normative, orthodox essence. In rehearsing the problems with each of the three forms of antimodern Christianity, I unpack the logic implicit within, a logic that necessarily distorts history even as it claims to recover it. I show the similarities between the conservative quest for Christian identity and the conservative quest for American identity, both of which involve reducing the complexity of the past to ahistorical principles. The problem at the root of this quest, I argue, is the pursuit of orthodoxy itself, which turns out to be the pursuit of a theological purity culture that requires the exercise of magisterial authority. The antimodern, antiliberal rule of faith ultimately ends up becoming a tool of authoritarian white Christian supremacy – the logic underpinning a theopolitics of Make Christianity Great Again.[109]

In the Conclusion, I turn from the diagnostic to the constructive in order to propose an alternative way to think about the rule of faith. As I have already argued, we cannot do without prescriptivism as such. We need norms if we are going to construct a liberating vision of Christianity that is able to live without fear in the face of social change. Central to that project is rethinking the rule not as a fixed account of Christian faith and practice but rather as an open, flexible, and translatable faith. My positive alternative will therefore not be a normative dogmatics outlining what I think Christians ought to believe about doctrinal topics such as Christology, atonement, and the trinity. I am not offering a new *regula fidei* or essence of Christianity, as if that would solve the problem. Instead, my approach will be to provide guardrails for how to think about normativity itself. What must the rule of faith be in order to embrace the diversity and flexibility of our world today? Lisa Isherwood and Dirk von der Horst helpfully frame religion as a way of "negotiating the poles of normativity and transgression," caught in a constructive tension between religion as something that "provides order and normativity" and religion as "a transgressive force." The danger with religious norms, they argue, is the temptation they provide to settle into sedate, safe patterns of normativity that refuse to upset unjust and unsustainable human relations. They point to resources in Christian theology for transgressing and challenging norms.[110] As helpful as this is, however, so long as normativity and transgression are placed over against each other, this way of thinking continues to reinforce the assumption that norms are inherently conservative, traditionalist, and reactionary. Isherwood and Horst are pushing against this assumption already by pointing to normative resources for engaging in socially transgressive actions. What I will argue here is that the rule of faith needs to be conceived in such a way that it empowers a *normatively transgressive Christianity*, by which I mean a Christianity that is constantly transgressing boundaries precisely as an expression of its internal norms.[111] We need a rule that helps Christian communities to cross old barriers and forge new identities and practices. Rather than a rule that guarantees uniformity, this will be a rule that guarantees diversity and pluriformity – what Alvin J. Reines, Catherine Keller, and Laurel C. Schneider each call "polydoxy."[112]

The pioneering German theologian Ernst Troeltsch wrote in 1913 that "the essence of Christianity differs in different epochs."[113] Similarly, we can say that the rule of faith differs in different epochs – indeed, that it differs among different individuals and communities. There are many rules and essences of Christianity, and that is something to celebrate. But that does not mean just anything goes. Embracing plurality does not necessitate a pure, absolute relativism. That would be another denial of prescriptivism and a relinquishing of our responsibility for thinking carefully about what it means to be Christian in modernity. My hope is that the following chapters will serve as both a diagnosis of our current theological condition and a prescription for how to address the crisis of modern Christian identity.

1

Modernizing the Rule

The Quest for the Essence of Christianity

A NDREW WALLS (1928–2021), the late missiologist and historian of Christianity, proposed a profound thought experiment in 1982. He imagined an interplanetary anthropologist and scholar of comparative religions who visited Earth at different moments to study Christianity: Jerusalem in 37 CE, Nicaea in 325, Ireland in the 600s, London in the 1840s, and Lagos in 1980. At each point in Earth history, this extraterrestrial scholar would observe the vast differences in religious belief and practice from other moments, including variations in standard of living, liturgical forms, relations with those outside their community, doctrinal beliefs, and the like.

What, Walls then concluded, unites these disparate modes of Christianity? How does our visitor from space make sense of these observations? Is the use of the label "Christian" deceptive and equivocal, being used in ways that are incommensurable with each other? Does shared religion ultimately depend on shared culture? Or is there a connection between these communities, a common essence or religious core that remains in some sense normative, even if the historical expressions of this core identity change dramatically from era to era?[1]

Walls uses his thought experiment as the basis for his theory of translation – translation referring not merely to the change from one language to another but to the process by which the gospel migrates from one cultural location to another. The move from London to Lagos in the present day requires cultural translation but so does the move from seventh-century Ireland to twenty-first-century Ireland. Both geography and chronology are significant in the question of cultural difference. Walls uses the term "gospel" to refer to the normative, prescriptive element in Christianity, while the term "culture" refers to the descriptive context in which Christian norms take root and flourish. His argument for translation aims to avoid reducing the prescriptive gospel to the descriptive context while also avoiding any abstract gospel free from context altogether. To explain this translation process, Walls proposes two principles for understanding the relation between gospel and culture: the "indigenizing" principle and the "pilgrim" principle. The former refers to the way Christian faith always inhabits a particular cultural form, while the latter refers to the way that Christian faith never leaves that form unchanged and always presses toward new forms – and finally to the eschatological horizon of God's kingdom.

Though more recent intercultural scholars have nuanced or moved beyond Walls's categories, his thought experiment remains theologically stimulating. What is the best way to theorize the relation between Christianity and culture in the wake of the increasingly rapid proliferation of diverse Christian communities around the world over the past century? Can we even speak of the "gospel" as a self-identical norm? What is "culture" now that anthropologists and cultural theorists have replaced old static notions of culture with models that recognize its plasticity and complexity? These are the kinds of questions raised by Walls's work, and they continue to be significant – as the rest of this book aims to explore in more detail.

But there is one important aspect of his hypothetical thought experiment that Walls does not point out – namely, the fact that we are able to consider his inquiry meaningful at all. Walls takes it for granted that the diversity of Christian communities throughout history poses a problem, a problem that his readers will themselves recognize and affirm. But that in itself presupposes a unique historical context, one in which the historical continuity of Christianity is no longer assumed as a given. Jesus followers in Jerusalem in 37 CE would, of course, not have perceived this issue at all, since there was no Christianity at this time; the issue then was whether gentiles could be included in the Jewish community. The differences between fourth-century Nicaea and seventh-century Ireland were rendered insignificant, if they were acknowledged at all, because they were held together by the ecclesiastical empire of Christendom, with its hierarchical structure of apostolic succession, the spread of authorized dioceses, and the recognition of priestly orthodoxy by the bishops.

Everything changes, however, when we move from Ireland in the 600s to London in the 1840s, and not merely in terms of the obvious differences of worship and doctrine. Not only do "religions after 1800 differ substantially from their pre-1800 forms," but the nature of their prescriptive norms changes as well.[2] Prior to the modern period, the norm of orthodoxy was defined over against heterodoxy, but there was no heterodox movement capable of challenging the institutional dominance of orthodoxy. The authority of orthodoxy was unquestioned. For this reason, the tension in the premodern world was between strict orthodoxy and lenient orthodoxy. Staf Hellemans calls this "orthodoxy from above," since it was "facilitated by the power of organisational elites in directing their organisational affairs," as seen paradigmatically in the Council of Nicaea.[3] It was only in the modern period, especially starting in the nineteenth century, that religious liberalism arose as a legitimate alternative, one that produced the corresponding reactionary norm of conservatism. The two binaries – orthodoxy and leniency, conservatism and liberalism – "became connected in modernity," as "the opposition between liberalism and conservatism was superimposed upon the older opposition between leniency and orthodoxy."[4] This superimposition had profound implications for both orthodoxy and liberalism. For one thing, a distinction between levels of doctrinal rigidity (orthodoxy vs. leniency) became a conflict between parties (conservatives vs. liberals). The opposition between orthodoxy and liberalism "acted as a binary conceptual scheme that permitted the convenient reduction of multiple projects to two warring sides," obscuring the fact that "there were always more than two projects."[5] This reduction also distorted the two parties. Orthodoxy, now understood predominantly as theological conservatism, hardened into a strict adherence to the authoritative tradition, while liberalism, now understood predominantly as lenient adaptation, became associated with the uncritical accommodation of modernity. As Hellemans points out, this was a misrepresentation of both positions. Orthodoxy had in fact vastly changed in modernity; it was now a program defined by its stern opposition to liberalism, as opposed to the earlier opposition to heterodoxy. Liberalism, for its part, was more than just leniency; it "had a programmatic base of its own: to unearth the essence of Christianity from the accretion of traditions."[6] As a strategy for defining religious identity, modern orthodoxy was more of a reaction to this liberal program than any straightforward continuation of the past.

Orthodoxy and liberalism in the modern period are also both chiefly "from below," defined not by the dictates of ecclesiastical elites but rather by lay individuals, parachurch organizations, and popular movements. Insofar as orthodoxy from above entailed forced conformity, as it did in the ancient and medieval worlds, virtually all forms of Christianity in modernity are from below. The most consequential difference between premodern and modern societies, the one described at length by Charles Taylor in *A Secular Age*, is not outwardly apparent, at least not without sustained experience in the modern world. It is the inner recognition that one is *choosing* to be Christian and that one could choose otherwise – to believe a different version of Christianity, a different religion entirely, or no religion at all. Not only can people choose otherwise but many of them do so on a regular basis. These constant, everyday choices create a social context in which faith, whether orthodox, liberal, or otherwise, is constructed and held together not by any authority – to the chagrin of many ecclesiastical leaders – but by the fragile decision of people to continue to participate in a particular form of religious practice. And increasingly people are choosing to abandon their religious communities, sometimes leading them to change their affiliation or even to disaffiliate from religion altogether. In other words, what makes Christianity in nineteenth-century London or twenty-first-century Los Angeles different from the previous versions identified by Walls are not necessarily the particular details of this or that worshiping community but the recognition of the multiplicity, contingency, and fluidity of all these communities.

The result of this ever-present awareness of Christianity's internal differences is that Christians in the modern, secular world of the Euro-American West are constantly asking themselves: What makes someone Christian? What binds these disparate groups together – if anything? Am I in communion with those people over there who also claim to be Christian? Do these polls truly represent me? Is there a "mere Christianity" underneath the centuries of doctrinal accretion and the decades of culture wars? Missiologists like Walls are often the ones most frequently posing these questions because they are intimately aware of the differences that exist in world Christianity today. But in our ultra-connected world, where anyone can digitally cross great distances in a matter of seconds, these questions have proliferated exponentially. And the questions are not a matter of merely abstract curiosity. They have deep existential significance, precisely because the boundaries of religious identity are no longer clearly defined.

The questions may have multiplied in recent years, but the underlying issue itself is an old one. For nearly a half-millennium, Christians in the West have been wondering what really defines Christianity. The problem was all too apparent. The Protestant Reformation gave rise to warring religious factions, with the so-called magisterial Protestants – that is, the Lutheran and Reformed churches – fighting between themselves over issues like the sacraments but also teaming up against the Roman Catholics, on the one side, and the Anabaptists and other Radical Reformers, on the other. As these divisions hardened into what we call denominations, splitting along national lines, it was hard to avoid the conclusion that one's religious identity was simply another way of describing one's cultural and ethnic identity, with Italian Catholics, Swedish Lutherans, Swiss Reformed, and British Anglicans. Moreover, the very nature of true, salvific faith changed in this period. "Following the Reformation," according to Peter Harrison, "the fragmentation of Christendom led to a change from an institutionally based understanding of exclusive salvation to a propositionally based understanding. Formerly it had been 'no salvation outside the Church.' Now, it had become 'no salvation without the profession of the "true religion."'"[7] Not only was orthodoxy questionable, but what counted as orthodoxy had changed – as well as how orthodoxy was determined and who had the authority to determine it. The scientific revolution and the Enlightenment philosophical revolution worked in tandem to disrupt matters further. While the Reformation wrested the question of Christianity's identity out of the hands of the Roman magisterium, these modern intellectual upheavals called into question all the sources and norms of Christian faith. If the Bible was not reliable in its description of the celestial heavens, could it be relied upon in its account of redemption in Christ? If knowledge required sensory experience, and was the result of our own minds interpreting that experience, then could we have any knowledge at all about God? And if we could, why should we trust the ecclesial authorities to provide us this knowledge? The critical floodgates had been opened. One could no longer assume the truth of Christianity. One now had to demonstrate that Christianity possessed a gospel that could survive these critical inquiries – an essence or core identity that could withstand the withering scrutiny of its biblical texts and dogmatic traditions. And so began the task of modern prescriptivism.

Already in his 1612 essay "Of Unity in Religion," Francis Bacon, the pioneer of the scientific method, distinguished between "the points fundamental and of substance in religion ... from points not merely of faith, but of opinion, order, or good intention."[8] As the waves of historical, scientific, and philosophical critique crashed against the shores of the church, the revetments of venerable tradition and learned dogmatics often did not hold, forcing new efforts at defining "the points fundamental." The outcome of this was the long quest for the "essence of Christianity," as it was called at the time – a quest that continues to this day.

This is the context in which Walls poses the idea of his hypothetical interplanetary scholar – a context marked by an ever-increasing pluralism, the persistent awareness of Christianity's tenuous position in the modern world, the search for a Christian identity that makes sense of the latest challenges to faith, and the manifest reality that there are virtually as many Christianities as there are Christians. For the descriptivists, this is how it has always been, insofar as history is nothing other than the messy, complex story of humans acting in diverse and contradictory ways; modern developments make for an interesting, sometimes tragic, chronicle but otherwise raise no concerns. For the prescriptivists and those trying to make sense of Christian faith today, however, all of this poses the dilemma: what unites Christianity, in all its complexity, across time and space? Is there a Christian essence? If so, who gets to define it and how? To the first two questions, Walls argues that the instances he picked out are held together in two ways: (1) historically, by means of a chain of cause and effect and (2) theologically and liturgically, by virtue of their shared conviction "that the person of Jesus called the Christ has ultimate significance," the use of the same sacred texts, and the special use of bread, wine, and water. He also notes "the continuity of consciousness," the sense each group has that they belong to a larger community that encompasses other communities throughout history, even ancient Israel. Moreover, Walls refers to all this as "an essential continuity in Christianity."[9] Regardless of what we make of Walls's answers – which are, by design, about as generic and anodyne as possible – the point remains that these are the underlying questions animating, even if only implicitly, the different quests for the Christian essence, both the modern liberal quest and the antimodern conservative reaction to it.

I refer to this long history as the quest for the essence of Christianity mostly because that is the language that was in vogue for most of this period, stretching roughly from the mid-eighteenth century to the mid-twentieth. This is the high period of liberal Christianity, which is hardly monolithic but broadly refers to those theologians, church leaders, and institutions that embraced the need to accommodate the new developments that came with modernity. Not all liberal theologians embraced the same developments of the modern age, so accommodating this period could look quite different from one person to another and from one period or region to another. Nevertheless, some common features remain, including the readiness to rethink the Bible and Christian doctrine in light of new scientific discoveries and the willingness to make use of new philosophical concepts as a way to adapt Christianity to the cultural moment. Given the radical upheavals that came with this period, there was still a felt need to identify what made a new theology recognizably "Christian." And that is what the idea of the Christian essence provided.

The language of "essence" is somewhat dated now and carries pejorative connotations for many who view it as overly static and disconnected from history, as if an essence is separate from and untouched by its concrete appearance. But other metaphors have the same or at least a similar problem: content and form, substance and accident, kernel and husk, core and exterior, center and periphery, norm and adiaphora, principle and application. There is no perfect language for whatever is the defining element or characteristic of something as historically complex as Christianity. Bishop and theologian Stephen Sykes titled his 1984 book on the subject, *The Identity of Christianity*, which was ahead of its time in its choice of terminology.[10] Seven years before his book appeared, the Combahee River Collective coined the term "identity politics," which helped unleash the widespread use of identity language that began in the late 1980s. Today we might speak of one's inner identity in contrast to their outward appearance – that is to say, how they "pass" or "present" in society, which does not move us past our linguistic dilemma. The language of identity is more common today than essence, but it has the same potential for critique and misunderstanding.

Whether we use essence or identity, or one of the other available options – and I will use them interchangeably in this book – does not matter here. For whatever reason, the word "essence" (*Wesen* in German) won the day and became the technical term for over two centuries, and it serves our purposes now just as well as it did then, with the same benefits and drawbacks. We regularly distinguish between essential and inessential aspects of things; and even if we no longer speak regularly about the "essence of Christianity," people are asking on a daily basis what constitutes the core identity of Christian faith. Church historian Rolf Schäfer observes that "the history of the concept 'essence of Christianity' grows out of the history of the concept 'Christianity,' for wherever one defines Christianity, there one defines its essence."[11] Faced with the challenges of religious division and disaffiliation, the existential problem of defining the essence of Christianity is more real to us now than it ever has been.

The increasingly vexed questions over Christian identity form the backdrop for the recent turn to the rule of faith among postliberal and conservative theologians and pastors. While the interest in the *regula fidei* is an effort to do an end run around the modern quest for the essence, effectively ignoring or denying that modernity happened, the reality is that the retrievals of the rule of faith today are dependent on this quest for the essence of faith whether they want to be or not – and for this reason they have to be understood as belonging to the quest, albeit antagonistically. "Anti-liberalism and anti-modernism," according to Hellemans, "are a way of thinking with regard to modernity ... and that is a genuinely modern undertaking."[12] Those who appeal to the rule of faith do so in a context in which such appeals are shaped by the transformations of society, including religion, that have occurred over the past several centuries. No one is untouched by these changes, even if the doctrines and liturgies remain identical. Someone who participates in the Divine Liturgy of Saint John Chrysostom today may be saying words that go back to the fifth century, but those words are received in a fundamentally different way by someone living in the twenty-first century. What is true for Greek Orthodoxy is even more true for Reformed Protestantism, which has undergone profound rifts and trans-formations over the centuries. As Evan Kuehn observes, few if any theo-logians today do their work "under any actual constraint of ecclesiastical censure, not even when they posture as if they were." For this reason, as loathe as some may be to admit it, "we are all liberal theologians now, and it has been quite a while since we were not all liberals."[13] While conservative Christians, according to Samuel Loncar, "have long argued that Liberalism is simply a bad compromise with the modern world," evangelicals and other antimodern traditionalists "suffer from the fantasy that modernity is optional, that they are not already, in every relevant sense, modern." Christian traditionalists of all stripes "have not yet recognized that the challenge is not *whether* to be modern but *how*."[14] If there is a distinction to be made, it is not between conservative and liberal Christians but between modern and antimodern liberals – or, to borrow from Winnifred Fallers Sullivan, between lowercase "protestants" and "catholics," respectively, the former referring to those (Protestant, Catholic, or otherwise) who accommodate modernity and the latter referring to those who resist it.[15]

The chapters that follow will look at the antimodern catholics. But before we can assess the recent antimodern attempts to answer the question of Christian identity by way of the rule of faith (*regula fidei*), it is first necessary to understand the modern quest for the essence of Christianity. In the rest of this chapter, I trace this quest from the Reformation through its modern liberal representatives, including Deists, mystics, historicists, existentialists, and liberationists. At this stage in our presentation, the point is not to argue for any particular account of the essence but to provide this history as the explanatory milieu for those who sought to counter the liberal quest with appeals to church tradition and ecclesial culture, whom I will discuss in the following chapters. This chapter will largely focus on the European tradition of liberal Christianity, both for the sake of brevity and because that is where the terms of the debate were set, before migrating to other parts of the world. At the end of this chapter, I will synthesize this history by outlining the different strategies for defining Christian identity that appear in the course of the modern quest.

THE REFORMATION ORIGINS OF THE QUEST

The history of the *quest* for the essence is different from the history of the essence itself. Every creed, every theological disputation, is either a direct or indirect exposition of what the faithful at a particular time and place considered the Christian essence – though the language of "essence" as we use it today is anachronistically applied to them. With respect to the ancients, we might more accurately call it the "substance" of the faith. Unlike the recent quest for the essential rule of faith that I am investigating in this book, however, there was no *ancient* quest for the rule of faith, because questing as such is a modern phenomenon. The ancient and medieval efforts at clarifying the Christian essence were not instances of a quest for the essence, because no quest was seen as critically necessary. Specific theologians had opinions about what defined a true Christian, but there was no existential need to figure this out because the authority of church tradition was not in doubt. Without a crisis of authority there can be no quest. By analogy, there were many theologians who made claims about the Jesus of history over the centuries, but there was no quest for the historical Jesus until the rise of historical consciousness and criticism of creedal Christology made such a quest necessary. To find the origins of the quest for the essence, we thus need to look to the origins of the modern crisis of authority, and for that we must turn to the Protestant Reformation.

It is a truism of recent scholarship on the history of Protestantism that the Reformation was more of a late medieval occurrence than an early modern one, and there is substantial truth to this observation. As Carl Ullmann (1796–1865) pointed out in his classic 1841 study of *Reformers before the Reformation*, there were numerous late medieval forerunners of the Reformation – Bernard of Clairvaux, the Brethren of the Common Life, John Wycliff, Jan Hus, Johannes von Goch, and Johann von Wesel, among others – and one needed the right social conditions to make a genuine Reformation possible.[16] Protestantism is the inheritor of these prior efforts at theological and ecclesiastical reform, as well as the beneficiary of serendipitous conditions, including the invention of the printing press and a favorable political environment. More recent research on the origins of Protestantism has only deepened this understanding of its medieval roots, countering the late nineteenth- and early twentieth-century German theologians who wanted to marshal Luther in favor of their national cause.[17]

We even find talk of an "essence" prior to Luther, as the work of Hans Wagenhammer has demonstrated.[18] Medieval theologians spoke about the *substantia fidei*, the substance of faith, which includes those matters that are necessary for one to believe in order to have saving faith. Thomas Aquinas, in his *Commentary on Lombard's Sentences*, says that the *substantia fidei* includes the belief that God is one and triune, among other things.[19] The late medieval German mystics, like Meister Eckhart and Johannes Tauler, generally did not talk about essences as static, metaphysical nouns. Instead, they talked about the life of ascetic virtue by which a person *becomes essential*. The "essential Christian" is the one whose life has been perfected through ascetic discipline so that they more fully experience participation in and union with the divine. The Bohemian Brethren and the Brethren of the Common Life, much like later Protestant pietism, distinguished between "the essential" and "the useful" aspects of the Christian life: the former referred to the virtues of faith, hope, and love, while the latter concerned details of doctrine and polity.[20]

While there were many reformist movements before the Reformation, it was Luther (1483–1546) who precipitated the modern quest for the essence. He was not the first to posit a new essence – nor was his account of the essence really new in the first place – but he was the first to do so in conjunction with a successful crisis of ecclesial authority. We must see both aspects, the negative and positive, together. Luther's critique of Rome's practice of indulgences was the critical counterpart to his constructive proposals for the essence of Christianity. In his 1518 *Heidelberg*

Disputation he articulated this essence as a "theology of the cross" (*theologia crucis*), which functioned for Luther as a hermeneutical norm by which to interpret the totality of God's revelation. He stated in thesis twenty, for instance, that a theologian must "understand the visible and posterior things of God seen through suffering and the cross."[21] The cross – which refers metonymically to a wider set of theological concepts, including justification, divine hiddenness, and the relation between law and gospel – serves as the core or principle of the early Luther's theology, providing a critical filter by which to evaluate scripture and doctrine and posing a direct challenge to the tradition and authority of Rome.

In other writings, Luther used the doctrine of justification to accomplish the same purpose. His 1518 sermon on two kinds of righteousness introduced the concept of "alien righteousness" or "alien justice" (*iusticia aliena*), which belongs to Christ alone and is "infused from outside of ourselves" and "by which he justifies through faith."[22] The alienness of grace provides not only a constructive norm for theology but also a critique of Rome's theology, which presumes that the church hierarchy possesses the authoritative deposit of faith (*depositum fidei*) and is authorized to mediate and dispense God's grace to those who partake of the sacraments. To declare that grace is alien is to acknowledge that no church institution or tradition can claim to possess it; if grace belongs to Christ alone then it is solely the work of God and is available equally to everyone for whom Christ is present by faith. By accepting this new doctrine of grace, this new Christian essence, one thereby accepts a new foundation for the church itself. For this reason Luther can say later that "if this article [of justification] stands, the church stands; if it falls, the church falls."[23] The distinction between human works and divine grace is so central to his thought that in his 1525 treatise *On the Bound Will*, Luther says that the distinction "between the power of God and our power, between the work of God and our work," constitutes the "total sum of Christianity."[24]

The question about the content of the Christian essence is inseparable from the question about its source and our access to that source. For this reason, Luther's account of the essence of Christianity goes hand in hand with his interest in the essential canon and the essential hermeneutic of scripture. Luther was influenced by the work of the humanists over the previous century, who had criticized the official texts and translations of scripture and challenged church leaders to focus more on the study of the Bible's original languages than on the fine points of scholastic theological debate. His own translation of the New Testament into German used the 1519 second edition of Erasmus's Greek New Testament. In addition to textual and philological study, Luther applied his account of the "sum of Christianity" to the biblical texts. His 1522 preface to the letter of James famously criticized its inclusion within the canon on the grounds that "whatever does not teach Christ is not apostolic." His guiding criterion for any text of the canon is not whether the church authorities have decided it but "whether it drives home Christ" (*ob sie Christum treiben*) – that is to say, whether it pushes, promotes, and emphasizes Christ.[25]

Luther further challenged Rome's authority when, in 1520, he introduced the principle that "scripture interprets itself" (*scriptura sui ipsius interpres*), rejecting the magisterium's exclusive right to interpret scripture and complementing the subversive theological concepts of cross and justification.[26] Luther combined this with a critique of the medieval fourfold exegetical method (known as the *Quadriga*) that emphasized spiritual and allegorical interpretation as the highest understanding of the biblical text. Luther elevated the literal (or historical) reading of the text, arguing that the spiritual interpretive methods are of no value "unless the same thing is expressed elsewhere in the historical sense."[27] Not only was this a criticism of traditional interpretive methods, but it also made the meaning of scripture accessible to common people who did not have the elite, esoteric knowledge of theological symbolism necessary to engage in spiritual interpretation, thus serving as the exegetical counterpart to his work on an accessible German text of the Bible. By identifying a publicly available, vernacular scripture as the source of the essence, and scripture itself as the hermeneutic for understanding this source, Luther identified a distinctively Protestant essence (or sum) of Christianity, one that subverts the traditional authority structure and democratizes our access to the knowledge and grace of God.

While he could never have anticipated what would happen in the centuries to follow, Luther's efforts made it possible to distinguish between the descriptive and prescriptive in a way that was inconceivable in the era of medieval Christendom, when the "true church" was simply identical with the visible church – that is to say, if you were a citizen of a Christian nation and participated in the customs of baptism and Mass, you were as much a Christian as anyone else. The Reformation exploded this identification. The true church was now essentially invisible, defined by an invisible, eternal act of election and an invisible, individual faith. Moreover, the source for defining the true church – the canonical scriptures – were available to anyone who could read, thanks to translation and the printing press. Anyone in principle could offer their own take on what makes someone a "true Christian." Prescriptivism became the common right of all. It was disruptive enough when the disagreements were merely over the understanding of Christ's presence in the Lord's Supper. But when the authority of the Bible and the reliability of our knowledge of God came under question, new efforts to define what makes someone Christian became necessary.

THE LIBERAL QUEST

For all of Luther's democratizing influence, the magisterial Protestant Reformation still took place within a late medieval context in which the authority of the church over society was presumed to be a given. Even appeals to nature and general revelation presupposed a social context in which everyone was already "Christian" by default. All of that changed as the scientific insights of Copernicus, Galileo, and Bacon transformed the intellectual landscape, resulting in the overthrow of the old "confessional regime."[28] Christians had always recognized that human reason could access truth apart from divine revelation on the basis that the same God who spoke the word of revelation also created the world and our rational capacities. All truth was God's truth, and thus the insights gained by reason apart from faith could not but cohere with the truths of revelation. But the scientific revolution upended that consensus. Telescopic observations that anyone could see with their own eyes disproved the geocentric Ptolemaic cosmos that ecclesiastical leaders understood as divine truth – a truth supposedly confirmed not only by common sense but also by the pages of holy writ. It was one thing for an Augustinian monk like Luther to claim that he had the correct interpretation of the apostle Paul's letters. It was quite another thing for anyone with the right scientific instruments to show that the old theories about the universe were wrong; indeed, even recognizing them as theories was itself scandalous. Entire metaphysical edifices had been constructed around these ideas, and once their certainty was no longer secure, the only question was: What else might crumble?

The answer was: quite a lot. Not everything crumbled right away, and different aspects of the classical world crumbled for different people. Moreover, people found widely divergent strategies for addressing these new developments. The most common and conservative approach was already on display in the Reformation. Calvin championed the idea of "accommodation" as a means of explaining the alien and often unsettling language of the Bible. If, in the Bible, God was accommodating the divine truth to the limitations of the human recipients of revelation, then one could explain geocentric statements, for example, as an act of accommodation to the cosmological views of ancient Israel. Some paired accommodation with an account of progressive revelation, whereby God gradually revealed new truths (or at least new clarifications of old truths) in line with humanity's progress in knowledge, especially with respect to the natural world. As attractive as this was for many, this approach came with significant drawbacks. For one thing, it assumed an anthropomorphic deity who willfully acts in discrete ways, choosing to reveal this or that according to specific human recipients. Such a concept of god might work at a popular level for those who imagine the divine as a kind of human figure, but theologically it was a nonstarter. Such a god could not be transcendent in the way the tradition had understood the one Jesus named as Father. Such a god would instead be more like the demigods of Greek lore, residing in their Olympian abode and deigning every so often to walk among mortals. The other problem was that it assumed a timeless, nonhistorical concept of revelation; it treated revelation as existing "out there" in some abstract, eternal form, which the deity then tailored for a specific historical moment. It failed to recognize that all truths are historical, enmeshed in the contingencies of culture.

The alternative to accommodation was the strategy of mediation, a term that refers to a two-stage process: first, the selection of a material principle or essence that summarizes the core of Christian faith; second, the mediation of all Christian doctrine in accordance with this principle. The process of mediation recognizes that all Christian theology is historical and open to new interpretations and accommodations. In place of a supposedly consensual, universal orthodoxy, mediation discards old doctrines and concepts if they no longer serve the purpose of expressing the fundamental essence of Christianity within the current moment. The theologian thus has the responsibility of identifying the principle or essence that best maintains continuity with the truth of Christianity while allowing for a more credible articulation of this truth. The choice of the essence is, of course, a highly contested one, and the arguments in theology within this context become arguments over the essence, as well as over related foundational starting points. Hence the reason for the heavy emphasis on prolegomena (introductory first principles) in modern theology. For the sake of simplicity, I will describe all theologies that engage in mediation as versions of "liberal theology," meaning any theology that embraces the challenges posed by modernity, such as the scientific revolution, the new epistemologies of philosophers like Immanuel Kant, the rise of historical consciousness and historical criticism in the nineteenth century, and the new sociopolitical and economic realities of mercantilism, imperialism, colonialism, and the Industrial Revolution. Liberal theology does not necessarily respond to all of these changes; it simply engages in the task of mediation in a way that constructs a theology more credible to this new world. Framed this way, all of the theologians surveyed in the rest of this chapter are liberal theologians, and the subsequent quests described below are not alternatives to the liberal quest but rather variations and developments of it.

In the wake of the Peace of Westphalia in 1648, many were disgusted with the way Roman Catholic, Lutheran, and Reformed Christians had allowed their theological differences to spill over into such bloody political conflict. Whether they had rightly interpreted the reasons for the wars or not, many concluded that the appeal to special revelation – the notion that God has specially disclosed hidden mysteries to select people, accessible by faith alone – was at the root of the conflicts. Each community believed it had exclusive access to God's truth, and that the others were heretical, perhaps even the agents of the devil. Such exclusivity was quickly falling out of fashion. The scientific revolution had already proven that knowledge about the natural world was available to anyone who made the empirical observations. Many drew the corresponding conclusion that general experience and observation of the natural world could grant people *religious* knowledge as well. These theologians, known as Deists, believed that reason, rather than revelation, was the source of true knowledge about God and the world.

Whether or not John Locke (1632–1704) belongs to the camp of the Deists – he understood revelation and reason to be complementary sources of religious knowledge – he at least paved the way for their arrival in his writings in the late seventeenth century. Like the Deists, he was appalled at the way commitment to irrational, supernatural doctrines had compelled people to behave in immoral ways. He opened his 1698 essay on "Error" with a critique of this distinction between orthodoxy and heresy:

> The great division amongst Christians is about Opinions. Every sect has its set of them & that is called Orthodoxie. And he who professes his assent to them though with an implicit faith & without examining he is Orthodox & in the way to salvation. But if he examines & thereupon questions any one of them, he is presently suspected of Heresie & if he oppose them or hold the contrary he is presently condemnd as in a damnable Error & the sure way to perdition. Of this one may say that there is nor can be nothing more wrong.[29]

In contrast to those who define religion in terms of propositional doctrines, Locke defined religion in terms of morality, the knowledge of good or bad actions, and he articulated Christianity's essence as the law or rule of God. The "divine law" refers to the "law which God has set to the actions of men, whether promulgated to them by the light of nature, or the voice of revelation."[30] The law of God must be wholly rational, for a person cannot assent to revelation if there is no "evidence of its being a revelation."[31] According to Locke, "reason must be our last judge and guide in every thing," including our examination of whether a supposed revelation "be a revelation from God or no."[32] His 1695 *Reasonableness of Christianity as Delivered in the Scriptures* developed his account, his liberal mediation, of what he considered to be the original, rational Christianity, which he interpreted as being focused strictly on the messiahship of Jesus and the kingdom of the Messiah – a kingdom of virtue and morality defined by the law of God. The law of God is identical with the moral and rational law of nature, but the advantage of Christianity is that one receives justification by faith despite failing to keep the law. By design, Locke restricted his analysis to the four Gospels and the book of Acts. The message of these texts, he says, is "obvious to any one who reads the New Testament."[33]

Unfortunately, the liberal Protestant message Locke found in the New Testament was not obvious to his detractors, who accused him of Socinianism – a label originally referring to the views of the anti-trinitarian Polish Brethren, who were guided theologically by the Italian Anabaptist Fausto Sozzini, though the term eventually became a generic label for anyone with heterodox beliefs. The Calvinist divine and controversialist John Edwards (1637–1716) wrote many works against the ostensible Socinianism of Locke. In *Socinianism Unmask'd*, Edwards argued that "besides the bare believing of Jesus to be the Messiah," it is necessary to believe a range of other doctrines, the whole set of them constituting "those *Evangelical Truths*, those *Christian Principles* which belong to the very Essence of Christianity."[34] Edwards perhaps had in mind the work of Richard Hooker, who was possibly the first to use the phrase "essence of Christianity," which he did in his well-known critique of Puritan theology and politics, *Of the Laws of Ecclesiastical Polity* (1594). Near the start of the third book, where he develops his direct refutation of Puritan ecclesiology, Hooker writes: "The visible Church of Jesus Christ is therefore one, in outward profession of those things, which supernaturally appertain to the very essence of Christianity, and are necessarily required in every particular christian [*sic*] man."[35] English theology thus typically saw the phrase "essence of Christianity" used not by liberals and Deists but instead by the conservative defenders of Christian tradition – foreshadowing the later interest in the rule of faith.

The opposite was the case on the continent. French mystics in the seventeenth century, such as Jean de Saint-Samson (1571–1636) and Madame Guyon (1648–1717), spoke of the "essence of the Christian religion" (*l'essence de la religion chrétienne*) to emphasize the contemplative experience of divine love above doctrines and practices.[36] For the mystics, like the pre-Reformation Brethren, talk of the essence of Christian religion was a way of refocusing the church around the virtues of faith, hope, and love. But the most significant developments happened in Germany, where talk of the essence of Christianity (*das Wesen des Christentums*) began to occur in the eighteenth century with the spread of Enlightenment thought. Johann Salomo Semler (1725–1791), the leading German rationalist theologian of that time, was influenced by English Deism and shared its rational and moral approach to Christianity. The school of German rationalist theology was known at the time as neology – the study of new things. In 1771 Semler defined the essence of Christian religion as the freedom of a person to use their rational faculties in distinction from official doctrine, and in 1779 he defined the essence as "a new moral or spiritual mindset" based on "the sublime teachings of Jesus."[37] The battle between the rationalists and the suprarationalists had reached a stalemate, with each side fixed in its understanding of Christianity as being about either natural morality or supernatural doctrine.

At the turn of the nineteenth century, Friedrich Schleiermacher (1768–1834) surveyed the available theological paths and found them wanting. Following his father's religious awakening, the young Schleiermacher was sent in 1783 to the religious school of the Moravian Brethren at Niesky. While this environment instilled in him a deep sensitivity to religious experience, the conservative doctrinal atmosphere stifled his inquisitive and critical mind. He ultimately broke with his father's pietist convictions and charted his own path, but some of what he learned from the Brethren stayed with him. Like the rationalists and Deists, Schleiermacher was critical of traditional orthodox doctrine, but he was just as critical of their replacement of a system of doctrine with a system of law and morality. His alternative, first formulated in the second speech of his famous *On Religion: Speeches to its Cultured Despisers* (1799), was to define the essence of religion as "neither thinking nor acting, but intuition and feeling."[38] Thinking and acting, or what he refers to as metaphysics and morals, are parochial and myopic; they think all that matters is what humans believe and accomplish. Religion, however, "wishes to intuit the universe, wishes devoutly to overhear the universe's own manifestations and actions, longs to be grasped and filled by the universe's immediate influences in childlike passivity."[39] The essence of religion, according to Schleiermacher, is a mystical sensitivity to the totality of life and nature, an openness to the holiness of all things. In distinction from both morals and metaphysics, "religion is the sensibility and taste for the infinite," by which he meant the divine.[40] In both his early and later work, he then defined the distinctive essence of Christianity as the manifestation of the infinite (God) in the finite, the way the finite resists and opposes the infinite, and finally the way the infinite overcomes this resistance through the reconciling work of Christ.

In his later systematic theology, *The Christian Faith*, Schleiermacher said that the essence of religion or piety that forms the basis for Christian community is "neither a knowing nor a doing but a distinct formation of feeling." The feeling he refers to here is the feeling of being "absolutely dependent" on God, the source of all life and existence.[41] For Schleiermacher, Christianity is rooted in a reality that is beyond the ability of our reason to grasp or our moral action to achieve, and what he called "feeling" was his way of describing the relation one has to this ultimate reality. The divine truth that theology seeks to bring to expression in language is therefore neither absolutely beyond reason (as traditional orthodoxy would have it) nor absolutely rational (as the Deists would have it). Instead, "all propositions of a Christian sort are super-rational in one respect, whereas in another respect they are all also rational." Theology is suprarational insofar as it refers to the transcendent reality that makes something "distinctively Christian," but it is rational insofar as it necessarily follows the same rules for language and meaning as any other discourse.[42] Schleiermacher thus found a way to carry out the mediation of Christian theology in a way that embraced the role of Enlightenment reason while also preventing the reduction of the Christian faith to something purely rational and natural.

HISTORICIZING THE QUEST

Schleiermacher was a pivotal turning point in the history of prescriptivism for the way he broke the standoffs between thinking and doing, on the one hand, and between reason and revelation, on the other. His novel alternative was to locate the essence of Christianity in prereflective feeling – the feeling of being absolutely dependent – and to understand the theological account of this feeling as both wholly rational and wholly suprarational. His mediating proposal provided a way for Christians to embrace modernity while preserving the essence of orthodoxy.

During Schleiermacher's influential life, another intellectual revolution was gathering momentum. Beginning by the late seventeenth century, the scientific revolution advanced beyond the study of the natural world to include the social world – the ideas, cultures, and societies of history.[43] Human history itself became a scientific object of study, open to analysis and critique on the basis of evidence. Modern humanity not only had scientific consciousness (i.e., the consciousness of living in a world governed by natural laws), but now it also had historical consciousness (i.e., the consciousness of shaping and being shaped by historical contexts). By the late eighteenth century, the accumulation of textual and archaeological evidence propelled the study of history out of the abstract realm of theology and political theory into a practical science that quickly came to shape how everyone sees the world. In the same way that people could no longer go back to a geocentric cosmos, so too people could no longer go back to a time when events were determined by divine law in a perfect synchronicity between the earth below and the heavens above.

Germany in the nineteenth century was at the vanguard of this revolution in historical understanding, and Schleiermacher's intellectual rival, G. W. F. Hegel (1770–1831), was the leading philosopher of history and historical consciousness. Both Schleiermacher and Hegel engaged in mediation in an effort to synthesize Christian faith and modern reason – Schleiermacher by means of an "eternal covenant" and Hegel by means of "reconciliation."[44] Both articulated an essence, but whereas Schleiermacher spoke of the essence of religion in more mystical and pietistic terms as a feeling that eludes rational articulation, Hegel defined the essence as spirit (*Geist*), which is rational self-consciousness, and this rational spirit has to work through its appearance within history in order to become reconciled with itself. For Hegel, historical consciousness was thus integral to the development of reason. The Hegelians split into two parties. The Hegelian Right, represented by the likes of Karl Daub and Philip Marheineke, identified the spirit with

God and found in Hegel's philosophy a way of historicizing traditional metaphysics. The Hegelian Left, including David Friedrich Strauss and Ludwig Feuerbach, appropriated Hegel's historical dialectic to critique orthodox Christianity, even religion itself – most powerfully in Feuerbach's work, *The Essence of Christianity* (1841). Picking up on a theme in Hegel's *Phenomenology*, Feuerbach (1804–1872) defined the essence of religion as the essence of humanity as such, which he regarded as self-consciousness: the consciousness of the infinite (religion) is nothing else than the consciousness of the infinite nature of consciousness itself.[45] Also worth mentioning here is Ferdinand Christian Baur (1792–1860), who straddled the divide between Schleiermacher and Hegel and was the first to develop a historical theology that employed historical criticism in the analysis of sources. Through a critical interpretation of the synoptic Gospels, Baur in his final years modified his understanding of the essence of Christianity and arrived at a position similar to that of Locke, in the sense that Baur came to define the essence in terms of Christianity's ethical character based on the moral teachings of Jesus.[46]

Those who followed Schleiermacher rather than Hegel could not avoid engaging in the historical analysis of Christianity that the Hegelians had promoted. The paradigmatic and defining figure of late nineteenth-century liberal theology, Albrecht Ritschl (1822–1889), began as a member of Baur's school but later abandoned the Hegelian method (including anything suggestive of metaphysics) in favor of a more Lutheran and Schleiermacherian approach that emphasized the experience of the religious community, particularly the experience of justification. Like Baur, he carried out his systematic theology by means of a rigorous history of doctrine. But for Ritschl the guiding principle of Christianity is not some abstract spirit or rational idea; instead, it was a soteriological essence defined by the historical and redemptive relation to the person of Jesus. Ritschl criticized what he called Socinian and Enlightenment theologians – here he had in mind the likes of Locke and Semler – for their "philosophical naturalism and religious and moral individualism," which led them to see "no natural connection ... between the forgiveness of sins and the historical position of Christ."[47] Ritschl, in this sense, was a strong defender of Christian tradition, but he interpreted this tradition in historical terms. He defended the tradition against rationalist critics without defending the metaphysical and supernatural doctrines that formerly communicated this tradition.

In contrast to Enlightenment individualism, Ritschl advocated a robust doctrine of Christian community and society under the rubric of the "Kingdom of God." A key feature of Ritschl's liberalism was his conception of God's kingdom as a social entity, a visible cultural community embodying the moral virtues of the Christian life in the world. The kingdom of God is the anthropological correlate of the doctrine of God. Insofar as "God is love," the kingdom is the civic society that embodies this universal love of neighbor.[48] The kingdom is therefore the human association, encompassing as many people as possible, characterized by moral action among its members that reflects the character of God. The difference between the church and the kingdom is that the church is strictly a "worshipping community" defined by "devotional action," whereas the kingdom is a civic community defined by "moral action." These are not two different communities but the same community in two different modes. "Those who believe in Christ, therefore, constitute a Church in so far as they express in prayer their faith in God the Father," while "the *same believers* in Christ constitute the Kingdom of God in so far as, forgetting distinctions of sex, rank, or nationality, they act reciprocally from love, and thus call into existence that fellowship of moral disposition and moral blessings which extends, through all possible gradations, to the limits of the human race."[49] The Ritschlian school of liberal theology thus consisted of both a critique of orthodox dogma and a fidelity to Jesus as the central historical fact and object of faith, and it connected both to an account of God's kingdom as the sociocultural context for and goal of the Christian life.

The apotheosis of nineteenth-century liberal and historicist theology appeared in the work of Adolf von Harnack (1851–1930), whose name is most associated today with talk of the essence of Christianity because of his famous and highly influential lectures on that topic in the winter semester of 1899–1900, published in German as *Das Wesen des Christentums* (The Essence of Christianity) and published in English as *What Is Christianity?*[50] Harnack was trained in conservative Lutheran theology but later gravitated toward Ritschl's combination of historical analysis and Jesus-piety. Both are on full display in his lectures on the essence of Christianity. In his opening lecture Harnack said "it is solely in its historical sense," using "the methods of historical science," that he would attempt to understand the Christian essence.[51] While he did not use this language, he made it clear that his aim was to provide a descriptivist account of Christianity in contrast to a prescriptivist. He rejected those approaches to the essence that were carried out by what he called apologists and philosophers of religion: the former referred to those who tried to defend Christianity's enduring value by showing how much good it has done for society; the latter referred to those philosophers and theologians, like Schleiermacher, who tried to identify a normative essence of religion in general, and then defined Christianity accordingly. Both of these approaches were so invested in a prescriptive, normative account of Christian identity that they failed to do justice to the historical diversity and development of Christianity. The purpose of his historical investigation was to be more honest about what Christianity essentially is, and this meant neither cherry-picking the examples that would prove how great Christianity is nor speaking about some abstract, timeless Christianity that bears little similarity to what we actually see on the ground. Whatever we make of Harnack's understanding of the Christian essence, we must keep in mind the intention of his project, which retains its validity regardless of the way he carried it out. In a way, Harnack was trying to answer the question posed by Andrew Walls at the start of this chapter: What holds Christianity together through all the twists and turns of history?

Harnack's descriptive approach meant that he placed no restrictions on the source material for his analysis of the essence, but since he was seeking to find the essence and not merely provide a descriptive history of Christianity, he was obliged to differentiate between the essential and inessential elements. This led him to his most famous – perhaps infamous – metaphor: namely, that his goal was "to grasp what is essential in the phenomena, and to distinguish kernel and husk."[52] The language of husk and kernel has been unjustly maligned in the decades since he gave this lecture. To be sure, the metaphor, taken literally, is crudely simplistic and suggests that within the messiness of history there is a clean, pure nugget of timeless truth just waiting to be discovered. Harnack meant no such thing, as he made very clear. The metaphor, like the other metaphors for the essence of Christianity that I presented above, is imperfect and prone to distortion, but only if taken out of the larger context of Harnack's argument and thus shorn of any nuance and explication. He explained what he meant by the "husk" in the following paragraph, where he stated that "Jesus Christ and his disciples were situated in their day just as we are situated in ours," and like us they "were bounded by the horizon and the framework" of their time and location.[53] They could not have been otherwise and still be human. The question, then, is whether one can differentiate between this horizon and something enduring – not necessarily timeless but at least meaningful in situations outside of its native context. Whatever that something is, that is the kernel. To deny that any such kernel exists is tantamount to denying any continuity in Christianity at all, for then every particular community would be trapped in its cultural and historical framework, incapable of drawing upon the past or bequeathing its wisdom to the future. Denying the distinction between husk and kernel would be the death of tradition as such. We can nuance and complicate this distinction, but rejecting it out of hand would mean each community is incommensurable with every other.

As a historian of Christianity, Harnack sided with those who see continuity over time, even if the tradition changes dramatically from one age to the next. He saw it as the central task and "highest duty" of the historian "to determine what is of permanent value" in each historical form of Christian life. But this does not mean the essence is changeless. Indeed, when it came to defining what this "gospel" is, Harnack wrote:

> There are only two possibilities here: either the Gospel is in all respects identical with its earliest form, in which case it came with its time and has departed with it; or else it contains something which, under differing historical forms, is of permanent validity. The latter is the true view. The history of the Church shows us in its very commencement that "primitive Christianity" had to disappear in order that "Christianity" might remain; and in the same way in later ages one metamorphosis followed upon another. From the beginning it was a question of getting rid of formulas, correcting expectations, altering ways of feeling, and this is a process to

which there is no end. But by the very fact that our survey embraces the whole course as well as the inception we enhance our standard of value of what is essential and of real value.[54]

Harnack here acknowledged, in contrast to those who assume his kernel was a static entity, that the essence of Christianity changes over time. As I pointed out already, the theologian Ernst Troeltsch, who wrote an important essay in 1903 on the essence of Christianity in response to Harnack's lectures, observed in 1913 that "the essence of Christianity differs in different epochs."[55] For this reason, Harnack's analysis of the Christian essence necessarily embraced, at least in principle, "the whole course" of Christianity in order to have as complete a picture as possible. But the historical theologian, according to Harnack, cannot simply repeat "the 'whole' Gospel," as if it were possible to make every detail and every permutation of Christianity normative. Each person is a child of their age, and for that reason we are tasked with the responsibility of discerning what is essential within the panoply of Christian history.[56]

What then did Harnack find to be essential? His answer was threefold: (1) "the kingdom of God and its coming," (2) "God the Father and the infinite value of the human soul," and (3) "the higher righteousness and the commandment of love."[57] Each of these was an aspect of Jesus's original message that retained its force throughout Christian history, even if the way people describe and interpret these ideas changes over time. Instead of the "kingdom of God" some speak of the commonwealth, reign, or "kindom" of God. Instead of "the infinite value of the human soul" we speak today of the dignity of each person. Instead of "higher righteousness" we might speak of Christian ethics or moral formation. The concept of the kingdom of God was a particularly vexing one for Harnack. While he was aware that what his contemporaries meant by this concept was a far cry from what Jesus and his early followers meant – though Harnack is perhaps not as sufficiently aware of this disparity as we are today, a point to which I will return below – he rightly pointed out the ambiguity surrounding this idea in the Gospels themselves, which speak of the kingdom at times as something "purely future" and external to us and at other times as something "already present" and within us.[58] This ambiguity resident in the biblical texts themselves makes it possible for later generations to interpret the kingdom in vastly disparate ways without abandoning their continuity with Jesus.

Well over a century since they were first given, Harnack's lectures are due for reconsideration. The details of his account of the essence are certainly dated and demand scrutiny, and since delivering the lectures the world has changed dramatically. Among other things, Harnack lived before the Pentecostal movement and globalization dramatically shifted the landscape of world Christianity. He lived at a time when the idea of miracles was no longer meaningful. While he acknowledged that "the Gospels come from a time in which the marvellous may be said to have been something of almost daily occurrence," that world no longer existed, at least not for him (or for myself, I must admit).[59] But for many today it remains alive and well. How then does one incorporate this into an understanding of the essence? Harnack's account arguably already makes space for this in his idea of the kingdom of God. The kingdom, he said, "is something supernatural, a gift from above, not a product of ordinary life." And even if religious people today reject the miraculous, they remain convinced that they are "not shut up within a blind and brutal course of Nature."[60] Some will interpret the "supernatural" character of God's kingdom to mean visible occurrences that are directly attributable to divine power, while others find any such competition between divine power and natural occurrences to be contrary to both reason and revelation. Nevertheless, the fact that both can find themselves in Harnack's category demonstrates the enduring power of his proposal.

ESCHATOLOGIZING THE QUEST

For all the insight of Harnack's historicizing of the quest, it marked the end of an age. The liberal synthesis of Christianity and modern European culture that began with the likes of Locke finally reached its conclusion with the generation of Harnack. This grand experiment in mediation was just as rich and profound, not to mention varied, in its results as was the medieval synthesis that preceded it. Whereas the medieval synthesis arose within an ecclesiastical empire, in which all things were determined by the church, the modern liberal synthesis had no such hierarchical guidance and thus took the form of a quest "from below" to discern what about Christianity could and should endure within the new world of modern science and human enlightenment. While much of this quest remains vital, it became clear around the time of Harnack's lectures that at least one essential feature of Christianity had been lost: eschatology. Seven years before Harnack's famous lecture series, Ritschl's son-in-law, Johannes Weiss, published a brief work on Jesus's preaching of the kingdom of God, in which he argued that the kingdom expected by Jesus was not a civil society of love and goodwill but rather the eschatological end of the world.[61] The book, and the research it instigated, highlighted the unbridgeable disparity between Jesus and modern Western society, but it was ultimately the devastation wrought by the First World War that brought an end to the Ritschlian liberalism that had grounded so much of its theology on the confidence that an enlightened European society stood in direct continuity with what Jesus had proclaimed.

In the wake of the war's wreckage, a new theological movement arose to provide a massive course correction to the quest. The movement was known as dialectical theology, and its originator was Karl Barth (1886–1968). He was joined by Rudolf Bultmann (1884–1976), Friedrich Gogarten (1887–1967), and Eduard Thurneysen (1888–1974), among others. The group was trained by the leading figures in liberal and historicist theology, including Harnack himself. The dialectical theologians criticized their teachers for turning the essence of Christianity into an objective feature of world history, a social and cultural fact accessible to anyone with the right scientific tools. Against this, dialectical theology argued that the essence of Christianity, the object of faith and theology, is a divine word, the act of divine revelation itself, and by definition this cannot be a historical object because God is not an entity within history. God stands over against the world in both judgment and grace as the "wholly other" God – not wholly other in an abstract, philosophical sense, but in the *eschatological* sense that one finds in scripture. In the second edition of his book, *The Epistle to the Romans* (1922; 1st edition, 1919), the book that launched this movement, Barth declared: "Christianity that is not wholly and completely eschatology has wholly and completely nothing to do with *Christ.*[62] Bultmann throughout his career said the same thing in a more historical register, arguing for the essentially eschatological nature of Christianity on the basis of its origins in the eschatological preaching of Jesus and the early community's understanding of itself as an "eschatological community" in which the "eschatological event" of redemption in Christ was "already being realized in the present."[63] Bultmann summarized his position in his 1955 Gifford Lectures: "In early Christianity history is swallowed up in eschatology. The early Christian community understands itself not as a historical but as an eschatological phenomenon. It is conscious that it belongs no longer to the present world but to the new Aeon which is at the door."[64] Gogarten followed the work of Barth and Bultmann on this point. In a book on the question of the essence of Christianity, titled *What Is Christianity?* (1956), Gogarten stated: "The Christian faith in its essence is hope for the future, so that we can even say it is quite truly the disclosure of the future."[65] Using similar language, Bultmann wrote in 1958 that Christianity can be understood "in its essence as an eschatological phenomenon." To be a Christian is to have an "eschatological existence," so that believers now see themselves as being removed from the world (what Bultmann called being "deworldized") while paradoxically remaining within the world.[66] This paradox of being simultaneously fully historical and fully eschatological is what dialectical theology understands as the essence of Christianity.

In addition to dialectical theology, this school of thought is also known as word-of-God theology and kerygmatic theology, because "word of God" and "kerygma" were the two terms, in addition to "revelation," that these theologians used to name the essence of Christianity as they understood it. Each term had its benefits and drawbacks. The word "revelation" was the most well-established already and thus the most widely used by this movement, though they had to expend significant energy countering the notion of natural revelation. While revelation rightly implies the disclosure of something new and previously unknown, it is also frequently treated as a static noun and conflated with the Bible. Barth often had to remind his readers that revelation, as he understood it, was always a *revealing* and never a *revealedness.*[67] Revelation for the dialectical theologians was not an object but an act and event – a divinely wrought occurrence in which the eschatological reality of God confronted people within history. For this reason, "word of God" and "kerygma" (derived from the Greek word meaning "proclamation") were more effective terms for naming this divine act.

Barth's theology from the start was focused on the importance of the word (and Word) of God.[68] In his 1924 lectures on dogmatics, Barth used the Latin phrase *Deus dixit*, "God has spoken," to refer to this revelatory word.[69] His later *Church Dogmatics* defined the norm and method of theology as "the revelation which Scripture attests as the Word of God."[70] The task of theology is to present and analyze the action of God that takes place in this word. Barth is reticent, however, to view God's word as the "essence of Christianity." He associates this term with a history that goes back to Protestant orthodoxy's notion of a "foundation of faith" (*fundamentum fidei*), which made a distinction between essential and inessential doctrines. Later rationalist and liberal theologians changed what they regarded as essential, but the overall structure remained the same. Barth's concern with this whole approach is that it settles down too comfortably with a fixed idea of what the object and content of theology ought to be. According to Barth, the object of theology cannot be reduced to "any view, or idea, or principle," because it is instead "the work and activity of God."[71] The place occupied by an essence or principle "belongs by right to the Word of God, and the Word of God alone." This does not necessarily rule out the essence of Christianity as such. Barth admits in the same paragraph that "dogmatics certainly has a basis, foundation, and centre," but the point is that "this centre is not something which is under our control, but something which exercises control over us."[72] Barth still has an essence of Christianity, but it is unlike the essences of previous generations, at least as he understands it. Whereas earlier accounts of the essence confined the word of God to a basic doctrine or theological principle, Barth understands the essence as an event – an eschatological event – that is "ready for new insights" and consists in an "openness to receive new truth."[73] In contrast to previous theologies, dialectical theology understands the essence to be "the Word of God itself" and "not a conception of it."[74] Whereas a concept of the word has nothing new to say, the word of God itself proclaims new truths in each new situation. For this reason, Sykes says that Barth represents "the most radical version" of the liberal "inwardness tradition" regarding the essence of Christianity, because the essence for him "is literally inexpressible, since it consists not of doctrines but of the disposition of openness, of expectant obedience. No mere doctrines are ever permanent or unchangeable, nor are any forms of church government."[75] In a sense, Barth has provided an essence that can make sense of the diversity of Christian history. Whereas Troeltsch pointed out that the essence differs in different epochs, for Barth this historical change does not undermine the essence of Christianity but instead confirms a different and more flexible account of the essence: one that is capable of changing in correspondence to the changes in history.

As a New Testament scholar, Bultmann used the term kerygma to serve the same purpose. The word had a long history already of being used to identify the essence of Christianity. In 1777, Semler pointed out that from "the beginning of the Christian religion" there was a distinction between *kērygma* as the essential truth of the Christian religion and *dogmata* as the religious doctrines that were true only for a particular time and place.[76] As I discussed above, Semler advocated for the rational critique of the latter in support of the former. Like Semler, Harnack used the term *kērygma* to refer to the beliefs about God and Jesus that characterized the earliest community of Jesus followers. There were "separate *Kerygmata* about God and Christ." The kerygma about God referred to God as the all-powerful creator, while the kerygma about Jesus referred to him as the fulfillment of prophecy and the "Son of God," and spoke of his death, resurrection, and return. These *kerygmata* were integrated into the baptismal formula, which became the basis for the *regula fidei* and the later creeds.[77] Martin Dibelius, one of the pioneers of New Testament form criticism, brought the term into New Testament studies in his 1919 work on the formation of the Gospels, where he identified the kerygma with the earliest preaching about Jesus, which he finds in paradigmatic form in places like Acts 2:22–24 and 10:36–41.[78] Bultmann then picked up the term from Dibelius. But it functioned strictly in this historical sense until Barth, in 1924, stated in his theological interpretation of 1 Corinthians 15 that "*kerygma* is based on revelation." Bultmann published a review of this book in 1926 and

commented on this passage, and from that point on he began to incorporate this theological understanding of kerygma into his work, in which
the kerygma is another way of naming the revelatory event of God's
word.[79] Understood this way, the kerygma increasingly took on an
eschatological meaning. This shift from history to eschatology also involved
shifting from a concept with a clear, objective definition to one that
could never be absolutely defined. Just as the eschatological God remains
wholly other and ungraspable, so too "the kerygma is just what theology
can never seize in definitive form." Because the kerygma is "nothing else
than God's word," it is as transcendent as God is and cannot be confined
to any linguistic expression – even something as simple as "Jesus, Lord"
(2 Cor 4:5).[80] Like Barth's concept of the word of God, Bultmann's
kerygma serves to ground theology on the act of God's revelation while
also empowering the translation of Christian faith into an unlimited
variety of historical forms.

While the dialectical theologians portrayed themselves as tireless
opponents of the quest for the essence of Christianity and were the most
vocal critics of the rationalist, liberal, and historicist theologians who
pioneered the quest, dialectical theology was in fact the pinnacle of the
quest, insofar as it implicitly advocated a concept of the essence of
Christianity that provided a theological grounding for the quest as a
whole. Many of the theologians reviewed above thought they had arrived
at the one correct account of the Christian essence, and this misplaced
confidence was what Barth and the other dialectical theologians rejected
as an encroachment on the eschatological transcendence of God. But
precisely in rejecting this confidence, they articulated a version of the
essence that affirmed the legitimacy, at least in principle, of these other
definitions. That was not how their work was received by English-
speaking theologians, however, as we will see in the following chapter.

LIBERATING THE QUEST

Speaking of anglophone theology, theologians in the United States made
a distinctive contribution to the quest that departed from the European
tradition and lay the foundation for the developments of the late twentieth century. We can describe this stage in the quest as the *politicizing* of

the essence. This development has its origins in the Lockean and rationalist account of the essence as the moral law, which then filtered its way through the American liberal tradition among Unitarians, revivalists, abolitionists, and moral reformers who readily dispensed with doctrine in favor of practice as the central criterion of genuine faith. The innovative revivalist Charles Finney (1792–1875) was paradigmatic of this mentality, writing in his 1835 work, *Lectures on Revivals of Religion*, that Christianity throughout history had become very good at producing people who were perfectly orthodox in their ideas while being entirely heretical in their actions. He argued, in contrast, that "the only design of doctrine is to produce practice, and it does not seem to be understood by the church, that *true faith* 'works by love and purifies the heart,' that heresy in *practice* is proof conclusive of heresy in sentiment."[81] Practice became the essence of Christianity for Finney, though he did not use that language. "Anything brought forward as doctrine, which cannot be made use of as practical," is not truly Christian and thus not true doctrine.[82] By contrast, he implied, anything that *is* practical for the faith is worthy of being considered doctrine.

What changed at the start of the twentieth century was that the moral and practical essence of previous decades became an explicitly *political* essence with the rise of socialist Christians who engaged directly with the policies and institutions of the political order. Walter Rauschenbusch (1861–1918) is the most notable of this group. In his diagnosis of where Christian went astray, Rauschenbusch went back to the second century, after which point "dogma came to be regarded as the essence of Christianity."[83] The result of this change, he argued, was the depoliticization of Christianity. As the early Christ followers became "a firmly organized, authoritative, and international ecclesiastical organization," the work of Christianity was reduced to the work of the church, focused on its own maintenance and expansion. The goal of the loyal Christian was to have the correct doctrine and preserve the apostolic tradition. "Christian ethics became churchly ethics," so that actions were moral if they served the cause of the church.[84] The church confined its radical vision to the spiritual interiority of the soul's salvation, leaving all politics to the state – to the empire with which it was in comfortable partnership. Christianity thus failed to accomplish the task of "social regeneration" that Rauschenbusch argued was part of its original purpose.[85] Implicit in his argument was the claim that the true essence of Christianity is socio-political transformation: the creation of a society defined by the message of Jesus. For Rauschenbusch, this meant partnering with socialism, whose views were "the most thorough consistent economic elaboration of the Christian social ideal."[86] Rauschenbusch was writing at a time when socialist mayors were running over two hundred small cities across the United States, filling people like Rauschenbusch with hope for the future.[87] He was critical of organized socialism, however, because of its own tendency toward dogmatic orthodoxy. In the same way that Christianity went astray by focusing on maintaining the church as an end in itself, so too Rauschenbusch was concerned that the socialist parties might solidify into "a narrow and jealous orthodoxy" focused on maintaining the party as an end in itself, something he also saw in the Republican Party and religious organizations.[88] Put another way, both Christians and political party activists needed to orient themselves around their proper practical essence.

The politicizing of the essence took a decisive turn with the rise of liberation theology in the wake of the civil rights movement and global student and antiwar protests. James Cone (1938–2018), one of the original architects of liberation theology, was unsatisfied with the notion that depoliticization was the problem, since the truth of the biblical story is "that God is not simply the God of politics but the God of the politics of the oppressed, liberating them from bondage."[89] From the vantage point of Black experience, the problem was not merely the institutional separation between Christianity and politics but the promotion of a false theology that led to a politics of the status quo. White status quo Christians "were wrong ethically because they were wrong *theologically*."[90] Cone's critique of white theology was reflected in his engagement with the question of the Christian essence. In his earliest works, in which he used the writings of Barth and other European theologians to lay the groundwork for his theology of liberation, Cone expressed his alternative to status quo theology as a clarification of the liberal tradition of the essence. Explicitly referring to Schleiermacher's *Christian Faith*, Cone wrote in *Black Theology and Black Power*: "Christ is the essence of Christianity. ... Christianity revolves around a Person, without whom its existence ceases to be."[91] The following year, in *A Black Theology of Liberation*, Cone said "the answer to the question 'What is the essence of Christianity?' can be given in the two words: Jesus Christ."[92] Cone's revision to this old white European question was to insist that "the essence of the biblical message" had to be united with "the struggle for black liberation," which ultimately meant insisting that "Christ is black" and even "God is black."[93] As Cone moved away from engaging European theology toward drawing on Black traditions of spirituals and blues as the source material for his theology, he left behind the quest for the essence at the explicit level, though his work was still an implicit contribution to the quest – one that stressed the importance of placing the liberation of the oppressed at the heart of the Christian story.

Cone's work was significant for the way it placed liberation at the center of Christian theology, but it was less concretely political than Rauschenbusch's work. It was the Latin American liberation theologians – including, *inter alia*, Gustavo Gutiérrez (1928–), Juan Luis Segundo (1925–1996), and Ignacio Ellacuría (1930–1989) – who emphasized the specifically political nature of liberation theology through their use of Marxian thought and their focus on class struggle. Gutiérrez thus defined theology as critical reflection on praxis, understanding praxis both historically in terms of political struggle and theologically as orthopraxis (right action).[94] Segundo countered what he called the "political taboo" head on by arguing that "every theology is political," and that "there is no such thing as Christian theology" without a "prior political commitment" – specifically, the personal commitment to the liberation of the oppressed.[95] For Segundo, this meant that the Christian norms have to be understood as political from the start, in the sense of being allied with a particular party and ideology. This decision or option to be on one political side is essential to having Christian norms in the first place. The attempt to impose supposedly apolitical Christian norms onto politics eventually turns into "third-way stands" that become counter-revolutionary in the face of a revolutionary moment.[96] In other words, the notion that Christian norms are originally apolitical is already a decision in favor of right-wing politics.

These Latin American works were not engaged in the European quest that had defined the broad tradition of modern liberal theology, but they, along with their North American counterparts, still offered a compelling answer to the basic question about the identity of Christianity, one that still reverberates in today's religious discourse. Whether in terms of support or opposition, the liberationist essence of Christianity set the terms of debate in the late twentieth century, as all discourse became highly politicized. While Rauschenbusch and Segundo thought it was self-evident that a genuinely Christian politics should be leftist, the rise of reactionary, counterrevolutionary theology in recent decades has, in effect, taken their account of the Christian essence and completely inverted it, generating an antiemancipatory, right-wing political theology governed by a preferential option for the status quo – even, in some instances, for the oppressors themselves.

THE QUEST FOR THE ESSENCE AND THE RULE OF FAITH

From a certain perspective, the liberal quest for the essence of Christianity – whose heyday lasted roughly from 1650 to 1950 – seems like a three-century-long digression from our main topic. Both before and, as I will explore in the following chapters, after the quest, the rule of faith generally dominated the discussion of what defines Christian faith and identity, insofar as there was any discussion at all. Proponents of the rule of faith today like to claim they are simply continuing the premodern tradition of the rule. The interest in the essence, according to this view, was a massive mistake, and to correct that mistake all we need to do is return to the consensus tradition of the church. But it's not that simple. The more recent interest in the rule of faith is quite different from the earlier rule of faith, even if the doctrinal propositions are the same, and we can only understand that difference by first grasping the intervening quest for the essence of Christianity and how it shaped the discourse about what it means to be Christian.

As much as some would like to blame the quest and all those who participated in it for the departures from what they consider orthodoxy, the reality is that the quest was not the initiator but the response to a rapidly and dramatically changing world. Today we name this period of change "modernity," which is shorthand for the many historical, institutional, scientific, and philosophical revolutions that transformed

Western society and the self-understanding of those who lived within these parts of the world. While some today claim it was an error for Christians to adapt to these new conditions, it would not be the first time Christianity learned to adjust to a new environment. Indeed, missiologists like Walls frequently observe that change has been part and parcel of Christianity from the beginning, starting with the Jerusalem Council (Acts 15). Walls's thought experiment is a way of highlighting how Christians have learned to accommodate radically different social, cultural, and political situations. Those who oppose the accommodation of Western modernity imply there are some cultural conditions that are incompatible with Christian faith, which ironically presupposes a more limited and inflexible understanding of Christianity than classical Christianity traditionally had.[97]

What the quest exposed is what should have always been plain to see – namely, that there is no single right way to be Christian. This had been harder to recognize when the ecclesiastical authorities were able to control the narrative and determine who was orthodox and who was a heretic. And in the days before mass media, ideas were preserved only when enough people wanted them preserved, and often this meant that marginal and heterodox ideas were only passed down by those who were writing *against* them. The rise of modernity coincided with, and was arguably caused by, the collapse of the authority structures and the easy spread of new ideas. Modernity thus forced people to make a heretical choice – heresy coming from *hairesis*, meaning "choice" – to decide where they stood vis-à-vis this new social context. Some embraced it and sought to adapt Christianity to modernity; others ignored it and pretended modernity did not happen; and still others opposed it and developed accounts of Christianity designed to counteract modernity.

Unfortunately, even the liberal theologians who embraced modernity still fought among themselves over which version of the essence was the "right" one. These disputes could often be vicious, leading to rival schools that viewed each other as enemies of the truth (e.g., the Left and Right Hegelians). The most notable example of this was the group of dialectical theologians, many of whom disparaged all liberal and historicist theologians as having abandoned revelation and genuine God-talk. Such overblown rhetoric did not make their own contribution to the quest any less a part of the modern liberal tradition. All it did was demonstrate the vast flexibility of liberal theology, even if their grandiloquence suggested that no flexibility was allowed. The task ahead of us is to glean what lessons we can from the history of the modern quest for the essence for constructing a better prescriptivism today, without repeating the tendency to declare one's account the only valid version.

This chapter has surveyed many, though by no means all, of the ways that theologians adapted Christianity to the modern period. To borrow from Schleiermacher, we can subdivide these different accounts of the essence into those characterized by *thinking, doing,* and *feeling* – or, put differently, reason, morality, and experience. These categories line up with the three dimensions of religiosity that Jocelyne Cesari, drawing on the work of earlier sociologists of religion, uses to understand religion in modernity: the "three Bs" of believing, behaving, and belonging.[98] These three aspects – creeds and beliefs, religious and social practices, and collective identity – correspond with Schleiermacher's categories and provide a useful rubric for mapping the liberal and conservative quests for normative Christianity.

Among those who embraced modernity, the ones who emphasized *thinking* tended to reject traditional Christian orthodoxy as irrational, still too bound up with myth. Hegel and the idealist thinkers who followed in his wake were a prime example of this. They identified the concept of God with Absolute Reason, which for some of them was the teleological fulfillment of human reason itself, while for others was the divine mind as a transcendent rational agent distinct from the world. But the rational and metaphysical reconstruction of Christianity was not the only available path. Barth would want to place many of the Protestant orthodox theologians in this category, those Reformed and Lutheran scholastics and suprarationalists who believed that divine revelation was something objective and doctrinal in nature and sought to use the tools of reason to their benefit. I would treat them as forerunners instead of the modern rule of faith, a precursor to those Protestant apologists in the late nineteenth and twentieth centuries, particularly in Great Britain and North America – such as William Paley, J. Gresham Machen, C. S. Lewis, and Gordon Clark – who mobilized rational proofs and observable evidence to defend what they understood to be the truth of traditional Christian teachings.

Others accommodated Christianity to modernity by taking the route of *doing* and locating the essence of the faith in its moral creed. Locke is a classic example of this approach, along with other Deist and rationalist thinkers, such as Semler. In the early American republic, the likes of Thomas Jefferson and John Adams followed in the footsteps of Locke and argued against doctrinal orthodoxy in favor of a liberal Christianity defined by natural religion and the moral law. In the Progressive Era, a more explicitly political approach to the moral essence arose in the work of Rauschenbusch and Vida Dutton Scudder, among others, and the liberation theologians took that further by connecting the Christian gospel with the struggle of the oppressed classes for emancipation. In a way, the moral interpretation of Christianity was the path of least resistance, since the Bible provides ample support for such a view. With the prophetic tradition in the Hebrew scriptures and the teachings of Jesus in the Gospels, a moral essence of Christianity has much to commend it. This was a version of Christianity that, at least compared to the speculative accounts of the Hegelians, made sense to the average layperson. One did not need to be a Deist or Unitarian to find this essence of Christianity attractive. Another advantage of this approach is the bridge it builds with other religions, particularly those with less investment in metaphysics and more focus on personal and communal formation. Beyond the potential for interreligious dialogue, common moral precepts, shared across religions, were seen by many as pointing to something fundamentally true, something deeper than any individual religion's account of revelation – a transcendent moral point unifying the religions and thereby all of humanity.

The path less traveled was the way of *feeling* that had its origins in the medieval mystics but reached its modern apotheosis in Schleiermacher. To describe this category using the term "experience" can be misleading, because Schleiermacher's feeling (a poor translation of *Gefühl*) is arguably beyond experience, or rather *before* experience, referring not to a specific sensation or awareness in human consciousness but rather what Thandeka calls "the rupture in human consciousness" that marks the "border point" at which "all individuation has been canceled."[99] Put another way, feeling is a way of trying to capture something that is utterly outside of our grasp and so completely incapable of being analyzed like a rational doctrine or enacted like a moral command. We might call this experience mystical or spiritual, though these words are equally prone to misunderstanding. Feeling, according to Schleiermacher, is the ineffable sense we have of being in unity not only with ourselves but also with all reality – existing in connection with other people, the world, and with God. The dialectical theologians had a crude understanding of Schleiermacher's theology as referring to some inner experience that could be grasped, manufactured, and manipulated, and they were rightly suspicious of this idea, even if they wrongly attributed it to Schleiermacher himself due to their contemporaries who claimed to be following Schleiermacher's lead. In truth, the dialectical theologians, with their eschatological concept of revelation, were far closer than their liberal colleagues to Schleiermacher, and we would have to locate the eschatological essence that dialectical theology articulated within the category of Schleiermacher's *Gefühl.*

What bearing does all this have on the topic of the rule of faith? As I show in the next three chapters, the rise of the rule of faith in modern – or, rather, antimodern – theology is a reaction to these various efforts at defining the essence of Christianity. While proponents of the rule of faith champion it as the "historic Christian faith," a norm impervious to the passage of time, the truth is that the rule cannot escape its historical location. In fact, the rule of faith as it has developed over the past two hundred years encompasses each of Schleiermacher's three categories: reason, experience, and morality – now transposed into orthodox doctrine, cultural identity, and conservative politics. In its doctrinal, cultural, and moral formations, it is contingent on the quest for the essence, even as it tries to claim timeless validity. Today's rule of faith, which has come to mean much more than just creedal Christianity, is just as modern as the essence of Christianity that it rejects.

2

Recovering the Rule

The Retrieval of "Historic Christianity"

T HE QUEST FOR THE ESSENCE OF CHRISTIANITY may have started in Europe, but it found a receptive home in the United States, where disparate interpretations of Christian faith flourished and multiplied. One of the most prominent proponents of this religious heterodoxy was the Unitarian minister and abolitionist, Theodore Parker. While initially drawn to the German liberal thought of theologians like Schleiermacher, he eventually came under the influence of the Transcendentalists, including Ralph Waldo Emerson and Henry David Thoreau. "The scales of ecclesiastical tradition fell from my eyes," he remarked later.[1]

On May 19, 1841, nearly four years into his pastorate at South Evangelical Church in the West Roxbury neighborhood of Boston, he preached "A Discourse on the Transient and Permanent in Christianity," a sermon announcing his definitive break with the norms of Christian orthodoxy – in particular the normativity of the Bible as the revelation of God and the normativity of the ancient creeds and doctrines. Parker argued that Christians throughout history had misidentified what is essential and nonessential, permanent and transient:

Any one who traces the history of what is called Christianity, will see that nothing changes more from age to age than the doctrines taught as Christian and insisted on as essential to Christianity and personal salvation. What is falsehood in one province passes for truth in another. The heresy of one age is the orthodox belief and "only infallible rule" of the next. Now Arius, and now Athanasius is Lord of the ascendant. Both were excommunicated in their turn; each for affirming what the other denied. Men are burned for professing what men are burned for denying.[2]

Parker had observed that, despite talk of infallible rules and eternal truths of faith, the supposedly permanent essence of Christianity changed depending on who was in power at a given time . For this reason, he argued that Christians have placed the emphasis in the wrong place. Christians have ignored the "true religion" that is "always the same thing, in each century and every land," and instead identified the essence with "forms and doctrines," which "are only the accident of Christianity; not its substance."[3] The very doctrines orthodoxy regards as fixed Parker contended were flimsy and ephemeral. The true substance, he claimed, was instead the natural religion and morality found in the words of Jesus, as well as in the teachings of all great religious leaders. This alone offered something actually stable throughout the vicissitudes of cultural change.

The sermon elicited a "great outcry," according to Parker's later recollections in a letter written to his congregation upon his forced retirement in 1859 due to tuberculosis. When the sermon was published, it was "vehemently denounced" and "most of [his] clerical friends fell off."[4] Having been ostracized from the Unitarians, Parker resigned his pastorate in 1846 and became the leader of a new community started by his followers called the Twenty-eighth Congregational Society. By that point he recognized that "I had thoroughly broken with the ecclesiastical authority of Christendom ... for I preferred the Jesus of historic fact to the Christ of theologic fancy."[5] A year after publishing his autobiographical reflections on the evolution of his beliefs, Parker died in Italy from the then-incurable disease.

While Parker had amassed quite the following, other Unitarians saw the need to go in a different direction. The same year Parker published his farewell letter, the pastor of First Congregational Church in New York City, Henry Whitney Bellows, gave an address on July 19 to the alumni of Harvard Divinity School expressing his concern that the time in which they were living "is not only an unreligious age, but it is becoming more and more unreligious."[6] Bellows still agreed with the Unitarian rejection of Christian orthodoxy – a position he regarded as faithful to the spirit of the Protestant Reformation – but he had come to believe freethinking liberalism had gone as far as it ought to go ("as Protestants of the Protestants, we are at the apogee of our orbit") and now there were aspects of orthodoxy that needed to be recovered, not in terms of doctrine but in terms of community.[7] Drawing on the recent conversions to Rome of John Henry Newman and Orestes Brownson, Bellows's solution to the irreligion of his day was "a new Catholic Church" – a church that would combine the rituals and mystical symbols of the Roman church with the intellectual freedom of Protestantism.[8] In his "Sequel" to the "The Suspense of Faith," delivered at his church on September 25, 1859, Bellows specifically criticized the liberal quest for an

> essence (so supposed!) of theologies and churches and of Christianity itself – in which at first only the old forms, dogmas, symbols, and rites of the Church, as a creed and an institution, were discarded as refuse or slag – as not essential and absolute; and in which at last the history and records and personality of Christianity itself were thrown off, as accidental or even excremental, or at any rate as non-essentials of a system, which had yielded its secret and soul to the crucible of metaphysical and scientific analysis – and now stood simplified and condensed in the phials of social philosophy.[9]

Bellows regarded the quest as a necessity, forced upon the church "by internal and irresistible laws of the mind and the age," but it had failed, in his judgment, because those who engaged in this quest "had not known how congenitally adapted to mortal wants is a positive revelation, an historical religion, an incarnated Divinity, an external apparatus of doctrines and symbols, possessing authoritative quality, tangible shape, and positive testimony."[10] In other words, ecclesiastical orthodoxy may be theologically flawed, but it is psychologically attuned to human nature.

Others, however, thought this did not go far enough. What was needed, according to some writers, was rather a return to what they considered historic Christian orthodoxy – not merely because it meets human psychological needs, but because it is true and essential to the faith. This was the argument of Episcopal minister John Cotton Smith. In his response to both Parker and Bellows, naturally titled "The Suspense and Restoration of Faith," he argued that the true essence of Christianity is the "Trinitarian and evangelical theology" of "historic

Christianity," a term he uses twenty-six times.[11] Smith shared none of Bellows's pessimism about the loss of faith and denies the need for a new church, claiming instead that traditional Christian orthodoxy provides everything that Bellows wants "and is the most powerful element in the Protestant world."[12] All we need, he argues, is "a return to the principles of evangelical or historic Christianity" – principles that Smith regarded as easily discernible from both the Bible and even a cursory study of history.[13]

We see in this snapshot from a small corner of American Protestantism in the nineteenth century a précis not only of the modern quest for a credible Christianity but also of its antimodern opponents, who are parasitically dependent on the questers for their raison d'être. This chapter and the following two explore these opponents – we could call them "counterquesters" – of the liberal reconstructions of Christian theology. Some of them, especially those in the nineteenth century, replaced the liberal essence of Christianity with their own more doctrinal, creedal version of the essence. Others rejected the language of "essence" altogether in favor of more traditional terminology. Chief among these options was the one favored by the ancient church, namely, the "rule of faith."

The rise of the antimodern interest in the rule of faith was not a single movement but rather a complex, polycentric development with sources in different traditions and communities. Just as modern, liberal theology arose in response to diverse stimuli and took a variety of forms, so too the formation of antiliberal (later postliberal), and often aspirationally – though not actually – premodern, theology was hardly a singular occurrence. As I explained at the end of Chapter 1, Schleiermacher's tripartite schema of thinking (doctrine), feeling (culture), and doing (morality) provides a heuristically useful rubric for analyzing the recent interest in the rule of faith. To be sure, all three aspects were usually always at play simultaneously, with some taking center stage and others moving into the background at different points. Distinguishing them involves telling the story in artificially one-sided ways, but it helps to highlight the different norms and logics involved in the recent battles over "true Christianity."

The *thinking* rule of faith, the subject of this chapter, took the form of the retrieval of "historic" creedal Christianity as the norm of true Christian faith. As rationalist and liberal theologians advanced interpretations of the faith intentionally at odds with more traditional accounts, the term "historic Christianity" became the watchword of those who claimed the mantle of orthodoxy, not only as a way of rhetorically giving themselves an air of authority by claiming continuity with an authoritative past but also as a shibboleth signaling their opposition to the modern quest for a credible essence. What different Christians mean by "historic," however, reveals their underlying assumptions about the essence. For many evangelical Protestants, the truly historic Christianity is not the rule of faith developed by the ancient church but instead the early apostolic community described in the New Testament. To retrieve this Christianity means bypassing the ancient and medieval tradition to recover some kind of original, and ostensibly authentic, Christian faith.[14] This is not the sense of the term that principally concerns me, though it is no less problematic. I am here interested in the other, more catholic (and Catholic) sense of "historic," referring to the doctrines of the ancient councils and creeds that have typically defined the meaning of Christian orthodoxy – what John Cotton Smith has in mind in the quotes above. For many Protestants, affirming the normativity of the ancient creeds was often seen as "Romanism" and thus a betrayal of the Reformation. The Bible and the rule of faith were seen as competing norms. Few have exemplified this tension more than John Henry Newman, whose Tractarian campaign on behalf of the rule of faith eventually concluded with his conversion to Rome. I devote attention to him here not only because of his influence on later retrievalist efforts, but also because he articulates with admirable honesty what the doctrinal adherence to the ancient rule requires theologically.

Though Newman was a cautionary tale for some at the time, in subsequent years many Protestants – here I am particularly interested in American Protestantism – began to affirm the conciliar, doctrinal tradition as normative for the faith. How this came about is too complex a story to tell here.[15] My purpose in this chapter is to set the stage for understanding the cultural turn that Protestants, both mainline and evangelical, would take in the latter half of the twentieth century, which will be the subject of Chapter 3.[16] For this reason, I have chosen two other Europeans who were contemporaries of each other and lay the foundation not only for Protestant affirmation of the rule of faith, but also for the cultural and moral agenda that accompanied it: Karl Barth and C. S. Lewis. While Barth made an appearance in the first chapter, here I am less interested in Barth himself and more concerned with the use (or misuse) of Barth's theology by the group of American neoorthodox theologians and church leaders who were inspired by Barth to criticize liberalism and recover "historic Christianity" – all in the name of the larger cultural goal of transforming American society. Lewis does much the same but for a lay audience, and after his death a largely American evangelical audience. While neither Barth nor Lewis saw himself as the champion of a reactionary Christian traditionalism – and in the case of Barth much of his work actually militates against this very outcome – their legacy is interwoven with the ways their critique of liberal theology became fuel for the culture wars.

THE DOCTRINAL RULE OF FAITH: FROM
INTELLECTUALISM TO VOLUNTARISM

The doctrinal rule of faith has a long history, going back to the second and third centuries when various accounts of the "rule of faith" or "canon of truth" – in Latin and Greek, *regula fidei* and *kanon tes aletheias*, respectively – were circulated by early Christian leaders in those decades before Christianity had a definitive biblical canon and an ecumenical creed. As Lorraine Daston points out, the terms *kanon* and *regula* originally referred to straightedges used by carpenters and masons to measure wood and stone. *Regula* was also associated with the word *norma*, which is perhaps derived from the Greek *gnomon*, both words referring to a carpenter's square for making right angles.[17] In short, three of the key terms in the social construction of religious boundaries – rule, canon, and norm – have their origins in physical construction, connoting mathematical precision. These terms also had a second cluster of meanings associated with the prescribed paradigms and models to imitate in art, grammar, and rhetoric, a meaning that became prominent thanks to the Rule of Saint Benedict, written in the mid-sixth century. The rule in this sense was a standard of beauty or virtue that others should emulate.[18] A third cluster of meanings, according to Daston, connects *kanon* and *regula* with *nomos* (law or custom) and *horos* (boundary), conveying the idea of a "limit that could not be breached without sanction," an idea that Christianity adopted in its imperial regulation of orthodoxy and heterodoxy.[19] By connoting mathematical accuracy, imitative ideals, and legal boundary-making, the use of these concepts with respect to Christian doctrine and practice indicates the kind of authority and consistency such rules and norms were intended to have.

The earliest articulations of the rule sought to answer the question of Rusticus to Justin Martyr: "What is your dogma?" Writing around 165 CE, Justin's answer included two key items, namely, belief in God the creator and belief in the "Lord Jesus Christ" as "the herald of salvation and teacher of good doctrines."[20] Irenaeus of Lyons, writing two decades later in *Against Heresies*, described the teachings held by Christians over against those he called the gnostics. His more elaborate and prototrinitarian accounts of the rule of faith clearly anticipate the later Nicene Creed. The faith of the church, he says, includes belief in "one God the Father Almighty" who created all things, "one Christ Jesus the Son of God" who "was made flesh for our salvation," and the Holy Spirit who has proclaimed the saving works of God.[21] As Everett Ferguson demonstrates in his summary of early Christian accounts of the *regula fidei*, the rule gradually became more complex, though the central points remained consistent. Tertullian's multiple accounts of the rule, for example, are generally in harmony with Justin and Irenaeus, focusing on God the creator and Jesus Christ's birth, death, and resurrection, though he adds new details such as being born from "the virgin Mary by the Spirit" and ascending "to sit at the Father's right hand."[22] Most importantly, according to Tertullian, "the rule of faith is entirely one, alone immoveable and unchangeable. ... This law of faith is constant."[23]

Within the contested period of early Christianity, the emphasis on the rule's singularity and immutability served rhetorically to identify who was orthodox, and thereby belonged to the true church, and who was not. In the case of Irenaeus and Tertullian, those excluded from the ranks of Christianity included the followers of Valentinus. But the purported immutability of the rule also served as an apologetic for the legitimacy of Christian faith. The authority of the rule, according to these early Christian apologists, was derivative of the original apostles' authority; the rule claimed to be the consistent articulation of their gospel. According to Irenaeus, the rule of faith is "the doctrine of the apostles."[24] That became a progressively more tendentious claim with each subsequent generation. Nevertheless, even if the claim is true that the apostles would recognize the rule of the second and third centuries as a continuation of their proclamation, the role of the apostles raises a fundamental question: Are the apostles authoritative because *they* are authoritative, or are they authoritative because they preached an authoritative *message*? For early apologists like Justin Martyr, the answer was clearly the latter.

For Justin, the rule is immutable because the *truth* is immutable, and this truth is not limited to the church. He argues, for example, that the Logos (truth or reason itself), which is Christ himself, spoke in and through Socrates and the pagans. Christ, he says, "is the Word of whom all humankind partakes. Those who lived by reason are Christians, even though they have been considered atheists: such as, among the Greeks, Socrates, Heraclitus, and others like them."[25] What was normative for Justin and for many Greek-speaking Christians was the rational Logos, the eternal truth as such, wherever and whenever such truth manifests itself. By identifying Christ with this universal Logos, Justin was able to argue that Christianity was nothing new but was merely the latest revelation of the same truth that has always been known to rational creatures. Novelty was the great heresy. The charge against Socrates was that "he introduced new divinities," and "now they endeavor to do the very same thing to us."[26]

Justin's position is an early, doctrinal version of a later, especially medieval, dispute in moral theology over the following question: Is something true and right because God wills it, or does God will it because it is true and right? The former became known as voluntarism and the latter as intellectualism. For the theological voluntarist, whatever God says is normative for the simple reason that *God* is the speaker; divine agency is what confers authority. For the theological intellectualist, however, God cannot say anything that is irrational or immoral for the simple reason that God is pure Rationality and Goodness itself; it is metaphysically impossible for God to act in a way contrary to God's own being, which is the ground for reality as such. The intellectualist answers an emphatic "No" to such classic questions as, "Can God make a square circle?" or, "Can God declare 2+2=5?" The intellectualist thus believes that truth is divine wherever this truth is found, regardless of whether a person knows its source or not. This debate developed primarily with respect to Christian ethics, with the intellectualists advocating for the normativity of natural law and common reason and the voluntarists arguing for obedience to the commands of God, however irrational and arbitrary they may be (or appear to be). But the terms of the debate apply well to the question of church doctrine.

As a strong intellectualist, Justin Martyr thus defends the normativity of Christianity by arguing that it does not teach anything that is not already understood to be true by reason. Such a position was easier to hold in the second century, before there was any biblical canon or doctrinal creed, when the new religion was still young and adjusting to the world in the wake of the indefinite delay of the Parousia – the return of Christ that the apostles and their disciples expected within their lifetime. It became increasingly difficult to sustain this intellectualist view with each passing decade, as the rule became ever more complex in response to new theologies and schools of thought deemed by some to be outside the bounds of the apostolic tradition. As more communities of Christ-followers were declared anathema, despite their commitment to the same rational Logos, it was only natural for those who saw themselves entrusted with protecting apostolic orthodoxy to shift the source of normativity from common reason to the consensus of ecclesiastical leaders. Irenaeus seems to be the turning point. As Ferguson points out, "With Irenaeus we reach the first Christian author to make frequent use of the word groups *paradosis/traditio*."[27] In his campaign against the so-called gnostics, Irenaeus claims that the gnostics appealed to a secret oral tradition as more normative than the written tradition, and thus he counters their appeal by emphasizing the authority of the apostolic tradition. He "consistently identifies tradition with what was delivered by the apostles and maintains that it was preserved in the churches."[28]

Implicit in this transition was a shift from doctrinal intellectualism to doctrinal voluntarism. This development, which has no single turning point but was a gradual process of institutionalization, was monumental in its implications. The authority of the Christian tradition was no longer verifiable by shared norms of rationality and common wisdom but instead received its normativity from the chain of apostolic succession. Returning to the question posed above, the apostles were no longer authoritative because they proclaimed a universal (and universally accessible) truth but because the apostles themselves were special – "on this rock I will build my church" – and only those whom subsequent church leaders considered representative of the apostles could share in their authority. In effect, normativity shifted from theology to politics, from shared ideas to the status and power of those who control the ideas. This development led directly to the political contest over apostolicity that Constantine sought to settle at the Council of Nicaea, in which the bishops used the imperial state (and vice versa) to resolve the vicious power struggles over whose Christianity would become normative. Since the public sources of authority, such as the scriptural texts and prior theological works, could be interpreted in multiple ways as supporting different ecclesial factions, the agonistic conflict at the heart of voluntarism required a magisterial authority, namely Constantine, to decide what counted as apostolic, "true" Christianity. The result, H. A. Drake argues, was the triumph of "a militant wing" of Christianity, represented by the bishops, who, in their commitment to ideological purity, used Constantine "to settle issues of internal cohesion" and "to enforce party discipline."[29] Theological voluntarism settled disputes by erecting a barrier between true, orthodox Christians and false Christians – or rather, heretics. The suppression of a "tolerant and inclusive Christianity" in favor of "a more coercive and intolerant form of Christianity" that occurred in the wake of the Constantinian consensus is a natural consequence of locating normativity in authoritative leaders.[30]

In the subsequent centuries of ecclesiastical empire, during which time the authority of God and the authority of the church were seen as coterminous, the question of doctrinal intellectualism naturally disappeared from theology – except on the esoteric outskirts, among those mystics and spiritualists who discerned a hidden transcendent essence lying beyond the official doctrines and practices. Modernity shattered the ecclesiastical empire and, as I explored in Chapter 1, empowered the search for universal (and often universally accessible) norms contrary to the consensus of church leadership. Two paths opened up in response to modernity, organized broadly around intellectualism and voluntarism. While liberal theology pursued various kinds of doctrinal intellectualism – rooted in general accounts of reason, morality, and experience – the traditionalist reactions to modern liberalism were conscious attempts to recover a robust doctrinal voluntarism in the face of new challenges from science, philosophy, and history. Liberal intellectualism pursued the essence of Christianity, while traditionalist voluntarism pursued the rule of faith.[31] The rise of the *regula fidei* in the nineteenth and twentieth centuries thus occurred in a context in which voluntarism was no longer presupposed as a given but now had to be consciously defended on the grounds that the church possessed special access to truth that one either accepted or rejected.

Broadly speaking, then, we can distinguish two approaches to modern doctrinal voluntarism: a Reformed Protestant version that located normative Christianity in the infallible text of scripture (i.e., it's true because God said it) and an Anglo-Catholic version that located normative Christianity in the creedal traditions of the church (i.e., it's true because the church said it).[32] I already touched on the former in the Introduction (and will discuss the Bible further in the following chapter), so I will focus my attention here on the latter, treating first the Oxford Movement in the nineteenth century and then Karl Barth (and the American neoorthodox theologians who appropriated him) and C. S. Lewis in the early twentieth century. All of this will then lay the groundwork for the discussion of the retrieval and *ressourcement* movements in the late twentieth and early twenty-first centuries that will be the subject of Chapter 3.

JOHN HENRY NEWMAN AND THE INFALLIBILITY OF TRADITION

Famous for his leadership of the Oxford Movement and his eventual conversion to Roman Catholicism in 1845 – and more recently for his canonization as a saint in 2019 – John Henry Newman (1801–1890) is an underappreciated figure in the history of the rule of faith and the search for a normative Christianity. He was not a systematic thinker; one can almost see him work out his views in his writings in real time. This is particularly the case regarding his view of doctrinal tradition, which lay at the heart of the ecclesiastical dispute that led to his abandonment of Anglicanism. For our purposes (setting aside his early years as an evangelical), we can split Newman's life into two parts: (1) his life before 1845, in which he wrote as an apologist for the Anglo-Catholic tradition and (2) his life after 1845, in which he wrote as an apologist for the Roman Catholic tradition.

While Newman's relationship with Rome understandably dominates the analysis of his life and work – as the most famous of those ex-Protestants who later wrote about their decision to "swim the Tiber" – in point of fact there is a remarkable consistency in Newman's thought in both periods of his life, especially when viewed against the backdrop of the liberal Protestantism that was spreading through Europe at the time. This is, of course, the period of Schleiermacher and Hegel and their respective schools of thought, which dominated the conversation in and around Germany. To be sure, England was not the continent. The Deism that had flourished there in the early eighteenth century had long since died out, and in the early nineteenth century English churches "remained almost completely untouched by the vast progress of the scientific thought of the educated classes."[33] Nevertheless, European idealism and romanticism were not wholly unknown. The Romantic theology of the poet Samuel Taylor Coleridge (1772–1834), who was a kind of "British Schleiermacher" and had joined the Church of England in 1814, was a conduit for German idealism into Great Britain. The Scottish philosopher Thomas Carlyle (1795–1881) was heavily influenced by the German idealist Johann Gottlieb Fichte. And perhaps most relevant of all: Newman's own younger brother, Francis William Newman (1805–1897), was himself a noted philosopher and activist who went in the exact opposite direction toward a kind of rational agnosticism. According to Otto Pfleiderer, Francis Newman's examination of the creeds in his 1850 book, *Phases of Faith*, demonstrates "the application of the intellect to the examination of the received authorities, resulting in the conviction of their insufficiency, and human and historical conditionality, and accordingly of their want of divine authority, and of their unfitness to serve as the firm ultimate bases of belief."[34] It is in this context that we can understand John Henry Newman's steadfast commitment to the authority and tradition of the church over against all modern, rational arguments.

During the 1830s, Newman was involved in the Tractarian or Oxford Movement as the initiator of the *Tracts for the Times*, a series of writings designed to give Anglicanism a firmer theological foundation in traditional orthodoxy. Tract 73, "On the Introduction of Rationalistic Principles into Revealed Religion" (1836), was written in opposition to two lay representatives of liberal thought, the Scottish theologian Thomas Erskine of Linlathen and the American writer Jacob Abbott, and included a postscript against Schleiermacher. While Newman does not use the language of essence here, his dispute with them, and Erskine in particular, is over their systematization of Christianity according to their normative principles and ideas. Newman objects to Erskine's notion of the "leading idea" of Christianity, which Erskine identifies with the "moral principles of the Deity." For Erskine, those doctrines are essential to Christianity that manifest "a direct and natural connexion" between the doctrine in question and the moral formation of a person.[35] Newman regards this as a kind of rationalism that sacrifices the orthodox mystery of revelation for a system guided by principles. As Stephen Sykes observes, Newman "fears that systematization of the kind proposed by Erskine and Abbott leads to a distortion of the language and ordinances of the Christian religion, as they were given."[36] Revelation, Newman claims, is "a doctrine *lying hid* in language," and while human language is never fully capable of expressing it, the language has to be preserved as the vehicle ordained to carry the message of God.[37] Newman appeals to the category of mystery as the reason why believers must accept the doctrinal messiness of the tradition as it is. To seek to make Christian theology internally consistent – thereby engaging in the work of mediation as described in Chapter 1 – is to lose the mystery of revelation. One either accepts the whole of tradition as it comes down to us, or none of it.[38] The rest of Newman's work was an attempt to develop this account of the normativity of the tradition.

Newman's primary effort in the Oxford Movement was to defend the distinctiveness of Anglicanism against both Protestantism and Roman Catholicism (which he often called Romanism). He called his position the *via media* (way of the middle). For Newman at this time, Anglicanism accepted everything in Romanism – including apostolic succession and sacramentalism – except what he considered its errors, which mostly had to do with the papal office. As he stated in his 1837 volume *Lectures on the Prophetical Office of the Church, Viewed Relatively to Romanism and Popular Protestantism* (later reissued as *Via Media, Volume 1*), "we Anglo-Catholics do not profess a different religion from that of Rome, we profess their Faith *all but* their corruptions."[39] It is instructive to note how Newman situates Anglicanism with respect to Rome and the Reformation. The Protestants acknowledge the fact of their separation from the Rome and each other, but Newman's Anglicanism regards this fact as a sin; there should be no separation, since there is one true tradition, and that tradition has one church. Rome, by contrast, agrees that separation is a sin but disputes Anglicanism's claim that Rome is the one who separated. Newman thus summarizes the state of affairs: "Our controversy with Rome, I have said, turns more upon facts than upon first principles; with Protestant sectaries it is more about principles than about facts."[40] The controversy with Protestantism, being a matter of principle, is the more deep-seated. Put another way, Protestantism and Romanism, according to Newman, each have a different criterion for what counts as normative in Christianity. For the Protestants, the criterion is scripture; for Rome, the criterion is the antiquity of tradition. The problem with the Protestant criterion is that we only have scripture, and only recognize it as normative, because of tradition – namely, the handing down of both the texts themselves and the practice of reading them as authoritative.[41] Moreover, Protestants have no institutional guardrails to avoid divergent interpretations of scripture and ensure the one true understanding of the faith. While Protestants make the Bible the standard or rule of faith, "no two agree as to the *interpreter* of the Bible, but each person makes himself the interpreter, so that what seemed at first sight a means of peace, turns out to be a chief occasion or cause of discord."[42] The problem with Rome's criterion, by contrast, is that it loses touch with scripture as the central authority of the faith. Once again, Protestants have the fact (scripture); Rome has the principle (antiquity). For Newman in 1837, all of this proves the superiority of the *via media*. In contrast to the Romanist who believes faith can rest on tradition without scripture, and in contrast to the Protestant who believes faith can rest on scripture without tradition, "our Church adheres to a double Rule, Scripture and Catholic Tradition." He adds that the phrase "Rule of Faith" applies to "the Bible and Catholic Tradition taken together. These two together make up a joint rule; Scripture is interpreted by Tradition, Tradition is verified by Scripture."[43]

The culmination of this period of Newman's thought appeared in his controversial 1841 *Remarks on Certain Passages in the Thirty-Nine Articles*, more commonly known simply as Tract 90. This tract, the last before his conversion to Rome, was written as a critique of prevailing Anglican views that scripture and the Thirty-Nine Articles on their own were sufficient in themselves to guide the church, when in fact, according to Newman in 1877, both were too vague in themselves and required an "authoritative interpretation" to ensure that the Anglican Church professed "what the Universal Church had from the beginning professed, and nothing else, and nothing short of it, that is, what had been held *semper et ubique et ab omnibus*" – here referring to Vincent of Lérins's oft-quoted maxim that Christians hold fast to what has been believed everywhere, always, and by all.[44] The opening section on scripture and church authority further explores Newman's dispute with popular Protestants and latitudinarian Anglicans over whether, as the latter claimed, scripture is itself the rule of faith. For Newman, this view was not only impossible, in light of scripture being too "ambiguous" to serve as a rule, but also a "recent adoption," being a departure from ancient tradition's decision to make "the Apostolic Tradition, as summed up in the Creed, and not the Bible, the *Regula Fidei*, or Rule."[45] The rest of Tract 90 goes through points of contention between Anglicanism and Romanism (e.g., purgatory, relics, transubstantiation, and the papacy), arguing for an interpretation that aligns the Thirty-Nine Articles with what he calls "primitive doctrine" or the "primitive church" as the hermeneutical criterion. When the articles are interpreted positively by the primitive church, as opposed to negatively against the Catholic Church, the differences between Anglicanism and Roman Catholicism, Newman suggests, begin to fade away.

From there, of course, it was but a short step to full affirmation of the Catholic Church's authority and tradition, but the final challenge was how to make sense of the developments in Catholic doctrine that

Newman had previously declared to be corruptions of the original apostolic tradition. This was the task he set for himself in *An Essay on the Development of Christian Doctrine*, published in 1845.[46] In doing so he addressed his own earlier objections to Romanism by demonstrating how its doctrines "developed logically and organically from the tradition of the early Church."[47] This pathbreaking work stands out from Newman's previous writings for its reversal of the conversation: whereas before Newman was concerned with demonstrating continuity of doctrine, in this book he develops an account of doctrinal change in an effort "to solve what has now become a necessary and an anxious problem."[48] Long before Adolf von Harnack and Ernst Troeltsch would take up the topic of the essence of Christianity and its historical development, Newman here explores the same set of questions. His argument – in certain respects akin to the German liberals and strikingly at odds with the Roman Catholic Church of his time, and which would not be officially adopted until the Second Vatican Council – was that Christian doctrine is not given all at once but necessarily undergoes development in history as a natural consequence of human involvement. As Bruno Forte points out, Newman is here caught in an apparent contradiction: "if truth is such, it transcends time; how then can it have a history?"[49] The book is his answer to this dilemma. It begins with Newman stating that Christianity is "a fact in the world's history" and "to know what it is, we must seek it in the world," a claim more commonly expressed by liberal theologians, which most traditionally orthodox theologians, Protestant and Catholic alike, tended to deny.[50] But like any apologist, Newman is convinced that history is on his side. While admitting that the history of Christianity does not obviously lead to the Church of Rome's system of doctrine, he does believe that history self-evidently excludes Protestantism: "Whatever be historical Christianity, it is not Protestantism. If ever there were a safe truth, it is this."[51] In the 1878 edition of this book, Newman added the now-famous line: "To be deep in history is to cease to be a Protestant."[52] From Newman's perspective, having recently undergone a close study of early Christian theology, it was self-evident that Protestantism was not a possible expression of the essence of Christianity. But that still left the question of how to explain the complex development of Catholic doctrine. Is the Roman Church an authentic representation of the apostolic tradition – the apostolic or primitive essence of Christianity – or is it a corruption of that tradition?

Newman's answer to this question sheds a great deal of light not only on his project but also on the conservative prescriptivism that appeals to the rule of faith as the baseline measure of Christian normativity. His argument in a nutshell is to argue for the development of ideas – the word "idea," as Lucas Laborde clarifies, can refer to both Christianity as a whole and to specific Christian doctrines – and his book seeks to articulate the conditions for authentic and inauthentic development of these ideas.[53] Newman provides seven tests to determine whether a development is the continuation or the corruption of the idea of Christianity, and the rest of the book applies these tests to particular points of doctrinal controversy.[54] But as David Bentley Hart acknowledges, "these criteria amount to little more than a transparently forced ideological reconstruction of the historical narrative," requiring both "willful narrative creativity" and "selective ignorance regarding those historical data that the preferred narrative cannot assimilate."[55] Reducing the complexity of history to the adaptability of an idea made it all too easy for Newman to reconstruct an account of Christian history that supported his argument, and any reconstruction under these presuppositions is "self-evidently specious," an exercise in "saving the appearances."[56] Newman's *Essay* is a stunning work of historical eisegesis, a retrospective reading of the past that already knows where history leads – namely, to his own position. His failure is thus an instructive one, serving as a cautionary tale for all those people, whether church leaders or Supreme Court justices, who wish to use history to prove the rightness of their beliefs.

To further nuance (or rather complicate to the point of obscurity) his account of what is normative in Christianity, Newman distinguishes between idea, type, principle, and doctrine. Newman uses the concept of idea to reject the essence of Christianity approach common among his liberal opponents. An idea "represents an object or supposed object" and is "commensurate with the sum total of its possible aspects," regardless of how these aspects might vary in the minds of individuals.[57] In other words, the idea of Christianity is an aggregate of all the aspects of Christianity and is irreducible to a single essence. Alluding to his

1836 tract against Erskine, Newman says that "sometimes an attempt has been made to ascertain the 'leading idea,' as it has been called, of Christianity." The problem with these diverse efforts to articulate the essence of Christianity is that "all these representations are truths, as being aspects of Christianity, but none of them is the whole truth. For Christianity has many aspects."[58] He adds in the 1878 version that "one aspect of Revelation must not be allowed to exclude or to obscure another; and Christianity is dogmatical, devotional, practical all at once."[59] The concept of idea here serves the same function as mystery does elsewhere: it emphasizes that Christianity is the sum of all its disparate aspects, which is another way of saying that Christianity is the tradition as it has developed. But Newman cannot stop there, for then he would lack the guardrails he needs to ensure the tradition endorses the Catholic rule of faith as opposed to Protestant biblicism.

The primary guardrail worth noting for our purposes is found in the concept of principle. Here we find that, despite his protestations against any "leading idea," Newman proposes his own essence of Christianity. Having acknowledged that doctrines arise and change over time, he uses the concept of principle to hold the multifaceted idea of Christianity together. Principles are the through lines that provide the continuity of tradition despite the outward changes in doctrinal formulation. He defines principles in distinction from doctrines in the following 1878 passage:

> Principles are abstract and general, doctrines relate to facts; doctrines develope [sic], and principles at first sight do not; doctrines grow and are enlarged, principles are permanent; doctrines are intellectual, and principles are more immediately ethical and practical. Systems live in principles and represent doctrines. Personal responsibility is a principle, the Being of a God is a doctrine; from that doctrine all theology has come in due course, whereas that principle is not clearer under the Gospel than in paradise, and depends, not on belief in an Almighty Governor, but on conscience. ... Doctrines stand to principles, as the definitions to the axioms and postulates of mathematics.[60]

The distinction between principle and doctrine provides Newman with a way to address the split between theological intellectualism and voluntarism. Doctrines pertain to "revealed facts" that are "special and singular," such as the incarnation of God. Principles, on the other hand, "are common to all the works of God" throughout nature and history. Newman connected the concept of principle to Bishop Joseph Butler's notion of an analogy between natural and revealed religion. Principles are thus the basis for intellectualism (truths that are known outside of a specific religion), while doctrines are the basis for voluntarism (truths that are only known within a religion). Newman made this point even more clear in his 1870 work, *Grammar of Assent,* in which he responds to the objection that Eastern religions are "older than Christianity by some centuries." He answers by claiming that "Christianity is only the continuation and conclusion of what professes to be an earlier revelation, which may be traced back into pre-historic times. ... As far as we know, there never was a time when that revelation was not."[61] Implicit in this connection between intellectualism and voluntarism is the assumption that the Christian church now is the exclusive domain for what was once a more universally known truth. Newman's theory of religious development provides additional support. Originally, this revelation was simple, like the tiny egg out of which a caterpillar hatches, and over time it becomes more complex, much like the caterpillar's transformation into a butterfly. But the butterfly is the exclusive continuation of what was originally an indistinguishable egg. This, at least, is how Newman uses the concept of principle to unify the voluntarist and intellectualist traditions.

When it comes to specifying what the principles of Christianity are, Newman suggests that it would be impossible to count all of them. He instead offers "nine specimens of Christian principles out of the many which might be enumerated." These are, in order: the principle of dogma, the principle of faith, the principle of theology, the sacramental principle, the principle of the mystical sense, the principle of grace, the principle of ascetism, the principle of the consciousness of sin's malignity, and the principle of sanctification. Newman then gives priority to four principles: faith, theology, scripture, and dogma.[62] One might reasonably ask at this point not only how Newman came up with this list but also how they provide a justification for Catholicism, given how vague and ambiguous they are. Upon closer examination, however, it becomes clear that the point for Newman is the sheer number and variety of

possible principles. He states that Christianity "has principles so distinctive, numerous, various, and operative" that it is "unlike any other religious, ethical, or political system that the world has ever seen."[63]
According to Newman, it is precisely the *difference* from other religions
that defines Christianity's type, which is the first of the seven tests of
doctrinal development. He describes the type of Christianity on the
analogy of organic development, the way a seed transforms into a tree,
thus radically changing its outward form while remaining the same type
of plant – a metaphor that is "fairly useless as applied to a history of
institutional adaptations and adjustments and transmogrifications."[64]

Lest his reader point out that organic metaphors provide little
guidance in determining whether a doctrinal development is a corruption, Newman clarifies that Christianity's type is simply a religion that
both rejects and is rejected by every other authority and community in
the world. He defines Christianity as the religion that is viewed by the
world as "irrational," promoting "gross superstition," holding to doctrines that are unknown and preposterous, and so treated with "with
curiosity, suspicion, fear, disgust."[65] Likewise, in turn, Christianity is a
religious communion that holds "all other religious bodies around it
heretical or infidel," is "a natural enemy to governments external to
itself," is "intolerant" of other ways of thinking, and seeks to construct
"a new modelling of society." He further claims (without proof) that
there is only one religion that fits this description.[66] In other words, what
makes Christianity distinctive is simply its otherness vis-à-vis the rest of the
world. Christianity is the religion supposedly persecuted by all and, in
turn, the persecutor of all. Newman has here constructed a purely
negative definition of Christianity, and one might be forgiven for
wondering whether he is defending or attacking it. The genuinely normative version of Christianity is therefore whichever communion is the
most at odds with everyone else, the most intolerant and exclusive in its
claims and values. For Newman, this was the Roman Catholic Church.
But Newman had not encountered modern evangelicalism, which took
his criteria of religious exclusivism and global persecution to an extreme
he could never have imagined, as I will discuss in Chapter 4.

All of this raises the crucial question: If we cannot specify a leading
idea or singular essence, and if we cannot give a more positive account of

Christianity other than its antithesis to the rest of society, what actually functions as the rule of faith that holds the tradition together? What is the normative element in Christianity if Christianity as such is an incomprehensible hodgepodge of strange ideas and practices? Newman's ultimate answer is that Christianity is held together by its commitment to "external authority," framed as a principle, and "the infallibility of the Church," framed as a doctrine.[67] He does not list this as one of his principles, presumably because it is the linchpin of his entire project and thus basic to the very idea of Christianity, as well as to every principle and doctrine. Newman ought to admit that this is his "leading idea," for that is what it is. In a remarkable passage, almost identical in both the 1845 and 1878 editions, he explicitly calls this notion of authority the essence of religion:

> It must be borne in mind that, as *the essence of all religion is authority and obedience*, so the distinction between natural religion and revealed lies in this, that the one has a subjective authority, and the other an objective. Revelation consists in the manifestation of the Invisible Divine Power, or in the substitution of the voice of a Lawgiver for the voice of conscience. The supremacy of conscience is the essence of natural religion; the supremacy of Apostle, or Pope, or Church, or Bishop, is the essence of revealed; and when such external authority is taken away, the mind falls back again of necessity upon that inward guide which it possessed even before Revelation was vouchsafed. Thus, what conscience is in the system of nature, such is the voice of Scripture, or of the Church, or of the Holy See, as we may determine it, in the system of Revelation.[68]

Here we find the key to Newman's entire system of thought, without which his arguments for the rule of faith and doctrinal development lack cogency. His belief that obedience to the infallible authority of the church is how he is able to hold together intellectualism and voluntarism, his acknowledgment of significant historical development and his belief in the exclusive truth of Rome, his acceptance of Christianity's messy complexity and his commitment to Christianity's consistency in idea, type, principle, and doctrine. Naturally, he acknowledges that one's commitment to external authority and the infallibility of the church increases in proportion to one's acceptance of developments in doctrine and practice.[69] Because Newman has rejected going the route of the mediating essence of Christianity – though, as the quote above indicates, he has his own account of the essence – his only recourse is to appeal to divine and ecclesiastical authority as the organizing principle of his thought.

While Newman is an important figure and worthy of attention in his own right, his work shows what a consistent rejection of the liberal tradition entails, namely, some account of external authority. For Newman, the only reasonable conclusion was that he had to join the Catholic Church. Over a century later, Protestants would make similar arguments for the rule of faith but without Newman's ecclesiastical commitments.

KARL BARTH, AMERICAN NEOORTHODOXY, AND THE RISE OF PROTESTANT RETRIEVALISM

For a long time Newman served as the model of what it looked like to make the rule of faith normative in Christian theology – not so much in what he wrote but in the fact he became Catholic. The lesson many Protestants took away from Newman was that investing so much importance in the ancient church and its theological tradition only led a person to Rome. As the Irish Presbyterian theologian Thomas Croskery wrote in *The Presbyterian Review* in 1885, Newman's Oxford Movement was an overreaction, one that led many Anglicans away from the Bible to Romanism. For Newman, wrote Croskery, "Liberalism was essentially irreligious ... and it could only be confronted and destroyed through the principle of authority as embodied in the idea of the Catholic Church." This reaction, however, "did not spring out of a fresh study of the Bible" but out of an abstract concept of the church. And in the end, Newman's *via media* was simply "the old Roman road made passable for English travelers."[70] Croskery here spoke for many Protestants who were vociferous in their opposition to Catholicism – and, by extension, to the rule of faith as the infallible norm of the church. Instead of following the *via media* and the *regula fidei*, Protestants doubled down on the normativity of scripture, as seen most clearly in the 1881 article on biblical inspiration in the same *Presbyterian Review* by the Princeton Presbyterian theologians A. A. Hodge and B. B. Warfield.

A half-century later, in the wake of the fundamentalist-modernist controversy that split the Presbyterians and carved out the liberal and evangelical camps we now know today, mainline Protestant leaders went looking for someone to provide direction for the church's future that rejected modernism without devolving into either biblicism or Catholicism. They found that direction in the figure of Karl Barth. What they found, however, was what they were looking for and not what Barth actually was. While Barth ended up facilitating the rise in the twentieth century of Protestant interest in the rule of faith and "historic Christianity" – what I will call Protestant retrievalism – this was highly ironic, given Barth's own (critical) stance on Christian tradition. Much was lost in the transatlantic translation of "Barthianism," as dialectical theology was often called. From the start, Barth was appreciated less on his own terms and more as a symbol of the rejection of liberalism – a rejection that was not fundamentalism but rather a return to the supposedly normative gospel of historic, ecumenical Christianity. In Chapter 1, I presented dialectical theology as an eschatological exten-sion of the modern liberal tradition. While accurate, this interpretation situates dialectical theology within the context of modern European history, where of course it belongs. The reception in North America, however, was an entirely different matter. In Europe, dialectical theology was a response to liberal historicism and offered a fresh take on the essence of Christianity that incorporated early Christian eschatology. In the United States, by contrast, dialectical theology was received as a way out of the impasse between a doctrinally rigid fundamentalism and a pragmatic, experientialist liberalism – while still remaining thoroughly and unapologetically Protestant. The result was the emergence of what became known as American neoorthodoxy.

The terminology for dialectical theology can be confusing. The fact that it was often identified with Barth does a great disservice to the other dialectical theologians – Eduard Thurneysen, Friedrich Gogarten, Rudolf Bultmann, and (to some degree) Emil Brunner – who developed the core theological ideas in their own ways. Though Barth originated many of the main insights, dialectical theology is *not* the school of Karl

Barth but a movement of which he became the most famous representative. In North America, the movement was originally called "crisis theology" or the "theology of crisis," but by the 1940s most people landed on the term "neoorthodoxy" as the preferred nomenclature, even though this was misleading at best and confused the Europeans with their North American advocates. Neoorthodoxy instead properly refers to the group of *American* theologians who adopted some, but not all, of the ideas of the dialectical theologians. This group includes Elmer G. Homrighausen (1900–1982), Walter Marshall Horton (1895–1966), Paul Lehmann (1906–1994), Reinhold Niebuhr (1892–1971), H. Richard Niebuhr (1894–1962), and Wilhelm Pauck (1901–1981).[71] According to Dennis Voskuil, "the term 'neo-orthodoxy' is so closely identified with the European religious movement which is also known as Barthianism, dialectical theology, and crisis theology, that it might appear to be simply an Americanized version of the European original. This is unfortunate, for while the formulators of the American movement appreciated Barth's critique of liberalism, they did not appropriate his theological propositions."[72] This is largely accurate, though Voskuil goes too far in denying that they appropriated Barth's theology. It was instead a partial embrace, which they mobilized for distinctively American purposes. Voskuil suggests that "neo-liberalism" and "religious realism" are more accurate labels for the American theological movement. Here I will refer to it as neoorthodoxy.

To understand how dialectical theology was received in the United States and how it "came to embody by the end of the 1940s a consensus point of view among mainline Protestant theologians," it will help to examine developments at Princeton Theological Seminary in the interwar period.[73] Princeton is an elite institution historically serving a single denomination – today's Presbyterian Church (USA) – but it had an outsized influence on theological developments in North America both because of its prominence and because it functioned as a key conduit for the diffusion of dialectical theology, and thus for the rise of neoorthodoxy and Protestant retrievalism, among English-speaking theologians. To set the scene, it is important to remember that, in the 1920s, the clash between the fundamentalists and modernists reached a climax with the Scopes Trial in July 1925, after which the fundamentalists began their retreat from mainstream institutions while modernist liberals proclaimed cultural victory. The fundamentalists at Princeton left to form Westminster Theological Seminary in Philadelphia in 1929 under the leadership of J. Gresham Machen (1881–1937), who had authored the 1923 broadside, *Christianity and Liberalism*. Machen and others formed the Orthodox Presbyterian Church in 1936 as an alternative to the mainline, northern Presbyterian Church in the United States of America. But despite the apparent victory by the liberals in the 1920s, by the 1930s the tables had turned and the liberals were now the ones facing a crisis.

If the crisis was largely a response to the disillusionment brought on by the First World War, it was Karl Barth who gave theological expression to this disillusionment. In Europe this occurred with the 1919 publication of his commentary, *The Epistle to the Romans*, but it took nearly a decade for his ideas to make their way across the Atlantic. Gustav Krüger lectured on Barth's "theology of crisis," as it was called at the time, at Union Theological Seminary in New York City in 1926.[74] But it was not until 1928 that Barth's own words became available in English. A 1920 sermon of his, "The Inward Man," appeared in *The Student World*, the publishing arm of the World's Student Christian Federation (WSCF). The same year saw the publication of Barth's book of essays, *The Word of God and the Word of Man*.[75] Emil Brunner lectured on the new theological movement at various seminaries and divinity schools in 1928 and published them as *The Theology of Crisis* the following year.[76] In 1931 John McConnachie and Wilhelm Pauck both published books on Karl Barth, indicating his significance as "prophet of a new Christianity."[77] Finally, in 1933, Edwyn C. Hoskyns published his translation of the second edition of Barth's *Epistle to the Romans*, giving English-speaking readers access to the work that launched the movement.[78]

While largely dismissed on both sides of the Atlantic by the old guard, dialectical theology found a hearing among the younger generation of liberal theologians who had been primed to rethink the overly sanguine nature of progressive Christianity. Active in organizations like the YMCA, WSCF, and the Student Volunteer Movement (SVM), young religious leaders like Francis P. Miller, Henry P. Van Dusen, and Reinhold Niebuhr read Barth's work and began to appropriate his ideas for their own critique of the older generation of American Protestant liberalism.[79] Van Dusen, later president of Union Theological Seminary, published an article in 1931 titled, "The Sickness of Liberal Religion."[80] His voice was not alone. As Voskuil points out, many liberals were raising serious concerns about the state of liberalism. Gaius Glenn Atkins, professor of homiletics at Auburn Theological Seminary, posed the question in 1934, "Whither Liberalism?" In 1935, Wilhelm Pauck asked more sharply, "What Is Wrong with Liberalism?" That same year the minister Harry Emerson Fosdick, who had famously preached "Shall the Fundamentalists Win?" in 1922, now preached, "The Church Must Go Beyond Modernism."[81]

It is worth pausing for a moment to look at Pauck's 1935 essay as a window into the rise of American neoorthodoxy. Pauck describes modern liberalism as the era in which "modern man released himself from the supernatural authorities of church, state, and society." Theological liberalism, in particular, is defined by "its opposition against ecclesiastical authority of tradition and against the supernaturalist system of orthodoxy."[82] Pauck observes that the "essence of Christianity" in modern theology "has taken the place of the authoritative creed or the inspired Bible or the supranatural church institution," as I pointed out in Chapter 1.[83] While Pauck agrees with liberalism's rejection of premodern supernaturalism, he also agrees with orthodoxy's claim that liberalism "stands in sharp contrast to the teachings of historic Christianity." In other words, while Pauck does not want to restore supernaturalism, he does want to reclaim the doctrinal voluntarism that comes with seeing the church's tradition as the defining norm for true Christianity. Pauck uses the phrase "historic Christianity" three times in his essay, in each case suggesting that the loss of this "historic" faith is central to what is wrong with liberalism. The person Pauck says has exposed all of this is none other than Barth: "It is Barth who has dramatically called attention to the fact that historic Christianity has lived of the gospel that the transcendent, eternal God has disclosed himself in Jesus Christ." According to Pauck, Barth has attacked liberal theology because it abandoned the truth of God's word "as it is proclaimed in the Bible and expounded in the doctrines of the church."[84] Historic Christianity, normed by the doctrines of the church, has a "profounder view" of

God and creation than liberalism, and Pauck praises Barth for provoking the church to recover this perspective.[85]

Pauck was hardly alone in these thoughts. By the end of the 1930s, Charles Clayton Morrison (1874–1966), editor of *Christian Century*, decided to put together a series on "How My Mind Has Changed" to assess what was happening. Thirty-four prominent professors, ministers, and Christian leaders contributed to the 1939 series, including Barth, Reinhold Niebuhr, Homrighausen, and Horton.[86] According to Morrison's concluding assessment, "the liberalism which had been for nearly a half-century the common presupposition of Christian scholarship had been for the first time effectively challenged in this decade. . . . The culture of Western civilization was under fire as based upon a philosophy which was now declared false." Elesha Coffman observes that Morrison "had in mind principally the advent of Barthianism, or neo-orthodoxy," especially since, as Morrison himself noted, nearly every contributor to the series referred to Barth, even if they only had the faintest knowledge of his work.[87]

Among the contributors to the *Christian Century* series was John Alexander Mackay (1889–1983), who was newly installed as president of Princeton Theological Seminary in 1937. His inaugural lecture on the theme of "The Restoration of Theology" argued that a return to serious dogmatic theology was necessary to address the "sense of uprootedness and spiritual homelessness" that had taken hold of many in the modern world, leading to "cultural crisis."[88] Mackay identified three contemporary models for how to address this crisis, each of which saw "the need of a luminous, authoritative principle amid our cultural anarchy": the first was Albert Schweitzer, who represented a modern, Enlightenment metaphysics and ethics; the second was Jacques Maritain, who represented the medieval Roman Catholic tradition of Thomas Aquinas's "Christian philosophy"; and the third was Karl Barth, who represented a move "back to the Reformation and to Holy Scripture." Of the three, Mackay saw the most promise in Barth. Mackay then recounted a story that Barth told him personally regarding a conversation the latter had had with Schweitzer, in which Schweitzer told Barth that both of them "started from the same problem of cultural anarchy, relativism, and uncertainty. But while I went back to the Enlightenment you went back to the

Reformation."[89] Barth's return to the Reformation – what Pauck saw as "historic Christianity" – was precisely what Mackay thought the church, and the world at large, needed. He went on in his lecture to talk about the rival "religious faiths" of the day, including communism, fascism, and nihilism. In order to resist these "new totalitarian faiths," the church required "a theology that will give it resistance-strength, communal cohesion, and expansive power," rooted in "the tradition of historic Catholic Christianity, a Theology of the Word."[90] Barth, Mackay thought, provided the necessary resistance-grade dogmatic theology.

One of Mackay's earliest decisions was to bring Brunner to Princeton Seminary for a one-year visiting professorship (1938–1939). That same year, he hired Homrighausen as professor of Christian education. These early hires laid the groundwork for Princeton Seminary to become the primary conduit of Barth's theology to the United States and the leading base of operations for American neoorthodoxy in the mid-twentieth century. For Mackay and other mainline Protestant leaders, Barth's theology was seen as the solution to the ideological ills of American culture and the intractable disputes in American Protestantism, largely because he circumvented the presuppositions of both conservative and liberal theologians by drawing on a new reading of scripture informed by theological commitments that were, or at least appeared to be, more ancient and ecumenical. Whether the Americans had read Barth correctly was not questioned until decades later. Ironically, Barth's actual theology was almost irrelevant for the rise of American neoorthodoxy for a few reasons: very little of his work was available in English (or being read by Americans in German) until the 1950s, early on Brunner had a more significant influence in the United States than Barth did, and it was more the general protest against liberalism that interested Americans than the particular nuances of Barth's thought.

In the American scene, Barth's theological work was largely reducible to two points. Kevin Vanhoozer even calls them the two "Big Bangs" of theology. The first and most important was simply the break with liberal theology, which Vanhoozer describes, borrowing Karl Adam's famous image, as "the bombshell dropped in the early twentieth century by Karl Barth on the playground of the modern theologians" – referring to the 1919 first edition of his *Epistle to the Romans*.[91] Adam's image of the bomb dropped on the theological playground, published originally in 1926, has been so widely used as to become virtually synonymous with Barth's legacy. It moved into English more quickly than Barth's actual writings did. The very same year it was quoted in *The Hibbert Journal*, followed by the *London Quarterly Review* in 1927, *The Methodist Review* in 1928, *The Spectator* in 1931, and *Crozer Quarterly* in 1932. People who had never and would never read Barth himself still knew, or at least thought they knew, that he had demolished the elite liberal theologians. And for many that was all they needed to know.

The second "Big Bang," according to Vanhoozer, was "Karl Barth's rediscovery of the Trinity." Never one to miss a rhetorical flourish, Vanhoozer piles on another scientific metaphor and calls this "a Copernican revolution in relation to the knowledge of God."[92] The notion that Barth "rediscovered" the trinity, like the trope that he dropped a bomb on the liberals, is frequently repeated by scholars, often without any interrogation.[93] The truth in the claim is that Barth was a key part of a trinitarian revival in theology that saw theologians across the ecclesiastical spectrum turning to the trinity as the solution to any number of theological and social problems – including the individualism of modern life, the hierarchical nature of patriarchy and state politics, and increasing disunity among Christians. Barth, for his part, saw the doctrine of the trinity as the solution to the problem of how genuine God-talk is possible. He began his *Church Dogmatics* in 1932 by declaring the *analogia entis* (analogy of being), and the whole project of natural theology that goes with it, to be "the invention of Antichrist."[94] Naturally, he also provided what he understood to be the antidote to natural theology, which was an account of the trinity as revealer, revelation, and revealedness: God is the subject of revelation (Father), the object of revelation (Son), and the means of revelation (Holy Spirit).[95] The opening part-volume of his *Church Dogmatics* (Volume 1, Part 1) containing this doctrine of the trinity first appeared in English, in a translation by G. T. Thomson, in 1936, the year before Mackay assumed the presidency of Princeton Seminary. The specific details of Barth's doctrine were not important to his reputation among Americans; it was enough that he became associated with the doctrine's "recovery." This was frequently connected to his rejection of liberalism, as Friedrich

Schleiermacher, the "father of modern liberal theology," was often (erroneously) viewed as having sidelined the trinity in his classic work of dogmatic theology, *The Christian Faith*, by placing the trinity at the end of his dogmatics rather than the beginning.

Barth's two "Big Bangs" led many to conclude that he stood resolutely in opposition to everything associated with liberal theology, including its rejection of church tradition and its quest for the essence of Christianity. Barth claimed, for instance, to have replaced the essence of Christianity with "the Word of God, and the Word of God alone."[96] His massive, unfinished project in dogmatic theology hearkened to an earlier time, reminding people of the works of classic theologians like Augustine of Hippo, Gregory of Nyssa, Thomas Aquinas, and John Calvin. But unlike many theologians in the ancient church, Barth had no interest in the intellectualist tradition. His resolute "Nein!" to natural theology signaled to readers that he was a strong, perhaps the strongest, proponent of the voluntarist position in theology, albeit in a distinctly Protestant mode that did not identify the tradition with the institutional church. Barth thus became symbolic for the return to "historic Christianity" among mainline Protestants. To follow his lead, many thought, involved working toward a new orthodoxy – indeed, what many regarded to be a more true and authentic orthodoxy. Barth had recovered in the minds of many the genuinely biblical and Christian message of the gospel after years of distortion by both liberals and fundamentalists.

Not everyone was convinced, however. Dialectical theology's "critique of modernism and return to orthodox doctrines did not much impress fundamentalists, for neo-orthodox theologians were no more orthodox than many moderate conservatives who had refused to join the funda-mentalist cause."[97] As historian George Marsden points out, "attitudes toward neo-orthodoxy had become an increasingly important issue as the postwar fundamentalist community was struggling to define its boundaries," and some, like Cornelius Van Til (1895–1987) and Carl McIntire (1906–2002) "were pressing anti-neoorthodoxy as a crucial litmus test."[98] In 1946, Van Til came out guns blazing in opposition to the theology of Barth and Brunner. In contrast to the idea of neoortho-doxy, Van Til called his book *The New Modernism*, indicating his judgment that Barth and Brunner represented a new version of liberal theology, not its antithesis. The seeds for this invective lay twenty years earlier. Van Til had attended Princeton Theological Seminary in the early 1920s, and after receiving his PhD in 1927 from Princeton University, he accepted an offer to teach apologetics at Princeton Seminary in 1928. The following year he was offered a full-time position, but he declined due to the reorganization of the seminary that had put modernists in control of the board. The restructuring of the seminary took place in response to faculty protesting the decision to appoint J. Gresham Machen the chair in apologetics and ethics. Van Til was then persuaded by Machen to join the new Westminster Theological Seminary, which claimed to be the successor to the Old Princeton of B. B. Warfield and Charles Hodge. It is in this context that we should understand his diatribe against Barth: it was nothing less than an attack on the theological program that had supplanted the Calvinist tradition at Princeton.

Van Til's attack was largely ignored by those aligned with neoorthodoxy, dismissed as little more than a curio from the fundamentalist backwaters. Paul Lehmann, who had befriended Dietrich Bonhoeffer while they were students at Union Theological Seminary in New York City, joined the faculty at Princeton the year after Van Til's book was published and was one of the few neoorthodox theologians to take the book seriously. In a review published in *Christendom*, he called it "a trenchant and arresting analysis of the present predicament of the Christian mind," though he also said the book "continues the polemical fervor and intransigeance that have come to be associated with Orthodoxy in American Protestantism."[99] Despite his serious engagement with it, Lehmann's critique of the book is notable for the way it displays the standard neoorthodox defense of the Barthian position. Lehmann argues that the problem with Van Til's book is not the critique of liberalism but its overly narrow definition of orthodoxy in terms of "classical metaphysics," as opposed to biblical authority. Van Til has shifted the goalposts of the conversation and thereby missed the fact that "the Bible and the Reformers are neither metaphysical nor anti-metaphysical."[100] They are concerned instead with God's self-revelation and redemption of sinful humanity, and this is what Barth and Brunner have recovered. Lehmann thus differentiates the neoorthodoxy of both Barth and Brunner from both liberalism and fundamentalism – providing a rhetorical model that would be repeated by Barth's defenders and proponents in the years to come.

While Van Til himself may have been ignored, the American neoorthodox scholars did everything they could to distance Barth from liberalism, highlighting the two "Big Bangs" as the definitive lens through which to truly understand Barth's thought. The motivation to do so was not due so much to Van Til as to the controversy over Rudolf Bultmann's program for demythologizing the Bible. Bultmann made his first visit to the United States in autumn 1951. On November 26, he visited Princeton Seminary, where Mackay let Bultmann speak about demythologizing only to the faculty, and not to the students, lest his remarks lead them toward liberalism. Bultmann was instead allowed to give a public lecture on the concept of freedom in Greek and Christian thought. After the lecture and the subsequent discussion, as Bultmann noted in his private reflections, "the president . . . emphasized in his words of thanks what the church owes to heretics, and how the most significant stimulation for theology has come from heretics. Thus here, as in certain German circles, I had to be regarded as a heretic, while everywhere else I was counted as part of 'neoorthodoxy' (Karl Barth is seen as the leader)."[101] At Princeton, and among the neoorthodox theologians more generally, it was important to protect Barth's name from being associated with Bultmann, whose work was considered by most in North America to exemplify liberal theology.

If Van Til had a chip on his shoulder about what happened at Princeton, those at Princeton were just as motivated to defend and protect the changes they had made – not only to Princeton Seminary but also to mainline Presbyterianism. Barth's theology had been instrumental in changing the landscape of interwar and postwar Presbyterianism in America, and since Mackay had hoped to transform American culture more widely with his recovery of theology, it was essential to protect the theological foundation for that transformation. Neoorthodoxy shared with Van Til the assumption that "historic Christianity," and not modern liberalism, was the future for the church. The question was whether Reformed orthodoxy or Barthian neoorthodoxy was the way to achieve this.

Barth's theology – or rather the American appropriation of it – may seem to have little in connection with Newman's impassioned plea to submit to the church's authoritative tradition. Barth had little patience for the idea of apostolic succession, and his followers did not speak about the rule of faith or the essence of religion. And yet American neoorthodoxy learned similar lessons from Barth, albeit framed in a distinctively Protestant way. Rather than submitting to the church's magisterium, Barth taught the church to embrace "its free submission to the sovereignty of the Word of God alone" – a divine Word that speaks the same message to Paul and Calvin as it does to the church today.[102] This message was understood to be defined by certain normative doctrinal tenets, including especially the doctrine of the trinity, but also corollary doctrines like the historical event of incarnation, the two natures of Christ, and the justification of sinners by grace alone. While Barth criticized the modern liberal quest for the essence of Christianity, he promoted his own account of the essence as the Word of God revealed in Christ and attested in scripture. He did not reject having an essence of Christianity, but rather denied that a *human* concept or principle could serve as the normative rule of faith. Barth instead claimed that a person must live "in full and free obedience to the Word of God," and this Word is "the work and activity of God," the divine command to the church.[103] He thus made traditional Protestant doctrines normative not because the church teaches them but because *God* says so. This too was a kind of voluntarism, albeit framed in terms of divine command, rather than church authority. To be sure, American neoorthodoxy paid less attention to how Barth redefined these doctrines and often seemed to have no ear for the way Barth characterized the normative essence as an *event* that often stood in opposition to the church and its traditions. What neoorthodoxy thus took from Barth was that the future for the church lay in recovering a normative, historical, and above all *theological* tradition of Christianity – a tradition that, in some sense, was authorized directly by God.

C. S. LEWIS AND THE IMMUTABLE FACTS OF "MERE CHRISTIANITY"

As significant as it was, Barth's influence was mostly limited to the academic elite – the faculty at theological institutions like Princeton and Yale and the leaders of organizations like the National Council of Churches and World Council of Churches. But his was not the only voice leading Protestants toward a "historic Christianity" and a doctrinal rule of faith. At the same time Barth was writing his *Church Dogmatics*, C. S. Lewis (1898–1963), the Irish novelist, apologist, and professor of English literature, was delivering the BBC radio talks that would become, in 1952, *Mere Christianity*. Barth and Lewis may seem to have little to do with each other, but the two are bound together in the larger quest for an essential, normative Christianity – though Barth spoke primarily to theologians and denominational leaders, while Lewis addressed the wider public.

Mere Christianity is in fact an anthology, composed of three shorter books published between 1942 and 1944, now divided into four books within the 1952 volume: "Right and Wrong as a Clue to the Meaning of the Universe," "What Christians Believe," "Christian Behaviour," and "Beyond Personality: Or First Steps in the Doctrine of the Trinity." Lewis's famous work is regarded as a classic in modern apologetics, and indeed this has been its primary influence, captured most notably in his argument regarding Jesus that "you can shut Him up for a fool, you can spit at Him and kill Him as a demon; or you can fall at His feet and call Him Lord and God."[104] Here, however, I will approach Lewis's work as an unwitting contribution to the quest for the essence of Christianity. The title alone suggests as much. In 1944 Lewis wrote an introduction to a new translation of Athanasius's *On the Incarnation* where he came close to making the connection. Speaking about the need for an antidote to modern accounts of Christianity, he stated: "The only safety is to have a standard of plain, central Christianity ('mere Christianity' as Baxter called it) which puts the controversies of the moment in their proper perspective. Such a standard can be acquired only from old books."[105] While Lewis borrowed Richard Baxter's 1681 antisectarian concept of "mere Christianity," in which Baxter claimed to be against all sects and parties, Lewis used the term precisely to oppose modern, liberal theologies, exemplifying the way appeals to the essence often claim to represent a universal and inclusive position at the same time that they exclude those who are regarded as beyond the pale.

Lewis, of course, would not have seen his work as a contribution to the quest for the essence. Unlike both Newman and Barth, Lewis took pains not to position his claims about "mere Christianity" as a polemical counterargument against alternatives that he saw as deficient or deformed – whether low-church Protestants and Roman Catholics in Newman's case, or liberals and fundamentalists in neoorthodoxy's. Indeed, Lewis took himself to be engaging in a purely *descriptive* task, explaining in broad ecumenical terms "what Christians believe," as book two of *Mere Christianity* states. His opening preface indicates that he sent the chapters on "what Christians believe" to clergy from four traditions: Anglican, Methodist, Presbyterian, and Roman Catholic (xi). He further clarifies that the *mereness* of "mere Christianity" is not "an alternative to the creeds of the existing communions" but rather "more like a hall out of which doors open into several rooms" (xv). His stated goal is to bring people into the hall, but then they are free to choose the room or communion that suits them best.

This ecumenical caveat notwithstanding, the book is a prescriptive statement about the essence – that is to say, what one person regards as the essence – whether Lewis and his readers acknowledge this or not. When he describes the book as "presenting an agreed, or common, or central, or 'mere' Christianity," he conflates descriptivism and prescriptivism, much the way Vincent of Lérins did when he defined the rule of faith as that which is held "by all" (xi). The goal of being purely descriptive is impossible when what one is describing are (what one takes to be) the normative beliefs of Christianity. Even a simple description of the Nicene Creed would still leave out many who consider themselves Christian. Lewis may write with the intention of articulating the common ground of all Christians, but such an effort was never realistic from the start. By his own admission, he does not even consult with Lutherans or Eastern Orthodox Christians, much less Anabaptists, Pentecostals, and the myriad other communities that fall under the Christian umbrella, including the different versions of Presbyterianism, Lutheranism, and the like. The notion that a single member of the Methodist clergy could speak on behalf of the Methodist church as a whole is obviously preposterous. If we factor in the passage of time, the matter becomes even more complex. Lewis cannot help but speak as a British Anglican in the mid-twentieth century. For that matter, he speaks also as a straight male whose homophobia and heteropatriarchal assumptions are evident throughout the pages of *Mere Christianity* – so much so that he thinks "there must be something unnatural about the rule of wives over husbands" (113). There is much in *Mere Christianity* that many would be hard-pressed to call "mere" in any meaningful sense. While Lewis talks about such doctrines as the trinity, incarnation, and atonement, he spends as much time, if not far more, discussing sexual morality and "Christian marriage." If these are part of the hallway, it is very narrow hallway indeed. Even if one limits the "mereness" to the chapters on "what Christians believe," one still finds claims that are fiercely disputed, such as the notion there is "a Dark Power in the universe" (45), that God made creatures with free will (47–48), and that "the central Christian belief is that Christ's death has somehow put us right with God" (54). The last of these most clearly displays the lack of engagement with Eastern Orthodoxy. One almost needs to posit a "merer Christianity" *within Mere Christianity*, but at some point the attempt to describe everyone ends up describing no one.

While Lewis's book fails as a genuine description of the Christian hallway (to use his metaphor), it works well as his account of prescriptive Christianity – his presentation of what we might call the rule of faith or the essence of Christianity. Lewis acknowledges as much explicitly. In response to the hypothetical question, "Who are you, to lay down who is, and who is not a Christian?" (xiii), Lewis turns to linguistics, using the example of how to define the word "gentleman." In other words, he turns to the very dispute (i.e., lexicology) that gave us the terms descriptivism and prescriptivism in the first place. He explains how the word used to have a clear, objective meaning ("one who had a coat of arms and some landed property"), but then the term gradually turned into a more generic compliment ("to be honourable and courteous"). The former is the prescriptive definition, while the latter is the descriptive definition. But Lewis regards the latter as "useless"; the only legitimate definition is the prescriptive one (xiv). By analogy, the word "Christian" has an objective, prescriptive meaning, and the purpose of his book is to clarify that meaning. He says that "we must therefore stick to the original, obvious meaning" of the word, referring to "those who accepted the teaching of the apostles." By his own admission, this definition excludes some from the ranks of Christianity:

> There is no question of [the word *Christian*] being extended to those who
> in some refined, spiritual, inward fashion were 'far closer to the spirit of
> Christ' than the less satisfactory of the disciples. The point is not a
> theological or moral one. It is only a question of using words so that we
> can all understand what is being said. When a man who accepts the
> Christian doctrine lives unworthily of it, it is much clearer to say he is a
> bad Christian than to say he is not a Christian. (xv)

Lewis thus advocates a timeless, universal definition of Christianity, so
that those who believe the correct doctrines are Christian regardless of
any other criteria, while those who do not believe are not Christians, no
matter whether they describe themselves as Christian, participate in
Christian community, or embody the Christian spirit. This explains why
he can blur the distinction between the descriptive and the prescriptive
in talking about "mere Christianity," and why he can claim to be speaking
on behalf of all Christians: only those who share the correct beliefs count
as "Christian" in the first place.

The same blurring of description and prescription occurs throughout
the book, most clearly in Lewis's decision to describe the doctrines of
Christianity using the language of scientific objectivity. Lewis uses the
word "fact" nearly twenty times in *Mere Christianity* when talking about
Christian teachings (as he understands them). A consistent refrain
throughout the book is that Lewis is not saying anything novel or unique
to him but is simply describing the facts about Christianity:

- "I am only trying to call attention to a fact." (7)
- "Christianity simply does not make sense until you have faced the sort
  of facts I have been describing." (31)
- "All I am doing is to ask people to face the facts – to understand the
  questions which Christianity claims to answer. And they are very terri-
  fying facts." (32)
- "I am telling you what Christianity is. I did not invent it." (115)
- "Up till now, I have been trying to describe facts – what God is and
  what He has done." (187)

The primary rhetorical purpose of these and other statements is paradoxically to secure Lewis's authority by denying any authority. In other

words, by downplaying any expertise for himself, he portrays himself as a simple reporter of the facts, a mere transcriber of the tradition, and thereby reinforces the authoritative nature of his book: Lewis, we are led to believe, is only presenting what has always and everywhere been true about Christianity. He even uses his lack of knowledge as part of his apologetic in defense of Christianity: "If Christianity was something we were making up, of course we could make it easier. But it is not. We cannot compete, in simplicity, with people who are inventing religions. How could we? *We are dealing with Fact.* Of course anyone can be simple if he has no facts to bother about" (165, emphasis mine).[106]

The secondary purpose of these statements is just as important. They subtly repackage as facts what are not facts at all but are instead *interpretations.* But interpretations would require Lewis to be the expert who offers prescriptive accounts of Christian doctrine that readers accept because they trust his understanding of the faith – and this is precisely what Lewis is unwilling to do. In order to avoid this role, he has to present what he says as a purely descriptive rendering of Christian tradition, and he does this not by demonstrating that his claims have a basis in the tradition – that too would require a level of expertise that Lewis does not have – but instead by simply asserting their factuality, by cloaking his claims in the language of scientific objectivity. In addition to the repeated use of "fact," he uses scientific and mechanical analogies and metaphors to illustrate his theological claims. For instance, he says that spiritual formation "is not merely the spreading of an idea; it is more like evolution – a biological or superbiological fact" (64); notice here the language of "fact" is first applied to science and then, by extension, to Christianity. Lewis uses an epidemiological analogy for evangelism, comparing the spread of the gospel to a "good infection" in which a person "catches" faith from another (177, 181). Seven times in *Mere Christianity* he describes the human person as a machine that correctly runs only one way, and religion provides the rules for proper operation. "God designed the human machine to run on Himself," he claims, and "Christianity is the total plan for the human machine" (50, 85). When talking about how a "man and wife" become "one flesh" in marriage, he says that Christians believe Jesus was "stating a fact – just as one is stating a fact when one says that a lock and its key are one mechanism" (104). These metaphors and comparisons suggest that the norms of Christianity are objective and self-evident, as clear as the way a key fits into a lock. They also allow Lewis to avoid the hard work of actually persuading his readers by simply asserting the supposedly obvious truth of his claims.

Rhetorical effectiveness aside, *Mere Christianity* suggests to readers that Christian doctrines are timeless, immutable facts. Indeed, Lewis says that, in general, "religion involves a series of statements about facts, which must be either true or false" (74). As a specific religion, Christianity is also, he argues, a series of factual statements. While he does not frame things in this way, Lewis is here contributing directly to the modern quest for the essence of Christianity. Like Schleiermacher or Newman before him, he first defines religion as such before identifying the distinctive essence of Christianity. For Lewis, religion in general is a series of propositional claims. The word Lewis uses for these religious claims is "myth," which he argues is a concrete expression of reality, from which can be derived innumerable abstract truths about the human experience. But as Lewis claims in his 1944 essay, "Myth Became Fact," "the heart of Christianity is a myth which is also a fact," and thus "to be truly Christian we must both assent to the historical fact and also receive the myth (fact though it has become)."[107] The distinctive Christian essence or rule of faith is thus found in the specific propositions regarding the triune God, the person of Christ, the immortality of each person, and the nature of salvation. To be a Christian is to believe these propositions: "That is the formula. That is Christianity. That is what has to be believed" (55). Faith is "the art of holding on to" these propositional beliefs through the vagaries of human experience (140). The purpose of this belief, he declares, is to transform a person into a "little Christ," about which he says: "This is the whole of Christianity. There is nothing else" (199).[108] Lewis has thus defined the whole or essence of Christianity as a person's rational assent to a series of propositions about myths-turned-facts – facts about what God is, what God has done, and how to run the human machine in order to become a Christlike person. And all of this, he claims, rests on God as "the rock bottom, irreducible Fact on which all other facts depend" (184).

Lewis uses the concept of "essence" explicitly in other writings from this period. In his 1946 response to the Welsh philosopher H. H. Price,

Lewis criticizes Price's claim that "the essence of religion is belief in God and immortality" on the grounds that this leaves out Judaism and Buddhism. Instead, Lewis argues that "the essence of religion ... is the thirst for an end higher than natural ends; the finite self's desire for, and acquiescence in, and self-rejection in favour of, an object wholly good and wholly for it."[109] Christianity is then "the completion, the actualization, the entelechy" of this essence – or as he also says, this essence has been "historicised in the Incarnation."[110] Much like Newman, Lewis seeks a union of the intellectualist and voluntarist traditions. Whereas Newman uses the term "principle," Lewis uses the word "myth" to refer to the universal truth or normative religious essence that unites all people, regardless of their culture or location in history. This is the constant, prereligious element that intellectualism seeks to affirm. Lewis then uses the word "fact" to identify the voluntarist position that the Christian church is now the exclusive bearer of the truth in its fullness – a specifically doctrinal truth codified especially in the church's ecumenical creeds. The myth-became-fact trope thus forms the basis of his apologetic: the truth is found in the church's factual teachings (voluntarism), but these teachings should be universally acknowledged because the facts are rooted in universal myth (intellectualism).

In an even more direct nod to Newman, Lewis compares the specific essence of Christianity to the "formal principles" of mathematics and language that are able to develop over time while still remaining essentially identical. His essay, "Dogma and the Universe" (originally published in two parts in March 1943), responds to the criticism that Christianity is something humanity has outgrown because the dogmas are unchanging while scientific knowledge is constantly advancing. Lewis defends Christianity by comparing dogma to the foundational principles of knowledge that must remain the same in order to make future discoveries possible. He gives as examples the "unchanging system of the alphabet" and the "multiplication table."[111] Much like Newman, who, in comparing unchanging dogma to the way an animal develops from an infant to an adult while remaining the same animal, writes that "young birds do not grow into fishes," Lewis likewise says "a small oak grows into a big oak; if it became a beech, that would not be growth, but mere change."[112] The difference between them is that Newman uses these examples to emphasize doctrinal *change*, whereas Lewis uses them to defend doctrine's *lack of change*.

Lewis is widely regarded as one of the foremost apologists of the twentieth century, but he was also, and perhaps more importantly, a key promoter of the doctrinal rule of faith among Protestants, especially Protestant evangelicals who embraced his work because of their interest in apologetics. In contrast to previous Protestant apologists who spent their time defending the authority and infallibility of scripture in the face of scientific challenges, Lewis modeled a different path. Lewis showed very little interest in biblical interpretation. Christianity for him was not defined by adherence to a certain reading of scripture but rather in his adherence to the essential doctrines – the doctrinal "facts" – that define the tradition. In this way, Lewis was the twentieth-century Newman, but whereas Newman grounded his account of the rule of faith in the infallibility of the church's authority (thus leading him to Rome), Lewis grounded his account in the immutability of doctrine, grounded in the eternal Fact that is God. Newman was able to allow for development and variation in doctrine precisely because the ecclesiastical institution provided the underlying foundation. Lewis, however, like his evangelical readers, did not have such an ecclesiology. For him, the immutability of doctrine is a necessary corollary of his belief in the immutability of God.

THE DOCTRINAL RULE OF FAITH IN
POST-DOCTRINAL AMERICA

Newman, Barth, and Lewis are by no means the maximal representatives of the doctrinal rule of faith. In each case, but especially in Barth's, there were conservative critics who found them to be insufficiently doctrinal. Moreover, I am not suggesting that their work is directly responsible for the more recent developments regarding Christian prescriptivism and normativity that I will cover in Chapter 3, though Barth is particularly important to that story. Instead, these writers are significant for the way they each contributed to a more general atmosphere conducive to doctrinal prescriptivism – in particular, among mainline and evangelical Protestants, groups that had not been as concerned about historic Christian doctrine, as Newman was wont to observe.

Newman, of course, castigated his fellow Anglicans for their lack of fidelity to ancient doctrinal norms and eventually converted to Rome out of a recognition that the theological ground for his doctrinal commitments rested on a concept of ecclesial authority the Protestant traditions could not supply. While committed Protestants generally did not listen to Newman, they eventually did listen to Barth, who made the rejection of liberal theology an intellectually fulfilled option without requiring the embrace of either Catholic ecclesiology or fundamentalist biblicism. Barth also did so in the name of a *Church Dogmatics* – highlighting both the churchly nature of his account of Christianity and its doctrinal content. Simultaneously, Lewis popularized the idea that Protestants stand within the churchly, doctrinal tradition of historic, or "mere," Christianity. Instead of a rule of faith, he talked of the law of nature that grounds the doctrines and practices of Christianity – thereby connecting doctrine to apologetics and morality. This apologetic strategy led Lewis to present himself as a descriptivist, even if, ultimately, his work was as prescriptivist as the other two.

In comparison to Newman's Anglo-Catholic fastidiousness with regard to the ancient rule of the church, Barth's Reformed Protestantism and Lewis's ecumenism led them to articulate more attenuated, less precise rules. Barth's rule was the "Word of God" (defined especially by the doctrine of the trinity) and Lewis's was the perennial myth that had become Fact (which ends up being, as he once said, whatever is in the Book of Common Prayer). The point being that the notion of a normative, prescriptive Christianity, even when defined in largely doctrinal terms, comes in different forms and can result in vastly different accounts of Christian doctrine. Part of what made Barth and Lewis so attractive to Protestants, especially evangelical Protestants, was precisely this doctrinal flexibility within their antiliberal vision of Christianity's essence.

Lewis died in 1963 and Barth died in 1968 – right in the midst of what William Hutchison has called the "transition from Protestant America to pluralist America."[113] It was also a transition from a doctrinal to a post-doctrinal America, as the robust theological systems of the "straight white male"–dominated Protestant America were no longer adequate to the cultural moment. The Confession of 1967, commissioned by the United

Presbyterian Church in the United States of America, represented the high-water mark of American neoorthodoxy. From its doctrine of scripture as the witness to the Word of God that is Jesus Christ to its doctrine of reconciliation as the organizing soteriological framework, the Confession of 1967 came close to making the *Church Dogmatics* the defining theology of the Northern Presbyterian denomination. But it came at the end of an era. The following year saw Mary Daly launch feminist theology with *The Church and the Second Sex*, and in 1969 James Cone initiated Black liberation theology with the publication of *Black Theology and Black Power*. A neoorthodox "church dogmatics" could no longer provide the normative parameters for Presbyterians, much less for other mainline Protestants. By comparison with the Confession of 1967, the later Brief Statement of Faith – commissioned by the Presbyterian Church (USA) in 1983 and adopted in 1991 – was doctrinally minimalist and represented a more inclusive and pluralist vision of Christianity, one that had repudiated the effort not only to police the prescribed boundaries of the faith but also to define what those boundaries were in the first place.

Those who still insisted on a doctrinal rule of faith felt compelled to abandon mainline Protestantism for the more hospitable climes of evangelicalism. Thomas Oden (1931–2016) is a paradigmatic example. In 1964 and 1969, respectively, he published books on the ethics of Bultmann and Barth, but a decade later he had turned his back on both liberalism and neoorthodoxy and instead promoted a new *Agenda for Theology*: paleo-orthodoxy, which he defined as "a return to the normative self-restrictions that have prevailed in Christianity's first millennium ... because of its close adherence to apostolic faith."[114] In his later memoir, where he charts his change of mind from mainline liberalism to evangelicalism, he acknowledges that "the almost comic term paleo-orthodoxy was an act of contrarian defiance to distinguish classic Christianity from neoorthodoxy."[115] Oden is an extreme example, for whom Barth's theology represented a hindrance to "historic" or "classical" Christianity. Evangelicals coming out of biblicist and fundamentalist traditions, however, often found Barth to be the solution to their problems. Bernard Ramm (1916–1992), for instance, writing a few years after Oden announced his agenda, saw in Barth's dogmatics "the future of evangelical theology," largely because, as he says, "I found him defending the ancient Christology of the church fathers as well as their doctrine of the trinity." For this reason Barth's theology provided evangelicalism with "new ways to maintain the old faith."[116] Ramm sums up "Barth's case against liberal Christianity" in the following way: "liberal Christianity is not Christianity as historically understood and is therefore not Christianity."[117] As Ramm reads him, like Pauck a half-century earlier, Barth advocates a kind of historical prescriptivism that defines "true Christianity" in terms of "historic Christianity," and any Christian who breaks with this historic essence is a #FakeChristian, as one might say today. Ramm, more than Oden, represented the direction of evangelicals in the late twentieth and early twenty-first centuries, as Stanley Grenz, Roger Olson, Kevin Vanhoozer, Daniel Treier, Mark Galli, and others advanced the school of American neoorthodoxy, but now from a more conservative direction.

Both Lewis and Barth became most well-known and appreciated in the United States after their deaths, as the rise of pluralist, post-doctrinal America prompted conservative reactions among Christians who found in these writers the needed theological inspiration for retrieving a more traditional and classic – and therefore, in their minds, true and essential – Christianity. Barth's theology became more widely influential after his death, as the mainline neoorthodoxy of John Mackay's Princeton Seminary was supplanted by the postliberal and evangelical versions of neoorthodoxy. The later repackaging of Barth leeched his work of any positive connection to the liberal tradition and solidified a version of Barthian theology amenable to the evangelical culture wars.

Lewis, who was not widely known in the United States before his death, exploded in popularity around the same time that American evangelicalism became a more mobilized demographic, thanks to the National Association of Evangelicals, Billy Graham's *Christianity Today*, the formation of new evangelical institutions of higher education, the schisms and conservative takeovers within major denominations, and the growing network of parachurch organizations. Lewis's own reception history tracks the changes in American Christianity. *Mere Christianity*, as George Marsden has documented, was initially warmly received by mainline Protestants. Princeton Seminary's *Theology Today* "offered nothing but praise" for Lewis in 1945, and the *Christian Century* offered additional praise in 1946.[118] By contrast, American evangelicals (at the time still known as fundamentalists) were cautious toward Lewis, if not outright critical of him. The same Van Til who was so critical of Barth and neoorthodoxy was also critical of Lewis, calling *Mere Christianity* "destructive of evangelical faith."[119] By the late 1960s, however, the situation was just the reverse. Lewis's star had waned among mainline Protestants – *Christian Century* published its first critical statement on Lewis in 1958 – at the same time that American evangelicals were claiming Lewis as one of their own, beginning most clearly with Wheaton College professor Clyde Kilby's defense of Lewis in 1958 against his critics in the pages of the new magazine *Christianity Today*.[120] In 1964, the year after Lewis's death, Kilby published *The Christian World of C. S. Lewis*. His forceful support for Lewis from the halls of Wheaton College ensured that "the future leaders of American evangelicalism, including many of its intellectual leaders, were going to have a high regard for Lewis."[121] Likewise, InterVarsity Christian Fellowship played an important role in the evangelical embrace of Lewis, beginning with the publication of an excerpt of his work in 1944 in the magazine *His*, and continuing with the use of Lewis in campus evangelism.[122] In 2005, marking the release of the new movie based on *The Lion, the Witch and the Wardrobe*, InterVarsity Press's publisher called Lewis "probably the greatest authority and example" of an informed Christian faith "outside of the Scriptures themselves," indicating just how highly esteemed Lewis had become among evangelicals and in American society more generally.[123]

The doctrinal prescriptivism of Barth and Lewis gained new adherents especially in the 1990s among those looking for a theological foundation for countercultural resistance to the cultural pluralism that posed a challenge to the future of "Christian America." But soon the prescribed margins of authentic faith had little to do with traditional creedal Christianity, as the rapidly changing pluralism provoked new cultural, moral, and political boundaries. The conservative enforcers of a normative Christian tradition began to replace doctrinal boundaries with more nebulous cultural boundaries that were more conducive to authoritarian control within an evolving society. The result of these changes, as Chapter 3 will show, was the culturalization of the rule of faith.

3

Inhabiting the Rule

How Christianity Became a Culture

I N 1963, the year that C. S. Lewis died, the Second Vatican Council was just getting underway. Pope John XXIII had opened the council on October 11, 1962, and after adjournment in December, preparations were being made for the sessions defining the nature of the church – sessions that eventually generated *Lumen gentium,* the Dogmatic Constitution on the Church, in 1964. At the same time as this landmark council was beginning its work, a very different event occurred on March 19, 1963: namely, the publication of Bishop John A. T. Robinson's "dynamite charge" of a book, *Honest to God.*[1] To be sure, Robinson's book was nowhere as significant as Vatican II, but in the year 1963 it was all anyone could talk about, eliciting comments from all the major theologians and Christian intellectuals of the day. The book sold nearly a half-million copies in the first year alone and came out in German the same year as *Gott ist anders* (God is other). Lewis was asked about it in one of his final interviews before his death, and Rudolf Bultmann felt compelled to write two articles in response to it, no doubt because of the way the Bishop of Woolwich appealed to Bultmann's writings in support of his views, even calling "a letter written by Bultmann" one of his "valued possessions."[2]

Juxtaposing Robinson's call for rethinking the meaning of the word "God" with the Roman Catholic Church's call for rethinking the meaning of the church highlights the two dominant responses to modernity in Western Christianity. Despite the overblown controversy regarding his book – which today seems rather tame, even traditional – Robinson represented the latest entry in the modern quest for the essence of

Christianity. Without using that language, Robinson asks whether Christianity must be "supranaturalist," "mythological," and "religious" – that is, whether these are essential to the faith – answering, in each case, in the negative.[3] He is, in other words, describing what the essence of Christianity is after we abandon the supernatural, mythological conceptuality of the premodern world. This became all the more clear three years later when William Hamilton, one of the cofounders in 1966 alongside Thomas J. J. Altizer of death-of-God theology (also known as radical theology), published a revised edition of his 1961 book on *The New Essence of Christianity*, featuring a preface by none other than Bishop Robinson.[4]

Vatican II may not seem like the opposite of *Honest to God* – and for many it was not. Certainly for Catholics accustomed to the Latin Tridentine Mass, the innovations that came with the council were nothing short of revolutionary, eliciting sharp opposition that continues today in the form of traditionalist communities and organizations that oppose the changes of Vatican II as a capitulation to modernism. And yet for the wider theological and ecclesiastical world, particularly for mainline Protestants, the council and the movements associated with it provided the impetus for a large-scale reaction against modernity and the liberal quest for the essence. By extending an ecumenical hand to other traditions, the Catholic Church invited Protestants, many of whom were exhausted with the focus on the Bible alone, to mine the depths of Christian tradition. The invitation could not have come at a better time. For (post)liberal Protestants weary of the wars over demythologizing and historical criticism, the ancient spiritual and figural methods of interpretation were like a swift spring breeze blowing open the exegetical shutters that had been closed by scholarly consensus. Vatican II alone was not the catalyst, but it came to symbolize the wider scholarly and popular turn toward the rule of faith, including both the creedal tradition and ancient liturgical forms, that arose in reaction to the quest for the essence that peaked in the 1960s. More than just a doctrine of the church or the renewal of classic liturgical forms, Vatican II and associated efforts embodied an alternative quest – not for the essence of Christianity but for what we might call *historic Christian identity*. This of course was a version of the Christian essence, but it was constructed in opposition to the concept of the essence that had developed in modernity.

In Chapter 2, I began my inquiry into the formation of this counter-modern identity by focusing on the *thinking* aspect of Schleiermacher's tripartite schema of thinking, feeling, and doing. The thinking or doctrinal version of normative Christianity typically entails the retrieval of the rule of faith, or what theologians tend to regard as traditional Christian orthodoxy. In the case of Newman, this involved the entire panoply of creedal propositions from virtually every conciliar decision. In the case of Barth's American followers, it involved a more constrained and focused emphasis on doctrines like the trinity and the Chalcedonian Definition of Christ's two natures, as well as items from the Protestant confessional tradition, such as justification by grace alone and Christ's substitutionary atonement. With Lewis, it was further limited to the trinity and atonement, seasoned with a dash of moralism. The lack of specificity regarding which doctrines were normative was not an accident but a key reason why Barth and Lewis were so appealing to American Protestants. The specific doctrines were less important than the broader normative Christian identity they served to define over against the liberal identity they aimed to oppose. Barth and Lewis were attractive for the way they gave their readers confidence that the truth of God's revelation and the facts of historic Christianity were on their side, whatever those facts may be. Even if many of Barth's neoorthodox readers disagreed with him or with each other over specific matters of dogmatic interpret-ation, they still shared what they took to be Barth's pursuit of a historic Christian identity over against all modern liberal alternatives. This common identity – more cultural than theological – precipitated the transition from neoorthodoxy to postliberalism that took place in the late twentieth century, in which culture, rather than doctrine, became the organizing essence of Christianity. The story of that transition is the subject of this chapter.

This chapter examines the second part of Schleiermacher's schema: feeling, or what I will analyze here in terms of culture.[5] But unlike doctrine, which has been important since antiquity, the story of how Christianity became a culture in the late twentieth century requires some explanation. It involves two different strands. The first, which will receive less attention, is the story of how the Second Vatican Council became a landmark event for American Protestants. This much is an extension of the story from Chapter 2 regarding how Protestants became increasingly interested in "historic Christianity." Protestants were not alone in this interest. Catholics were embarking on a similar quest, one that led to a new movement of *ressourcement* – the recovery of ancient sources for the purpose of renewing the church today. In the wake of Vatican II, the Catholic and Protestant quests intersected. But in order to understand why that intersection was so fruitful, we need to explore the second and more complicated strand. This aspect of our story takes us back to the American neoorthodox theologians at Princeton Theological Seminary, who did more than simply aim at the recovery of historically orthodox Christianity. At the center of their program was a new and distinctively American effort at biblical theology, which had the stated goal of restoring the Bible's normative authority for the church – and therefore for American society as a whole. The story of this movement and its eventual collapse sets the stage for the rise of what has become known as postliberalism, at the heart of which is what I call cultural ecclesiocentrism – an account of Christianity that makes the church, understood as a countercultural institution of identity formation, normative for Christian faith and theology. While this cultural account of the faith is closely connected to the doctrinal account, the purpose of this model of normative Christianity was to avoid the scholastic disputes over the finer points of doctrine that often divided otherwise closely aligned traditions. Rather than get caught up in the old conflicts over issues like the real presence of Christ in the eucharist, cultural ecclesiocentrism redirected Christian apologetics against a common cultural enemy: secular modernism.

The cultural rule of faith became a fundamentally new way of distinguishing the "true Christian" from rival claimants. By completely redrawing the lines regarding inclusion and exclusion, the cultural account of Christianity's essence laid the groundwork for new ecclesial alliances in the ecumenical age. Moreover, the plasticity of culture as the basis for normative Christianity made it a ready vehicle for the fluid political landscape that emerged in the late twentieth and early twenty-first centuries. As predominantly white Christian leaders denounced ever-new attacks in a "war on Christianity," the cultural rule of faith became a rallying cry to mobilize the faithful for the front lines. The boundary lines defining "true Christianity" became trenches in cultural warfare. But to understand how we arrived where we are today, we first need to go back to the early twentieth century.

THEOLOGICAL RENAISSANCES: PROTESTANT RETRIEVALS, THE LITURGICAL MOVEMENT, AND *RESSOURCEMENT*

The dialectical theologians were not the only ones engaged in a new theological movement during the early decades of the twentieth century, nor were they alone in retrieving earlier theological work. This was a period of numerous theological renaissances – not only a renewed interest in orthodoxy but also a renewed engagement with past theologians.

The dialectical theologians themselves were involved in what became known as the Kierkegaard Renaissance that began in Weimar Germany and spread to France, Great Britain, and the United States. Karl Barth himself is often credited with initiating this renaissance with his *Epistle to the Romans*, though it was likely his friend Eduard Thurneysen who stirred his interest.[6] The global enthusiasm for Kierkegaard is in fact "unthinkable without Barth's stormy personality and instant fame." Prior to his famous work on Romans, the reception of Kierkegaard "came only in a drizzle," but afterwards the "publications by and about the Dane poured forth from the German presses in a torrent."[7] Almost instantly Barth's connection to Kierkegaard was the subject of conversation, leading Anders Gemmer and August Messer to publish *Sören Kierkegaard und Karl Barth* in 1925, with Gemmer discussing the former and Messer the latter. Regarding this book, Barth remarked to Thurneysen: "I can only grin painfully."[8] Following Barth, the other dialectical theologians – especially Emil Brunner, Rudolf Bultmann, and Friedrich Gogarten – joined in the party, quoting Kierkegaard frequently in their writings.[9] Barth quickly grew wary of this growing interest. He had already started to distance himself from Kierkegaard by late 1924 after reading the work of the Danish Kierkegaard scholar Eduard Geismar.[10] Things took a sharp turn, however, in the mid-1920s when the Danish thinker caught the attention of more liberal German theologians. Among these, Emanuel Hirsch is particularly important. Hirsch was Barth's colleague at Göttingen, after Barth joined the faculty in 1921, and the two of them disliked each other from the start. Hirsch, who later became a prominent Nazi theologian, first published on Kierkegaard in 1926, the same year that Gogarten and Bultmann published works that referred to the Dane, and from this point onward Barth soured on Kierkegaard and the renewed interest in his writings.[11]

At the same time as these developments were taking place, an even more prominent retrieval effort was occurring in Weimar Germany: the Luther Renaissance (1917–1933).[12] As with the Kierkegaard Renaissance, this retrieval of Luther occurred within a fragile and unstable period in political history, in a society still shaken by the horrors of the Great War and seeking cultural stability. Kierkegaard's existential grappling with anxiety spoke to the fears and yearnings of those living in the Weimar Republic, especially the avant-garde socialists and budding fascists who were critical of the young regime and concerned about authentic individuality.[13] Luther caught the attention of some of the same scholars (Hirsch especially), but he served a different function, coming to represent the foundation of modern German culture and serving as the patron saint of German nationalism. Inspired by the quatercentenary of the Reformation in 1917 and the (re)discovery of Luther's 1515–1516 *Lectures on Romans* (published by Johannes Ficker in 1908), Lutheran scholars, inspired by Karl Holl's pioneering work, began retrieving a version of Luther who could address their religious, political, and existential concerns.[14] As Christine Helmer has pointed out, the theologians of the Luther Renaissance were concerned about "Germany's moral collapse" and looked to Luther, or at least their version of him, to "function as hero for Germany at a time of its great nadir."[15] The Luther they promoted provided the theological grounding for a society of law and order, in which each person was committed to their leader through self-sacrificial obedience. It is hardly a surprise that this provided a fertile basis for the rise of National Socialism, as seen especially in Erich Seeberg, Eric Vogelsang, and Hirsch.[16]

Both of these retrieval efforts in Weimar Germany were particular to their time and place, but they exemplified a larger, more global interest in addressing modern cultural crises by turning to earlier thinkers who could provide the needed sources of renewal. Not long after the dialectical theologians, Kierkegaardians, and Lutherans pursued their respective theological movements in Germany, Switzerland, and the Netherlands, a group of French Catholics began to push against the neoscholastic or "manualist" Thomism that had come to dominate Roman Catholic theology in the wake of the First Vatican Council (1869–1870), and especially after Pope Leo XIII's 1879 encyclical *Aeterni Patris* made the theology of Thomas Aquinas the basis for Catholic seminary education. Exiled from France as a result of decrees designed to separate church and state, the Jesuits and Dominicans relocated, respectively, to the Channel Island of Jersey and Belgium, taking refuge in two seminaries – the Maison Saint-Louis and Le Saulchoir – where they began a renewal movement in Catholic thought.[17] The new movement came to be known as *ressourcement* theology (a theology that "returns to the sources"), though its detractors called it *la nouvelle théologie*, "the new theology" – a highly pejorative term within Catholicism. The movement went through four phases, according to Jürgen Mettepenningen, beginning in the mid-1930s and reaching a climax with the Second Vatican Council, which officially endorsed much of this "new theology."[18] The theologians who initiated *ressourcement* theology – Marie-Dominique Chenu, Henri de Lubac, Yves Congar, Jean Daniélou, and Henri Bouillard – sought to recover the ancient sources of theology in early Christianity. As used by their critics, the adjective "new" was meant to imply they were "rejecting, rather than retrieving, the Catholic tradition," while the *ressourcement* theologians "saw themselves as retrieving the ancient texts in order to renew tradition."[19] Patricia Kelly points out that the *ressourcement* theologians "latched onto and indeed developed" the ideas of Newman regarding the way revelation unfolds over time, thus necessitating the historical development of doctrine. While both Newman and the *ressourcement* theologians were seen as suspect by a Catholic leadership steeped in neoscholasticism, such views would soon become popular and exert significant influence on the church.[20] Both Newman and the *ressourcement* theologians also promoted the reading of early Christian theology by making primary sources more widely available. Between 1838 and 1881, members of the Oxford Movement, led especially by Edward Bouverie Pusey, edited the *Library of the Fathers*, a fifty-volume series of writings by the theologians of the ancient church.[21] Similarly, Daniélou, de Lubac, and Claude Mondésert founded *Sources chrétiennes*, a still-ongoing series of ancient and medieval texts that now numbers over 600 volumes. This interest in the study of entire texts, rather than just canonical selections and authorized definitions, was a hallmark of *ressourcement* theology. While the actual theological views of these theologians were important – including their well-known innovations on the relation of nature and grace – for the purposes of my argument here, the key legacy of this movement was the more general call for a return to the authoritative texts from a supposedly more pristine period in the church prior to later ecclesiastical declension.

The theological *ressourcement* movement found further support from the liturgical renewal movement that likewise reached its culmination in the reforms of Vatican II. The liturgical movement had its origins in the eighteenth-century discovery and study of ancient sacramentaries that led to the 1786 Synod of Pistoia's call "for a return to the pristine liturgy of the early church," but this early liturgical *ressourcement* was set back in 1794 when Pope Pius VI condemned the Synod.[22] Liturgical innovations at French, Belgian, and German Benedictine monasteries in the nineteenth century made the matter a live issue again. The Belgian monastery, Mont César Abbey, became a hub for liturgical renewal thanks to the efforts of Lambert Beauduin and his belief, articulated in a 1909 lecture, that the church's internally focused worship and externally focused social mission should be connected. At the Maria Laach Abbey in Germany, Odo Casel argued that the sacraments originated in the ancient Greek mystery religions. Theologically, these renewal efforts found support in the work of nineteenth-century German Roman Catholic theologians, such as Johann Adam Möhler – the so-called Tübingen School of Catholic theology – who developed the idea of the church as the Mystical Body of Christ, which eventually led to two papal encyclicals by Pius XII, *Mystici Corporis Christi* (1943) and *Mediator Dei* (1947).[23] Möhler's work was important to the *ressourcement* movement more widely, and the French translation of his 1825 work *Unity in the*

Church was published as the second volume in the *Unam Sanctam* series on ecclesiology that Congar introduced in 1937.[24]

As Frank Senn points out, the liturgical movement was brought to the United States by the monks at St. John's Abbey in Collegeville, Minnesota. From there it exerted influence among the mainline Protestant denominations, though the reception of a deeply communitarian liturgical ethos among highly individualistic Americans was always tenuous.[25] Senn observes that one of the goals of the liturgical movement "was the return to an earlier, more biblical tradition," moving behind the medieval scholasticism to the first several centuries of Christianity. He says that this "ought to have connected with American Protestantism" but largely did not, because American Christianity, he argues, is not only "biblicistic" but also "gnostic" and "mythical," disconnected from both the "historic liturgy" and "historical Christianity." For this reason, retrieving the "historic liturgy" will therefore "have a pervasively counter-cultural quality" to it within American culture.[26] Senn here participates in a long-standing tradition of prescriptivism, going back to Irenaeus, but it has been reconfigured for a modern Protestant context as a *retrievalist* prescriptivism. According to this viewpoint, not only is the ancient liturgy, and the "historic Christianity" that grounds it, the *authentic* practice of Christian faith, but it is also a lost version that must now be recovered as a countercultural way of life. Despite his sweeping claims about American gnosticism, by the time Senn published these words in 1997, retrievalist prescriptivism had been making inroads into American Protestantism for some time and was just starting to break into American evangelical circles, even if the liturgical *ressourcement* that concerned Senn remained of less interest to these groups.

The *ressourcement* and liturgical movements reached their institutional climax with the Second Vatican Council that lasted from October 1962 to December 1965. But in terms of the larger story of prescriptivism and the rule of faith, that was only the beginning. From there, Protestants picked up the mantle of retrievalism – effectively constituting the fifth phase in the *ressourcement* movement. There were several motivating factors for this interest in "historic Christianity" among Protestants that all collided in this period. In Chapter 2, I explored the renewed emphasis on traditional, "orthodox" doctrine among mainline Protestants, inspired in large part by Barth and American neoorthodox theologians. These doctrinal efforts were explicitly pursued against the backdrop of social and political upheaval, as mainline Protestants were enlisted in the struggle against what they saw as the threats posed by communism and secularism. The need to rectify a crisis posed by modern culture was a consistent theme in these retrievals, whether the retrieval in question was early Christianity, Luther, Kierkegaard, or orthodoxy more generally.

The felt need for retrievalism among mainline Protestants was reinforced practically in two ways. First, the ecumenical movement motivated many to find points of common ground among the different traditions and denominations. The ecumenical movement had its origins in the nineteenth-century missionary movement, but it was the 1910 World Missionary Conference in Edinburgh that generated the momentum to form the World Council of Churches (WCC) – established in principle in 1937 and then officially, following the war, in 1948. The National Council of Churches (NCC) followed in 1950. The WCC and NCC were symbolic of a widespread ecumenism that saw alliances form between denominations with respect to both polity and social witness. Ecumenical partnerships were the practical counterpart to theological retrievals of earlier theological work, and together they created an environment in which Christianity was defined by certain shared doctrines and a shared mission to proclaim the message of Christianity – a view that was fortified by the work of the International Missionary Council (IMC), which joined the WCC in 1961, and Vatican II's *Ad gentes* (1965).[27] Second, the institutional approval of the liturgical movement that occurred in 1963, with the Second Vatican Council's adoption of the Constitution on the Sacred Liturgy (*Sacrosanctum concilium*), led to the replacement of the old one-year lectionary, the Tridentine Roman Missal, with a new three-year lectionary, the *Ordo lectionum Missae*, in 1969. As the liturgical and ecumenical movements grew in influence with Protestants, there was growing Protestant interest in adopting a similar lectionary among the mainline denominations. Guided by the work of the Consultation on Church Union, the Consultation on Common Texts, and the English Language Liturgical Consultation (previously the International Consultation on English Texts), these ecumenical Protestant organizations eventually produced the Common Lectionary in 1983, followed by the Revised Common Lectionary in 1994 – establishing a shared text of scriptural readings among the major Protestant denominations. These ecumenical and liturgical partnerships also had doctrinal implications, resulting most famously in the 1999 Joint Declaration on the Doctrine of Justification between the Vatican and the Lutheran World Federation, later adopted by the World Methodist Council in 2006 and the World Communion of Reformed Churches in 2017.[28]

While there were significant efforts, as in the Joint Declaration, to establish doctrinal unity on especially contentious matters, the final decades of the twentieth century in fact saw mainstream Christian communities move away from the view that doctrine defined the essence or rule of Christianity. The *ressourcement* and liturgical movements, which were initially perceived by the church authorities as undermining Catholic doctrine, shifted the focus from the letter of doctrinal propositions toward the deeper spirit and underlying language, logic, and practice of the tradition, rooted in the all-encompassing culture of the church. This shift manifested itself theologically among Protestants in what became known as postliberalism, but in order to tell that story we first need to understand how Protestants came to separate the normative essence from the Bible.

TENABLE FUNDAMENTALISM: BIBLICAL THEOLOGY AND THE SEARCH FOR AUTHORITY

It is no small irony that the period of ecumenical agreement *between* traditions was also a period of great strife and division *within* them. The growing Protestant interest in "historic Christian tradition" and ancient liturgical practices coincided with heated disputes between the liberal and conservative wings of the mainline denominations over how to interpret the Bible. The reason for this was the growing crisis of authority, as Protestants confronted the crucial questions about what provided the norm or rule for their Christian identity. Before American Protestants were ready to engage in their own *ressourcement* and let antiquity serve as a criterion for authentic faith, they first had to struggle with their long-standing commitment to the normativity of the Bible.

The Westminster Confession of Faith (1647) marked a decisive shift in the history of Protestant, and especially Reformed, theology by identifying the (Protestant) biblical canon as "the rule of faith and life," characterized by "infallible truth and divine authority" and also serving as "the infallible rule of interpretation of Scripture."[29] This contrasted with the earlier position of the Second Helvetic Confession (1561), which followed Augustine of Hippo in interpreting scripture according to "the rule of faith and love," referring to the ancient ecumenical creeds and the love of neighbor.[30] The position of biblical infallibility became a hallmark of the Old School Calvinism associated with Princeton Theological Seminary, under the leadership of Charles Hodge, A. A. Hodge, and B. B. Warfield. It faced challenges, however, from the growing field of historical-critical research. In 1893 Charles Augustus Briggs was excommunicated from the Presbyterian Church for heresy over his denial of biblical infallibility and his promotion of what was then called "Higher Criticism." This event, along with other developments, eventually culminated in the fundamentalist-modernist controversy, which reached a climax in the mid-1920s. Two years after he preached "Shall the Fundamentalists Win?," Harry Emerson Fosdick delivered lectures at Yale on *The Modern Use of the Bible*. He astutely recognized that the dispute between the fundamentalists and modernists was not primarily over the Bible itself but over two different accounts of the essence of Christianity – that is, over what is permanent and enduring in Christian faith. "To-day there are two parties in the churches," according to Fosdick. "The crux of their conflict lies at this point: one party thinks that the essence of Christianity is its original mental frameworks; the other party is convinced that the essence of Christianity is its abiding experiences." For the former (the fundamentalists), the concepts and cultural forms used to articulate God's word in the past are permanently binding on all future Christians, whereas for the latter (the modernists), what is essential and enduring are not the conceptual vehicles of revelation but rather the personal experience of faith "that phrase and rephrase themselves in successive generations' ways of thinking."[31] Following the controversy, and the subsequent separation of the two sides into separate churches, the modernist theologians explored far more experimental "rephrasings" of the tradition, leading to the crisis of liberalism discussed in Chapter 2. Gaius Glenn Atkins summarized the situation in 1932 in hyperbolic but telling fashion: "In 1890 the 'liberal' was debating whether there were two Isaiahs; in 1930 the extreme 'modernist' was debating whether there was a personal God."[32]

The neoorthodox reaction to theological modernism took as its inspiration Karl Barth's declaration of a "strange new world within the Bible" – a phrase that first appeared in the 1928 publication in English of *The Word of God and the Word of Man* but only gathered momentum among American pastors and theologians in the 1940s. As former liberals embraced American neoorthodoxy, there was a felt need for a new approach to the Bible to replace the fundamentalist and modernist options of the previous generation. Fosdisk's "two parties" were no longer adequate. Postwar Protestant church leaders wanted guidance on how to read the Bible that maintained traditional confidence in the Bible as God's word, as the source and norm for theological reflection, but also respected historical scholarship and was not inerrantist. Biblical theology provided the answer. Once again, Princeton Theological Seminary is key to this story. In 1937, as John Mackay began his tenure as the seminary's new president, Princeton Seminary hired Otto Piper (1891–1982), a New Testament scholar in exile from Hitler's Germany, to be a visiting professor. Four years later he was made a chaired faculty member, beginning a long and distinguished career. With his new position, Piper began teaching a course on the "Biblical Theology of the New Testament." In a way, Piper was carrying on a venerable tradition at Princeton, where Geerhardus Vos (1862–1949) had championed what he called "biblical theology" under the terms of the Old Princeton Calvinism before retiring in 1932. But Piper's program was distinctively post-liberal and neoorthodox.[33] Piper was largely importing this approach from Germany, where biblical theology had become popular a decade earlier. But in the United States, as it was developed by the likes of Piper, James D. Smart, G. Ernest Wright, John Wick Bowman, Joseph Haroutunian, and Donald G. Miller, among others, biblical theology took on a characteristically American flavor, leading Brevard Childs and others to refer to this period as the "biblical theology movement."[34]

Piper's lectures remained unpublished, but in 1946 he was invited to write a series of four articles for *The Christian Century* on the topic, "What the Bible Means to Me," which "forced the issue out of the theological seminaries and into the churches."[35] In the first article, he recounted his time in the 1920s as Barth's colleague at the University of Göttingen, where he "realized that biblical theology as it was taught at that time was unsatisfactory." He closed the article by acknowledging that he has had "to endure the vitriolic attacks of fundamentalists who denounced me as a disguised modernist and the haughty disdain of liberals who could not understand that a critical scholar should believe that the Bible is the Word of God."[36] With his theological centrism, Piper represented exactly what American post-liberal and neoorthodox pastors and theologians were seeking. The second article stated that biblical criticism has a "legitimate place in the church" but subordinate to faith's claim that the Bible is "the infallible source of true religion." Piper criticized the "ultra-orthodox schools" like Westminster Seminary for a static approach to the Bible that led to literalism, and he offered instead a tempered traditionalism that seasoned the old fundamentalism with a dash of historical humility.[37] While American neoorthodoxy sought to carve a path between the ruins of the old fundamentalist-modernist controversy, they were also addressing their cultural anxieties about the present. As Chapter 2 showed, Mackay launched his theological agenda at Princeton with an eye toward addressing the cultural and political dangers that he saw facing the church at the time. Piper shared these anxieties and integrated them into his message about biblical theology. At the end of his fourth article in a series ostensibly on biblical theology, he says that God has given Christians a "comprehensive purpose" to bring about a "new order" on earth, a "Christian civilization" that "constantly assimilates elements taken from its environment." This process of assimilation has taken different forms, including the "ecclesiastical civilization" of antiquity, the "corporate civilization" of the Middle Ages, and now the "Protestant civilization of the Western world." Whatever the form, this civilization requires "the Spirit of Christ as its sustaining power," which is why "our Western civilization ... is so rapidly disintegrating." The secular humanists, according to Piper, hope to sustain it without faith, but "that hope is vain. Standards alone will not do. We need power." To generate this power, Piper calls on the church to avoid conforming to secular society and to focus "on preserving its

peculiarity as a Christian church" and to be unwavering in its commitment to making the world "subject to the power of [Christ's]
Kingdom."[38] The culture war playbook that evangelicals and other
Christian nationalists would later perfect was initially developed by
mainline Protestants, and especially those informed by American
neoorthodoxy and Christian realism.

Around the same time as Piper's articles, two new Presbyterian jour-
nals arose to address the growing interest in a renewed theology rooted
in a view of the Bible as the authoritative and infallible Word of God –
Theology Today, founded by Mackay at Princeton Seminary in 1944, and
Interpretation, launched at Union Theological Seminary in Richmond,
Virginia in 1947. Much like the interest in "historic Christianity," the
concern with the Bible was animated by the idea, as seen in Piper's
writings, that a deeper engagement with the Bible would restore
Western society. Mackay's inaugural editorial for *Theology Today* in April
1944 announced that the first aim of the journal would be "to contribute
to the restoration of theology in the world of today as the supreme
science, of which both religion and culture stand in need for their
renewal."[39] The basis for this renewal, Mackay thought, was the authority
of the Bible. Indeed, as he put it in a later editorial, "to make the Bible
known by the people of today is the supreme cultural task of our time."[40]
Mackay believed that the Bible, "which was rediscovered by the
Reformation, must be rediscovered again." Without abandoning the
advances achieved through biblical criticism, Mackay thought the Bible
needed to be understood in its "essential unity" as the word of God
containing the "progressive revelation" of God's redemption.[41] He was
even willing to call his position a "tenable fundamentalism," indicating
neoorthodoxy's much closer alignment with the fundamentalist rather
than the modernist side of the earlier conflict.[42] This alignment was
especially clear in Mackay's call for a "new crusade" that would come
about through the rediscovery of historic Christian truth – an understanding of truth that "has a coercive quality, like a belt that binds, that
braces up those who are bound by it, for creative quest and crusading
action."[43] He concluded his first editorial by stating that the recent
"history of religion and civilization ... has given increasing significance
to 'the strange new world within the Bible' which was then rediscovered"

by Barth.[44] The rest of the articles in the opening issue of *Theology Today* took up the call for a "new crusade": Paul Minear wrote on the need for biblical theology, Holmes Rolston wrote on Barth's commentary on Romans, and Frederick William Dillistone praised the circle of neoorthodox theologians "who are dissatisfied with a rigid fundamentalism on the one side and a destructive liberalism on the other" and have recovered the "Apostolic Gospel" of "Historic Christianity."[45] Josef Hromádka, another scholar who, like Piper, fled the Nazis and found a new home at Princeton Seminary, wrote on "Civilization's Doom and Resurrection." While he did not comment on the role of the Bible, he admitted that "we find ourselves in a panicky state of mind" and argued that "we civilized nations cannot be saved unless our mind bows before *the* authority which is absolute and final."[46] American neoorthodoxy found support for their concerns in Emil Brunner's 1947–1948 Gifford Lectures on *Christianity and Civilisation*, which began with Brunner declaring that the future of "Christian civilisation is at stake and its survival is questioned."[47] Anxiety about the decline of Western civilization was the watchword among these mainline church leaders, and the proposed answer was a "tenable fundamentalism" that could provide the necessary spiritual authority – indeed, authoritarianism – to right the cultural ship. As Mark Thomas Edwards has observed, Mackay and the group of neoorthodox and Christian realist ministers and theologians involved with *Theology Today* "launched a coordinated assault on religious privatization."[48] They wanted nothing less than to establish global Christian supremacy – what Edwards calls "God's totalitarianism" – and they did so by appealing to the authority of the Bible as God's revelation.

If *Theology Today* was the organ of biblical *theology*, then *Interpretation* was the organ of *biblical* theology. The editors announced this clearly in the opening of the journal's third editorial: "*Interpretation* has committed itself to the cause of biblical theology."[49] Authors and editors alike sounded a clear reason for such commitment: the times demanded it. As the journal's first editorial put it, "the urgency of this task" is "prompted by desperate conditions." There is, they say, a "universal urge to go back to the Bible."[50] The editors of *Interpretation* were not as brazenly supremacist as those involved with *Theology Today*, but they exhibited the same anxious energy – prompted, no doubt, by the postwar conditions.[51] In his article for the inaugural issue, "The Relevance of Biblical Interpretation," the British Baptist and Old Testament scholar, Harold Henry Rowley, stated that the journal's appearance is "a symptom of our time," since they were living in an age that was keenly aware of the loss of "Christian standards of life."[52] Modern scholarship, according to Howley, had broken the Bible into historical pieces, and thus the goal of the journal, and the task of biblical theology more generally, was to recover the Bible in its full, divine unity. The editors of the journal likewise warned against the "fragmentation" of the Bible that resulted from modern biblical studies in the nineteenth century. Biblical theology, they claimed, gave access to the "whole counsel of God."[53]

All of this was taking place at the same time that theologians in Germany were debating the controversial program to "demythologize" the Bible proposed by Rudolf Bultmann, and we can understand better now why Bultmann had the reception he did in 1951 when he visited the United States. The neoorthodox church leaders were not merely concerned with the reputation of Barth's theology; they were also deeply immersed in a quest for a culturally authoritative religious norm, which they sought to find in the Bible as interpreted by biblical theology. Critical biblical scholarship, the kind Bultmann was famous for developing, was perceived as the enemy of American neoorthodoxy's project of re-Christianizing the West and establishing a new global Christendom. When Bultmann visited in the fall of 1951, he was walking into a cultural land mine. The atmosphere became even more explosive in 1953 with the publication of the first *Kerygma and Myth* volume, a partial translation of the original *Kerygma und Mythos* that appeared in Germany in 1948. A second English volume, which bore even less resemblance to its German counterpart, was published in 1962.[54] With these books and the flood of scholarly commentary that ensued, the debate over demythologizing that had started in Germany a decade earlier made its way across the Atlantic.

Bultmann's original lecture, presented in April and June 1941 to a group of theologians associated with the Confessing Church, had two targets: first, the Hitler-supporting German Christians who had bought into a mythologized, heroic, Aryan Christianity; and second, much of the Confessing Church itself, which had countered the German Christians by doubling down on the doctrines of Lutheran orthodoxy in the belief that the main problem with the Nazi supporters was their deviation from Christian tradition. While Bultmann was an active member of the Confessing Church, he found himself increasingly at odds with the leadership. This is what he had in mind when, in speaking to this group of theologians, he criticized "contemporary Christian proclamation" that expects people "to acknowledge the mythical world picture as true."[55] Myth, for Bultmann, refers to a particular cultural context – namely, an ancient one. Myth is not true or false; it is either relevant or irrelevant, one's own culture or someone else's. The norms of Christian faith, which he called the kerygma, were in his view independent of the mythical or any other world picture, and thus one of the tasks of theology and preaching is to translate these norms from their original, mythical context to the cultural environment of the theologian or preacher. The problem he had with some in the Confessing Church was that they insisted this was impossible, that the norms of Christian faith are permanently defined by the confessions and creeds of the past – a past that is culturally foreign (i.e., mythical) to the church today. Naturally, the result was outrage on the part of the conservative Lutheran faction. In March 1942, Hans Asmussen told Bultmann's friend Ernst Wolf that the general convention was "shocked by the statements themselves" and dismayed that the church's resources were being used to support such ideas.[56] A few days later Dietrich Bonhoeffer came to Bultmann's defense, arguing that these "rather stupid" protests on the part of "several blowhards" was "a real scandal for the Confessing Church."[57] Despite support from Bonhoeffer and others, by the end of the decade heresy charges were being drawn up for Bultmann. The forces of doctrinal prescriptivism in Germany could not tolerate one of their own breaking with tradition.

Much as what happened to Barth in the 1930s, the original political context for Bultmann's lecture was often lost in its transatlantic translation. When it arrived to English-speaking readers in the postwar fifties, the Nazi-era audiences of the lecture were largely forgotten. The essay instead entered a fraught contest over the future of American society, in which some Christian leaders sought to leverage a credible and popular account of Christian faith to gain cultural influence and societal advantage. Biblical theology, by presenting a unified theological message, played a crucial role in these efforts to shape the direction of the American church. But demythologizing, and the critical hermeneutics that came with it, threatened to undermine these efforts. At the heart of this conflict was an implicit dispute over prescriptivism. For biblical theology, what was normative or prescriptive was the Bible itself, read as the unified, canonical, infallible revelation of God that is eternally and identically relevant to each person throughout history. "Lying at the center of the new concern for a theologically oriented study of the Bible," according to Childs, "was the conviction that the Scriptures were highly relevant for modern man."[58] Joseph Haroutunian, for example, wrote in 1940 that "we have discovered a new kinship between us and the Biblical people. We can once again recognize them as men like us."[59] This was precisely what Bultmann called into question. His lecture on demythologizing began by announcing that the authors and audience of the biblical writings were *not* like us at all but belonged, in fact, to an utterly alien world. The Bible was not self-evidently relevant to people today; it had to *become* relevant through the process of interpretation and conceptual translation.[60] What was normative for Bultmann was not the Bible itself but rather the kerygma, an elusive and ultimately indefinable event available to faith alone – and thus unusable for any project of cultural domination. Though Bultmann was known in Germany as a representative of biblical theology thanks to the publication, starting in 1948, of his *Theology of the New Testament,* his theological and hermeneutical program could not but be anathema to American audiences seeking a foundation for their social agenda.

While the downfall of the biblical theology movement is often ascribed to the publication of James Barr's *The Semantics of Biblical Language* (1961), in truth this was merely the final and most incisive blow.[61] Childs lays some of the responsibility at the feet of Bultmann himself, whose work captured the imagination of younger scholars with its radical embrace of historical criticism, despite "the sustained polemic against Bultmann on the part of the Biblical theologians."[62] In March 1963, the *Christian Century* called Bultmann the "stone of stumbling" dividing the ministers into "pre-" and "post-" Bultmann: "Pipe-smoking, tweedy Rudolf Bultmann has been the biggest stone of

stumbling, the hottest topic, in the past quarter-century of theology. . . .
Bring up his name at such [ministers'] conferences and you will soon
find the topic changed or the conference majority intensely unified."[63]
To be sure, Bultmann's influence was itself a symptom of a larger
fracture within the field of biblical studies that was emerging in the
sixties. The story of what happened, which has been told by scholars
over the years, is ultimately the story of the parting of the ways between
history and theology, between descriptivism and prescriptivism. Biblical
theology had a methodological dilemma: it was premised on the har-
monization of historical biblical research and normative Christian theology. The biblical theologians were committed to the prescriptive claim
that the Bible is the infallible revelation of God, but they simultaneously
wanted to engage in textual and historical analysis – and thought the
latter could support the former. This led them to treat the language of
the Bible as a perspicacious window into normative theological judgments, something Barr exposed as ahistorical. With the discovery of the
Dead Sea Scrolls and Nag Hammadi library, along with greater attention
to other ancient extrabiblical sources, the work of descriptive historical
work became not only highly technical but also far more nuanced in its
understanding of antiquity, nuances that were increasingly incompatible
with the simplistic theological narrative of salvation history to which the
biblical theologians were dedicated.

The field of biblical studies faced a crisis: whether to remain allied
with theologians in the effort to transform society or to restrict themselves to the descriptive task of historical research. The majority chose
the latter, exemplified by Krister Stendahl's 1962 article on biblical
theology, in which he argued, following Johann Philipp Gabler (1787)
and William Wrede (1897) before him, that biblical scholars must distinguish between what the text *meant* and what the text *means* – restricting
biblical theology to the former and handing the latter over to dogmatic
or systematic theology.[64] It would take those who were dissatisfied with
this forced binary another decade or more to figure out an alternative
path that would retain the prescriptivist approach they favored, and
when they did so it would be in partnership with the ecumenical and
liturgical movements that were occurring at the same time. The result of
this confluence of trends was postliberalism.

FROM THE BATTLE FOR THE BIBLE TO THE CULTURE WARS:
THE RISE OF POSTLIBERALISM

With the fracturing of the biblical studies guild and the growing skepticism toward both biblical authority and confessional doctrine that came with the erosion of "Protestant America," the former mainline Protestant binary between the "orthodoxy" of the biblical theologians and the "heresy" of the demythologizers – between those who made the Bible the rule of faith and those who located the rule in something existential or experiential outside of the church's control – crumbled into a theological *bellum omnium contra omnes* ("war of all against all"), with each party laying claim to the biblical texts. It was no longer as simple as asking whether the Bible was the authoritative rule of faith or not. The question now was *in what sense* and *according to which interpretive method* was it the rule of faith? The result was intellectual dissension in the ranks of American Protestantism. While the term "battle for the Bible" is associated with the discord among conservative evangelicals in the 1970s over biblical inerrancy, theirs was neither the first nor the only battle taking place at that time. Indeed, the battle for the Bible was taking place on all sides as Protestant ministers and theologians struggled to define what constituted the essence and identity of Christianity.

A notable early book in this regard was *Theology in Conflict: Barth, Nygren, Bultmann* by the Swedish theologian Gustaf Wingren (1910–2000) – published originally in 1954 and translated into English in 1958. Wingren used the differences between Barth, Bultmann, and fellow Swedish theologian Anders Nygren as case studies in his argument that every theologian operates with presuppositions, specifically hermeneutical presuppositions (referring to how the Bible should be read) and anthropological presuppositions (referring to human nature and the cultural situation).[65] While Wingren believed certain presuppositions were more genuinely Christian than others, ultimately his study proposed that the task of systematic theology is "to answer the question: What is the essence of Christianity?"[66] Wingren was still operating under the assumption there was a "right" way to answer this question, but his study at least had the virtue of presenting the issue in a fresh way.

A more programmatic take on the same question appeared the following year in *Authority in Protestant Theology* by Robert Clyde Johnson (1919–2002), a former Presbyterian minister who at the time was professor of theology at Western Theological Seminary in Pittsburgh (later Pittsburgh Theological Seminary) and later became dean of Yale Divinity School. Johnson's book arose out of the growing consciousness of theological pluralism that was developing within Protestant America. For many decades the situation was framed in the starkly dichotomous terms of either "blind acceptance of a heteronomous norm" or "an autonomous rejection of any theological authority whatsoever."[67] But Johnson argued this was an inadequate framing of the situation that failed to recognize the tensions in Protestant theology stretching back to the Reformation. Instead of splitting people into two camps – those who accept the norm and those who reject it – Johnson differentiated between the norm (referring to the singular, permanent, and absolute authority over theology) and the criterion or *discrimen* (referring to one of many derivative authorities). The term *discrimen* here functions as a synonym for "essence" or "material principle." Having an absolute norm is not the only way to establish authority or boundaries in theology – nor can it be. Even when theologians make scripture the norm, as Protestant orthodoxy did, they must still make use of a *discrimen* to guide their interpretation of scripture and the construction of theology. Every Protestant Christian must therefore make what Johnson called a "theological decision" regarding which *discrimen* to embrace, such as the contextual approach of Paul Tillich, the scientific approach of Nygren and Gustaf Aulén, or the confessional approach of Barth – options that Johnson presented in the final part of his book. "Even the refusal to choose is in itself a choice, made by default."[68] Setting up the Bible as the norm does not absolve one of the responsibility of clarifying the *discrimen*, and it is precisely this failure to clarify the criteria "that pervades Protestantism in the mid-twentieth century."[69] The lack of clarity leads to false alternatives and the tendency of leaders to declare that their theology alone is the definition of orthodoxy. "The absolutistic threat is always with us," Johnson wrote, "and has to be met in every generation." The way to do so, he argued, is to recognize that God alone is "the absolute, normative authority." Contrary to the fundamentalists (who now fashioned themselves as evangelicals), as well as more than a few of the neoorthodox, "the Scriptures are not the norm of Christian theology, but are one of the criteria within its theological *discrimen*."[70]

Johnson was ahead of others in the United States in recognizing the need for each Protestant theologian to clarify their *discrimen*, their account of the essence and authority of Christianity. He wrote his book amid the biblical theology movement, before its demise fully laid bare what many saw as the theological chaos – from a different perspective, the perennial diversity and pluriformity – in American Protestantism. A decade later, on the other side of this demise and after Vatican II opened up new ways of thinking about Christian norms, books started appearing more frequently on the question of biblical authority and interpretation. Robert H. Bryant, a professor at United Theological Seminary of the Twin Cities who had completed his PhD under H. Richard Niebuhr at Yale University, published *The Bible's Authority Today* in 1968. His opening chapter was titled "The Strange New World in the Bible," which he used not only in Barth's sense but also as a reflection on the strange new situation that Christians found themselves in, with Protestant and Catholic leaders alike "urging theological renewal" and forcing many to ask, "What is the guiding authority for the church's proclamation and ministry?"[71] Two years later, J. Christiaan Beker, professor of biblical theology at Princeton Seminary, wrote a postmortem for his discipline in the journal *Interpretation* in which he acknowledged that the hope of biblical theology's cultural renewal "has now collapsed." The "strange new world" of the Bible "has become so strange to the average student." Because biblical theology was wedded to neoorthodoxy, and neoorthodoxy itself has collapsed, "biblical theology seems to have given birth to the crisis of the biblical field."[72] That same year, James Smart, an emeritus professor at Union Theological Seminary in New York City often associated with American neoorthodoxy, published *The Strange Silence of the Bible in the Church: A Study in Hermeneutics*. Smart attributed the growing silence of the Bible to "what has been happening in Biblical scholarship in this century," during which time "Biblical interpretation has become ever more complex," leading many to ignore the Bible out of confusion over how to understand it.[73] Barr, the scholar who helped bring an end to biblical theology, reflected in

1971 on the silence of the Old Testament in contemporary theology, which he attributed to the demise of neoorthodoxy and the "larger crisis of biblical authority in general" that resulted from this.[74] In 1975, David H. Kelsey published to wide acclaim *The Uses of Scripture in Recent Theology*, using Johnson's distinction between norm and *discrimen* to analyze the different ways theologians appealed to the authority of scripture to underwrite their theological programs. Quoting Wingren, Kelsey recognized that the decision of the *discrimen* "entails a judgment about the nature of 'Christianity,'" and therefore "the most basic decision a theologian makes is his answer to the question, 'What is the essence of Christianity?'"[75] The answer to this question, according to Kelsey, is decisive for how a theologian understands scripture and its role in theological argumentation.

The sum effect of these and other writings was the conclusion that *everything is in flux and open to change*, right down to the very norms of theology and even the definition of Christianity itself. The old doctrinal prescriptivism seemed extinct. The triumphalism and supreme confidence exhibited by the neoorthodox Christian realists in the 1940s was gone by the 1960s. Now it looked as if each theology was based on little more than arbitrary individual decisions or the changing social context. In addition to Robinson's *Honest to God*, a number of theologians positively engaged the growing secularism of Western society, including Gabriel Vahanian's *The Death of God* (1961), Harvey Cox's *The Secular City* (1965), Ronald Gregor Smith's *Secular Christianity* (1966), and Thomas Altizer and William Hamilton's *Radical Theology and the Death of God* (1966).[76] The rise of theologies that made individual identity and experience a source and *discrimen* only compounded the situation, with pioneering works by Mary Daly and James Cone appearing in 1968 and 1969, respectively.[77] From the perspective of those seeking intellectual law and order, the scene in seminaries and churches looked like theological anarchy – the academic reflection of what many considered the social anarchy occurring in the streets, as Black rebellion against police violence in the late sixties prompted President Lyndon Johnson to declare a "War on Crime" in 1968.[78] The theological upheavals, combined with the wider cultural and political upheavals regarding civil rights, gender equality, and secularization, posed a threat to the old ecclesiastical order.

The "battle for the Bible" – in both its mainline and evangelical manifestations – was thus symptomatic of the anxiety that church leaders were experiencing regarding the loss of certainty and control. Harold Lindsell's diatribe, which appeared in 1976, was a particularly inflammatory reaction to this anxiety – a public "burn book" that chose to call out everyone Lindsell thought was insufficiently committed to biblical inerrancy, including the Lutheran Church Missouri-Synod (LCMS), the Southern Baptist Convention (SBC), Fuller Seminary, North Park Theological Seminary, and the Evangelical Theological Society, among others. The LCMS had experienced its crisis two years earlier due to the removal of John Tietjen as president of Concordia Seminary, leading to the "Seminex" controversy; Fuller Seminary had moved away from strict adherence to inerrancy in the early 1970s; and in the case of the SBC, Lindsell hoped to provoke its leaders into a controversy. Two years later, in the fall of 1978, evangelical leaders produced the Chicago Statement on Biblical Inerrancy, declaring that the Bible's inerrancy was not "limited to spiritual, religious, or redemptive themes" but included "assertions in the fields of history and science."[79] The following year the fundamentalists orchestrated their takeover – what they call the "conservative resurgence" – of the SBC. While the debates occurring among the fundamentalists and so-called neoevangelicals were vastly different from those in mainline circles, the underlying issues were the same: the challenge of historical criticism, the growing split between theology and biblical studies, and the awareness of the role of theological presuppositions. Mainline developments were also having a direct impact on the evangelicals. As Harold Ockenga noted in his foreword to The Battle for the Bible, one reason for the founding of Fuller Seminary in 1947 was the fact that Park Street Church had twelve members attending Princeton Theological Seminary, where "authoritative Scripture was not taught."[80]

Reading Lindsell, or any other inerrantist literature from this time, one cannot but be struck by the superficial nature of their arguments compared to the literature by the mainline theologians wrestling with the crisis in biblical authority. The evangelicals in the 1970s, like the neoorthodox in the 1940s, had reduced the question to whether one accepted the authority of the Bible or not – and authority for the evangelicals had been further reduced to whether the Bible was free of what they considered to be factual errors. The question of the essence of Christianity was beyond their purview, even if it was implied throughout their writings. Lindsell spent a chapter of his book defending inerrancy, which he thought could be done by defending the scientific accuracy of particular verses. For instance, he addressed the measurements of the molten sea in 2 Chronicles 4:2 by examining the formula for the circumference of a circle, leading to statements like the following: "If we allow for the eight inches for the two sides of the molten sea, it means that the diameter was 180 inches, less eight inches, or 172 inches. And when 172 is multiplied by 3.14 (the value of *pi*) the result is 540.08, which is quite accurate."[81] This is indicative of the kind of reasoning Lindsell used throughout his book. Matters of history and culture were seemingly irrelevant, and even a potential threat. He warned against "the field of biblical interpretation" as having the potential to undermine biblical infallibility.[82] For him and other evangelicals, belief in the authority of scripture implied certain hermeneutical presuppositions that could not be articulated without opening up the possibility of multiple interpretations, something that evangelical leaders could not permit. Despite Lindsell's repeated assertions about upholding "historic orthodoxy," the only thing historic about his view was the belief that church leaders ought to forcefully remove everyone considered to be a heretic.[83] He compared the matter to communism, with which one could live at peace only if one "capitulate[d] to their demands." The alternative was either "peace at any price" or "the purity of the church" – and Lindsell demanded purity.[84] His was a militant doctrinal prescriptivism: not only were those who disagreed with him not true Christians, but they should be speedily forced out of their positions in the church and academy.

In many evangelical circles this militancy never wavered; each new social or ecclesial panic provided new reasons to double-down on inerrancy as the mechanism by which to exclude those whose views did not align with one's own.[85] But some did put aside the concern regarding inerrancy, not because of any acceptance of historical criticism but because policing a person's doctrine of scripture turned out to be a poor indicator of one's actual theological and ethical positions. Evangelicals were slow, and often loathe, to admit it, but it was undeniable that two people who held equivalent accounts of biblical authority could come to very different interpretations of the text. It would take another twenty years or more before evangelicals found an alternative solution, and when they did, it was by turning to the mainline Protestants who had regrouped after the demise of biblical theology to form the new movement of what became known as postliberal theology.[86]

To understand what transpired, we need to go back to the late 1960s. After virtually a decade of working in obscurity, the forty-five-year-old Yale professor, Hans Frei (1922–1988), delivered a lecture at Harvard Divinity School in December 1967 announcing what he had been working on since he completed his (unpublished) dissertation in 1956 on Barth's doctrine of revelation. Frei declared early in the lecture that "my aim is to take a first step toward getting at the question: What is the essence of Christianity?" In this regard, he was contributing to the conversation with which Wingren, Johnson, and Smart were all wrestling. But unlike the others, Frei proposed something unusual: "My plea is that this be done in a nonperspectivist way if possible."[87] By "nonperspectivist" Frei meant that he wanted to understand the essence of Christianity in a way that did not involve the subjective perspective of the theologian. In contrast to the many proposals about hermeneutical and theological presuppositions, Frei wanted an objective approach to the problem, and his proposed answer was to "start with the synoptic Gospels" because of "their peculiar nature as narratives."[88] What Frei meant by this became more clear in 1974, a year before Kelsey's book and two years before Lindsell's, when he published his first book, *The Eclipse of Biblical Narrative*. Frei argued that both conservative and liberal theologians in the twentieth century were operating under the same modern assumption about how to understand the Bible – namely, that the meaning of the text consisted in its reference to something outside of the text, whether a historical event, the intention of the author, or the subjective experience of the reader. This assumption, Frei claimed, arose in the eighteenth century and broke with the precritical understanding of the Bible that held from the early church to the Reformation, according to which there was no world outside of the text; the reality or subject matter of scripture was identical with the text itself. Drawing on the work of literary critics like Erich Auerbach and the New

Criticism, as well as the philosophical work of Ludwig Wittgenstein and Gilbert Ryle, Frei argued that the narrative of scripture "rendered that reality itself to the reader," enabling the reader to become a participant in the narrative.[89] Within the precritical mindset, figural interpretation was simply "a natural extension of literal interpretation," but with the modern gap between text and reality, literal and figural interpretation fell apart – the former becoming historical-critical reconstruction and the latter becoming biblical theology.[90] The solution to the current crisis of authority, Frei seemed to be suggesting, was to abandon our modern assumptions and return to a precritical, premodern essence of Christianity, one that no longer fretted over whether something "really happened" or what the original authors "truly meant" and instead simply embraced the literal sense of the text.

Frei could sound like both the biblical theologians of the 1940s and the evangelicals of the 1970s in his defense of Barth's "belief in the objective, literal truth of the eschatological, *heilsgeschichtliche* [salvation-historical] events of Scripture," but he argued that such realism distinguished itself from "a fundamentalist, literalist interpretation of these events. For the Biblical realists generally proclaimed the objective truths of the events set forth in Scripture and avoided the problem of either reconciling them to or contradicting the concepts of modern philosophy and *Weltanschauung* [worldview]."[91] In other words, Frei criticized the "fundamentalists" for being *too modern* in light of their concern with proving the veracity of what they took to be the Bible's claims – for example, by verifying the historical factuality of events in the biblical narrative, reconciling the creation account with modern science, and proving the biblical accounts of the miraculous. Frei thus represented what Jason Springs calls an "unapologetic theology" – borrowing a term made prominent by Frei's student, William Placher – meaning Frei did not think theology ought to "justify itself in nontheological terms."[92]

Not surprisingly, this attracted attention from evangelicals, in particular Carl F. H. Henry. A cofounder of Fuller Seminary and the founding editor of *Christianity Today* (succeeded by Lindsell), Henry had established himself as the leading evangelical theologian. During his tenure at *Christianity Today*, Henry had interviewed Barth during a trip to Europe that produced a series of articles on the state of modern theology. In the fourth article, published in December 1964, Henry quoted Barth on the topic of "salvation history" (*Heilsgeschichte*), a concept developed by Barth's colleague Oscar Cullmann and promoted by the biblical theologians in the United States. Barth, however, rejected this concept on the grounds that it encouraged people to turn away from the biblical witness itself "to something behind the witness and existing independently of it" – such as the historical Jesus – when Barth wanted to focus solely on the Christ of the New Testament.[93] Despite some disagreement over the terminology, Henry must have noticed the resemblance between Barth's position in the 1960s and what Frei was proposing a decade later. But Henry, like other evangelical theologians at the time, was not yet ready to embrace Frei's Barthian-narratival approach to theology on the grounds that it undercut the ability to engage in apologetics. Specifically, Henry wanted Christ's resurrection to be an objectively and historically verifiable event that could be used to convince others of the truth of Christianity. For Henry, the essence of Christianity was located in the historical factuality (or inerrancy) of scripture. When Barth visited the United States in 1962, Henry had asked him if the resurrection was "of such a nature that newsmen would have been responsible for reporting [it] as news," something Barth denied.[94] Henry had the same concern with respect to Frei.

In November 1985, Henry gave lectures at Yale providing an evangelical response to narrative theology. Henry was deeply concerned about the "exegetical relativism" that had emerged over the previous decades with the multiplicity of hermeneutical theories and methods offering competing ways of interpreting the Bible.[95] He acknowledged the uniqueness of Frei's narrative theology, which focuses on the text itself using the tools of literary criticism as opposed to historical criticism. But like his interview with Barth, Henry raised his concern about the lack of assurance regarding the "historical factuality of the divine redemptive acts," such as the resurrection. Henry wanted a way out of the morass of hermeneutical ambiguity that still retained the apologetic potential to compel belief and obedience, and the way to do so, he claimed, was to assert the "objective cognitive authority" and "objective inspiration and inerrancy" of scripture.[96] Lacking this emphasis on objective authority, Frei's narrative approach to theology was, in Henry's judgment, "not fully befitting the historic Christian faith."[97] In his appreciative rejoinder to Henry, Frei began by making his now-famous statement that "we need a kind of generous orthodoxy which would have in it an element of liberalism ... and an element of evangelicalism. ... I don't know if there is a voice between those two, as a matter of fact. If there is, I would like to pursue it."[98] But what this meant for Frei only became clear later, when he said that he rejected the pursuit of a "theory-neutral, trans-cultural" language that could serve an apologetic purpose by bridging theology and nontheological disciplines, such as historical research and philosophy. This meant he disagreed with "a view of certainty and knowledge which liberals and evangelicals hold in common."[99] According to Frei, both liberals and evangelicals wanted a universal, perspective-free understanding of Christianity, something he considered impossible.

We naturally might have expected Frei to be more sympathetic with Henry. Certainly the Frei in 1967 who sought a "nonperspectivist" approach to the essence of Christianity sounded much closer to Henry in 1985 than to Frei himself, who now seemed to reject a "nonperspectivist" posture.[100] In 1967 Frei claimed to be on a quest "for categories of understanding *detached from the perspectives we bring to our understanding*, including our commitments of faith."[101] This is precisely what Henry was searching for with his "trans-cultural" concepts that were not dependent on subjective perspectives and commitments. What changed for Frei in the course of those twenty years? The answer is that, a year earlier, his Yale colleague George Lindbeck (1923–2018) had published his groundbreaking book, *The Nature of Doctrine: Religion and Theology in a Postliberal Age*. Narrative theology had been subsumed into the project of postliberalism.

Frei was an idiosyncratic theologian whose narrative theology was not synonymous with what became postliberal theology, though his project laid an important part of the foundation for this later movement.[102] While his dissertation referred to "Barth's post-liberal theology" because of Barth's commitment to "Biblical realism," it was his affiliation with Lindbeck – along with Frei's opposition to the revisionist school at the University of Chicago associated with David Tracy – that solidified his connection to this new theological movement.[103] Born in China to Lutheran missionary parents, Lindbeck brought a special sensitivity not only to the ecumenical and interreligious dialogue that was occurring at this time but also and most importantly to the fundamentally *cultural* nature of these debates. Frei was focused on the methodological questions involved in reading the Bible and constructing theology, so that it sometimes seemed, at least in his earlier work, as if the solution was simply a matter of adopting a premodern or postcritical hermeneutic. But Frei knew well that biblical realism on its own could not generate Christian unity, and Lindbeck supplied the missing piece. The principal lesson of *The Nature of Doctrine*, developed with the aid of Clifford Geertz's anthropological research and Ludwig Wittgenstein's philosophy of language, was that the basis for both divisions and alliances between religious communities was irreducible to propositional doctrines or subjective experiences. What divided a Protestant from a Catholic, or a Christian from a Hindu or an atheist, could not be defined in terms of a particular doctrine, method, or interior experience, but rather it was one's "cultural-linguistic" way of viewing the world "that shapes the entirety of life and thought."[104] Religious differences went far deeper than how one exegetes a particular text; they were a matter of religious *grammar*, the way a community uses and understands language itself. Different cultural-linguistic communities may therefore have "incommensurable notions of truth, of experience, and ... of what it would mean for something to be most important (i.e., 'God')."[105] It is not enough to have a common text; one has to develop a common language and common practices for using that language.

When postliberals like Lindbeck talked about the cultural-linguistic interpretive community, they had, of course, a very particular community in mind – namely, the Christian church. To be sure, what they meant by "the church" is a matter of some question, to which we will return in a later chapter. But for now it will suffice to observe that it referred to what they identified as the "consensus Christianity" of the orthodox, conciliar tradition. What differentiated the postliberals from those who held to a doctrinal rule of faith was the conviction of the postliberals that doctrines were second-order accounts, one step removed from the more fundamental matter of the community's culture: those underlying linguistic norms and social presuppositions that differentiate one community from another.[106] Here the postliberals were attempting to make sense of the ecumenical movement that was at its peak during this time. If mainline Protestants, Roman Catholics, and Eastern Orthodox Christians were not going to budge regarding their defining doctrinal commitments, was there another way to understand ecumenical unity? Indeed there was. These communities could be understood as sharing a common consensual Christian culture, or historic Christian identity, more basic than their doctrines. In *this* sense, they belonged to the same capital-C Church, even if they were members of otherwise separate communions. At the same time, anyone who criticized their theological agenda, even if they identified as Christian – indeed, even if they identified as part of the same ecclesiastical tradition – could be seen as belonging to a foreign cultural community. The cultural-linguistic approach relativized every perspective as one culture among others, thus allowing its adherents to redraw the lines of inclusion and exclusion ad hoc without regard for the old denominational and institutional structures.

The cultural turn in theology that postliberalism promoted reconfigured the meaning of objectivity and subjectivity that had defined the crisis of authority up to this point. Prior to this moment, the story went something like this: Old Protestantism had supreme confidence in the objective inspiration of the Bible and the objective truthfulness of Christian doctrine. The norms of Christianity were an inviolable, indisputable reality, and one either embraced or rejected them. This confidence was chastened and challenged by the rise of liberalism and historical criticism. The neoorthodox conservatives embraced this chastening but sought to use the tools of biblical studies and modern theology to forge a new objectivity. In the effort to achieve a "Christian America" they regrouped under the banner of biblical theology – until the methodological problems with this approach brought about its demise, along with the split between the theological and biblical studies disciplines. At this point the crisis of authority fully set in, with the result that objectivity seemed out of reach, as well as the unity that presumably would follow from such objective authority. It is no surprise that one saw an uptick in discussions of the essence and identity of Christianity during this period; everything seemed up for grabs. Pluralism, both cultural and academic, was here to stay, and the challenge now was how to navigate a world characterized, both scholarly and socially, by ever-increasing difference.

Frei's literary approach to the question of Christian norms suggested a way to recover the old confidence by simply bracketing off all methods or inquiries outside of the text. Frei wanted the text itself to define reality, but it was increasingly impossible to avoid the question, "For whom is this biblical language meaningful?" As literary criticism shifted from New Criticism to reader-response theory and deconstruction, and as cultural studies and the concept of collective identity became more prominent, it was natural for postliberalism to shift from a focus on the *text* being read to the community of *readers* doing the reading.[107] Within this cultural-linguistic community, the norms remained as objective as ever, so that Frei's earlier concern for a "nonperspectivist" approach to the essence of Christianity could still be affirmed. Inside the circle of the Christian linguistic community, the essence was given in the biblical narrative; outside this circle, however, the norms were meaningless and untranslatable.[108] Postliberalism thus redefined the objectivity of Christian norms from a universal objectivity located in a public object (i.e., the Bible) to a cultural objectivity within the confines of a particular linguistic community. Frei therefore stated in 1986 that the "plain" or "literal" reading of the Bible, which in theory could authorize any number of readings, was in fact "governed" by "the creed, 'rule of faith' or 'rule of truth'" and was a "crucial instance" of the way "interpretive traditions of religious communities tend to reach a consensus on certain central texts."[109] In other words, postliberalism shifted the locus of normative authority from the text to the interpretive tradition (i.e., the cultural norms) of the church. These norms, like the grammar of a language, were untranslatable to outsiders. Any attempt at translation would be the abandonment of Christianity's cultural essence. "Culture lives by language," according to Robert Wilken, and "if there is a distinctly Christian language, we must be wary of translation." The task is not to translate but to assimilate: "There must be translation *into* the Lord's style of language, bringing alien language into the orbit of Christian belief and practice and giving it a different meaning."[110] Postliberalism thus radicalized the early church's shift from intellectualism to voluntarism: if Christianity is essentially a culture, then the only way to understand it is to become enculturated into it. The essence of Christianity was now not only unusable for apologetics but also, and more importantly, immune to all critique: if you were within the community, you already shared the cultural essence; if you were outside the community, you could not understand the essence and thus all criticisms could be ignored. Postliberalism was therefore a "protective strategy" that privileged the "insider" claims of adherents while all others remained "outsiders."[111]

Postliberalism's replacement of universal doctrines with culturally incommensurable norms and practices undermined traditional apologetics, but it did not necessarily mean that postliberals withdrew from the earlier project (embraced by both fundamentalist and neoorthodox theologians) of Christianizing American culture; it simply changed the tactics. A cultural-linguistic model of Christian identity meant that there were now two primary ways of engaging the wider society. One could take the path of *separatism* and isolate one's community from alternative cultures viewed as antithetical to and incommensurable with one's own. Or one could take the path of *imperialism* and assimilate other communities and cultures into one's own dominant community. While postliberals have tended to prefer one path or the other – Stanley Hauerwas and William Cavanaugh adopting the former, and John Milbank, Phillip Blond, and R. R. Reno going with the latter – in fact most of those who have embraced the Christianity-as-culture model have moved back and forth between the two paths, choosing whichever seemed most expedient in the moment. By way of example, Rod Dreher promoted the separatist Benedict Option in 2017, but he followed this up two years later by signing an "America First" manifesto regarding a new "consensus conservatism" that openly "embrace[d] the new nationalism" of the "Trump phenomenon."[112] The two paths are not necessarily at odds and both share a common presupposition: the notion that Christianity is essentially a distinct and normative culture. If the imperialist option has come to define postliberalism's legacy, that is likely because it was the path promoted, however unwittingly, by both Frei and Lindbeck. Lindbeck stated that his program of "intratextual theology redescribes reality within the scriptural framework rather than translating Scripture into extrascriptural categories. It is the text, so to speak, which absorbs the world, rather than the world the text."[113] As he said later, "the biblical world absorbs all other worlds," and this world-absorption leads to world-creation – the "Christianization of culture."[114] Frei is somewhat more circumspect but otherwise echoes these views. In the conclusion to his 1986 essay on "The 'Literal Reading' of Biblical Narrative in the Christian Tradition," he says that intratextual theology, or what he calls "Christian self-description," can help Christianity regain its primary vocation as a religion, "after its defeat in its secondary vocation of providing ideological coherence, foundation, and stability to Western culture." Once Christianity reestablishes its autonomy, it "might then contribute once again to that culture" and may once more carry "the future of the culture of the West."[115] From American neoorthodoxy to biblical theology to postliberalism, the consistent thread tying them together – besides the interest in Barth's theology – can be expressed in the phrase: "Make Christianity great again!"

While Frei's famous phrase of "generous orthodoxy" was sometimes taken – as in Brian McLaren's book of the same name – to be a liberalizing of evangelicalism, in actuality the period of theology inaugurated with Frei's work was the *evangelicalizing of liberalism.*[116] The evangelicals had replaced mainline Protestantism as the group most actively concerned with renewing Christian culture, and the postliberals noticed they had found a receptive audience among them. In retrospect, we can see why. The postliberals had normalized and mainstreamed the protectionism that evangelical inerrantists had originally developed. Whereas evangelicals simply asserted the superiority of "insider" experience and the uniquely supernatural character of the Bible, postliberals supplied a cultural theory that achieved the same goal but in a way that provided academic legitimacy – something evangelicals had long desired and pursued.[117] It was only natural for postliberals and evangelicals to see each other as allies in a common project. Frei's effort in 1985 at a rapprochement with Henry's conservative evangelicalism was but one prominent example. Lindbeck's lecture at the Wheaton Theology Conference in the spring of 1995 – where he said that postliberalism was "more likely to be carried on by evangelicals than anyone else" – was another.[118]

In a lecture given in September 1995, Lindbeck interpreted Barth's "strange new world" of the Bible to mean that the Bible is "all-absorbing" and "purports to provide a totally comprehensive framework, a universal perspective."[119] He then used the term *Weltanschauung* or "worldview" to describe this comprehensive framework, arguing that this is what Frei's realistic narrative as understood by the premodern church aims to provide.[120] The use of this term was hardly neutral. While the word had its origins in German Enlightenment thought, its use in North American theology had been defined by Reformed evangelicals. The two most important works in this regard were the 1890–1891 Kerr Lectures on *The Christian View of God and the World* by the Scottish Presbyterian James Orr (1844–1913), who later contributed to *The Fundamentals* that established American fundamentalism, and the 1898 Stone Lectures at Princeton Theological Seminary on *Calvinism* by Abraham Kuyper (1837–1920), who established modern Dutch Reformed theology, also known as neo-Calvinism.[121] From the start, conceiving of Christianity as a *Weltanschauung* was bound up with a culture-war mentality. As David Naugle observes, Orr was convinced that "only by presenting Christianity as a comprehensive system of belief that embraced all aspects of reality would any progress be made in this all-determinative culture war."[122] The worldview concept then filtered throughout evangelical philosophy and theology thanks to the writings of Gordon Clark, Arthur Holmes, and James Sire.[123] Holmes had retired from Wheaton College in 1994, the year before Lindbeck gave his lecture, and his influence was felt throughout evangelical higher education. Carl Henry, who studied under Clark at Wheaton College, was also a key promoter of worldview language. The opening volume of his six-volume work, *God, Revelation and Authority*, described the "clash of cultural perspectives" due to the "conflicting convictional frameworks" or worldviews that characterized the "new Dark Ages" that was currently "engulfing the civilized world."[124]

Evangelicals, according to Molly Worthen, "were overfond of this word, *Weltanschauung*," and "they intoned it like a ghostly incantation whenever they wrote of the decline of Christendom."[125] But evangelicals were not alone in doing so. Mainline postliberals shared their militant opposition to modernity and liberalism, as well as their anxiety about Christianity's tenuous future.[126] Henry and other evangelicals were expressing many of the same anxieties about the world that the mainline neoorthodox biblical realists had expressed three decades earlier. Both also were invested in reasserting their source of authority (located especially in scripture) to address this anxiety. Postliberalism, whose realistic biblical narrative descended from the earlier biblical realism, claimed that the problem could not be solved by simply changing one's system of doctrinal propositions and principles – that is, one's "worldview," as Orr had defined the term.[127] The postliberals contributed the idea that the problem was not a "clash of cultural *perspectives*" so much as a clash of *cultures*: the basic practices and linguistic forms that shape a particular community.[128] Lindbeck's cultural-linguistic model was thus a mild corrective to evangelical rationalism, but his use of *Weltanschauung* is evidence of how much more closely aligned postliberalism and evangelicalism had become.

The cultural-linguistic model that initially provided a way for postliberals to forge ecumenical and interreligious unity had become a new weapon in the countercultural resistance to liberal modernity. The differences between evangelicals and postliberals over particular doctrines were finally irrelevant; what united them was a shared sense of cultural warfare, the clash that characterized Christianity's relationship with the wider world. If Christianity was a worldview (whether defined doctrinally or linguistically), then it was, like all worldviews, "untranslatable and competitive," claiming to be universally comprehensive. According to Lindbeck, this meant Christianity was necessarily caught in a struggle with other worldviews, since "only one, if that, can be ultimately successful" and "the prize winner stands alone."[129] The more aggressively militant postliberals took this lesson to heart, leading to the formation of Radical Orthodoxy following the publication of Milbank's *Theology and Social Theory* (1991). The evangelicals were learning the same lesson, albeit from different sources, and in the twenty-first century, after their doctrinal apologetics proved fruitless in the effort to Christianize society, they would come to adopt the cultural turn – bringing about the convergence of evangelicalism and postliberalism that had been slowly building over the previous half-century.

THE ECCLESIAL WORLDVIEW: THEOLOGICAL INTERPRETATION OF SCRIPTURE AND THE TURN TO THE CHURCH

The alignment between postliberalism and evangelicalism was nowhere more apparent than in the successor to the biblical theology movement that developed in the late 1980s and 1990s: theological interpretation of scripture (TIS). According to Stanley Porter, James Barr's critique "set the entire field of biblical theology into a period of initial decline and then revisionism until it developed the proper foundation for its work." That foundation – which I would identify as postliberalism – gave rise to "a revised form of this movement in the Theological Interpretation of Scripture."[130] The connections between biblical theology and TIS went deep: they recognized the same sources of inspiration, were criticized by some of the same scholars, and pursued the same ends. Even more so than biblical theology, the proponents of TIS traced their origins to Barth's *Epistle to the Romans*, especially the heavily revised second edition of 1922. Daniel Treier called Barth the "pioneer" of theological exegesis and the "motivation and model" for theological interpreters today.[131] Angus Paddison, in his contribution to *A Manifesto for Theological Interpretation*, described Barth's *Romans* as "the opening salvo in the twentieth-century's renewed theological engagement with Scripture."[132] While this may be so, it is also the case that, in both form and content, there is little similarity between Barth's commentary and the work produced by TIS. Barth's *Romans* pioneered TIS much the same way that Barth's critique of liberal theology established American neoorthodoxy: whereas neoorthodoxy was inspired by Barth's rejection of his liberal teachers, TIS was inspired by Barth's protest against "the sterility of the historical-critical method predominant in biblical interpretation."[133] In both cases the connection is largely superficial and does not shed much light either on Barth or on what makes TIS distinctive.[134]

The more relevant pioneer was, of course, Hans Frei's *Eclipse of Biblical Narrative* and the postliberal interest in precritical, countercultural theological interpretation (and historic Christian identity more generally) that blossomed from it. In the wake of Frei, David C. Steinmetz (1936–2015), the historian of Christianity at Duke Divinity School who earlier had graduated from Wheaton College, published his 1980 article on "The Superiority of Pre-Critical Exegesis" in *Theology Today*, an essay that has since been anthologized and is viewed as one of the founding documents of what became TIS.[135] Five years later, the journal *Ex Auditu* was launched at Princeton Theological Seminary – under the leadership of Thomas Gillespie (president of the seminary and original editor of the journal), Dikran Hadidian, Ben Meyer, and Peter Stuhlmacher – for the purpose of publishing the papers from the Frederick Neumann Symposium on Theological Interpretation of Scripture. The first issue of *Ex Auditu* reprinted Steinmetz's essay, along with other articles from *Theology Today*. After three years the symposium and journal left Princeton and migrated into evangelical circles, first Fuller Theological Seminary, where Robert Guelich served as editor for two years, followed by North Park Theological Seminary, which has been the home for the symposium since 1990.[136] Lindbeck published "The Story-Shaped Church" in 1987, a germinal essay that tied the work of Frei directly to the task of TIS.[137] In the late nineties, postliberals and evangelicals began to work together more constructively, leading to the emergence of a reformist group of evangelical theology described as "postconservative" – the evangelical parallel to postliberal.[138] For the postconservatives, like the postliberals, "the Bible absorbs the world and is our authoritative narrative."[139] In 1998, the postconservative theologian Kevin Vanhoozer published *Is There a Meaning in This Text?* and brought the emerging hermeneutical conversation into the fold of evangelicalism. That same year Craig Bartholomew started the Scripture and Hermeneutics Seminar to discuss the work of Vanhoozer and others, which resulted in an eight-volume series of books published by Zondervan beginning in 2000. In 2005, Vanhoozer, along with Bartholomew, Treier, and N. T. Wright, coedited the *Dictionary for Theological Interpretation of the Bible*; that same year Baker started publishing the Brazos Theological Commentary on the Bible (edited by Reno); and in 2007 the *Journal of Theological Interpretation* began publication, featuring an editorial board of both evangelical and mainline postliberal scholars.[140]

Frei set the terms for this movement in a twofold way. In a negative sense, Frei's work was a wholesale critique of historical criticism as a modern, and therefore problematic, departure from the precritical interpretation that he claimed characterized the consensus of the church for a millennium and a half. TIS rejected the modern decision, going back at least to Johann Salomo Semler, to treat the Bible like any other book.[141] In a positive sense, Frei argued that a precritical interpretation meant reading the Bible in accordance with the rule of faith within the context of the cultural community that was normed by this rule. The emphasis on the community is crucial. If anything unites the various streams of TIS together, it is the notion that such interpretation is conducted by the church and for the church. In his programmatic essay for the inaugural issue of the *Journal for Theological Interpretation*, Richard Hays begins his definition of TIS by stating that "theological exegesis is *a practice of and for the church*." Joel Green says that TIS is "identified especially by its self-consciously ecclesial location." Likewise, Bartholomew and Heath Thomas have defined theological interpretation as "interpretation of the Bible for the church."[142] This emphasis on the church as normative for the task of theological interpretation only brings into relief the gap between TIS and Barth's *Romans*, where we read that "in the Church, all manner of divine things are possessed and known, and are therefore not possessed and not known. ... The opposition between the Church and the Gospel is final and all-embracing: the Gospel dissolves the Church, and the Church dissolves the Gospel."[143] Naturally, the church appears nowhere in Barth's methodological prefaces where he reflects on how he approached his commentary. It would be hard to find a starker contrast between this and TIS. For TIS, by contrast, the church *does* possess the gospel and all manner of divine things, and for this reason the community alone is capable of rightly interpreting the scriptural text.

For TIS, interpreting the Bible for the church is inseparable from interpreting the Bible by the rule of faith. This is a somewhat curious development that deserves more critical attention than it has received. The article by Steinmetz that has been so influential to proponents of TIS says nothing about the rule of faith – or any rule at all. By "precritical exegesis," Steinmetz meant the distinction between the literal and spiritual meanings of the text that early Christian theologians like Origen and Augustine pioneered, as well as the fourfold sense of scripture developed by medieval interpreters. These hermeneutical distinctions made possible the highly creative and allegorical interpretations for which the ancient church is known. It is important to take stock of the context of this essay. It was published in a special issue of *Theology Today* expressly put together in response to Lindsell's *The Battle for the Bible* and its 1979 sequel, *The Bible in the Balance*. The editorial by Bernhard Anderson pointed out that "in recent years a strong tide of conservatism has swept people into worship services where the Bible is forcefully proclaimed as the veritable Word of God, indeed the inerrant Word of God," and he referred to Lindsell's work as the preeminent example of this. After discussing the alternative position of Barr, Anderson wrote that, while some "hope that we can move into a post-critical era when the Bible will once again be the normative basis for the church's understanding of God's revelation," the fact remains that "we are modern persons" and "there is no harbor safe from the winds and tides of the modern world."[144] In other words, placed in historical context, Steinmetz was responding not only to historical criticism but also to the rigid literalism of evangelicalism. Precritical exegesis is superior, he was arguing, because it frees the Bible for *more* readings, not because it tethers the Bible to the orthodox tradition of the institutional church. The problem with modern hermeneutics is that it restricts the text to "a single meaning," when in fact there are multiple levels of meaning.[145]

This makes the emphasis on the rule of faith in recent years so distinctive. If one looks at the early issues of *Ex Auditu*, one finds few if any references to the *regula fidei*. When Stuhlmacher discussed it in 1986, he identified it as "dangerous" because it could lead to further division among the churches. For this reason he recommended sticking with the hermeneutical parameters set forth in the biblical texts themselves.[146] A decisive shift occurred in 1994, however, when David Yeago published his article, "The New Testament and the Nicene Dogma," in which he argued that "the exegesis underlying classical Christian doctrines is in certain crucial respects methodologically superior to the 'critical' exegesis which has claimed to invalidate it."[147] Here we find a more relevant concept of superiority than the one in Steinmetz's article where the origins of today's TIS are concerned. Brevard Childs, the Yale colleague of Frei and Lindbeck, said he was "fully supportive of Yeago's challenge" and called it "courageous and bold because it flies in the face of the whole scholarly biblical guild."[148] The work of Yeago and Childs, along with Frei and Lindbeck, set postliberal and evangelical theology on the path toward the adoption of the rule of faith as the hermeneutical norm for a theological reading of scripture. We can see the fulfillment of this in more recent writings on TIS. Green devotes a chapter of his book to the relationship between scripture and the *regula fidei*, arguing that use of the rule of faith provides the necessary "hermeneutical lenses" for interpretations that are "worthy of the name 'Christian.'"[149] Even as an evangelical who advocates placing the authority of scripture over that of the church, Treier still states that "not to read with the Rule is not to read as a Christian."[150] Walter Moberly goes even further and says that "if one wishes to engage with God [!], then a rule of faith, among other things, must come into play in the way one uses the Bible."[151] Hays argues that we learn to read "with the eyes of faith" when we are "trained by *the Christian tradition*," referring to the doctrines of Christian orthodoxy.[152] In his series preface for the Brazos Theological Commentary on the Bible, R. R. Reno similarly but more provocatively claims that "our vision is darkened" and corrupted by the world, and thus "we need training and instruction in order to cleanse our minds." The "body of apostolic doctrine" codified in the *regula fidei* provides the purifying instruction, he says. If we ask where we can find this apostolic doctrine, Reno names "the Nicene tradition," "the Niceno-Constantinopolitan Creed," "ancient baptismal affirmations of faith," "the Chalcedonian definition," and "the creeds and canons of other church councils." Anticipating the objection that many important aspects of the tradition are not defined in official creedal documents – and those creedal statements are not self-interpreting anyway – Reno goes on to say, as I have pointed out already, that the rule of faith is not "limited to a specific set of words, sentences, and creeds. It is instead a pervasive habit of thought, *the animating culture of the church in its intellectual aspect.*"[153] By now we are in a position to understand not only why Reno has defined, and in effect, redefined, the rule of faith in terms of the church's culture (and he is by no means alone in doing so) but also what the significance of that decision is. The rule of faith in TIS represents the fusion of the doctrinal rule I discussed in Chapter 2 with the cultural rule that postliberalism promoted. The result is that to be a "true Christian" is to belong to a particular culture – a culture that is identified with antiquity by means of a vaguely defined orthodoxy. The TIS movement, along with postliberalism more generally, thus embodies what I call *cultural ecclesiocentrism*: a theology centered on the church understood as a distinct culture.

Put another way, TIS represents what we might call an *ecclesial worldview theology.*[154] Like a previous generation of American evangelicals, it espouses the notion that Christianity is a *Weltanschauung*, an all-encompassing perspective by which alone the true nature of things is known – and by which our otherwise perverted minds are purified and redeemed. But this worldview has been filtered through the postliberal cultural turn so that only those who belong to a specific cultural-linguistic community – namely, the church – are capable of sharing this *Weltanschauung*. As with other instances of worldview thinking, TIS is thus a quintessential example of "thinking whitely," given that its universalizing gaze reimagines "the whole world as fitting within the framework of their thinking." By further aiming constructively at the formation of the cultural world of the church, TIS embodies the homogenizing, colonizing project of whiteness.[155] Because this homogenizing project eliminates external voices of critique, TIS also continues the protectionism of postliberalism and brings it fully within the realm of New Testament studies.[156] Of course, there is nothing magical about the church; simply belonging to this community does not automatically give one access to this worldview. One must *practice* and *use* this worldview. What proponents of TIS mean by this is that one must make the church the *norm* for one's interpretation of the text, and in turn one's interpretation of scripture must seek to provide, or rather reaffirm, the norms for the community. According to Hays, the goal of theological exegesis is "to read the Bible as normative for a community."[157] John Thompson of Fuller Seminary stated that his goal is "to establish and implement a *normative* function for Scripture in our contemporary world" for the purpose of forming "Christian culture."[158] In other words, it is not enough to *think* whitely; one must engage in the colonizing formation of whiteness, meaning a space in which everyone is tasked with the responsibility of eliminating heretical differences and laboring to strengthen and spread the normative ecclesiastical culture. The result is a normative hermeneutical circle: the church norms interpretation, and interpretation norms the church. The hermeneutical circle of TIS is thus hermetically sealed; anyone who contests the norms is subject to exclusion from the community, and anyone outside the community has nothing relevant to contribute to the conversation. Much like the European encounter with Indigenous nations, the outsider is voiceless unless and until they convert.

One obvious advantage of adopting a worldview model for biblical studies is the ability to relativize competing methodologies as alternative worldviews or cultures. Stephen Fowl, for instance, points to genocidal conflicts, quantum physics, Marxist ideology critique, and other developments as indications that "we never perceive or comprehend the world and its past without some set of lenses." This observation – self-evident to the point of banality – leads Fowl to the conclusion that historical criticism is merely "one among many sets of scholarly interpretive interests," and this recognition means "there is now room for theological concerns to re-enter the scholarly realm."[159] Every reading of the Bible is a "culturally located" or "interested" reading, and therefore every reading is as good as any other. Setting aside for the time being whether this is a responsible use of cultural relativism, the more important consequence of this position is the implied assumption that any interpretation *for the church* is necessarily a theologically normative one. Other readings might have something interesting to say, but they will primarily be for *other* communities, only tangentially relevant at best to Christian readers. Much the same way that postliberalism limited theology to "Christian self-description" in a concerted effort to exclude extratheological sources of knowledge and critique, so too TIS limited biblical interpretation to the reaffirmation of the orthodox Christian tradition.

While cultural relativism supposedly gave TIS an equal claim on the text, many proponents of TIS have not been willing to be as generous in return. Indeed, they were often prone to claiming that, since the Bible was written by people of faith and handed down by people of faith, their ecclesial-theological approach was the *only* valid way of reading the Bible. Hays offers the most vivid example of this in his 2007 article. He criticizes Heikki Räisänen, Michael V. Fox, and Wayne Meeks each for promoting critical biblical scholarship that is self-consciously written for a secular, pluralistic world. Hays chides Meeks for rejecting the traditional effort "to find 'normative' meanings in texts," which would mean "that NT scholars should abandon their role as teachers of the church," something Hays regards as self-evidently intolerable.[160] Hays singles out Hector Avalos for special scorn because of the latter's self-description as a "secular humanist" and his claim that the Bible "has no intrinsic value or merit." In response to Avalos's critique of the Society of Biblical

Literature and his admission that he no longer wishes to continue studying the Bible, Hays responds: "Given the opinions expressed in Avalos's essay, this is probably a wise vocational discernment." Hays concludes that the study of the Bible "outside of faith communities" is "intellectually incoherent." He quotes Robert Jenson's position that "outside the church, no such entity as the Christian Bible has any reason to exist." Jenson (1930–2017), one of the strongest advocates of the notion that Christianity is a culture, even goes on to say in this essay that interpretation of the Bible outside of the church "must be arbitrary, uncontrollable, and finally moot."[161] We see here the Janus-faced character of worldview-thinking: on the one hand, it relativizes all theories and theologies as equally legitimate participants on the playing field of worldviews, but, on the other hand, it authorizes a totalizing and totalitarian perspective that delegitimates any perspective other than its own. Ecclesial worldview thinking uses pluralism to give itself a seat at the table, which it then uses to burn the table. In this way, TIS continues the authoritarian legacy of biblical theology.

THE RULE OF FAITH AS CULTURAL CONSTRUCTION

In January 1949, H. Richard Niebuhr presented a series of lectures at Austin Presbyterian Theological Seminary on the topic of *Christ and Culture*. These lectures, published in 1951, quickly became a classic, and Niebuhr's famous typology – Christ against culture, Christ of culture, Christ above culture, Christ and culture in paradox, and Christ the transformer of culture – became a template for future conversation and a sparring partner for later theologians, spawning numerous rebuttals and variations. By "Christ," Niebuhr was contributing to the conversation regarding the essence of Christianity, even if he did not use that precise terminology. He declared early on that a Christian is "one who counts himself as belonging to that community of men for whom Jesus Christ – his life, words, deeds, and destiny – is of supreme importance as the key to the understanding of themselves and their world."[162] Though Niebuhr recognized the manifold ways that Christians have defined Christ, he insisted there remained a "fundamental unity" rooted in the text of the New Testament, a position that perhaps anticipated the later work of his student, Hans Frei. Behind all the different theologies there was still "the essence of the Jesus Christ who is one and the same."[163]

What Niebuhr did not anticipate, however, was that by the end of the century, Christ, and by extension the community of those who belonged to him, would himself be understood as a culture. In 2003–2004, Jenson would even publish a series of articles with the title, "Christ as Culture."[164] The essence of Christ, and thus the essence of Christianity, had substantially changed, so that one could not relate Christ and culture as two distinct categories. In the wake of postliberalism, to speak of "Christ and culture" was instead to speak of "Christian culture and other cultures." It was, in other words, to speak of a culture war.

It is time to draw the threads of this chapter together. I have recounted this long and complex story to understand how large swaths of Protestant America came around to embracing the idea that Christianity's essence is its culture. More pointedly, both mainline and evangelical Protestants shifted from a doctrinal or biblical rule of faith to a cultural rule of faith. They did so in large part because doctrine and scripture were no longer capable of holding Christians together. Doctrine failed to do so after the fundamentalist-modernist controversy (followed by the collapse of mainline Protestant America several decades later), and scripture failed to do so after the failure of the biblical theology movement and the irreparable breach between theology and biblical studies that opened up in the 1960s. These developments created a veritable emergency among church leaders looking for a stable solution to the theological pandemonium. The solution that seemed most plausible to many of the leading figures in the late twentieth century was to conceive of Christianity in terms of a culture. A distinct advantage of this approach was the ability for Protestants to make common cause with post–Vatican II Catholics by marginalizing their doctrinal differences in favor of liturgical and cultural points of connection. This is why it is important to see the shift from biblical theology to TIS against the backdrop of the *ressourcement* movement that was occurring simultaneously. Many of the Protestants most heavily involved in the *ressourcement* and liturgical dialogues were also the ones advocating for narrative and postliberal theology. In many respects, it was a single conversation directed at different audiences: to the Catholics, these Protestants were able to claim a common cultural tradition of historic Christianity; to the evangelicals, these same Protestants could claim to be upholding a normative and authoritative scripture free from the errors of modern historical criticism. It was a win-win-win all around. Culture came in to save the day, and the result was the construction of a historic Christian identity that claimed to be the consensus of two millennia of Jesus followers, irrespective of the many doctrinal and institutional schisms.

To be sure, there is much more to this story that I have not been able to tell here. A not insignificant aspect of this shift is the way cultural discourse infiltrated every intellectual corner of the American landscape by the end of the twentieth century, so that it became nigh impossible not to see everything as expressive of culture. In one sense, this was a positive development. For many, "postmodernism" signified the recognition that we are all situated within historical and cultural contexts that have shaped what we see and how we see it, so that any purportedly universal or timeless claim has become dubious at best. Such an acknowledgment was not original and can hardly be attributed to something called postmodernism, but however people came to this insight, it represented an advance on claims of universal, ahistorical rationality. There is no culture-free gospel, and thus no Christian essence that can stand outside and above the fray of some cultural location.

In retrospect, however, the rage about postmodernity was a proxy for a more important and genuinely new shift in the American consciousness – namely, the creation of individual (psychological) and group (sociohistorical) identity, and the fragmentation of identity that necessarily followed. Gerald Izenberg has traced this development in his magisterial work.[165] Suffice it here to say that what developed in postwar America, thanks especially to Erik Erikson, was not merely the realization that *Christianity* is cultural but that *Christians* are cultural, that each person's identity is defined by the culture(s) to which they belong. The story I have told in this chapter – especially the history of the biblical theology movement and TIS from the 1940s to the early 2000s – is the story of various efforts to reinforce a sense of social identity in the face of challenges to that identity. The liberals who regrouped in the 1930s in the wake of Barth's "bomb" sought to overcome the fragmentation between fundamentalism and liberalism by drawing on a theological reading of the Bible as a single story of salvation history. These post-liberal (but not yet postliberal) Christians placed their hope in biblical theology to be the vehicle by which they would Christianize American society anew, defeating communism and Catholicism in the process. When this failed so spectacularly, it produced an identity crisis – a group identity crisis. What did it mean to be Christian in America now? The postliberals offered what seemed initially to be a compelling answer: a Christian culture that not only could unite Christians across denominational and institutional boundaries but also did not depend on salvaging "Christian America." It was therefore durable even in the face of American social fragmentation and the collapse of Western Christendom.

This was all well and good so long as the relevant issues were simply doctrinal disagreements, denominational decline, and liturgical renewal. Talk of Christian culture in that relatively anodyne sense helped to give people a sense of community in the face of so much institutional upheaval, as denominations split and merged to create new formations. But of course these developments did not occur in a vacuum. Alongside and behind these institutional changes was a cultural sea change of massive proportions that overshadowed all of the biblical, hermeneutical, liturgical, and cultural conversations – namely, the *politicization* of identity. It is no accident that Lindbeck crafted his cultural-linguistic model of Christianity against the backdrop of the Reagan Revolution. Even if the cultural rule of faith was constructed to address an ecumenical problem, it was used almost immediately to advance a political agenda. The postliberals were not only willing participants; they helped lay the groundwork for the Christian culture war that had been mobilizing for decades and has since engulfed the churches – and the American people as a whole. The cultural rule of faith has today become the *political* rule of faith.

4

Weaponizing the Rule

Making Christianity (and America) Great Again

"**W**E GOT RID OF THE JOHNSON AMENDMENT," President Donald Trump boasted at the National Day of Prayer Service on May 2, 2019, referring to Executive Order 13798 on "Promoting Free Speech and Religious Liberty" that he signed two years earlier on May 4, 2017. "You can now speak your mind and speak it freely. ... They took away your voice, politically. And these are the people I want to listen to, politically, but you weren't allowed to speak."[1] The Johnson Amendment was legislation that Senate minority leader Lyndon B. Johnson proposed in 1954 to deny tax-exempt status to nonprofit groups that "participate in, or intervene in (including the publishing or distributing of statements), any political campaign."[2] While rarely enforced, the amendment theoretically prevented churches and other religious nonprofits from openly supporting specific candidates for public office. Conservative religious leaders and activists, such as Ralph Reed and Jerry Falwell Jr., had been trying to repeal it for years in order fully to fuse religious practice and political activity. In opposition to Barack Obama's campaign for the presidency, the Alliance Defending Freedom (ADF) launched the "Pulpit Freedom Sunday" event in 2008 to challenge the Johnson Amendment directly by enlisting pastors to connect the Bible to politics in their sermons.[3] Knowing well that white evangelicals were his primary supporters, Trump had campaigned on the promise to "totally destroy" the amendment, a view he had reiterated at the 2017 National Prayer Breakfast – the annual event organized by the secretive Fellowship.[4]

Trump, of course, had not gotten rid of the amendment, despite his characteristically false claims to the contrary. Even with the excessive increase in executive power, he did not have the ability to rewrite the tax code by presidential fiat. Following his executive order, Trump pursued his agenda through the Republican tax reform bill, known as the Tax Cuts and Jobs Act of 2017, that he eventually signed into law in December. The version that passed the House included a repeal of the Johnson Amendment, but this was removed during the reconciliation with the Senate version because of its violation of the Byrd Rule, a piece of news that disheartened evangelicals and was reported by *Christianity Today*.[5] There was a further effort in 2018 to prevent the IRS from using any funds to investigate churches for violating the Johnson Amendment, but this too failed to make it into the final Consolidated Appropriations Act of 2019 – though it hardly mattered given how reluctant the IRS has been even to conduct an audit of a church, much less strip one of its tax-exempt status.[6]

Even so, it was nevertheless appropriate that Trump made his errone-ous boast on the National Day of Prayer, an annual occurrence that began on July 4, 1952, after Billy Graham called for Congress to enact such a day in a speech earlier that year at the Capitol on February 3. The day after Graham's speech, Tennessee representative Percy Priest introduced a resolution in response to the challenge "made on the east steps of the Capitol by Billy Graham." Representatives John McCormack and Jack Brooks both concurred, noting their hope that "all creeds" and "all denominations" would participate, "whether they be Catholic, Protestant, or Jew."[7] Eleven days after Graham's speech, Senator Absalom Willis Robertson, father of the future televangelist Pat Robertson, introduced Public Law 82-324 to the Senate by declaring the nation's special need for prayer in light of the critical state of world affairs – a crisis that was, in the senator's mind, both religious and political at the same time. According to Robertson, "we are threatened at home and abroad by the corrosive forces of communism which seek simultaneously to destroy our democratic way of life and the faith in an Almighty God on which it is based." Robertson continued by appealing to the religious spirit of the "founding fathers," who "based their Declaration of Independence upon a firm reliance on the protection of Divine Providence."[8] The official Senate Resolution 276 that the Senate unanimously approved resolved that it would be appropriate for the nation to have a day of prayer in light of "the challenge of communism to religious freedom and the fundamental tenets of democracy, which are based on faith in God and the teachings of His Holy Word."[9]

Trump's executive order may have been toothless, but it followed a long-standing script of Christian nationalism that has been entangled with the history of the United States from the beginning. That script has undergone a "dramatic change," as Jared Goldstein has pointed out. Christian nationalists in the nineteenth century viewed the United States Constitution "as a godless document unworthy of a Christian nation" and so campaigned for decades to amend it. Today, however, "Christian nationalists laud the Constitution as the highest expression of the nation's Christian identity."[10] While hearings on the Christian amendment to the Constitution took place as late as 1975, Goldstein traces the turning point to the election of President Dwight D. Eisenhower in 1952 – the same year that Congress established the National Day of Prayer. That year there was a "renewed religious agenda in Washington" as both parties "refused to be outfaithed" by the other. In an effort to demonstrate their spiritual commitment to defeating communism, politicians used "societal resources to stimulate a religious revival" in what amounted to a state-sanctioned religious program that Jonathan Herzog has called the "spiritual-industrial complex."[11] Shortly after his inauguration, which was a uniquely religious ceremony compared to previous inaugurations, Eisenhower was baptized at National Presbyterian Church on February 1, 1953, in the first and only presidential baptism in the nation's history.[12] Later that year the first National Prayer Breakfast took place, and in 1954 the words "under God" were added to the Pledge of Allegiance. By the time of Eisenhower's election, the strictly Christian nationalism of the Christian amendment movement had broadened into a generic religious nationalism that valorized the "Judeo-Christian heritage" of the nation.[13] In the fight against godless communism, it did not matter what creed, denomination, or even religion one adhered to, so long as one adhered to *something*. The "God" of Americans, as Will Herberg famously observed in 1955, was "religion itself"; what truly redeems, according to postwar religious Americans, was simply "the 'positive' attitude of *believing*."[14] The essence of American Christianity that was emerging during this period was largely reducible to the practice of religion in general, specifically as this practice was a mark of one's patriotic commitment to the nation. In this sense, the Constitution – shaped as it was by the Lockean deism of the founders – was a thoroughly Christian document.

What Goldstein reveals is that, at the very same time that mainline American Protestantism was struggling to clarify the essence of Christianity, the nation as a whole was clarifying the essence of Americanism. The position that emerged in the 1950s and eventually became the settled creed of American civil religion is what Goldstein calls "constitutional nationalism," which is "the belief that the essence of American identity involves a shared commitment to principles found in the Constitution."[15] The explicit creed provided cover for the implicit, ascriptive norms that characterized American society, particularly norms regarding whiteness, patriarchy, and cisheteronormativity. Just as the Bible or the "historic Christian" creeds did not directly provide the essence of Christianity, despite claims to the contrary by fundamentalists, evangelicals, and neoorthodox theologians, so too the Constitution did not actually supply "the essence of what it means to be American" but instead "served as a magic mirror onto which Americans have gazed and found projections of themselves and their dreams for the nation."[16] Prescriptive claims about what constitutes true American identity have thus functioned at the civic level much the same way that prescriptive claims about true Christianity have functioned at the religious level: they create "national mythologies" that allow Americans to police those who do not conform to a prescribed idea of "what the nation truly is," while at the same time excluding all the shameful parts of American history as anomalous episodes that "do not reflect who we really are."[17] As scholars have constructed more nuanced – and deflating – descriptive accounts of United States history, those whose identities are bound up with the myths have doubled down on the purified essence of Americanism, even as the insistence on this singular, infallible essence allows the injustices of the past to remain unexamined and uncorrected.

The quest for the essence of American identity has run parallel to, and been an integral part of, the quest for the essence of American *Christian* identity. Just as the former has been deeply religious in character, so the latter has been deeply political. The myths associated with American identity are often mirror images of the myths associated with Christian identity, particularly in the antimodern versions of each. Both are tied to founding texts: the Constitution for the one, the Bible and creeds for the other. Both employ normative hermeneutical methods: originalism (or strict constructionism) for the one, historical-theological biblicism for the other.[18] Both make the imagined community normative for their respective interpretations: nationalism for the one, ecclesiocentrism for the other. Both are exceptionalist accounts of their respective identities: regardless of the past, American identity and Christian identity are deemed fundamentally *good*, even superior to alternatives. The two are also historically connected. The United States, and the resulting contests over American identity, were born out of the same Enlightenment liberalism that produced the theological quests, both liberal and counter-liberal, for Christian identity, and those antiliberals who have sought ever since to "make America great again" have often been the ones seeking to "make Christianity great again" as well out of a recognition that these two prescriptivist projects are bound up with one another.

Of these two quests, this chapter, like the rest of the book, focuses on the Christian quest – but here specifically with respect to its entanglement with American politics and political identity. This brings us back to the heart of this book, back to where we started. While much has been written about the rise of the Religious Right,[19] my goal here is to see these developments in the wider context of the modern quest to define a prescriptive, normative Christianity in the face of changing conditions. Traditionalists sought to recover the doctrines of "historic Christianity," the subject of Chapter 2. The postliberals I explored in Chapter 3 proposed rethinking Christianity as a culture as the way to address the crisis of authority within an increasingly secular and fragmented society. Having looked at *thinking* (doctrine) and *feeling* (culture), to use Schleiermacher's schema again, we turn now to *doing*, which here refers to politics and morality. The political rule of faith drew upon the doctrinal and cultural rules to define true Christianity in terms of proper Christian practice – a practice that could, at various times, include not only formal liturgical participation but also white supremacy, male headship, antiabortion natalism, and heteronormativity. Both of the rules described in the previous chapters were already deeply interwoven with political concerns and motivations, and despite being led initially by mostly mainline Christians (including many associated with liberal theology), the doctrinal and cultural rules laid the groundwork for a new war of religions fought now over sociopolitical positions that have no basis in the dogmas, doctrines, and practices of classical orthodoxy. The cultural turn was the linchpin that forged the connection between ancient doctrines and contemporary politics. Once the creedal rule of faith was reconceived as a cultural worldview – a worldview that was adaptable to whatever political battles were being waged at the time – it became possible for Christians to think that their efforts to exclude LGBTQ persons, for example, were a direct extension of the ancient church's anathematizing of what came to be regarded as heresies.

This chapter will explore the way this culturalized historic orthodoxy was weaponized by the Christian right – or rather weaponized anew for a pluralistic, (post)secular society, because this was not an original tactic but one that has repeated itself in various historical moments. The rule of faith in this period became far more than a way of distinguishing the "true Christian" from rival claimants. Instead of merely an effort at retrieving traditional doctrines, it became a program for restoring an entire way of life, the long-lost culture that proponents considered not only ideal but prescriptive for Christianity. Whether such a culture ever existed is beside the point; it was the vision of this society that has served as the basis for new political alliances, legal claims, and religious boundary-making. Moreover, the plasticity of culture as the basis for normative Christianity made it a ready vehicle for the fluid and rapidly evolving political landscape that emerged in the late twentieth and early twenty-first centuries. As predominantly white Christian leaders denounced attacks on their religious freedom and way of life in a supposed "war on Christianity," the rule of faith became a rallying cry to mobilize the faithful for the front lines. The boundary lines defining "true Christianity" became trenches in cultural warfare.

THE POLITICAL RULE IN A LIBERAL SOCIETY: SLAVERY, SPIRITUALITY, AND THE STATUS QUO

To speak of the political rule alongside the doctrinal and cultural rules can be somewhat misleading. Unlike with doctrine or culture, reactionary critics of modernity have rarely framed their accounts of true Christianity in explicitly political terms. That has instead been the strategy of liberationist and other leftist theologians, who have framed Christianity in political terms to expose the underlying politics that conservative Christian leaders have often been able to avoid acknowledging directly. To understand the peculiar nature of this situation requires understanding the liberal political order of the United States and its implications for the relation between religion and politics.

The old European model, going back to antiquity, is what some call Christendom, or what Ernst Troeltsch more accurately described as "church-directed culture": an ecclesiastical civilization that united "the immutable Divine with the mutable human in a cosmos of ordered and organized functions."[20] Religion and politics within this ecclesiastical culture worked hand in hand, with religion providing the metaphysical and moral foundation as well as the transcendent goal, and politics operating within the immanent and worldly domain to arrange human affairs in light of the religious scaffolding. Religion and politics formed a single, coherent totality encompassing both the immanent and the transcendent, the penultimate and the ultimate. Human beings were thus simultaneously *homo politicus*, as Aristotle argued, and *homo religiosus*.[21] When the consensus about this cosmic picture fell apart, "a new relationship of religion to political governance was created," making it necessary to figure out how to arrange human society in a way conducive to the common good without relying on everyone's assumption of a religious foundation on which there was no longer agreement. The result was the modern liberal project. For the first time since Constantine established an ecclesiastical culture, "national and religious identity no longer necessarily went hand in hand. ... Religion was thereby politically and legally divided into modern and antimodern."[22] While religiously conservative antimoderns[23] have repeatedly charged liberalism with creating a public-private split that confines religious faith to the interior realm of individual conscience, one could equally describe it instead as an effort to create social cohesion in the midst of religious and ideological pluralism. Of course, for conservatives who believe the only true cohesion is the one supplied by normative religious identity, this amounts to the same thing.

William Wilberforce (1759–1833), for example, bemoaned the decline in Great Britain of what he called "real Christianity" and the consequent decline of society in general. Though Wilberforce acknowledged that even "false Religion" had the capacity to "prescribe good morals" and enforce a productive society, "true Christianity, from her essential nature, appears peculiarly and powerfully adapted to promote the preservation and healthfulness of political communities."[24] This was the case, he argued, because the "peculiar doctrines" of Christianity "laid the foundations of a superstructure of morals proportionably broad and exalted." Because these doctrines have faded from view, so too has the moral superstructure that holds society together.[25] Much depends at this point on which morals one holds up as the highest aim of society – obedience and order or love and generosity. Wilberforce, to his credit, sided with the latter and opposed the slave trade as a result. He saw Christianity as providing support for a diverse, liberal society. The primary defect of human nature, in his view, was selfishness, and Christianity offered the needed remedy. He criticized "nominal Christians" because "they know Christianity only as a system of restraints. She is despoiled of every liberal and generous principle: she is rendered almost unfit for the social intercourses of life, and is only suited to the gloomy walls of that cloister, in which they would confine her." By contrast, "*true Christians* consider themselves not as satisfying some rigorous creditor, but as discharging a debt of gratitude," which frees them for "the large and liberal measure of a voluntary service" and fills the true Christian "with the desire of promoting the temporal well-being of all around him."[26] Wilberforce thus defined normative or true Christianity in terms of a liberal service toward others, and so the nominal or "fake" Christian was the one who failed to connect Christian faith to one's social existence, opting instead to keep religion within the walls of the church. It is easy to see why present-day religious conservatives find much to appreciate about Wilberforce. His argument about the importance of religion, and specifically Christianity, to the health of society anticipates today's postliberal and antiliberal proponents of religious nationalism. But unlike the latter, Wilberforce has a distinctly different account of what religion teaches and how it relates to political community – one that fosters the "temporal well-being of all."

Compared to Wilberforce, things could not have been more different across the pond. Many of the key architects of the United States held a vastly different view of orthodox Christianity – indeed of any orthodoxy at all.[27] Among the reasons for the collapse of the old ecclesiastical culture were the bloody Wars of Religion, and the subsequent Peace of Westphalia, which left a deep impression on Locke and his American followers, including John Adams (1735–1826), Thomas Jefferson (1743–1826), and James Madison (1751–1836). In a letter to Mathew Carey, author of the political bestseller *The Olive Branch*, Jefferson distinguished moral principles from "dogmas of religion," noting with respect to the latter that "all mankind, from the beginning of the world to this day, have been quarrelling, fighting, burning and torturing one another, for abstractions unintelligible to themselves and to all others, and absolutely beyond the comprehension of the human mind."[28] Likewise, Adams, in an 1825 letter to Jefferson, referred to the blasphemy laws that existed "throughout the whole Christian world," making it illegal "to deny or doubt the divine inspiration of all the books of the old and new Testaments" – punishable in most of Europe "by fire at the stake, or the rack, or the wheel," or in England "by boring through the tongue with a red hot poker." Such laws were not only embarrassing but also "great obstructions" to a free society.[29] The problem with religious orthodoxy, according to these founders, is that it refuses to acknowledge the legitimacy of alternative perspectives and thereby to make space for pluralism, for the freedom of thought. The American framers understood Christian orthodoxy to be a prescriptivism that insists on its normative account of Christianity as the only and infallibly true perspective on the world. A nation that endorsed the policing of Christian orthodoxy could therefore only lead to a society structured by the violent suppression of the heterodox, an idea that seems to delight more than a few among today's Religious Right.

Whatever its faults – I will turn to those in a moment – liberalism is an attempt to deal with irreconcilable ideological differences at the societal level, and one way to deal with these differences is to distinguish, however simplistically at times, between religion and politics. Naturally, this places liberalism at odds with a rule of faith, at least at the institutional level. John Jay (1745–1829) wrote in his charge to the

Grand Jury of Ulster County, following the recent adoption of the New York Constitution of 1777, that "no opinions are dictated; no rules of faith prescribed; no preference given to one sect to the prejudice of others."[30] Privately, Jay's views were not all that dissimilar from Wilberforce. In an 1816 letter to John Murray, Jay expressed his opinion that peace would "prevail among all nations" if they all had Christian rulers like "our Christian nation," because "*real* Christians will abstain from violating the rights of others, and therefore will not provoke war."[31] Such was not the view of Adams. When John Quincy Adams, who expressed interest in both Calvinism and the ancient creeds, wrote his Unitarian father in January 1816 about his openness to the idea of the Bible as the "rule of faith" (and thus of God as trinity), the elder Adams, pointing out the diversity of texts and their discrepancies, replied with undisguised derision: "'*The Bible a Rule of Faith.*'! What Bible? King James's? The Hebrew? The Septuagint,? [*sic*] The Vulgate? ... Which of the thirty thousand Variantia are the Rule of Faith?" Adams further cast scorn upon orthodox doctrine: "An incarnate God!!! ... My Soul Starts with horror, at the Idea, and it has Stupified the Christian World. It has been the Source of almost all the Corruptions of Christianity."[32] The reference to corruptions indicates that Adams, like other Unitarians, did not reject a prescriptive account of religion entirely. Rather they rejected the doctrinal rule of faith and replaced it with a moral rule of faith. As Adams declared in his 1825 letter to Jefferson, "the substance and essence of Christianity as I understand it is eternal and unchangeable and will bear examination forever but it has been mixed with extraneous ingredients, which I think will not bear examination and they ought to be separated."[33] Akin to the Unitarian minister Theodore Parker thirty years later, the eternal essence of Christianity for Adams was found in the moral teachings of Jesus, whereas the later orthodox doctrines were the "extraneous ingredients" that he thought should be discarded. Adams, like Locke and Jefferson, believed that orthodox Christianity, with its doctrinal accretions and the "culture of authority" (*Autoritätskultur*, to use Troeltsch's term) necessary to enforce these doctrines, was incompatible with a liberal social order, but it could be made compatible once stripped back to its moral essence.[34]

Cutting religion down to size has the virtue, in theory, of fostering a pluralistic society, but it can also have the effect of silencing any religious critique of the sociopolitical order. When David Osgood, minister at the Unitarian Church of Medford, Massachusetts, preached a discourse against Jefferson on April 8, 1810, Boston postmaster Aaron Hill sent it to Jefferson, calling it a "political sermon" that had substituted "federal prints" – referring to the federalist newspapers that Osgood apparently favored – "for the Bible as rule of faith & practice."[35] The implied assumption seems to be that, had Osgood kept the Bible alone as the rule of faith, he would not have preached a political sermon against the president, which assumes the Bible is not already deeply political. Indeed, Osgood based his sermon on the story of Absalom usurping David's throne in 2 Samuel 15. Osgood thus transgressed a cardinal rule of liberal society: as George Washington (1732–1799) said to a group of universalists in 1790, "in our nation, however different are the sentiments of citizens on religious doctrines, they generally concur in one thing, for their political professions and practices are almost universally friendly to the order and happiness of our civil institutions."[36] Religious communities are thus expected to play nice with the civil institutions in exchange for the free exercise of religion. But this presupposes that one's free exercise will not undermine the order of these institutions.

Of course, it is one thing for a minister to criticize a president for having a pro-French bias, as Osgood did, and quite another to criticize him for enslaving people. It is impossible to overlook the fact that, with the notable exception of the Adams family, most of the other founders were enslavers who were willing participants in the creation and maintenance of what Paul Finkelman has called "a slaveholders' republic."[37] The sectional crisis over the future of the slave system, in which each side claimed to represent God's will, is the most well-known instance of the politicization of Christianity. As Mark Noll has observed, the Civil War was a "theological crisis."[38] But the crisis for Christianity in the Americas goes back much further to its settler-colonial origins. According to Katharine Gerbner, the slave system was something to which Christianity adapted itself, as Christians involved in the colonial enterprise embarked on their own quest to rethink the norms of Christianity in a way that could accommodate enslaving people. Initially this involved what Gerbner calls "Protestant Supremacy," an early version of white supremacy in which one's identity as a Protestant marked one as superior to others.[39] In seventeenth-century Barbados, the definition of Christian underwent a change. Whereas in the 1640s the term "Christian" referred to a doctrine or belief, by the 1660s "Christian" became "shorthand for 'nonslave'" and was increasingly "used as an ethnic indicator."[40] The doctrine of Protestant Supremacy that arose in this period established a religious caste system that ranked people based on their religious belonging, with magisterial Protestants having mastery, followed by non-conforming Protestants, Jews, and Catholics, while "heathen" slaves were excluded from the established Protestant churches.[41] Those Christians who embraced this normative vision refused to evangelize the enslaved population, since conversion to true Christianity was incompatible with one's status as a slave. As the free Black population grew, however, the religious caste system became a racial caste system, with "white" replacing "Christian" in the 1690s as the indicator of mastery.[42] The resistance to baptizing slaves changed later with the evangelical awakenings, as missionaries and evangelists like George Whitefield and George Fox denounced the norm of Protestant Supremacy in an effort to Christianize and reform slavery, arguing for their position on the grounds that all people are spiritually – though not socially – equal before God and capable of conforming to the moral and spiritual norms of the gospel. Unwilling to apply the doctrine of spiritual equality to the question of earthly equality, these revivalists redefined the norms of Christianity again to accommodate the conversion of all without challenging the slave system. The result was a theology of "Christian Slavery" that reconciled the norms of Christianity with perpetual bondage and brought "slaves within the Protestant community."[43]

All of this provides crucial background for the later controversy over "political preaching" that broke out in the antebellum United States. The dispute provides one of the most pointed examples of the challenge Christian critics of the civil institutions often face in trying to correct distortions of the Christian essence, made all the more difficult in the case of the sectional crisis because the essence of Christianity (as well as the essence of Americanism) had previously been adapted to the Atlantic slave trade and the American slaveocracy. The settler-colonial slave system had already constructed both religion and politics, thus stacking the deck against abolitionists and other reformers. When the system Christians are criticizing as immoral or unchristian is protected by the rule of law, then any appeal to a religious rule, such as the Bible, can be criticized as an illegitimate politicizing of the faith, while the conservative defenders of those institutions can be equally political without talking about politics at all. As Congregationalist minister and Christian abolitionist George B. Cheever (1807–1890) observed, abolitionists were charged with bringing politics into their sermons when they preached against slavery, while the enslavers they were preaching against "would be glad to find some support of slavery, some shield for it in God's word." Indeed, if a person used the Bible to proclaim that slavery is right, "he might do *that* from the pulpit *ad infinitum*, and they would not regard it at all as political preaching, but as simply the genuine meekness of wisdom preaching peace by Jesus Christ, and the very perfection of gospel conservatism."[44] Cheever recognized just how specious the line between religion and politics often was, and how this line could be used to serve the interests of white supremacy. "The moment any sin passes from the individual to the nation, and is sanctioned by law," he observed with wry irony, "then instantly the speech against it is branded as political preaching." To authorize any violation of religious norms, "you have only to make it legal and national, and you have given it a tabernacle."[45] That is to say, if you move something across the line from religion to politics, it becomes ostensibly immune to religious critique – or at least this is how white supremacists treated denunciations of the sin of slavery.[46]

Those ministers and theologians who supported the slave system could comfortably remain what they regarded as being "nonpolitical." Southern Presbyterians – as well as many Northern Presbyterians – referred to the "spirituality of the church," the term they gave the doctrine that the church's business was purely spiritual, as opposed to the civil and political matters that were the business of the state. James Henley Thornwell, the foremost Southern defender of the church's spirituality, claimed – in a speech on African colonization – that the church is "exclusively a *spiritual* organization" and "has no mission to care for the things . . . of this world," a convenient position to hold for someone who viewed the conflict between enslavers and abolitionists – like every culture warrior since – as a conflict, respectively, between "Christianity and Atheism."[47] The doctrine of the church's spirituality was hardly limited to Presbyterians, though Marcus McArthur points out that "most other denominations did not have a specific name for this doctrine."[48] For many, the idea that church and state operated in separate spheres and should not interfere with each other was largely taken for granted. As Luke Harlow notes, Southern evangelicals dating back to the colonial era "had refrained from wielding religion in direct political engagement, believing the church to be a purely spiritual institution that should not meddle with the purely secular affairs of state."[49] McArthur calls this "apolitical theology," but such a term privileges the insider perspective of those making these claims. It would be more accurate to call it *status-quo theology*. We could also call it *cultural-exile theology*, since advocates of this position understood themselves to be at odds with the dominant political culture and tended to cultivate a persecution complex. In any case, these preachers were hardly neutral in their commitments. As McArthur observes, "the doctrine came to be intimately connected to proslavery religion," and these ministers "increasingly employed it in their opposition to numerous Northern social reforms, especially slavery." Given their support of the slave system, the preachers naturally "found the doctrine consistent with their interpretation of the Bible and useful in their argument for the peculiar institution" – that is to say, *politically* useful. "If the church was strictly a spiritual institution," they argued, "then the clergy were responsible only to preach the Bible, which they believed included slavery in the divinely ordained social order, leaving the question of the legality of slavery to its proper sphere – the state."[50] Their belief that the essence of Christianity was spiritual was also ecclesiastically useful, as it allowed the Southern Presbyterians to claim that the schism in the Presbyterian church was the fault of the Northern Presbyterians for their politicization of the church – as if those in the South were simply morally principled Christians holding fast to the historic orthodoxy of the Reformation and did not have a vested political interest in the divide.

McArthur is right, in one sense, to point out that this status-quo theology was a "preexisting doctrine" that predated the sectional crisis, though this hardly absolves the doctrine of its connection to the slave system, much less makes it any less political.[51] Insofar as we can trace it back to the magisterial Protestant reformers, it was a doctrine tailor-made to curry favor with the imperial rulers who could provide the reform movement with political protection – hence the *magisterial* nature of this Protestant tradition, in distinction from the Radical Reformation. Historian Jack Maddex has argued more pointedly that antebellum Southern Presbyterians "were proslavery social activists who worked through the church to defend slavery and reform its practice."[52] Presbyterians (as well as most Protestants) in both the North and the South were theocrats who, like Wilberforce, believed that the nation ought to be guided by Christian norms.[53] The "apolitical" or status-quo theology was primarily found among conservative Christians in the border states (the subject of McArthur's study) who tended to be proslavery but also antisecession. Abolition and secession were the "twin heresies" that had to be rigorously opposed by what they regarded as true Christianity.[54] In the wake of the North's victory, Southern Presbyterians adopted the "spirituality of the church" doctrine because it suited their narrative of moral self-righteousness over against the politicized North and provided them with a way to rebut Northern claims that they had "formed a 'political alliance' with slavery."[55]

But it was not only the South that found refuge in this doctrine. In 1887, a decade after the end of Reconstruction, the General Assembly of the Northern Presbyterian denomination declared its unanimous agreement with the Southern assembly regarding "the spiritual or non-political character of the Church," meaning that the church is "entitled to speak only where [Christ] has spoken, and to legislate only where he has legislated."[56] What this meant in practice was a willingness to tolerate racial injustice (i.e., to view theological consensus as more important than social equality), as seen in the reunion of the Northern church with the Cumberland Presbyterians in 1906 despite the fact that the Cumberland church included racially segregated presbyteries.[57] Even so, the spirituality doctrine did not have the same force in the North as it did in the South. The same year the Northern church declared its agreement with the South in fact marked the initial unraveling of the consensus around the church's spirituality, as Presbyterians in both North and South began to campaign against intemperance and express support for prohibition policies. At the same 1887 General Assembly, James H. Baird brought a complaint against the Synod of

Pennsylvania for endorsing a prohibition amendment, but the assembly ruled that it was not in violation of church doctrine.[58] In the South, where the spirituality doctrine was far more entrenched, most remained opposed to any church action regarding prohibition for the same reason they opposed abolitionism, a point that becomes clearer if prohibition is seen, as Mark Lawrence Schrad has argued, as a "progressive shield for marginalized, suffering, and oppressed peoples to defend themselves from further exploitation."[59] Ultimately, even the Southern Presbyterians came to soften their position on the apolitical nature of Christianity by 1910, when the denomination ruled against W. I. Sinnott, in his complaint against the Presbytery of North Alabama for their support of an Alabama prohibition amendment – an echo of Baird's earlier complaint in the Northern church.[60] When it suited their social agenda, therefore, those Christians who had previously claimed to be apolitical were willing to abandon commitment to the church's spirituality. If, following Maddex, we see the spirituality doctrine as a thoroughly, albeit implicitly, political doctrine serving the interests of theocratic Christians who wanted to see the society molded according to certain moral norms, then the strengthening or softening of the doctrine in accordance with the winds of cultural change is precisely what we would expect to see.

In the 1940s and beyond, the spirituality doctrine was used in the South to suppress church support for desegregation and the civil rights movement, even leading the Presbyterian Church in the United States (PCUS) to disapprove of participation in the 1963 March on Washington for Jobs and Freedom.[61] Increasing resistance to the old ecclesiology – and the status-quo theology underpinning it – led to the formation of A Fellowship of Concern in 1964, which declared, as one of its principles, the goal of seeking "a more vital role in the struggle for social justice."[62] They were opposed by a group that called themselves Concerned Presbyterians, who insisted the church should stick to a purely spiritual mission of saving unbelievers. Concerned Presbyterians also rejected the Fellowship's proposal to reunite with the Northern denomination, the United Presbyterian Church in the United States of America (UPCUSA), which southern Presbyterians viewed as overly "political," meaning overly invested in matters like racial integration. By the 1970s, the Concerned

Presbyterians were actively planning to secede from the PCUS, even pushing for a reunion vote in 1972 as an excuse to break with the denomination. The following year a group of conservative Presbyterians gathered in Birmingham to form the Presbyterian Church in America (PCA), stating their support for the spirituality of the church and their opposition to union with the UPCUSA.[63] By this point in the story, it should be clear that what counts as "political" versus "spiritual" is itself a deeply political – as well as theological – question, one rooted in the politicized struggles over defining the norms of Christianity itself.

Status-quo or cultural-exile theology in the present is no more limited to Presbyterians than it was in the 1860s, but many of the leading representatives are associated with the Presbyterian splinter denominations: both the Orthodox Presbyterian Church (OPC) that broke away in 1936 due to the fundamentalist-modernist controversy and the PCA that formed in 1973 – in each case to defend what they regarded as "historic orthodoxy" and "true, spiritual Christianity." Westminster Seminary California (WSC) is a particular hub for this theology. David VanDrunen, a former OPC pastor and current professor at WSC, is the most notable proponent of what he calls "two kingdoms" theology, arguing that the work of the Christian is not to redeem or transform culture but instead to "recognize that for the time being they are *living in Babylon* . . . as sojourners and exiles in a land that is not their lasting home."[64] McArthur, who is on staff at WSC, has written for *The Gospel Coalition* in defense of "apolitical theology," arguing that Christians today should "be cautious" about engaging in politics in light of the Civil War–era ministers in both the North and the South who "stoked the war's fires through political preaching" – implying that "both sides" are to blame.[65] They represent an alternative to the Kuyperian neo-Calvinist model of cultural transformation that advocates a single kingdom of God over all the various spheres of life, a position that has found a home among a broad range of American evangelicals who were inspired by Francis Schaeffer to overcome the fundamentalist isolation from cultural engagement.[66] A weaponized version of Kuyper's Christian worldview, which claims there is an "antithesis" between the Christian and modern worldviews, became the template for the brash and aggressive orchestrators of the Religious Right movement – such as R. J. Rushdoony, notorious for the dominionist theology of Christian Reconstruction – who operated out of an unshakeable conviction that the world would be better if it were remade in their own image.[67]

Whereas the "apolitical" spirituality of the church was once an effort to maintain the ecclesiastical and political status quo (including slavery and segregation), the current interest in the church's spirituality stems from a rejection of the activist work of today's mainline Protestant churches as well as a protest against the rapid changes in sociocultural norms, especially those related to gender and sexuality. As postwar society has become more thoroughly political and polarized, a point documented by Lilliana Mason in her work on how politics became our identity, status-quo theology has become more explicitly a cultural-exile theology, expressed by some through a longing for a supposedly less political past – meaning a time when the politics of conservative Christians was reflected more in the society and media (e.g., "Make America Great Again").[68] The pining after a version of the nation in which these Christians were superficially able to be apolitical is how a person can espouse the spirituality of the church one moment and militant Christian nationalism the next. "True Christianity" too often seems to mean "one kingdom" when Christians have cultural power and "two kingdoms" when they do not.

In Chapter 3, on the cultural essence of Christianity, I argued that defining the rule of faith in cultural terms leads to one of two options where the relation between religion and society is concerned: either *separatism* (church and society represent two permanently opposed cultural worldviews) or *imperialism* (the church can absorb other cultures into its own). Something similar proves to be the case in the context of what I am describing as the political essence of Christianity. The history of antimodern, counterliberal Christianity's relationship to politics within American liberal society follows the same pattern, much as we would expect given the connection between culture and politics. The first option is the path of a *two-kingdoms separatism*, represented especially by the claim that the church is an apolitical institution concerned strictly with the spiritual business of preaching the gospel of salvation. The second option is the path of a *one-kingdom imperialism*, characterized by the conviction that Christians are called to redeem the civil order in accordance with the Pauline injunction to "take every thought captive to obey Christ" (2 Cor 10:5) – a claim frequently invoked by Christians who take this approach.[69] Both paths involve a political rule of faith, the protests of the former group notwithstanding. Put in political terms, the first path advocates what we might call an *exilic politics*, while the latter promotes a *redemptive politics*. (Besides its theological resonance, the language of "redemption" was the term that Southerners gave their policy of ending Reconstruction and restoring white supremacy in the late nineteenth century.)

Rather than representing two mutually exclusive theologies, it is rather the case that American religious discourse alternates between these two approaches depending on the ends to which they are put. Kathleen Sands describes these theologies as different forms of religious rhetoric: separatism represents what she calls "wall rhetoric" (as in the "wall of separation"), while imperialism represents "foundation rhetoric." Christians who object to churches being forced to abide by COVID-19 mask mandates employ wall rhetoric, but those same Christians may call for a Christian America, thus engaging in foundation rhetoric.[70] There is no contradiction here from the perspective of these Christians, because both forms of theological rhetoric stem from the conviction that Christianity is a particular culture, whose theological and political norms ought to be protected and empowered against whatever one perceives as a threat.

Despite the differences in their practical implications, both politicizations of the Christian essence share two fundamental features that pertain to the identity and normativity of Christianity. First, both presuppose a strong church-world binary, in which the (antimodern, counterliberal) church stands in contrast to (modern, liberal) society. This opposition can be a permanent conflict, as in the separatist model, or it can be a temporary one in the imperialist model – temporary only because the church eventually subsumes the world until everything is the church. Second, both view themselves as the representatives of classical orthodoxy and historic Christianity, the inheritors of the true faith. Like the doctrinal and cultural rules, the political rule thus defines "true Christianity" in opposition to an Other – liberal Christianity, other religions, cultures, or worldviews, even the world as a whole – and constructs a political identity built around this opposition. It would be far too much to attempt to survey the history of counterliberal Christian politics in the United States, and others have already done this work. In what follows I instead will focus on two key parts of this history that pertain to the construction of a normative Christian identity designed to buttress a reactionary politics: first, the formation of a global Christian identity by means of a politicized ecumenism and, second, the formation of a historic (and heteronormative) Christian identity through the construction of a politicized gnosticism as the perennial enemy of the true faith.

THE WAR ON CHRISTIANITY: CONSTRUCTING A GLOBAL CHRISTIAN IDENTITY

"Missouri will ever be conspicuous in the annals of history as the only State in the American Union to inaugurate and authorize a formal opposition to Christianity, as an institution, and legalize the persecution of ministers of the gospel, as a class." So wrote the Reverend William M. Leftwich in his 1870 hagiographic account of *Martyrdom in Missouri*, a two-volume work dedicated to the "moral heroism" of the "martyrs of Missouri" who stood up for "a pure, unsecular Christianity," referring to ministers in the Union who, during the Civil War, refused to declare loyalty to the cause of the North.[71] The use of martyr language was hardly limited to the Christians in the border states who were accused of disloyalty. Southerners latched on to the martyr motif in their construction of the Lost Cause myth. A month after Robert E. Lee died, his widow wrote to Lee's cousin that the late Confederate general was "now only the Hero of a lost cause, yet as the blood of the Martyrs built up the Church so may the sacrifice of this Martyr yet produce fruit for his country that we know not of" – a reference to the famous line by Tertullian often loosely translated as: "The blood of the martyrs is the seed of the Church."[72] Likewise, in 1871, Wade Hampton, the Confederate officer and later one of the "Redeemers" who restored white rule in the South, described Jefferson Davis – who was very much alive and had recently been released from prison – as a Christ figure who "lived to bear vicariously for us in his own person, with the sublime endurance of a martyr, the sufferings, the humiliations, the wrongs of the whole South."[73] Not only was every fallen Confederate soldier "a martyr for the truth," but all Southerners "were holy because martyrs like Davis had redeemed them." Later, when Confederate monuments began to be erected around the South, there were speeches about honoring the "blood of the martyrs."[74] Such an explicit fusion of religious and political identity was hardly new, but the Civil War radicalized this way of thinking in the American context – in both the South and the North.

As the infallibility of the Bible and the certainty of Christian doctrine became the subject of dispute, an increasingly reliable indicator of whether a person was a true Christian was whether they experienced persecution. Jason Bruner has traced how persecution became a criterion for true Christianity over the course of the twentieth century, becoming in effect a moral or practical rule of faith that superseded doctrinal and cultural differences to construct a global body of Christians defined by their experience – real or, more often, imagined – of oppression. The use of martyrdom as the norm for Christianity marks a clear distinction from the role that martyrdom played in the ancient church. To be sure, martyrdom was certainly used in early Christianity to identify true Christians. As Bruner notes, "Eusebius worked to separate true Christianity from what he believed were aberrations and heresy by compiling dramatic snapshot accounts of Christian martyrs from across the Roman world."[75] But for everyone from Eusebius to John Foxe, a person did not count as a martyr simply because they suffered for their faith; a person counted as a martyr only if they met the prescriptive, doctrinal conditions of orthodoxy. "One Christian sect's martyrs were another's illegitimate, foolish dead," Bruner observes. During this time there was no "common Christian identity that transcended what were held as fundamental theological schisms."[76]

A decisive change had taken place by the time of the Hamidian massacres of Armenian Christians that occurred in the Ottoman Empire in the mid-1890s. To understand why the response to this event was so different, it is necessary to understand these events against the backdrop of both (a) the nineteenth-century missionary movement that created an "informal spiritual empire" by globalizing Protestantism[77] and (b) what Ian Tyrrell has called "America's moral empire," referring to the informal expansion of American moral and cultural institutions and influence between the 1880s and the 1920s that "either occurred through the work of missionaries or mimicked the missionaries."[78] During this period there was a synergy between the emergence of a Protestant reform movement that aspired "to create a more Christian and moral world" and the rise of American imperialism and colonialism that sought to expand American influence through the acquisition of territories and the spread of Americanism.[79] These efforts at moral and cultural imperialism piggy-backed on the missionary societies that had already established trans-national networks of communication and influence, beginning in the early nineteenth century with groups like the American Board of Commissioners for Foreign Missions (ABCFM), founded by Congregationalists and Presbyterians in 1812. The ABCFM, as Bruner notes, had been sending missionaries to the Ottoman Empire since the 1820s with the goal of converting the supposedly "nominal" Christians who resided there – including the Armenian Orthodox, Melkite Greek Catholic, and Chaldean Catholic – to American evangelicalism. When the massacres occurred, however, the ABCFM "attempted to leverage a common Christian identity over and against an Islamic threat in order to motivate a broadly Christian public in the United States and Western Europe to aid in the plight of the Eastern Christians."[80] To do so required "a new way of imagining Christianity worldwide," one that did not depend on "doctrinal agreements or personal testimonies of conversion to determine who might be regarded as truly Christian."[81] Instead of using a rule of faith to determine shared identity, this new imagination defined Christianity in terms of being targeted for persecution based on their religion. People who would not have otherwise been regarded as Christian by Protestant evangelicals were suddenly regarded as truly Christian on account of persecution. The very people who had been the target of missionary activity were now fellow Christians. The result of this process was "an internationalized vision of a common Christian identity that extended beyond tradition."[82] This new shared global Christian identity was neither doctrinal nor cultural, but instead what we might call moral – and as the experience and endurance of suffering became weaponized domestically, the identity also became political.

The weaponization occurred with the rise of the anticommunist movement in the interwar and especially postwar periods.[83] This took place at the same time that American neoorthodoxy was seeking to Christianize America through biblical theology, which was also when American Christians more generally began to embrace constitutional nationalism. Globalism, and global ecumenism in particular, was already in the air, with the establishment of the United Nations in 1945 and the World Council of Churches (WCC) in 1948. Moreover, the "political mobilization" of Protestant churches had already occurred in the late nineteenth and early twentieth centuries through the missionary societies that put American denominations in touch with global politics, as seen in the situation of the ABCFM above.[84] The politicization of the mainline missionary movement occurred through the work of the Federal Council of Churches (FCC), which advocated for universal human rights and desegregation, but the more the ecumenical leaders promoted "this liberal agenda for domestic and foreign affairs, the more they angered the evangelicals."[85] The evangelical response was to mobilize politically by forming alternative alliances and constructing new moral and political versions of Christian identity that broke with the standard confessional, denominational, and institutional markers found among the ecumenical Protestants.

Beginning in the late 1940s – in the midst of what Matthew Bowman calls "an age of religious anxiety," when American evangelicals were concerned about the growing specters of communism abroad and materialism at home – "a generation of young fundamentalists trooped overseas to win the world for Christ," picking up where the mainline Protestants had left off and laying the groundwork for what Andrew Preston has termed "evangelical internationalism."[86] The evangelical global mission movement, which climaxed with the Lausanne Congress of 1974, was never a purely spiritual effort to "save lost souls," but was an integral part of a developing "evangelical foreign policy lobby," as described by Lauren Turek.[87] Evangelizing the world was part of a coordinated effort to defeat communism and had all the urgency of a global war, one where the missionaries were God's soldiers battling the ever-present forces of evil. The anticommunist movement included popular evangelists like Billy Graham (1918–2018) and Billy James Hargis (1925–2004) as well as more expressly political activists like Fred Schwarz (1913–2009), founder of the Christian Anti-Communism

Crusade.[88] The evangelical foreign policy lobby argued for human rights as well, but as Turek points out, evangelicals largely reduced this to the right of religious freedom, and especially the freedom to evangelize.[89] The simplification of the agenda also facilitated its weaponization. "Christian America," with its providentially ordained Constitution, became the beacon of religious freedom, while communism became the all-purpose symbol for the denial of freedom. The spiritual battle-field was thus at the same time a political battlefield.

By so focusing on the need for freedom of religion, evangelicals ended up constructing an account of Christian identity based around the *lack* of such freedom: true Christians were the ones who were denied the freedom to practice their faith. This new political rule allowed evangelical internationalists to identify a global body of genuine Christians without having to verify this identity using the traditional metrics of doctrine, culture, church membership, or individual conver-sions. A person was a true Christian if they believed themselves to be a victim of a war on Christianity – whether they were or not was irrelevant. Internationally, this included those Christians who belonged to the so-called underground church and were suppressed by communist regimes.[90] The most explosive version of this was the Romanian Lutheran pastor Richard Wurmbrand (1909–2001), who had been imprisoned and tortured off and on between 1948 and 1964 for preach-ing against communism and in favor of Christianity. He fled his native Romania and came to the United States in April 1966. On May 6, he testified before the US Senate, taking off his shirt to show his scars: "I show to you the tortured body of my country, of my fatherland, and of my church, and they appeal to the American Christians and to all freemen of America to think about our tortured body. . . . You cannot be a Christian and praise the inquisitors of Christians."[91] The following year Wurmbrand published the runaway bestseller *Tortured for Christ* and formed the organization Jesus to the Communist World, later renamed The Voice of the Martyrs (VOM).

Wurmbrand, as Bruner points out, characterized imprisoned Christians as having a purer and more authentic faith like the Christians of the early church, defined not by the Bible or doctrine but simply by the experience of persecution, which "erased history, making context irrelevant."[92] Persecuted Christians throughout history were united in a kind of spiritual ecumenism, defined by the suffering Christ: "Those who experience persecution that is related to their Christian faith, community, or identity are therefore determined to have had genuine faith, regardless of the tradition or denomination they might belong to."[93] Wurmbrand contrasted the true faith of persecuted Christians outside of the West with the compromised faith of Western Christians who had grown comfortable and indolent. Those Christians in the United States who wanted to have a genuine faith needed to experience their own persecution, which they readily found in the cultural, legal, and political shifts that occurred during this time, including the banning of school segregation in *Brown v. Board of Education* (1954), the *Engel v. Vitale* case that outlawed school prayer (1962), and the Civil Rights Acts of 1964 that denied all racial discrimination. That last event led to the decision by the IRS in 1970 – eventually confirmed by the Supreme Court in 1983 in an 8–1 decision – to revoke the tax-exempt status of Bob Jones University because of its complete exclusion of Black applicants due to its prohibition against interracial dating.[94] It was this decision, rather than the legalization of abortion, that led elite activists to mobilize the evangelical Religious Right, as historian Randall Balmer has pointed out.[95] American evangelicals were already primed to see themselves as victims in a war on "historic," "biblical" Christianity, waged by liberal politicians and judges, because of the school prayer decision (and for some because of the Confederacy's defeat), but the loss of the privilege of tax exemption is what galvanized the movement – and continues to galvanize evangelicals, as seen in the fight to repeal the Johnson Amendment. The persecution narrative, having been established during this earlier period at the height of the Cold War, was then easily reinforced later, with cases like *Roe v. Wade* (1973), *Hustler Magazine v. Falwell* (1988), *Lawrence v. Texas* (2003), *Christian Legal Society v. Martinez* (2010), *Obergefell v. Hodges* (2015), and *Bostock v. Clayton County* (2020).

The combination of the "war against communism" and the "war against Christianity" narratives created a conflicting picture of the West, represented for American evangelicals by the United States. According to the anticommunism narrative, the democratic West, ostensible beacon of religious freedom, was superior to the communist non-West. According to the Christian persecution narrative, however, the persecuted non-West was superior to the privileged West. The political mobilization of American evangelicalism arose from the confluence of these two accounts, which generated an idealized definition of the nation as the bearer of freedom and a politicized definition of global Christianity as those denied freedom. This explains why paeans to Christian America occur alongside condemnations of America's attacks on Christianity: the mythical image of God's chosen nation conquering the communist threats to religious freedom is projected into the past like a protological mirror image of the eschatological kingdom of God, serving as a permanently unreachable yet normative vision of both religious and national identity.[96] The call to "make America great again" has always been inseparable from the parallel call to "make Christianity great again." The connection was exemplified by the way Wurmbrand made his appeal before the Senate to "American Christians," encouraging them, and thus the nation as a whole, to identify themselves with those who had been denied religious freedom – and thereby to restore both the nation and the church to their pure, essential natures. To this day, the protological vision of Christian America has proved remarkably effective in mobilizing a broad coalition of antimodern Christian activists. Locating the national ideal in the past allows Christians to declare that *this* is what the nation originally was (and still essentially is), while simultaneously being able to denounce anything they dislike in the present as evidence of a war on their faith. The flexibility of Christian nationalist protology reflects the same strategic flexibility of constitutional originalism, which claims to access the original meaning of the Constitution while being able to freely wield this vision of the past in a political battle against policies and positions that were entirely unknown to the American framers.[97]

Wurmbrand's VOM and related organizations contributed to evangelicalism's increased interest in the global church – not merely as the recipient of American missionary efforts but increasingly also as the source of a more pure and vital Christian faith that can serve as an inspiration to the languid churches in North America. In 1974, the year of the Lausanne Congress, the British missionary Patrick Johnstone, serving at the time in South Africa, published a book called *Operation World* that provided a "brief survey" of the prayer needs of each country with respect to world evangelization.[98] The purpose of *Operation World* was to give Christians anywhere a sense of connection to those in other parts of the world – a connection that was based simply on statistical data and was reinforced through the act of prayer. Ralph Winter, a speaker at Lausanne who was a professor at Fuller Seminary's School of World Mission from 1966 to 1976, and George Verwer, the founder of the evangelical missions agency Operation Mobilisation, helped bring *Operation World* to a worldwide audience, republishing it in 1976 as the *World Handbook for the World Christian*.[99] Beginning in 1978 the book regained its original title of *Operation World*. In 2006 *Christianity Today* listed it as one of the "top 50 books that have shaped evangelicals."[100]

In 1982, drawing in part on Johnstone's work but especially on his own travels, British missionary David B. Barrett (1927–2011) compiled statistics on world Christianity into the *World Christian Encyclopedia* (*WCE*), a work that was expanded in 2001 and revised again in 2020. The *WCE* originated as the sixth edition of the *World Christian Handbook*, an evangelization reference work that was published by the World Dominion Movement – founded in 1923 by the wealthy businessman Sidney J. W. Clark – in five editions between 1949 and 1968, before Barrett was handed the reins.[101] Unlike *Operation World*, the *WCE* was meant to be an authoritative resource on world Christianity, though as Jan Jongeneel and Mark Noll have pointed out in reviews, the data presented in the *WCE*, at least in the second edition, were greatly inflated, seemingly to give a very rosy picture of world evangelism (i.e., domination).[102] Barrett was inclined to count anyone as Christian who had the remotest connection to the religion. According to Gina Zurlo, Barrett discovered through his travel experience "a lack of traditional, institutional unity in Christianity," but instead posited "a new source of Christian unity – ironically, in secular, social scientific methodology." Adopting a *descriptive* rather than prescriptive approach to Christian identity, Barrett defined Christianity in terms of "self-identification in the church."[103] The result was a kind of statistical ecumenism, in which evangelical quants identified many as Christian whom American evangelicals would not consider fellow believers. Perhaps in response to this,

Barrett also created the category of "Great Commission Christian" to refer to people who are not only committed to the faith but also actively contributing to global Christian expansion by obeying the call in Matthew 28:16–20. Such a category seems intended to identify the *truest* Christians, replacing the old pietistic language of being "born again." But even here Barrett was extraordinarily generous: in the 2001 edition of the *WCE* he identifies roughly 62 percent of American Christians, and 85 percent of regular churchgoers, as "Great Commission Christians."[104]

Bruner has identified a similarly loose counting strategy at work in the literature associated with tracking the global persecution of Christians. The quantification of Christian persecution, like the quantification of world Christianity more generally, operates on the basis of an alternative ecumenism to the official ecumenical movement associated with the FCC (later NCC) and WCC. We could justifiably call this a *political ecumenism*, not only because what binds these people together under a common denominator is the experience of being persecuted (typically in the context of political conflict), but also because the quantification of this persecution "has become central to political efforts on behalf of perse-cuted Christians."[105] The connection between these two kinds of quanti-fication (world Christianity and Christian persecution) is hardly coincidental. After publishing the *WCE* in 1982, Barrett moved his World Evangelization Research Center (WERC) from Nairobi, Kenya, to Richmond, Virginia, in 1985. Todd M. Johnson joined WERC in 1989 and became a coauthor, along with George T. Kurian, of the second edition of the *WCE*. Following this, WERC moved to the evangel-ical Gordon-Conwell Theological Seminary and became the Center for the Study of Global Christianity (CSGC), where Johnson served as dir-ector. While Barrett began counting "Christian martyrs" in 1986, the CSGC began tracking annual data more systematically once it was launched at Gordon-Conwell, releasing data on the average number of martyrs each year. The numbers are eye-popping, with an annual average of over 160,000 martyrs in the 1990s and over 100,000 martyrs annually in the first decade of the twenty-first century.[106]

Johnson and Gina Zurlo, coauthors of the 2020 edition of the *WCE*, acknowledge that they take an "inclusive approach" to counting Christian martyrs. They define martyrdom as dying prematurely "in situations of witness," which includes "the individual's entire lifestyle, regardless of whether or not he or she was actively proclaiming at the time of death."[107] Their stated reason for this is to include people like Dietrich Bonhoeffer, Martin Luther King Jr., and Óscar Romero among the martyrs, but it also means that any genocidal or mass killing of a population that the *WCE* counts as Christian (whose numbers are already inflated) counts as a mass martyrdom. As Bruner points out, the CSGC counts as martyrs "*all victims* from the Rwandan Genocide" as well as "a significant percentage of the reported '5.4 million' deaths from the subsequent wars in the Democratic Republic of the Congo (DRC) between 1996 and 2010."[108] Not only does the CSGC use the highest casualty estimates, often far beyond estimates by independent inquiries, but the numerical data obscure the fact that the perpetrators of these mass killings were largely all Christian as well. The stories associated with such figures tend to highlight some non-Christian political threat (e.g., ISIS or Boko Haram), but the figures are only as high as they are because of atrocities that were as much committed by Christians as they were experienced by Christians. If these numbers are supposed to show that there is a "global war on Christians," then we would have to conclude that this has been "*almost entirely* a civil war."[109] Moreover, as in the case of the Hamidian massacres, the people being touted as fellow persecuted Christians are in many instances people that missionaries in the past, and even some in the present, have sought to convert to a supposedly true, evangelical Christianity, on the assumption that their particular form of Christian belief was nominal or unorthodox.

In light of the inflated numbers, the lack of transparency about Christians being the persecutors, and the often arbitrary and opportunistic use of ecumenism, it is difficult to avoid the conclusion that much of the literature regarding worldwide Christian persecution is thinly veiled propaganda aimed at politically mobilizing American evangelicals to lobby the United States government in support of religious liberty policies under the pretense that there is a "global war on Christianity." Sometimes it is not veiled at all. The 1997 book by Paul Marshall, *Their Blood Cries Out: The Worldwide Tragedy of Modern Christians Who Are Dying for Their Faith,* has chapters titled "The Advancing Jihad" and "Communism's Continuing Grip," and then criticizes American

Christians for pursuing "peace at any price," targeting apathetic evangelicals, mainline Christians, and the WCC. Marshall's book is the neoconservative Christian counterpart to Samuel Huntington's *The Clash of Civilizations*, situated between the end of the Cold War and the beginning of the Global War on Terror. In an appendix, Marshall defines religious persecution as "the denial of any of the rights of religious freedom," and in another appendix, titled "The Meaning of Religious Freedom," he stresses that religious freedom includes "the right to *change* one's religion."[110] This leads Marshall to claim that any effort to restrict missionaries and evangelists "from trying to share those beliefs with others" is an act of persecution against Christianity.[111]

As historians of mission have long pointed out, global evangelistic efforts by Western Christians frequently involved "the export of certain elements of U.S. ideology and culture" to the global South, a point that C. René Padilla criticized in his message at the 1974 Lausanne Congress.[112] In many cases the spreading of Americanism (or, in previous generations, some version of Eurocentrism) was done unintentionally out of a naïve lack of awareness of the way Christianity had been enculturated in the West. But in other cases, this cultural imperialism was quite intentional, whether in the transatlantic colonial missions of early modernity or, more recently, in the efforts by American evangelicals to export homophobic policies to African nations – most famously in the case of Uganda's Anti-Homosexuality Bill of 2009, known as the "gay death penalty" bill because of its original provision of capital punishment for "aggravated homosexuality."[113] The bill finally became law in 2014 after replacing the death sentence with a maximum sentence of life in prison, but it was ruled invalid by the Constitutional Court. On May 26, 2023, Uganda's president, Yoweri Museveni, signed into law the Anti-Homosexuality Act of 2023. The new legislation criminalizes speech in support of LGBTQ civil rights and authorizes the death penalty as the maximum punishment for what it calls "aggravated homosexuality."[114] As Zambian pastor and activist Kapya Kaoma has documented at length, "one of the main organizations promoting homophobia in both Africa and the United States over the last decade [i.e., first decade of the twenty-first century] is the Institute on Religion and Democracy (IRD)," a prominent neoconservative think tank founded in 1981 to capitalize on the Reagan Revolution as an opportunity to apply conservative political activism to Protestant mainline churches.[115] After working to oppose African liberation efforts, the IRD later switched to promoting the view that homosexuality is "un-African," exploiting both anticolonialism and homophobia in Uganda and other African nations in an effort to characterize mainline pro-LGBTQ churches "as neocolonialists who are working to destabilize and corrupt African morals."[116] Having fanned the flames of anti-LGBTQ sentiment among global South Christians, groups like the IRD could then point to a shared conservative sexual politics as further indication that white American evangelicals, who opposed the liberalization of American society regarding gender and sexuality, belonged to a global body of marginalized evangelicals that represented the true church. This is the context in which to understand the claim that "Christians are the single most widely persecuted religious group in the world today," as Eric Metaxas wrote in the foreword to *Persecuted: The Global Assault on Christians*, Marshall's latest book on this topic, a book dedicated "to the great principle of religious freedom, known to Americans as the 'first freedom.'"[117] By defining persecution as any restraint on religious freedom – including the freedom of Western missionaries to spread their message of the gospel, whatever else that message might include and regardless of who might be funding them – Marshall, IRD, and other Christian Right organizations created a politicized ecumenism that united global Christians based on the notion of being oppressed by Western liberal elites who supposedly were suppressing the liberty of American evangelists and forcing non-Western Christians to embrace their "gay agenda." Marshall, it is worth noting, happens to be the current chair of IRD's Board of Directors, as of this writing.[118]

It is not hard to see why American evangelicals would support a presidential candidate who sought to undermine the "liberal world order" and who claimed "we're all victims" when liberal institutions, such as democratic voting, did not support him.[119] In May 2017, shortly after Trump assumed office, the Billy Graham Evangelistic Association, led by Franklin Graham, hosted the World Summit in Defense of Persecuted Christians. Originally planned for Moscow, which had become a key hub for global Christian Right activism, the summit was moved to

Washington, DC, after Russia passed the so-called Yarovaya law limiting evangelism to religious settings.[120] In his speech at the summit, US Vice President Mike Pence described Donald Trump as "a champion of the freedom of religion" and said that "the Christian faith is under siege" throughout the world by "radical Islamic terrorists" who harbor "hatred for the Gospel of Christ" and are committing "genocide against people of the Christian faith." Pence went on to say that "the terrorists will not stop until we stop them. And under President Donald Trump, we will stop them." He thus framed the conflict in terms of Christians as the oppressed and Muslim terrorists as the oppressors and presented the US military, with Trump in charge, as the global agent of religious freedom.[121]

After Kansas governor Sam Brownback was appointed by President Trump in 2018 to be Ambassador at Large for International Religious Freedom, the IRD hosted a Global Christian Persecution Summit in Washington, DC on May 10, 2018, for the purpose of "examining why American Christians have failed persecuted Christians overseas and aiming to inject concern for the Persecuted Church into the very DNA of American churches."[122] The summit used the identifying label of "Christian" to construct a theologically amorphous but politically advantageous identity by which those attending the summit could understand the suffering of the global persecuted church as their own. By presenting Christians as "belonging to a single metaphysical community of the body of Christ," speakers at the summit could place ethical and political obligations upon their listeners.[123] In a call to arms, Brownback declared in his opening remarks that "we've got a global religious war going on" and "there is more persecution going on now than ... in any time in history."[124] Such claims had, by this point, become so politicized that there was no longer any meaningful distinction between true Christianity and true Americanism. The struggle to "make Christianity great again" by mobilizing Christians to address this global religious war was simultaneously the struggle to "make America great again," a point that Brownback reinforced by stating that "this [Trump] administration is strongly focused on religious freedom."

The larger goal is not only to remake America but to remake the world, using the catholicity of Christian identity as the basis for the universality of conservative politics. The IRD is but one of many organizations forming what Clifford Bob has called the "global right wing."[125] The "interconfessional partnership" between these organizations constitutes the institutional structure of the new politicized ecumenism – what Andrey Shishkov has termed "conservative ecumenism" or "Ecumenism 2.0." Chrissy Stroop simply calls it "bad ecumenism," but this should not be taken to mean that the old liberal ecumenical movement, what Shishkov calls "classical ecumenism," was therefore good without qualification.[126] The ecumenism pioneered by mainline Protestant liberalism, represented by the likes of John Mackay, in many respects laid the groundwork for the rise of the right-wing cultural revanchism that characterizes the Christian Right in the twenty-first century, as I have shown in previous chapters. One of the key Christian Right organizations forming this new conservative ecumenism is the World Congress of Families (WCF), a group that was founded in 1995, in the aftermath of the Cold War, by the American historian Allan C. Carlson of the Howard Center for Family, Religion and Society in Rockford, Illinois (now called the International Organization for the Family) and the Russian sociologist Anatoly Antonov of Moscow State University for the purpose of promoting "a traditional, heterosexual family model and conservative gender roles."[127] The WCF also played a key role in promoting anti-LGBTQ policies in Africa and held a "pro-family" conference in Nigeria in 2009, the same year Uganda proposed its infamous bill.[128] The WCF exemplifies the way Christian Right NGOs took advantage of the new geopolitical situation to globalize and politicize the culture wars. At the WCF IX gathering in Salt Lake City on October 27–30, 2015, Alexey Komov, the WCF representative in Russia, spoke about how Russians, who had experienced antireligious persecution in the past, were now well-equipped to "help our brothers in the West" resist the "new totalitarianism" of the LGBTQ sexual revolution.[129] A year earlier, an email hack revealed that Komov had discussed with the Russian Orthodox oligarch Konstantin Malofeev his view that "open persecutions against Christians in the West will soon begin." The hack further revealed that Malofeev and Komov believe that pro-LGBTQ rights are leading to the end of civilization because the "sodomization of the world" is destroying the white birthrate.[130] In addition to waging their theopolitical culture war by spreading pro-Russian politics through far-right parties in Europe, Komov and the Russian funders of the WCF proposed countering this global persecution of natalist Christians by working with lawyers from the ADF, one of the leading conservative Christian legal organizations responsible for decisions like *Burwell v. Hobby Lobby Stores* (2014), *Masterpiece Cakeshop v. Colorado Civil Rights Commission* (2018), and *303 Creative LLC v. Elenis* (2023). Organizations like ADF focus on the issue of religious freedom because it allows them to adopt a "persecuted identity" that "sees itself constantly struggling against a secular, antagonistic majority," thereby shifting the narrative from an offensive attack against LBGTQ persons to a defensive protection of a supposed religious minority.[131]

Given such a politicized account of Christian identity, the "persecuted church" has increasingly shaded into the "persecuted right." In the wake of the prosecution of those involved in the Capitol insurrection on January 6, 2021, for example, Republican activists began organizing events valorizing the imprisoned insurrectionists as "martyrs" and "political prisoners."[132] But the shift from religious to political identity with respect to global persecution is most clearly on display in the right-wing reaction to "cancel culture." The very idea of "cancel culture" is part of the same persecution imagination that Bruner analyzes with respect to American Christianity. Like the CSGC's database of global Christian martyrs, there is a Canceled People Database (CPD) that tracks those who have been "canceled" around the world, which includes everyone from a French teacher who was beheaded for showing students a cartoon caricature of the Prophet Muhammad to the actress Gina Carano, who was fired from the Disney show *The Mandalorian* after suggesting that being a conservative in the United States was like being Jewish in Nazi Germany.[133] What binds these people together is the vague sense that they have been "canceled," an identity that the database constructs by placing them together on a list. In an interview on National Public Radio's *On the Media*, Michael Hobbes, cohost of the podcast Maintenance Phase, pointed out that the CPD is an example of how "moral panics ... lump together all of these events that really have nothing to do with each other," much like the way the CSGC lumps together deaths and calls them martyrdoms, or the way Marshall lumps together any infringement on what he regards as religious liberty and calls it persecution.[134]

The categories of "the martyred," "the persecuted," and "the canceled" construct common identities that elide contextual details in an effort to mobilize people to action. This is as true for the Christian right as it is for the political right more broadly. As Alexandria Ocasio-Cortez pointed out in a 2022 interview, "You cannot really animate or concentrate a movement like that [i.e., white nationalism] – you can't coalesce it into functional political power – without a sense of persecution or victimhood. And that's the role of this concept of cancel culture."[135] The identities of the persecuted simultaneously construct the identities of the persecutors: the anti-American (or anti-Christian, which are usually conflated) liberal at home or the communist/jihadist abroad – in both cases typically racialized as nonwhite. While the persecutors are constructed as the racial and ideological Other, the specific identities and histories of the persecuted are largely erased in the name of a color-blind body of authentic, persecuted Christianity or global body of "canceled persons" – those who have been oppressed by the Other, whether religious extremists or woke liberals.

THE WAR ON GNOSTICISM: CONSTRUCTING A CISHETERONORMATIVE ORTHODOXY

In spring 2007, Barrows Auditorium at Wheaton College's Billy Graham Center hosted the annual Wheaton Theology Conference. The topic of that year's conference was "The Ancient Faith for the Church's Future," featuring some of the key names in Protestant *ressourcement*, including Christopher A. Hall and D. H. Williams. The conference itself was a response to "A Call to an Ancient Evangelical Future," a document published in May 2006 by Robert Webber and Phil Kenyon and sponsored by evangelical institutions, including InterVarsity Press, Baker Books, Northern Seminary, and Webber's Institute for Worship Studies.[136] Webber, who began teaching at Wheaton College in 1968, had been the leading evangelical proponent of retrievalism for three decades, beginning in December 1976 when he brought together a committee of evangelicals to establish the National Conference of

Evangelicals for Historic Christianity.[137] The committee gathered to organize a conference held on May 1–3, 1977, in Warrenville, Illinois, for the purpose of producing "The Chicago Call: An Appeal to Evangelicals."

At the conference, all forty-six attendees were given a packet containing three other statements that appeared in the 1970s: the 1973 Chicago Declaration, the 1975 Hartford Appeal, and the 1976 Boston Affirmations. The packet instructed attendees to "study these statements as forerunners to THE CHICAGO CALL."[138] The Chicago Declaration of Evangelical Social Concern, written by a group of fifty evangelical leaders who were organized by Ron Sider on Thanksgiving weekend in 1973, became the creed for the "moral minority" of progressive evangelicals.[139] By contrast, "An Appeal for Theological Affirmation," largely written by Peter Berger and Richard John Neuhaus and signed by twenty-five of the leading postliberals – eighteen of whom were present at the Hartford Seminary Foundation on January 24–26, 1975, where the statement was approved – represented the quintessential antimodern declaration of the late twentieth century. It was, as Shishkov observes, "the forerunner for the current conservative ecumenical initiative."[140] Signers included Avery Dulles, Stanley Hauerwas, George Lindbeck, Richard Mouw, Louis Smedes, and Robert Wilken – a veritable "Who's Who" of the post-Vatican II ecumenical postliberal establishment.[141] The question of what constitutes a normative Christianity was at the center of the Appeal. In a modern version of the ancient anathematization of heresies, the Hartford Appeal identified thirteen "false and debilitating" themes of modern Christianity, beginning with the idea that "modern thought is superior to all past forms of understanding reality, and is therefore normative for Christian faith and life." Similarly, in response to the tenth theme, the Appeal rejected the notion that social, political, and economic welfare programs are "ultimately normative for the Church's mission in the world."[142] The Hartford Appeal thus encapsulated, in one brief statement, the interest in historic Christianity and the separate culture of the church, both of which are implicitly politicized in the statement. The Appeal marked the rise of conservative ecumenism and symbolized the shift from postwar mainline liberalism to the Reagan-era New Christian Right, which did not spring only from fundamentalist and evangelical sources but was a political river fed by tributaries from both the separatist and mainline wings of antimodern American Protestantism. The Appeal led to Neuhaus's founding of the Institute on Religion and Public Life in 1989 and the subsequent publication, starting in March 1990, of what soon became the premier right-wing Catholic magazine, *First Things*.

The statement generated intensely polarized reactions. In a symposium published the following month, Harvard Divinity School theologian Harvey Cox, author of *The Secular City*, denounced it as "the great Hartford heresy hunt" that represented a "bland admixture" of "ecclesiastical triumphalism, two-kingdoms piety, and neoclericalism." The statement "suffers from a pervasive Church/World dualism" due in part to the complete absence of "any Christological center."[143] Gregory Baum identified Berger's commitment to neoorthodoxy, with its sharp distinction between God and the world, as the source of Hartford's antimodern dualism – as seen most clearly in the Appeal's criticism of those who "denigrate God's transcendence."[144] Cox responded by working with the Boston Industrial Mission – an ecumenical ministry to scientists and engineers in the research and development industry, based on the models of the Detroit Industrial Mission and Sheffield Industrial Mission – to produce a counterstatement called "The Boston Affirmations," which rejected "religious spiritualizers" who abandon the world in an escapist retreat into the church.[145] Apart from Cox and Max Stackhouse, however, the Boston Affirmations had little star power compared to Hartford. With the demise of the industrial mission movement, due in large part to the neoliberal financialization of the economy in the 1980s and the corresponding decline of US labor and manufacturing (the Boston Industrial Mission shut down in 1986), there was no institutional voice for the kind of theological concerns represented by the Boston statement. The antimodern postliberalism of the Hartford Appeal became the dominant Protestant vision in the post-Reagan era, embraced in various ways by mainline and evangelical thinkers alike.

It is within this context that we must understand Webber's Chicago Call and the evangelical *ressourcement* movement that followed. On one level, the Chicago Call and the Evangelicals for Historic Christianity who put it together represent the evangelical version of the Oxford

Movement, a comparison that was not lost on the participants. Webber himself noted the similarity in his "behind the scenes" account of the statement, with the exception that, in contrast to John Henry Newman, these evangelicals saw no reason to reject the Reformation. In fact, the authors of the Call, along with the corresponding book titled *The Orthodox Evangelicals*, go out of their way to stress the unity and continuity between the ancient church and Protestant Reformation.[146] But the repeated talk of "the biblical and historic faith" was about much more than simply the emphasis on ancient creeds and orthodox doctrines. The discussion of the Chicago Call belongs in this chapter, rather than the earlier chapter on the retrieval of "historic Christianity," because, like the previous declarations of the 1970s, it was a sociopolitical statement that deployed talk of the ancient faith as a way of countering social and cultural trends.[147] The Call was centrally a reaction against what Webber called the fragmentation and superficial "pop-evangelicalism" that had become dominant, likely referring to the phenomenon of mass media televangelists, such as Pat Robertson (who started in 1961), Jimmy Swaggart (1971), and Jim and Tammy Faye Bakker (1974).[148]

In addition to its internal critique of evangelicalism, the Chicago Call was also an external critique of the secular, liberal world. Some of this was softened in the final version. The original draft of the Call included a section on "A Call to Servanthood and Stewardship" that began by describing the problem: "The world is faced with the demise of the Christian perspective and value system. . . . The holistic Christian world-view has been replaced by a fragmented secularism espousing material-ism, self-interest and personal security. The result of this is alienation, oppression, injustice and suffering in all its forms." In the margin of his copy, Webber had written: "the loss of a norm." Below this, he wrote: "the recovery of the norm." This mention of recovery was in reference to the second part of the statement, which said that "sin is at the heart of all these problems," and thus the church must "subject every ideology to the critical judgment of the gospel" and form a response based on "the historic, biblical faith." In part this entailed "reshaping both private and public life in conformity with the will of God" and "rediscovering and establishing the order and harmony which God has intended for his Creation."[149] Even if the political views of this group were relatively moderate by comparison, such statements were not dissimilar to those of Christian Reconstructionism and anticipated the views of the Moral Majority that began two years later. The original prologue to the Chicago Call framed the entire statement as a response to the fact that "the Church today is confronted by division within, godless secularism without, and urgent human need in the world."[150] While this material was eventually modified or replaced – the section on servanthood became a section on sacramental integrity – these themes and ideas still reverberate throughout the final version.

Crucially, the Chicago Call used claims of "historic continuity" with the ancient church to legitimate its sociopolitical critique. Ancient catholic doctrine served a social function, not only to reject recent developments in evangelicalism as faddish departures from the tradition, but also to ground its particular social agenda as being the "historic consensus." The section on recovering the creeds, for instance, was titled "A Call to Creedal Identity" and was less concerned with specific doctrines or creeds than with the ability of the church to "state its faith over against heresy and paganism" and thereby to exclude persons and ideas that did not conform to its vaguely defined rule for true Christianity.[151] The purpose of this call was to construct contemporary evangelical identity in terms of what I have called historic Christian identity, and in that sense the vagueness of the rule of faith was essential in two respects. First, much like the National Association of Evangelicals or the Moral Majority, it enabled the organizers of the Chicago Call to mobilize a diverse coalition of Christians from various theological and ecclesial traditions. Casting as wide a net as possible in his chapter on creedal identity, Morris Inch narrated the history of this identity in terms of an unbroken continuity from the baptismal formula in the Gospel of Matthew to the Lausanne Covenant of 1975, thereby securing evangelicals' claim to historic Christian identity.[152] Second, the responsibility of a creedal identity is to preserve the purity of that identity against distortion, and the vagueness allowed proponents to exclude whomever they regarded as outside the bounds of the community. Inch stated that "Christian orthodoxy generally appears as a correction of one or another deviation from the truth."[153] Despite whatever misgivings the organizers had about the fundamentalist movement, the Chicago Call stood broadly in the tradition of *The Fundamentals*, which "pioneered a means of creating an evangelical 'orthodoxy' out of an ever-shifting bricolage of beliefs and practices." Like *The Fundamentals*, the Chicago Call created "whatever 'orthodoxy' the present moment required," even if it sought to define this orthodoxy in ostensibly "historic" terms.[154]

The Chicago Call was set against an encroaching secularism, as was fitting given the widespread talk of secularization in the 1960s, but by the time Webber issued his Call to an Ancient Evangelical Future (hereafter CAEF) in 2006, secularization was no longer the concern. Berger, who was one of the key contributors to secularization theory in the years before his work on the Hartford Appeal, announced in 1999 that his earlier assumptions were "false" and "essentially mistaken."[155] The problem was no longer the decrease in religion but the increase in *false* religion. The prologue to the CAEF stated that "today, as in the ancient era, the Church is confronted by a host of master narratives that contradict and compete with the gospel." Webber clarified what narratives he had in mind: "Ancient Christians faced a world of paganism, Gnosticism and political domination." Ancient Christians, he claimed, held to the true faith "in the face of heresy and persecution." The CAEF later reinforced the point by referring to "false spiritualities" like "New Age Gnosticism" that lead to a "dualistic rejection of this world and a narcissistic preoccupation with one's own experience."[156]

The double reference to gnosticism highlights the evolution of antimodern Christianity over the course of the late twentieth century. What began as a war against communism in the post–New Deal era became a war against secularism in the 1960s, which became a war against gnosticism in the wake of the Reagan Revolution and the New Christian Right. Gnosticism succeeded so well as the object of attack because it was such a malleable category, capable of referring at times to completely opposite phenomena. Like communism, gnosticism was associated with progressive politics, but unlike communism, those who attacked gnosticism did not have to work hard to convince people that it was an alternative religion: that job had already been accomplished by early Christian apologists. As the original heresy of the ancient church, it symbolized the enemy of "historic Christianity," and because it had persuasive purchase in both religion and politics, it served the purposes of the New Right coalition.[157]

The rise of gnosticism as the catch-all heresy was a gradual process, beginning largely with the publication in 1952, the year of Eisenhower's election, of *The New Science of Politics* by Eric Voegelin (1901–1985), who was one of the "twentieth-century master painters of liberal disorder."[158] Voegelin, who left Nazi Germany for the United States in 1938, burst onto the scene of conservative political thought with his announcement that "the essence of modernity [is] the growth of gnosticism."[159] Gnosticism, according to Voegelin, was any effort to establish certainty and stability in the midst of the instability of history and could thus lead to opposing agendas: either the disavowal of the world in favor of some mystical, speculative fancy, or the attempt to transform the world into one's future ideal – the latter giving rise to William F. Buckley's famous phrase, "Don't immanentize the eschaton!" Both the cult leader who forms a separatist enclave and the dictator who sends millions to death camps are examples of "Gnostic activists."[160] Any attempt to address the world's problems was thus liable to the charge of gnosticism, and henceforth the conservative political agenda became the protection of the status quo and the obstruction of progressive policies – even though, ironically, today's militant Christian Right exemplifies precisely what Voegelin was criticizing. To be sure, the details of Voegelin's argument were, in Edmund Fawcett's judgment, "unconstrained and hard to follow," but what endured was the idea that gnosticism was the persistent error of human history, beginning at the dawn of Christianity and reaching its apotheosis in modern liberalism.[161] It helped that charges of (neo)gnosticism were proliferating in other spheres. In his 1959 review of Rudolf Bultmann's Gifford Lectures, a young J. I. Packer stated that "Bultmann's own version of the gospel is really a new Gnosticism," a claim that became increasingly widespread with the rise of postliberalism.[162] The British New Testament scholar N. T. Wright popularized this charge against Bultmann but extended it to include whole swaths of modern theology, on the grounds that their work reflected gnosticism's "three-stage narrative" of (1) the sinner prior to the arrival of the gospel, (2) the event of grace and faith, and (3) the renewed Christian living by grace.

If this were true, it would mean virtually all Protestant theology is gnostic – a claim Wright often seems to endorse.[163]

Someone who explicitly made this very claim was the Canadian Presbyterian pastor Philip J. Lee, author of the 1987 work *Against the Protestant Gnostics*. Lee opened his book by referring to Voegelin and others who had explored the gnostic tradition in recent years, but whereas these thinkers (he claimed) viewed the heresy as being "*outside* the Christian community," Lee contended that it was "firmly ensconced *within* the churches," specifically the Protestant churches.[164] Nevertheless, for Lee, gnosticism was still outside *true* Christianity. Throughout the book he lamented the "decline of an authentic Protestantism" in North America, where he claimed gnosticism ran rampant.[165] Lee defined gnosticism in a more conventional way than Voegelin, characterizing the gnostics as spiritual elites who believed they had a saving knowledge that allowed them to escape the world and who disdained the ordinary masses for being bound to materiality. Lee then isolated each component of his definition – alienation, private knowledge, escapism, narcissism, elitism, and syncretism – and used the presence of that component to show how gnosticism was "in ascendance in North America."[166] This method allowed him to lump disparate groups under the same heretical label, even if they did not share every feature of his definition. We see in both Voegelin and Lee the plasticity of the category of gnosticism – a polyvalence that has allowed conservative polemicists to weaponize it against almost any perceived threat. Lee, for instance, finds gnostic tendencies at work in both evangelicals who attack the body as corrupt and libidinal liberals who overly celebrate the body.[167]

That last example regarding sexuality is the most prominent way that gnosticism has been weaponized in recent decades. In the wake of the gay liberation movement and the rise of civil rights victories for LGBTQ persons – along with the challenge to traditional Christian norms regarding gender and sexuality posed by queer theology – one strategy used by antimodern Christians seeking to reinforce a moral and political rule of faith has been to characterize the movement for LGBTQ liberation, especially with respect to transgender persons, as essentially gnostic. In 1982, the postliberal Christian ethicist, Oliver O'Donovan, wrote a pamphlet titled *Transsexualism and Christian Marriage*, which sought to evaluate whether a transsexual (the language of transgender had not yet become standard) could participate in a Christian marriage. O'Donovan answered in the negative, on the grounds that sex-reassignment surgery could not change the given biological sex, and since "the marriage will not be the union of a man and a woman," it thus "will not be a marriage at all."[168] In the course of making this cisheteronormative argument, he asserted that differentiating one's true "sex" – the distinction between sex and gender was not on his radar – from what was assigned at birth was gnostic: "If I claim to have a 'real sex,' which may be at war with the sex of my body and is at least in a rather uncertain relationship to it, I am shrinking from the glad acceptance of myself as a physical as well as a spiritual being, and seeking self-knowledge in a kind of Gnostic withdrawal from material creation."[169]

O'Donovan's statement, one of the earliest pieces of Christian commentary on this issue, spread like a viral meme. A 2003 report by the Church of England's House of Bishops, entitled *Some Issues in Human Sexuality*, quoted this very passage from O'Donovan, as well as the judgment by British psychologist Fraser Watts that O'Donovan's essay was "far and away the best piece of Christian writing about transsexualism."[170] The same report also quoted at length from Christian ethicist Robert Song's work on medical technology, which distinguished between gnosticism and orthodox Christianity on the question of whether "one's true self [is] to be found in separation from or identification with one's body," aligning gnosticism with the former. Medical intervention was permitted when it was "genuinely therapeutic," while attempts to "transcend the created order" were gnostic.[171] Much like debates over what counts as true Christianity, setting up this kind of moral rule of faith thus requires clarifying what counts as *true* therapy. Transgender priest Christina Beardsley wrote a rejoinder to *Some Issues* in 2005, pointing out how "disturbing" it was for the bishops to connect a contemporary issue with an ancient "heresy" and thereby place transgender Christians outside the church as enemies of the truth.[172]

The gnostic meme has nevertheless continued to spread. Kevin Vanhoozer quoted both O'Donovan and *Some Issues* in his 2009 essay for the volume, *Four Views on Moving beyond the Bible to Theology*. In the course of six pages on the "lie" of transsexuality, he asserts that this idea "flirts with a gnostic, even docetic, disregard for bodily reality."[173] On August 3, 2017, *The Times* of London published a letter to the editor by N. T. Wright, who, as bishop of Durham from 2003 to 2010, was part of the House of Bishops when they released their report. The letter was a response to articles by Clare Foges and Hugo Rifkind on the transgender debate, and as someone who was already prone to describing opponents as gnostics, Wright's position was not a surprise:

> The confusion about gender identity is a modern, and now internet-fuelled, form of the ancient philosophy of Gnosticism. The Gnostic, one who "knows", has discovered the secret of "who I really am", behind the deceptive outward appearance (in Rifkind's apt phrase, the "ungainly, boring, fleshy one"). This involves denying the goodness, or even the ultimate reality, of the natural world. Nature, however, tends to strike back, with the likely victims in this case being vulnerable and impressionable youngsters who, as confused adults, will pay the price for their elders' fashionable fantasies.[174]

Others have made the connection to gnosticism without referring explicitly to O'Donovan or the Anglican bishops. Evangelical theologian Peter Leithart described the prohibitions in the state of Washington against transgender discrimination in public restrooms as "invasive Gnosticism."[175] Drawing on the work of Irenaeus, Catholic theologian and media entrepreneur Robert Barron, who at the time was professor at the University of Saint Mary of the Lake and is now bishop of the Diocese of Winona-Rochester, described the "lionization of Caitlyn Jenner" as "an embracing of Gnosticism." Barron's statement prompted a response by the trans Catholic Anna Magdalena Patti, who observed that "the word 'Gnostic' has become to Catholicism what 'Communist' was to McCarthy-era Americans."[176] But not only to Catholics, as we have seen.

Not content with the limited application of gnosticism to the gender identity debate, Catholic natural law theorist Robert P. George claimed in 2016 that all aspects of "expressive individualism and social liberalism" in modernity stem from gnosticism, including "abortion, infanticide, euthanasia, sexual liberation, the redefinition of marriage, and gender ideology."[177] Writing for *First Things*, George lumped all of these together under the label of "gnostic liberalism," making it easy for other antimodern, counterliberal Christians to condemn as heretical anything they regarded as liberal. Five years later, R. R. Reno, the editor of *First Things*, wrote a piece on "gnostic politics," drawing heavily on Voegelin's work to support his rejection of all progressive agendas. For Reno, who was writing during a feverish outcry by conservatives about critical race theory and cancel culture, talk of "liberation," "inclusion," and the singular "they" was essentially gnostic, all part of a sinister "Woke Revolution" sweeping through American life. The quintessential gnostics, according to Reno, were thus the "Woke Revolutionaries [who] preach inclusion while ruthlessly cancelling laggards who fail to keep up with their escalating demands," as if asking people to use one's preferred pronouns were a punishing burden.[178]

The antignostic discourse has become such a mainstream feature of antiliberal politics that even an atheist like James Lindsay, most famous for his part in the so-called grievance studies hoax, frequently uses the term gnostic with respect to "woke" identity politics to bolster his claim that leftist critical theories about race, gender, and sexuality represent a "new religion" that he calls "Social Justice."[179] Framing the left as an alternative religion has made Lindsay popular among the Christian Right, and his New Discourses website is owned and funded by the conservative Christian activist Michael O'Fallon, president of the far-right Christian nationalist group Sovereign Nations.[180] In their book *Cynical Theories*, Lindsay and Helen Pluckrose refer to the "gnostic 'epistemologies'" of "Social Justice" on the grounds that these theories "rely upon feelings, intuition, and subjective experience," as opposed to the supposedly "objective reality" and "objective knowledge" that were pursued by the "old religions," like Christianity and Enlightenment science.[181] As with George and Reno, the term "gnostic" has become a convenient catch-all term to describe any idea about a human person that does not fit within the traditional, orthodox boundaries – what they regard as "objective reality," as if their perspective is the only perspective. By defining any appeal to personal experience as gnostic, Lindsay has created a category that allows him to reject as heretical any viewpoint other than his own: if he acknowledges it, then it must be objective; if he does not, then it must be based on another's subjective feelings. The category is tailor-made to target the LGBTQ community. On June 17, 2022, Lindsay introduced the term "Queer Gnosticism" as part of his campaign to characterize LGBTQ persons as "groomers," another term he popularized.[182] In late December 2022, after being reinstated on Twitter by Elon Musk the previous month, Lindsay began speaking about gnosticism on an almost daily basis, often referring to the "cult of Queer Gnosticism" in order to claim that affirming the LGBTQ community, and especially transgender persons, has nothing to do with secular liberalism but rather involves subscribing to a new religious cult – one that must be opposed in a "world war."[183]

While there is no evidence of an LGBTQ cult, there is ample evidence of the war against it. In the wake of the 2015 *Obergefell v. Hodges* decision that legalized same-gender marriage, the battle over moral norms switched from marriage to gender identity. The same year Robert George wrote about widespread gnostic liberalism, the first state law was passed that prohibited transgender individuals from using the restroom of the gender with which they identify (North Carolina's Public Facilities Privacy & Security Act).[184] An onslaught of similar antitransgender bills soon followed. By 2020 there were 79 antitrans proposals on matters such as athletics, healthcare, and bathroom access. In 2021, the year Reno complained about gnostic politics and the "Woke Revolution," the number of bills nearly doubled to 147 – out of over 250 anti-LGBTQ measures – and a record 13 bills against transgender youth were enacted into law. The number has continued to grow, with over 300 bills in 2022. That year Alabama became the first state to make it a felony to administer gender-affirming medical care.[185] In 2023, the legislative war against LGBTQ persons entered a new phase, with ten anti-LGBTQ laws already on the books across six states and over eighty such bills passing at least one chamber of a state legislature by March 2023.[186]

Many of the antitrans bills are paired with education bills that seek to intimidate teachers and police the access of information available to minors, following and extending the model set by Florida's "Don't Say Gay or Trans" bill and Texas Governor Greg Abbott's directive to teachers and medical professionals to report parents who help their children receive treatments to align their bodies with their gender identity. In Arkansas, for instance, Republican Governor Sarah

Huckabee Sanders signed S.B. 294 into law (now Act No. 237) on March 8, 2023, which bans classroom instruction regarding gender identity and sexual orientation, in addition to sexual reproduction in general and critical race theory. Less than a week later, on March 13, the governor signed S.B. 199 (now Act No. 274) into law, a measure that claims to "protect minors from medical malpractice" by allowing for private lawsuits for "injury" resulting from gender-affirming care, defined broadly as "any physical, psychological, emotional, or physiological injury."[187] In 2022, the Idaho House passed a bill (H.B. 675) that would make it illegal to receive out-of-state medical treatments for trans youth – a ban that echoed a similar bill in Missouri criminalizing out-of-state abortion care.[188] After the bill died in the Idaho Senate, it was replaced in 2023 by H.B. 71, which contains largely the same text banning gender-affirming care but without the out-of-state provision and with additional explanations. The authors of the new bill apparently fancy themselves scientists and philosophers, since they declare, without support or documentation, that "biological sex is an objectively defined category that has obvious, immutable, and distinguishable characteristics."[189] Likewise, the Idaho Senate has passed S.B. 1071, a bill that prohibits instruction on human sexuality, sexual orientation, and gender identity before the fifth grade.[190] The militancy of the effort in Idaho is not surprising given the strong presence of far-right Christian nationalism in the state. In 2020, Idaho became the first state to ban transgender women and girls from playing on sports teams with cisgender women and girls thanks to H.B. 500, the so-called Fairness in Women's Sport Act.[191]

Christian organizations have been central to this political agenda. While the WCF has pursued a more globalist agenda by promoting natalist and heteronormative policies in Eastern Europe, Australia, Africa, and the United Nations, the WCF belongs to a coalition of right-wing Christian organizations, such as the ADF and the American Family Association (AFA), that have focused on promoting a domestic anti-LGBTQ agenda. As Bethany Moreton points out, the "Don't Say Gay or Trans" bills proposed in Florida and other states echoes the 2013 ban in Russia on "gay propaganda," supported and funded by WCF and other Christian Right organizations.[192] The AFA was at the forefront of raising panic about how transgender bathroom rights would lead to sexual predators preying on women and girls. In 2016 they organized a petition pledging to boycott Target over their inclusive bathroom policy.[193] Journalist Imara Jones has documented how the ADF was integrally involved in crafting the antitransgender legislation in Idaho, which became a template for the bills in other states.[194] Idaho House Representative Bruce D. Skaug, who is the managing attorney of Skaug Law and who sponsored the recent bills banning gender-affirming care (H.B. 675 and H.B. 71), has worked closely with the ADF. When transgender athlete Lindsay Hecox brought a lawsuit against Idaho in April 2020 regarding its sports ban, Rep. Skaug joined ADF lawyers to support H.B. 500 by issuing a memorandum in opposition to Hecox, eventually bringing two cisgender female athletes on board to serve as intervenors. The latter complained of losing to a transgender Montana athlete, whom the lawyers misgender and call a "male." As of this writing, the case is still pending.[195]

While the anti-LGBTQ political and legal agenda pursued by groups like WCF and ADF may seem rather remote from the antignostic rhetoric of conservative Christian theologians, the two are indeed linked by Christian Right theorists. Allan Carlson, the founder of WCF and member of the Lutheran Church-Missouri Synod, published his natalist book, *Conjugal America: On the Public Purposes of Marriage*, in 2007. In this work he characterizes the opponents of his "pro-family" politics as the new gnostics, claiming that gnosticism "despises procreation" and "posed a stark danger" not only to early Christianity but also to "our own time as well."[196] Much like Philip Lee, Carlson claims that gnosticism took two forms with respect to sex: one emphasizing sexual license and the other opposing sex altogether. Both of these "devalue marriage," by which Carlson means procreative monogamous heterosexual marriage. He describes the "anti-human fanaticism of the Gnostics" as one of the "sexual disorders" of the ancient world, against which Christianity waged a moral battle in defense of a "new marital morality."[197] Today's proponents of an LGBTQ-inclusive society are bringing back the "Gnostic idea" in "new guise," from which "nothing that is natural, traditional, cultural, religious, social, or moral is safe." Proponents of abortion rights are likewise engaged in heresy, he claims, because abortion "would surely have pleased the baby-hating Gnostics."[198] While the gnostic heresy-hunting focuses especially on gender and sexuality, these are inseparable from the racism and white supremacy that have been central to all forms of American Christianity, particularly evangelicalism. A senior editor at *Touchstone* magazine – which describes itself as a "journal for mere Christianity" and has become the mouthpiece of conservative ecumenism – Carlson wrote a glowing review in early 2022 of Voddie T. Baucham's book *Fault Lines*, which applies the label of "Ethnic Gnosticism" to promoters of critical race theory, who supposedly believe, according to Baucham, that "people have special knowledge based solely on their ethnicity."[199] Carlson, in his review, claims that this "new Gnostic heresy" is "every bit as dangerous as that which almost destroyed the early Christian Church 1,800 years ago" and is now persecuting the church by destroying careers and tarnishing reputations. The clear message, once again, is that these racial and sexual gnostics must be opposed in an all-out religious war to defend true Christianity.

We can see at this point how the discourse around the global war on Christianity intersects with the discourse around gnosticism: talk of a global war frames Christians, particularly those who are supposedly "canceled" within progressive society, as persecuted victims of modern liberalism, while talk of gnosticism frames the supposed persecutors as heretics who must be actively opposed by the true followers of God. The two discourses thus construct an embattled Christian identity by manufacturing a cultural war that legitimates an aggressive response. The former frames this identity in *global* terms, allowing conservative Christians in the United States to appropriate the moral capital and persecuted status of majority world Christians. The latter frames this identity in *historical* terms, allowing Christians to frame their new moral orthodoxy regarding patriarchal cisgender heteronormativity as continuous with the early Christian orthodoxy of Irenaeus and the ecumenical creeds. Both discourses are framed in *martial* terms – one as an unjust war on true historic, biblical Christianity and the other as a righteous war by authentic Christians against its oldest enemy. Such language justifies actual persecution of transgender persons while claiming that the people challenging gender norms were the original aggressors and persecutors. Just as the statistical data on global Christian persecution obscures the way Christians were often the ones committing the violence against other Christians, so too in the culture war against purportedly "gnostic" LGBTQ persons, Christians are frequently leading the charge – often against fellow Christians.

THE NEW WARS OF RELIGION: COALITIONS
OF TRADITIONALIST DISCOURSE

In *After Utopia*, her 1957 analysis of the twentieth-century revolt against the Enlightenment, the political theorist Judith Shklar traced the way romanticism, with its "opposition to all historical and social optimism," planted the seeds of rebellion against modern society that had taken hold in both secular liberal and Christian thought.[200] A key manifestation of this romantic revolt was the rise of what she called "social theology," referring to the interconfessional school of thought that viewed totalitarianism and other sociopolitical ills as the result of a religious decline from a prior golden age, usually located in a nebulous Middle Ages. For thinkers like Emil Brunner, Christopher Dawson, T. S. Eliot, and Jacques Maritain, humankind is essentially religious and the rise of irreligion in the West has forced people to look to secular ideologies for the source of community and meaning. According to social theology, these ideologies are in fact not secular at all but are rather rival religions driven by the single-minded purpose of destroying true Christianity. Communism, Dawson claimed, was the "Kingdom of the Antichrist" in political form and thus "a *counter-church* with its own dogmas and its own moral standards."[201] The apotheosis of this way of thinking was found in Voegelin's claim that "all modern political thought, liberal, socialist, and totalitarian, is descended from a religious heresy, the 'Gnosticism' of Joachim of Floris, and that in their general character *all* political theories since Hobbes are the same, since all are secular religions."[202] The "grand simplicity" of this way of seeing the world boiled down to the claim that we are living in a "new war of religions – possibly the final battle."[203]

While the conservative social theologians laid the blame for this war at the feet of modernity for bringing about the rise of false secular religions, we can instead implicate these social thinkers for creating the war itself, insofar as they constructed the religious framework that interpreted all political conflicts through a theological lens and saw "every reverse in political fortune as a cosmic disaster."[204] Shklar was uniquely perceptive in her analysis, in the way she connected the dots between neoorthodox Protestants, neo-Thomist Catholics, and British Anglo-Catholics, among others. These theologians and philosophers disagreed on various points of doctrine and polity, but they formed an early version of the same conservative ecumenism that has been weaponized by the New Right coalition. Today, instead of Brunner, Eliot, and Maritain, we have Sohrab Ahmari, Patrick Deneen, Rod Dreher, Yoram Hazony, and Adrian Vermeule. What binds together both versions of conservative ecumenism is the "reverence for tradition," which is "not simply social conservatism," though it is that, but also a sense of "historical solidarity" that supposedly unites each generation into a single continuum that forms the "dogmatic basis for conservatism."[205] Ahmari calls this the "unbroken thread" of tradition that purportedly provides the cultural ballast in an "age of chaos." It should come as no surprise that he contrasts this "thread" with gnosticism, which he claims is against all order and tradition.[206] If this religious – or at least philosophical – solidarity is lost, so the theory goes, then all social and political solidarity will naturally crumble. Religious, and especially Christian, traditionalism believes that its institutions and norms are the "natural" state of humanity, according to God's will, and that they are inherently superior to all other institutions and norms.[207]

One way to think about these forms of political ecumenism is by drawing on Maarten Hajer's concept of "discourse coalitions." As Emil Edenborg explains, Hajer's discourse analysis shows "how people who do not fully understand each other and may have fundamentally different ideological outlooks and worldviews" can nevertheless "coalesce around certain shared discursive elements which provide a starting point for political action."[208] A discourse coalition is a group of actors who share "a particular set of storylines over a particular period of time" in the context of engaging in "an identifiable set of practices."[209] The use of shared storylines and metaphors constructs a common narrative that connects allied actors. Hajer's work on environmental policymaking points to the example of "acid rain" as one such storyline. Edenborg applies this theory to the storylines of "traditional values" and "protecting children" that have come to dominate in Russia and the global right wing.[210] Bruner's work points to the storyline of the "global war on Christianity" that shapes so much of today's religious and political discourse. According to Hajer, "discourse institutionalization" occurs when a coalition gains in strength to the point that it compels other actors to adopt the new discourse and takes on institutional form – something that has certainly occurred in the rise of Christian nationalism, the anti-LGBTQ movement, and the efforts to reverse abortion rights, all in the name of defending traditional values and protecting religious freedom.[211] Discourse institutionalization helps explain how people who may not be on board with the most extreme political goals nevertheless participate in the discourse. For instance, it is surely the case that not all who write about the gnosticism of the modern age – such as the benighted think pieces about the gnosticism of transhumanism and virtual church gatherings – are also advocates of antitransgender legislation.[212] But they are unwittingly contributing to a discourse coalition that is actively advancing the aims of anti-LGBTQ activists.

From Shklar's vantage point in the 1950s, Christian traditionalism was the basis for Christian fatalism, a resignation to the destruction of religion and culture. While religious tradition, according to those mid-century conservatives, was the grounds for culture and civilization, it also depended on this culture for its own survival. And since the possibility of re-Christianizing society was seen as obsolete, the only remaining position was despair. Certainly a lot of what Shklar observed remains the same today, in particular the way a certain kind of conservatism and traditionalism has entrenched itself among liberals, both political and religious. Shklar recognized that the problem was hardly limited to the card-carrying fascists and religious fundamentalists, a truth that continues to elude many today.

At the same time, quite a lot has changed since Shklar wrote her first book. We may still live "after utopia," but the traditionalists are no longer in despair about the world. On the other side of the Reagan Revolution and the New Right movement, Christian traditionalists are instead in full militancy mode. Ahmari wrote in 2019 against the polite conservatism that he called "David French-ism," arguing instead that the current "cultural civil war" requires dispensing with civility and engaging in political battle "with the aim of defeating the enemy and enjoying the spoils in the form of a public square re-ordered to the common good and ultimately the Highest Good."[213] The two-kingdoms separatists are a diminishing cohort these days. With the Republican Party remade in the image of Trump, a US Supreme Court biased toward Christians claiming to be persecuted, integralists proudly writing in major media outlets, and global heads of state like Vladimir Putin supportive of the right-wing agenda, those advocating a traditional rule of faith are feeling as bullish as ever.

The revolt against modernity that Shklar analyzed as a "decline of political faith" I have here analyzed in terms of Christian faith – specifically, the essence of Christianity. The precipitous decline of interest in the modern liberal Christian essence was matched by a meteoric rise of interest in an antimodern, counterliberal essence. The doctrinal and cultural forms of this essence surveyed in previous chapters laid the dogmatic basis for the political form of this rule of faith – a rule that claims to have the global church and historic Christianity on its side, and which mobilizes and weaponizes them against the "heresy" of gnostic, liberal society. The new wars of religion, or what Stroop calls the "inter-confessional culture wars," raise profound questions about Christian identity, as each side lays claim to the labels of historic orthodoxy and what Wilberforce called "real Christianity."[214]

This chapter has documented the climax of this antimodern rule of faith, reached in the systematic effort to impose repressive social policies targeting especially gender and sexual minorities in the name of defending Christians from global persecution and advancing the true gospel of Jesus Christ. The tale I have recounted can be best understood as the gradual institutionalization of a discourse coalition organized broadly around the storyline of "making Christianity great again": "great again," because the ideal lies somewhere in a vaguely defined past; "Christianity," because this is a quest for the supposedly true Christian faith; and "making," because this is a religious identity that must be constructed. This coalition comprises a diverse array of theological voices, including the work of John Henry Newman, white Presbyterians and other conservative American Protestants, Karl Barth and his reception by American neoorthodoxy, the biblical theologians and later postliberals, and the fundamentalists and evangelicals who amassed enough political clout to institutionalize their cultural norms. The actors within this coalition were sometimes at odds with each other, but they contributed to an antimodern, fear-driven narrative that bore social and political fruit, some of it unintentional. However benevolent some of these actors were, the storyline they constructed has produced a Christian essence that only reinforces a martial and antagonistic religious identity, one that stands in conflict with a pluralistic society and tends toward precisely the kind of weaponization that has occurred in recent decades. If there is going to be a form of Christian community that can live peacefully in the world while contributing toward a more liberating social existence, then it will be necessary to develop an alternative account of Christianity – an account that abandons the attempt to find a singular "true" prescriptivism. It is to that constructive project that I turn in the final chapter.

Rewriting the Rule

Christianity without Orthodoxy

"**E**VANGELICALS ARE THE NEW LIBERALS**," wrote Samuel Loncar, editor of the *Marginalia Review of Books*, in 2014. "They just don't know it." Loncar wrote these words in a review article reflecting on the histories of mainline Protestant liberalism and conservative American evangelicalism. Placed in conversation, the two histories made it abundantly clear that both groups, often viewed as rival traditions within Protestantism, have been grappling with the same dilemma: how to accommodate modernity without abandoning the essence of Christianity. Evangelicals, along with other traditionalists, think that Protestant liberals failed in this effort "to remain Christian in the modern world." But as Loncar points out, evangelicals "do not realize or openly acknowledge what they are doing." They are convinced they are simply adhering to what they regard as the historic biblical tradition, supposedly unchanged over the many centuries. They believe that "modernity's assimilation is a choice that confronts them rather than a reality that defines them," and so, in the absence of critical self-reflection, they continue to accommodate modernity without any awareness of how modern they are and have always been.[1]

If the previous chapters have demonstrated anything, it is that the conservative attempt to reinforce a traditional Christian identity was indeed thoroughly modern, and not merely because the social and historical pressures to do so were a feature of modernity. The situation goes far deeper. For one thing, the quest for a normative Christianity was originally carried out by liberal Protestants who were sensitive to the new cultural conditions, and it was in reaction to these theological efforts to accommodate modernity that conservative church leaders began to double down on traditionalism. Not only that, but many Protestant liberals – chastened by global war, the work of Karl Barth, and the ecumenical and *ressourcement* movements – began to abandon liberalism in favor of a turn toward the idea of historic Christianity. This shift precipitated various conservative mainline efforts to establish a normative Christian essence that could form the foundation for public Christian witness in the mid-twentieth century. When doctrinal and biblical efforts unraveled, these former liberals (postliberals in retrospect) turned to the concept of culture as the way to achieve this stable identity.

The cultural turn had two main consequences for this story. First, it aligned the religious movement(s) to establish true Christian identity with the broader political movement(s) to establish true American or Western identity, since both identities are defined by their antimodern storyline about the decline of Western society as a result of the modern era. Both identities are thus characterized by their engagement in a culture war – an organized attempt to "make the West great again." The dual quests for traditionalist Christian identity and traditionalist American identity are deeply interwoven, each empowering the other in a feedback loop that has created a situation in which church services are indistinguishable from political rallies and political rallies are indistinguishable from church services.[2] Second, and more surprisingly, the cultural turn aligned the postliberals with the evangelicals who in the meantime had been developing their subcultural networks and building their movement to assume political power. As the evangelicals shed the separatism of their fundamentalist forebears and embraced mainstream status, it became increasingly clear that they would be the ones who carried on the postliberal program of antimodern, countercultural Christianity.

The evangelicals – a term that today refers to an antimodern religious coalition invested in a conservative theopolitical identity – are truly the new liberals, in the sense that they are searching for what it means to be Christian in modernity and often coming up with a variety of answers. But unlike the liberal Protestants of old, the evangelical traditionalists have constructed a very different rule of faith, one that is defined as much by what it opposes in the modern world as by anything that can be found in the tradition. For today's antimodern Christians, the anathemas of the ancient creeds have been largely transposed from naming doctrinal heresies and heretics to naming cultural and political heresies, these being the new markers of religious identity.[3] The anathemas have, moreover, all but displaced the confessional affirmations. The conservative rule is essentially exclusionary: it is primarily an exercise in excluding what (or who) does not belong, whether these are heretical doctrines, foreign cultures, or liberal politics. The antimodern essence of Christianity is purity culture writ large; it is an effort, however fantastical, to keep the ecclesial and political body pure from the taint of modern society.[4]

It would be sufficient for the historian to stop here, for the historical task is to describe what people have done and thought – not to prescribe what people today should think.[5] But as a theologian invested in the question of norms, I began this book by arguing that we need some kind of prescriptivism, and it would be a dereliction of my responsibility to avoid finishing that line of thought. What follows will not provide a specific set of prescriptive norms for others to adopt but will instead explore what *kind* of prescriptivism would be salutary in our present situation – negatively in this chapter and then more positively in the Conclusion.

The previous chapters have documented the way that the traditionalist quest for truly Christian doctrine, culture, and politics has institutionalized an antimodern discourse coalition that uses the norms of an imagined past to oppose practices, policies, and communities in the present that are deemed a threat to a genuinely authentic Christian identity. I am not arguing, I hasten to add, that any defense of orthodoxy and the rule of faith necessarily entails supporting the right-wing culture wars. It is theoretically possible to be a defender of ancient Christianity and an advocate of liberal democracy, civil rights, and social justice. But such advocacy is increasingly difficult when one is committed to defending and promoting "historic Christianity," a concept that is inextricably bound up with a storyline about the heretical and pernicious errors of modernity and involves protecting a normative Christian antiquity against adaptation to new historical conditions. Not only does this idea involve policing certain doctrinal and cultural boundaries, but it claims that the entire era in which we live is corrupt and must be opposed. Such thinking is inevitably a form of culture war rhetoric, even if it is not expressed in the same martial tones as it is in political discourse. It should thus come as no surprise when a coalition defined by antimodern rhetoric becomes weaponized for political ends to which some of those participating in this coalition do not personally subscribe.

In short, while defending orthodoxy is not in itself the problem, it thrusts one into a discourse coalition that is at the root of religious participation in the culture wars. Once the advocacy of orthodoxy becomes the advocacy of a supposedly ideal form of Christianity that lies in an irretrievable past – or rather a past that its proponents claim is retrievable with the right people in positions of power, though in fact it is not – the hydra of toxic Christian prescriptivism has reared its head(s). The argument here is not causal but viral: antimodern, counterliberal ideas that mandate certain norms regarding how to think about Christianity quickly spread through religious and cultural networks, adapting to new social circumstances and political contexts. As they evolve, they reinforce each other and create an environment conducive to extreme and exclusionary versions of Christianity. The idea of "retrieving ancient Christianity" can thus support both an academic protest against historical-critical hegemony in biblical studies and a political campaign against same-gender marriage – and the social legitimacy of the former buttresses the latter. Without subscribing to the contested terrain of cultural meme theory, we can still describe the quest for the rule of faith today as a kind of memeplex – a group of memes or cultural ideas that have formed a coalition, working together, often unintentionally and unknowingly, to advance a campaign against modernity as antithetical to true religion.

None of this is inevitable or necessary. While the forces concerned with decrying "cancel culture" and advancing anti-transgender legislation have strong motivations outside of religion, it is nevertheless the case that religion has provided the foundation for the antimodern agenda and remains central to the channels of power and influence that sustain exclusionary and reactionary policies – as the work of the World Congress of Families attests. But this discourse coalition is more than just right-wing politics, even if the political dimension suffuses every aspect. The discourse includes the revival of the creedal rule of faith among previously biblicist evangelicals, the liturgical and theological *ressourcement* among American Protestants, the reactionary turn toward historic and original versions of Christianity, and the rigorous policing of orthodoxy through heresy trials and terminations of employment – from Charles Briggs in the 1890s because of historical criticism, to Rudolf Bultmann in the 1940s and 1950s because of demythologizing, to the myriad examples of job terminations in the late twentieth and early twenty-first centuries because of evolution, gay marriage, universalism, or wearing a hijab in solidarity with Muslims.

The damage wrought due to anxiety over the loss of tradition has been incalculable. While those defending their version of the faith blame modernity, I place the responsibility instead on the very idea of a divinely authorized, orthodox tradition – not tradition as such but the notion there is one *right* tradition to the exclusion of all others. The violence and cruelty that stems from defending this tradition long predates the rise of the modern era. We see it in the anathematization of those deemed heretics in late antiquity; in the medieval execution of mystics, scholars, and those who published dangerous ideas; and in the way pre-Enlightenment Protestants executed those who denied the trinity, "rebaptized" believers, were declared to be "witches," or converted to Judaism. Though such outward, bodily violence became (mostly) unacceptable in the modern period, this only occasioned the transition toward forms of violence that did not leave a visible mark: public scorn, termination of employment, and the withdrawal of the support of local communities. These consequences are morally disturbing in themselves, but the problem begins with the incoherence of the concept of orthodoxy itself, and it is there that we must begin. In what follows I look again at the three aspects of the modern quest for the rule of faith – doctrine, culture, and politics – not only to better understand why the quest went awry, but also to understand how we might change course in the future.

THE IMPOSSIBILITY OF HISTORIC CHRISTIANITY

In celebration of the 1976 bicentennial of the Declaration of Independence, religious publishers released a flurry of books on the

Christian status of the country, with titles like *America: One Nation Under God, A Nation under God?*, and *America: God Shed His Grace on Thee.* The Episcopal Church even published *This Nation under God: A Book of Aids to Worship in the Bicentennial Year 1976.* Most of the books looked to an idealized version of the nation's supposedly Christian past as an inspiring resource for American Christians in the present to reclaim the country for God, under the assumption that "we must know the past . . . to clarify our spiritual identity and our origins."[6] Reflecting on the resurgence of Christian nationalism during the bicentennial, the deans of evangelical history – Mark A. Noll, Nathan O. Hatch, and George M. Marsden – noted that "at times of crisis it is a natural human reaction to turn to the past for support." In the case of perceived cultural crisis, "one of the calls to reform America in our day becomes an appeal to recover the Christian roots . . . to regain what we have lost."[7]

The same turn to the past occurs in situations of perceived religious crisis, which throughout the United States in the twentieth century has often been inextricable from the anxiety over the decline of "Christian America." The quest for true Christianity has often been a quest for the true America – a nostalgic look to something original that might serve as the basis for spiritual identity. But this talk about the past is mere artifice. Despite the rhetoric about recovering so-called historic Christianity, the retrievalist project is deeply ahistorical. It depends, as David Bentley Hart has observed regarding John Henry Newman's work, on "an illusionist's trick," a historical sleight of hand that "retains its power to enthrall and persuade only so long as one studiously maintains one's willing suspension of disbelief and, so to speak, keeps one's seat."[8] There are overt parallels here between Christian retrievalism and American retrievalism that are worth exploring at length because they help expose the (il)logic involved.

On November 2, 2020 – the eve of the national presidential election – Donald Trump issued Executive Order 13958 on "Establishing the President's Advisory 1776 Commission."[9] The directive was a response to the furious pearl-clutching among conservatives over the 1619 Project published by the *New York Times Magazine* in August 2019 and organized by Nikole Hannah-Jones.[10] That project made the claim that, to understand the United States, we need to reckon with the institutionalized racism that stems from the fact that enslaved Africans had been brought to this land in 1619, long before the country was ever established in 1776. While such a claim was amply supported by the historical record, as demonstrated by the scholars and journalists who participated in the project, it struck at the heart of what Jared Goldstein calls "constitutional nationalism" – the conservative American mythology about the nation as a land of liberty and justice supposedly enshrined in its founding documents.[11] If "historic Christian orthodoxy" is the quintessence of theological prescriptivism, then "constitutional nationalism" is the quintessence of political prescriptivism.

Trump's 1776 Commission was a full-throated embrace of constitutional nationalism. The executive order (EO) began by describing the president's goal of "better enabl[ing] a rising generation to understand the history and principles of the founding of the United States in 1776." The word "history" is here defined entirely by the word "principles," a term that appears multiple times in the text. The reason for this is straightforward. A central claim of conservative defenders of the United States is that it was founded on the ideals of liberty and equality for all, while progressive critics have repeatedly pointed out the hypocrisy of claiming these ideals while continuing to participate in the enslavement of human beings. The conservative counter is to insist that "true America" is defined by these principles, not the historical details associated with the founding. This is the same prescriptivist move made by defenders of Christianity in the face of scandals and other criticisms. When someone points out that Christians, whether in antiquity or today, were patriarchal, anti-Jewish, involved in corruption, or some other sign of hypocrisy, the protectionist response is to say that Christianity is defined by its normative principles (e.g., "all of you are one in Christ Jesus"), not by the historical conditions for the construction of those principles – much less by what later Christian leaders have done. There is a deep harmony here between Christian prescriptivism and American prescriptivism that reinforces the evangelical Christian alignment with a Republican Party that embraces a prescriptivist conception of the United States.

Trump's EO, for instance, declares that the American nation is exceptional because it represents "the formation of a republic around these principles," marking "a clear departure from previous forms of government." The EO then narrates the history of the nation as "our Republic's exploration of the full meaning of these principles," constructing "a clear historical record of an exceptional Nation dedicated to the ideas and ideals of its founding." Remarkably, this supposedly "exceptional" exploration of the nation's political principles apparently includes even "civil war, the abolition of slavery, Reconstruction, and a series of domestic crises and world conflicts," as if the American Civil War and later civil rights movements were simply a natural unfolding of the nation's founding ideals rather than a crisis exposing profound structural flaws – the nation's "original sin." The EO sees America as a list of "great heroes" from Abraham Lincoln to Martin Luther King Jr., all engaged in a "great moral endeavor" defined by "a shared identity rooted in our founding principles," all the while ignoring that both Lincoln and King were assassinated for challenging the system of white supremacy that the founders kept intact.[12] The EO's guiding philosophy of history is (white) American supremacy, governed by the conviction that America is essentially good and pure, and references to the inviolable principles of the founding serve as permanent exculpation from any historical trespass.

Signed into law by Governor Ron DeSantis on April 22, 2022, Florida's House Bill 7, officially called the Individual Freedom Act but known more widely as the Stop the Wrongs to Our Kids and Employees (W.O.K.E.) Act, is a further example of the prescriptivist manipulation of history. According to the text of the bill, "American history shall be viewed as factual, not as constructed, shall be viewed as knowable, teachable, and testable, and shall be defined as the creation of a new nation based largely on the universal principles stated in the Declaration of Independence."[13] In addition to reinforcing the right-wing prescriptivist notion that American history is defined by normative, universal principles, this bill also dictates how history itself should be viewed, making the notions of history being "factual" and history being "constructed" mutually exclusive, despite the irony that viewing history as factual and testable is itself a construction. The irony goes deeper in light of the Florida Department of Education's adoption of rule number 6A-1.094124 on June 10, 2021, amending the state's curriculum requirements. The amendment says that instruction on historical events "must be factual and objective." Examples of instruction that "distort historical events" include "material from the 1619 Project" and anything that "define[s] American history as something other than the creation of a new nation based largely on universal principles stated in the Declaration of Independence." The rule also bans "the teaching of Critical Race Theory, meaning the theory that racism is not merely the product of prejudice, but that racism is embedded in American society and its legal systems in order to uphold the supremacy of white persons."[14] These materials are judged not to be factual without any factual evidence, purely on the grounds that they violate the highly subjective interpretation of American history as the story of a supposedly colorblind nation "based largely on universal principles." American conservative prescriptivism demands that the nation be an exceptional, blameless agent of good in the world, and it achieves this by overriding whatever descriptivist evidence scholars might point to in the name of the normative principles of the Declaration.

In addition to redefining history based on their chosen norms, political and legal conservatives frequently appeal to the authority of history and tradition in a way that reflects how theological conservatives appeal to the authority of historic Christianity. To take a notable recent example, Supreme Court Justice Samuel Alito, in his majority opinion in *Dobbs v. Jackson Women's Health Organization* striking down the precedent set by *Roe v. Wade*, claimed that "a right to abortion is not deeply rooted in the Nation's history and traditions," drawing on the criterion established in the liberal ruling by Justice Lewis F. Powell, Jr. in *Moore v. City of East Cleveland* (1977) to expand the definition of "family" and weaponized twenty years later in the conservative ruling by Chief Justice William Rehnquist in *Washington v. Glucksberg* (1997) that upheld a ban on physician-assisted death.[15] In the case of Alito, the appeal to history and tradition is used to bypass the legal precedent for abortion rights set by previous rulings that go back a half-century. Ignoring the principle of *stare decisis*, Alito reverts instead to the English common law of the thirteenth century, quoting Henry de Bracton's treatise *De Legibus et Consuctudinibus Angliae* (c. 1235), as well as other common-law treatises from the seventeenth and eighteenth centuries.[16] His stated aim is to show that "during the relevant period – i.e., the period surrounding the enactment of the Fourteenth Amendment," abortion was viewed as a crime, and therefore the substantive due process jurisprudence used to support abortion rights is supposedly invalid. Alito's logic here is simply the rejection of substantive due process altogether, since the whole point of this principle is to allow for the protection of rights not enumerated in the Constitution or held at the time the text was written. Indeed, if the jurisprudence supporting abortion is rejected (i.e., the right to privacy), then any number of other rights connected with this are also potentially on the chopping block, including the right to use contraception (*Griswold v. Connecticut*), the right of parents to raise their children as they see fit (*Pierce v. Society of Sisters*), and the right to engage in same-gender sexual relations (*Lawrence v. Texas*), not to mention the many other decisions based on other aspects of substantive due process.

My concern here is not to wade into the legal thicket surrounding constitutional interpretation – though I will return to the Constitution in the Conclusion as I sketch out an alternative for how Christians might relate to their own history – but the point is to see how the appeal to history has become (and has always been) a weapon used to gain leverage over opponents and enforce conformity to a certain vision of how things ought to be – in this case, the way things were in 1850, or even 1250.[17] If something can be shown to be "historical" and "traditional," it is thereby more authentic, so the thinking goes. The past becomes the prescriptive ideal that the present must recover and restore.

The issues of abortion rights and the 1776 Project provide vivid examples of a practice that Christianity long perfected, namely, the manipulation of history for the purpose of policing orthodoxy and imposing the prescribed identity. Each example represents what Svetlana Boym describes as "restorative nostalgia," which has no interest in a nuanced account of the past but rather seeks to "rebuild the lost home" by engaging "in the antimodern myth-making of history by means of a return to national symbols and myths" – or religious myths in the case of Christian nostalgia. Restorative nostalgics do not believe they are nostalgic at all, because "they believe that their project is about truth," and such truth is timeless.[18]

But all these cases, and especially the case of Christianity, must face a dilemma: there is no historical origin to recover, even if we could agree on what that was. It simply does not exist. Certainly the *past* exists insofar as we know that events occurred before the present moment, but the very act of articulating those prior events immediately falsifies them, at least in the sense that we think we are grasping hold of the past itself and establishing some connection with it. This is hardly a new insight; philosophers of history have been saying this for decades. But when it comes to Christian identity, these are hard lessons to learn, since so much of this identity is typically premised on continuity with the past. Indeed, Judith Lieu claims that "without continuity there can be no identity," but as she points out in her study of early Christianity, the nature of this continuity is hardly straightforward and involves as much subjective invention as objective discovery. She thus finds that, throughout Christian history, "continuity is transformed into discontinuity, and discontinuity into continuity."[19] Churches have papered over the problem of historical continuity by relying on ideas like "apostolic succession" or the Protestant alternative of viewing the continuity of the gospel message (whatever that is) as a historical constant, even though it is nothing of the sort. And yet the impossibility of historic Christianity remains the thorn in the side of normative Christian theology and practice – a thorn whose wound continues to fester even though theologians try to mask it behind doctrine.

In the same way that Americans establish continuity with their origins by conflating the historical context of the Constitution with the ideas found in the Constitution, so too Christians establish continuity with their origins by conflating the historical context of the Bible or the early church with the doctrines and beliefs found in these ancient texts. By transforming history into a principle, one is thereby able to trick oneself into thinking that holding on to this principle in the present is the same as having continuity with the past. This is the illusionist's trick, the sleight of hand used in the quest for historical Christianity.

The work of postliberal Lutheran scholar David Yeago provides an example of how theologians pull off this illusion. In his 1994 article on "The New Testament and the Nicene Dogma" – the essay referred to in Chapter 3 as a turning point in the use of the rule of faith in biblical interpretation – Yeago sought to explain how the Nicene Creed could be continuous with the New Testament, despite the fact that the theological terms used in the creed, such as *homoousias* (of one being/essence), are not found in the scriptural texts. To solve this dilemma, Yeago made a now widely used, though rarely interrogated, distinction between *judgments* and *concepts*. This distinction is analogous to other distinctions I have been using throughout this book, including content and form, essence and accident, principle and application. According to Yeago, the Nicene term *homoousias* is a historically contingent verbal resource, a feature of its time and place – in itself no more special than any other concept. Every concept, he argues, is the historical clothing for a normative judgment. Concepts are the props used to perform an action, the tools employed to bring an underlying judgment to expression, a judgment that has no necessary relationship to the concepts used to articulate it. When the apostle Paul, for instance, speaks of Jesus as *kurios* (lord) and being "in the form of God" (Phil 2:6) these are the concepts used to express a theological judgment, which Yeago argues is equally expressed in the fourth century by the concept of *homoousias* (of one being/ essence). Both concepts are "saying the same thing."[20]

"Unity in teaching," Yeago claims, "must be sought at the level of judgements and not at the level of concepts, for discourse only *teaches*, makes claims that can be accepted or rejected, insofar as it passes and urges judgements."[21] Embedded in this statement is the underlying logic of historic Christianity. Yeago is saying here that what is normative in the New Testament texts has to be found at the level of judgments rather than concepts, but what he does not say – what he instead assumes from the outset – is that the New Testament is a text whose purpose is to *teach* readers throughout all times and places. The New Testament is not a historical artifact for Yeago but a divinely appointed teacher. This is the presupposition that he and others in the school of postliberal theological interpretation of scripture bring to the text. With that assumption, it becomes necessary to posit something like a judgment in order to find something transcultural in scripture. This allows the reader to establish "unity in teaching," which is their way of saying "historical continuity" between then and now. The text as *teacher* – that is to say, the text as the mediator of timeless judgments or principles – is a text that can be cleanly extracted from its historical context and relocated anywhere in history.

With Yeago's distinction in hand, it becomes possible to find continuity with virtually anything throughout Christian history. Jordan Barrett finds continuity between the "biblical judgments regarding justification" and the Protestant Reformation doctrine of imputed righteousness, an idea that biblical scholars have widely criticized.[22] Kevin Vanhoozer, who uses the judgment-concept distinction in almost every one of his writings, finds continuity between "what Scripture teaches about itself" and the even more widely criticized doctrine of biblical inerrancy – the teaching that scripture is completely without error.[23] Vanhoozer's promotion of this distinction addresses a dilemma for American evangelical theologians. As evangelicals, they are committed to biblicism, the notion that all divine truth can be found in the Bible. As theologians interested in the Christian tradition, however, they want to make use of doctrines and concepts from the creeds and later theologians. Yeago's distinction provides the desired bridge. Suddenly the entire theological tradition becomes "biblical," since every later doctrinal concept can be viewed as a variation on a biblical judgment. It is a masterful trick. The entirety of "historical Christianity" is now also potentially "biblical Christianity," resulting in the unity of biblicist Protestants and traditionalist Catholics that Newman thought was impossible. Is it any accident that this theological unity was forged in the late twentieth century, precisely when they were developing a political unity?

Like any trick, however, it only works so long as you do not look at the details. Take Yeago's original article on the question of Christ's divine status, for instance. Yeago makes a number of assumptions about Judaism in antiquity that have become stock features of conservative biblical scholarship functioning as Christian apologetics (e.g., N. T. Wright, Larry Hurtado, and Richard Bauckham). These assumptions include: ancient Judaism held to a strict monotheism in which YHWH was the only deity; the god of the Jewish people existed at a transcendent remove from the created order; and thus the relation between Jesus and YHWH was an either-or binary that can be described as either identity or nonidentity. Together these assumptions compose what Paula Fredriksen calls "purely Jewish monotheism," and it forms the basis for historical apologetics about Christian belief in the trinity. Unfortunately, as Fredriksen points out, purely Jewish monotheism "never existed."[24]

Indeed, the term "monotheism" is of modern vintage and does not adequately describe anyone in the ancient world. "Antiquity's universe was a god-congested place," and thus "*all* ancient 'monotheists' – be they pagan, Jewish, or, eventually, Christian – were, by modern measure, 'polytheists.'"[25] Paul calling Jesus *kyrios* means Jesus has some kind of superior divine status, but that in itself means very little. The more important question is why this divine status matters. The proponents of a proto-Nicene "early very high Christology," as Fredriksen calls it, lose sight of the historical context for the New Testament.[26] When Paul and the other Christ loyalists proclaimed the crucified Christ's resurrection, they were announcing the end of the age and the imminent arrival of God's kingdom. It was their eschatological conviction, and not their belief in the unique identity of Jesus, that was the source of their excitement and the motivation for their evangelistic activity. The resurrection of Jesus was a sign of the impending apocalypse, not an indication of his metaphysical status. The proto-Nicene apologists, much like the bishops at Nicaea, have ignored this end-times expectation and replaced eschatology with Christology. Their "diminuendo of apocalyptic eschatology is of a piece with [their] *haut* divinization of Christ."[27]

If there was a "judgment" among the New Testament writers, it was less a judgment about Christ's uniquely divine identity and much more a judgment about his role in the end of days. The notion that the earliest Christ loyalists were making doctrinal judgments at all is anachronistic; their attention was on the imminent arrival of God's kingdom, and consequently they "scarcely noticed" the theological differences that were amply on display in their communities.[28] Insofar as there was a judgment about the person of Jesus, it cannot be the same judgment as that of Athanasius. Whether it was simply a "high, human Christology," as J. R. Daniel Kirk claims, or a high Christology in which Jesus is the greatest of YHWH's divine agents, who was involved in the creation of the world and now ushers in the end of the world, either way the judgment, historically considered, does not trespass on the singularity and exclusivity of YHWH's identity.[29] Because they miss this point, the proto-Nicene apologists also fail to take account of how theology developed in the years between Jesus and Nicaea, as attention shifted to the person of Jesus himself at the expense of eschatology. Theologians in the second century, like Justin Martyr, viewed Jesus as an angel and a second god. Others viewed him more as a phantom appearing in flesh. The Logos Christology that eventually dominated was only one among many options and had multiple versions that were worked out over centuries. The Arian controversy that led to the Nicene council would hardly have occurred if the texts were as unambiguous as today's apologists claim.[30]

None of this necessarily means that the Nicene dogma is thereby *wrong*, as if a doctrine is illegitimate unless it can be traced back to the original disciples. There is no disputing the fact that it is *possible* to develop the doctrine of the trinity from these texts – it's been done thousands of times. As Hart points out, any historical development will "retain some trace of its cultural or material or conceptual antecedents," so it will always be possible to represent a later doctrine "as a natural and rationally necessitated advance upon what preceded it."[31] Nicaea instead raises the question of norms and the role history is supposed to play in deciding what is normative. When historical continuity becomes the basis for religious (or national) identity, then it is all but guaranteed that history will be distorted to support the norms with which one already identifies. Yeago's judgment-concept distinction is only one way of achieving this, and one of the most flexible. Robert Jenson, one of the key postliberal proponents of Christianity as culture, bypasses the need to find later orthodox judgments among the early Jesus loyalists by connecting all stages of Christianity through his account of the Holy Spirit, in essence subsuming the original community into the later church. Jenson creatively replaces a historical continuity in terms of "hanging on to what is already there" with an eschatological continuity as "receiving what must come," which makes later dogma normative as part of the Spirit's fulfillment of the original event.[32] N. T. Wright takes the opposite approach by nullifying later church history on the grounds that historical research reconstructs a more normative account of true Christianity than the one theologians have provided. Wright goes so far as to naturalize history as an objective reality open to public scientific inquiry. The historian is "like the scientist" who forms hypotheses and puts them to the test, and history is a form of natural science that investigates "real life, real space-time-and-matter existence" and produces "*real knowledge*" that is as secure as anything attained by the biologist or chemist.[33] Wright's work exemplifies just how modern the conservative Christian effort to establish authentic Christianity is. His work also exposes the illusion, since it only succeeds so long as we do not ask whether history really operates the way he says it does.

These are all ways of establishing some version of historic Christianity, and all are premised on the assumption that history is, in some sense, normative. But this is a category error. Theology aims to clarify what something *means* to people today. History, at its best, tells us what something *meant* to people who are utterly strange to us, and "what a text *meant* cannot but be different from what it, within a current community, *means*."[34] The concept of "historic Christianity" refers to an impossibility that has never existed and could never exist. No matter the theological mechanism devised to claim continuity between then and now, there is no bridging the cultural and historical chasm between an ancient text and its present-day readers. This is not to suggest that any connection between past and present is impossible, that theologians and historians are doomed never to speak meaningfully to each other. But any such bridging – and this is the crucial point – will never be the historical establishment of the single normative religious viewpoint. There will not be continuity but there may be *communication*. And every act of communication with the past will always only be part of the ongoing quest for Christianity and thus a *contemporary proposal* of the rule or essence of faith, normative for no one beyond those who choose to embrace it.

THE PERIL OF CHRISTIAN CULTURE

In the face of the ahistorical nature of historic Christianity, it may seem both logical and desirable to find continuity and normativity in the construction of Christian culture. Such was the effort of the postliberals that I examined in Chapter 3, who recognized, to their credit, that doctrine does not exist as some abstract entity in a free-floating state apart from culture. Every propositional formulation of a doctrine is an expression of one's cultural context, the historical location in which one is situated. The error of both biblical and doctrinal literalists consists in the fantasy that their beloved text – whether scripture or creed – effectively comes straight from heaven, without the messy intermediary of historical development. The postliberals thus took up the mantle of Newman but translated his ideas into the language of cultural formation. So far, so good.

The problem is that the postliberals shifted to thinking in terms of culture while retaining all of the normative authority that traditionalists previously ascribed to doctrinal propositions. Instead of focusing on thinking the right doctrine, the concern became inhabiting the right culture. This way of viewing Christian norms provided postliberals with a response to the ecumenical movement's effort to bring about church unity. They recognized that any effort to find a universally normative doctrinal tradition that could unite past and present was bound to fail. In place of doctrine, they appealed instead to a normative *way of life*, defined by the language, grammar, and practices of Christian community. The church is united so long as everyone inhabits the same normative culture. Ultimately, this led mainline postliberals to make common cause with evangelicals, especially Reformed evangelicals, regarding the idea of a Christian worldview: an all-absorbing cultural framework designed to shape and order "every square inch" of one's life, as well as all of society. The result was a theological and political program that was often implicitly, and sometimes quite explicitly, integralist – or dominionist, in evangelical parlance.[35]

To be sure, most postliberals typically frame their position in more insipid ecumenical terms (e.g., "we must interpret the world in light of Christ's redemption"), but the political payoff is the same: a counter-liberal social vision that subordinates everything to the church, understood as an authoritative premodern culture existing alongside modern society as an alien and antagonistic presence. David Yeago, once again, provides a characteristic example. In a 2012 article in *First Things* titled "Modern but Not Liberal," Yeago articulates how he thinks "classical theology" might respond to modernity regarding social issues, such as racial discrimination. Classical theology, as Yeago understands it, is a worldview that interprets "the human race in the context of the scriptural narrative construed according to the rule of faith," and then it uses the "interpretive potency of the scriptural narrative" to survey, judge, and assimilate the "diverse cultures" of the world. From this vantage point, "alien cultures, threatening bodies of thought, and historical cataclysms only provide new opportunities to discover once again" that all knowledge is "hidden with Christ."[36] The church has the one true culture, and all other cultures are alien and potentially threatening, in need of redemption by being brought into Christ's culture. The postliberal, in Yeago's articulation, engages the world with the supreme confidence that the church has all the answers, and if only the church could control the levers of society, all would be made right with God's help. It is not hard to see why some decided to abandon the ecumenical niceties as a relic of liberalism and embrace a fully integralist social policy.

These consequences were virtually inevitable once the postliberals embraced the idea that Christianity is a culture. To some, this may seem to be hyperbolic, for surely, they might say, the language of culture is a neutral and highly flexible term. Without getting into the weeds of anthropological disputes – any definition of culture will suffice to make the point – the term culture is typically used to refer to "the complex of values, customs, beliefs and practices which constitute the way of life of a specific group."[37] In itself, there is little controversial about this concept. The problem arises when the idea of culture is connected to Christianity, which historically brings with it the assumption of normativity (i.e., orthodoxy) – namely, that there is a right way to be Christian. Normativity leads to the related assumption of uniformity: if there is a right way to be Christian, this ideally should apply to all Christians across space and time. If we now understand this "way of being Christian" as a culture, then it follows that all Christians are supposed to belong to the same culture.

The problem starts to become clear at this point. If Christianity is not just a culture but a normative culture, characterized by the orthodox requirement of remaining essentially the same over time, this requires Christian identity to overmatch and ultimately suppress all other marks of cultural identity. Indeed, it places Christianity in outright conflict with other cultures, including the cultures that exist within the orbit of the church. The postliberals who advanced this concept of Christianity almost by definition had to view culture as a kind of static, self-contained entity, quite in contrast to how cultural theorists and anthropologists understood it. The notion that culture was fluid and hybrid was anathema to the postliberals, since that was incompatible with the idea of an orthodox tradition. If culture is hybrid, then Christian culture is syncretistic – and that would defeat the whole purpose of talking about Christianity as a culture. The postliberals thus imposed the norms of orthodoxy upon the concept of culture, resulting in a theological version of purity culture. In her critique of the postliberals on this point, Kathryn Tanner argued that Christian identity is instead "essentially impure and mixed, the identity of a hybrid that always shares cultural forms with its wider host culture and other religions."[38] The "boundaries between Christian and non-Christian ways of life" are not clearly defined but "fluid and permeable," and thus Christian identity is "no longer a matter of unmixed purity, but a hybrid affair established through unusual uses of materials found elsewhere."[39] Tanner's critique fell on deaf ears among the traditionalist postliberals, for it would mean the dissolution of their entire project, which was to set a clear boundary between true Christianity and modern Western society. The pursuit of purity was the point. But that pursuit could only ever lead to the imperialistic suppression of difference and the instigation of cultural and religious warfare.

In my prior work on this topic – most clearly in my dispute with the postliberal biblical scholar R. W. L. Moberly in a series of articles between 2012 and 2018 – I framed the problem in terms of mission, though our disagreement began originally over the task of biblical interpretation.[40] Moberly argued that the church is the "presupposition" for all biblical exegesis, drawing on Augustine's statement that "I would not believe the gospel if the authority of the Catholic Church did not move me."[41] My main rejoinder to his argument was that everything depends on how we understand the church and its role as a presupposition. I distinguished between two kinds of presuppositions: a weak version that views the church as the interpretive *context* and a strong version that views the church as the interpretive *norm*.[42] The former, I said, is largely (but not entirely!) uncontroversial. Most people are not going to be interested in interpreting scripture unless they belong to a church in some capacity. This much is straightforward but does not achieve what Moberly means by presupposition. He has something more normative in mind, as evidenced by the fact that, in his final response, he uses the example of how "the supposed 'level playing field' of much historical-critical biblical scholarship is less level than often assumed, precisely because of certain preconceptions that may profoundly influence the accounts offered and the judgments made."[43] Any preconception or presupposition that "profoundly influences" the interpretation is by definition normative. The question, as always, is which norm we are talking about. Moberly rejects the norms of historical criticism in favor of the norms associated with the church understood as a "plausibility structure," a sociological term developed especially by Peter L. Berger to understand the way our social context constructs our understanding of reality. But as I pointed out in my 2017 rejoinder to Moberly, Berger uses the term plausibility structure as a synonym for "cultural world," which is what Charles Taylor calls a "social imaginary" and what others call a worldview.[44] My central concern has been the way that talk of Christianity as culture legitimates the violent antagonism with modernity that we see in culture war rhetoric, and the term plausibility structure repeats the same problematic dynamic. As Berger and Thomas Luckmann point out, "the plausibility structure must become the individual's world, displacing all other worlds, especially the world the individual 'inhabited' before his alternation."[45] If Christianity is a culture that one must inhabit, this places a person in an antagonistic and potentially authoritarian relationship with others, one that makes it difficult, if not impossible, to create pluralistic spaces of difference.

The mission of the church enters the picture at this juncture.[46] While mission is often associated with evangelism and proselytism, at its core the concept applies to any relationship between a religious norm (e.g., the Christian gospel) and culture, however that is understood. The study of mission is the study of how religious norms navigate different cultural contexts, as in the example of Andrew Walls's extraterrestrial anthropologist that I described in Chapter 1. For Walls, the norm of the gospel is something distinct from culture, even if it never exists outside of culture. But what happens, then, if we now conceive of the norm itself as cultural? This is the problem that postliberalism, in all its variations, presents us. As I laid out in Chapter 3, once Christianity is understood as a culture, there are two basic options for how Christianity relates to those who are considered culturally other: either it can take the path of separatism and remain closed off to difference (e.g., new monasticism, intentional communities, the "Benedict Option"), or it can take the path of imperialism and assimilate whatever is different so that it becomes the same. The latter is the path that most postliberals and virtually all evangelicals have taken, though many seem to vacillate between the two options depending on whether they (or the group with which they are affiliated) are in power or not. Whereas the separatist approach avoids mission by staying closed off from others, the imperialist approach engages in a form of mission as diffusion, in which the spread of Christianity becomes the spread of the culture of the missionaries. Christian history is littered with examples of such cultural imperialism, for which the postliberal model of the church offers fertile theological support.

In my previous writings, I used the example of the German Christian Faith Movement (*Glaubensbewegung Deutsche Christen*), the group of German Christian nationalists who saw the Nazi regime as the manifestation of a truly Christian order for the German state, as a point of comparison. In part, this was because Moberly began our exchange with a criticism of Rudolf Bultmann, who was a member of the Confessing Church that opposed the German Christians. Moberly, I argued, failed to see that what he criticized Bultmann for (i.e., not making the social context of the church normative for biblical interpretation) was precisely what enabled Bultmann to criticize the German Christians. The issue is instructive, even if deeply uncomfortable. The postliberals who are engaged in theological interpretation of scripture are by no means closet Nazis, but some of them are Christian nationalists, and that is no accident. At the risk of bordering on the *reductio ad Hitlerum*, it is important to examine the theoretical links between these two kinds of imperialism: the postliberal idea of the church as a culture and the German Christian idea of the church as an ethnic-national people (*das Volk*).

There is a propensity to dismiss any link here on the grounds that only one of these groups is genuinely Christian. In my discussions with German Lutherans, I have found a tendency to characterize the German Christians as a *pagan* movement, something controlled by influences and norms alien to Christianity. There are, to be sure, legitimate grounds for this, given the way propagandists like Alfred Rosenberg drew on Norse mythology to flesh out their idea of the Aryan race. But we see the same tendency to highlight paganism in discussions of Christian nationalist movements in the United States, most clearly in the insurrection of January 6, 2021. Alongside people holding Bibles and a picture of Jesus wearing a MAGA hat, there was Jacob Anthony Chansley, known as the "QAnon Shaman," who came dressed in a horned Viking headdress and covered in Nordic body art. But Chansley, also called Jake Angeli, led the crowd in a prayer in the Senate chamber thanking the "heavenly Father" for "blessing us with this opportunity to stand up for our God-given inalienable rights" and "for allowing us to send a message to all the tyrants, the communists, and the globalists that this is our nation and not theirs." He went on to thank the "divine, omniscient, omnipotent, and omnipresent creator God for filling this chamber with your white light of love ... for filling this chamber with patriots that love you and that love Christ."[47] As the QAnon movement picked up steam in 2020, evangelical commentators, like Katelyn Beaty, were quick to describe it as an "alternative religion," though surveys soon revealed that over a quarter of white evangelicals subscribed to the QAnon conspiracy theories, and most of the others in the movement identified as some version of Protestant or Catholic.[48] Sociologist Samuel Perry described white Christian nationalism as "imposter Christianity." When this was picked up by journalist John Blake in July 2022 and applied to the January 6 insurrectionists, it prompted the same backlash over descriptivism and prescriptivism as the earlier #FakeChristian discourse, leading other experts on this topic, like Kristin Kobes Du Mez and Annika Brockschmidt, to point out that authoritarian Christian nationalism is indeed Christianity – even if it is not *all* of Christianity.[49] As tempting as it may be to exclude QAnon supporters and the aspiring insurrectionists from the bounds of Christianity, this move is precisely what Chrissy Stroop and others have criticized as a version of Christian supremacy for the way it preserves Christianity as something inviolably innocent.[50] The same temptation applies to the German Christian movement. Descriptively at least, both groups were composed of Christians claiming to represent their Christian faith, and thus it behooves us to examine what account of Christian norms might lead to these actions or are at least implicit in them.

The postliberal concept of the Christian church as its own culture is, I argue, the mirror image of the German Christian concept of the church as *Volk*.[51] The German Christians conflated Christianity with the plausibility structure of the German nation, while the postliberals conflated Christianity with the plausibility structure of the Western church. The fact that the content is different cannot obscure the fact that a similar logic (i.e., Christianity as culture/plausibility structure) applies in each case. Both groups understand their prescriptive norm as cultural – something defined by and generative of a normative cultural form. To belong to their respective "orthodoxies" is to inhabit a specific culture that ought primarily to define your identity. In the case of the German Christians, the culture in question is the fascist imaginary of an Aryan race defined by those who have true "German blood."[52] In the case of the postliberals, however, things are decidedly less clear. Robert Wilken refers to "a distinctly Christian language" that cannot be translated without being lost.[53] R. R. Reno, the editor of *First Things* and the Brazos Theological Commentary on the Bible, speaks about "the animating culture of the church" as "a habit of mind rather than a list of propositions."[54] In a breathtaking act of appropriation, Robert Jenson says that Christ is the culture of Israel, so that "a relation between, say, Christ and Chinese culture is in itself a relation between Jewish culture and Chinese culture." The church has "a culture of her [*sic*] own" and claims "to continue the culture of Israel." Because the church can "lose her identity" if it does not "cultivate her culture," the church has to be discerning regarding what it can absorb from the world, for "there are some elements of other cultures that it can assimilate and others that it cannot without self-destruction." Among the latter, Jenson says, are Enlightenment ideas about autonomy, so it is no surprise that he, along with most other postliberals, joined the antiabortion movement. Lest we miss the political implications, Jenson points out that "Christ," referring to the culture of the church, "is a political fact among and in competition with the polities of this world," in relation to which "all earthly would-be sovereigns" are "extensively in rebellion."[55] The consequence of this is clear: those who belong to the Christian church inhabit a culture that is in open warfare with other cultures, particularly those cultures shaped by Enlightenment modernity. The ambiguity around what exactly constitutes this Christian culture not only gives postliberals plausible deniability when it comes to issues of nationalism, racism, and homophobia, but it also makes the postliberal view of Christianity a flexible component of the conservative discourse coalition, allowing it to adapt to every new stage of the culture war without requiring the laborious process of a new church confession.

Is there anything to prevent the amorphous culture of the church from being conflated with the dominant national culture in which one lives? Arguably, what Reno calls the "animating culture of the church" is already a version of this, being the residue of the Roman imperial culture of late antiquity filtered through the colonialist histories of Western Europe. The postliberal effort to construct Christianity as its own separate – and, crucially, normative – culture is an attempt to create a color-blind version of Christian history that is ostensibly neutral with respect to race and ethnicity, able to spread innocently throughout the world while disavowing any responsibility for its relationship with European colonialism.[56] The failure to recognize the doctrines, practices, and habits of Western Christianity as already cultural, national, and racial is precisely what scholars of critical race theory identify as the chief characteristic of whiteness – namely, that it operates by remaining invisible (but is no less pernicious for being invisible).[57] The German Christians made their worldview easy to criticize by appealing so explicitly to myths of racial superiority, but the structure of their ideology was little different from what others have done in the effort to establish hierarchies of power, both in Europe and elsewhere in the world. More importantly, there is nothing in postliberalism to prevent it from slipping into a kind of militant Christian nationalism. The framework is already in place for this to happen. Is it any accident that Reno became an ardent supporter of Donald Trump's presidency and published a book in 2019 on restoring Western culture, titled *Return of the Strong Gods: Nationalism, Populism, and the Future of the West?*[58]

Kevin Vanhoozer recognized this implicit danger in the "cultural-linguistic" theory of postliberalism when he observed that "many Evangelicals have unknowingly made the cultural-linguistic turn already, though the cultures they have appropriated have not been altogether holy."[59] But his "canonical" alternative simply repeated with respect to the Bible the same cultural and racial blindness that mainline postliberals have with respect to church tradition. The canon is no more historically unimpeachable than the church, and indeed was born from the same exercise of authoritarian power. But acknowledging this means bracketing all questions of authority and viewing the Bible descriptively, rather than prescriptively. The problem is the same in each case: once something becomes timelessly normative, its historical situatedness must be suppressed. What is true for constitutional nationalism in relation to the US Constitution is true also for Christian prescriptivism in relation to both the Bible and church tradition. In each case, the tradition in question is reduced to ostensibly innocent principles that occlude the culturally alien and historically troubling features of the tradition. The peril of postliberalism – and any theology that valorizes the past as prescriptive – is that it further empowers the invisibility of whiteness and the suppression of historical context by bathing everything in the pious light of normative Christian tradition, making it not only possible but probable that those who subscribe to its theology and participate in the discourse coalition of antimodernism will be less likely to recognize when they are aiding efforts at white Christofascist nationalism – or why it might be wrong to do so.[60]

One might argue in response that there are unobjectionable examples where Christianity has been conflated with a cultural plausibility structure. Not every instance of cultural Christianity is Anglo-American, German, or Afrikaner. The case of the Black Church in the United States is a case in point, a situation where Christianity has been integrated with cultural norms that are specific to that community – norms that generated the resilience and resistance necessary to propel the fight for abolition and civil rights. What makes cases like this different from the others, however, is not merely the issue of race (white vs. Black) or power (systemic privilege vs. marginalization), as important as these are. Instead, the crucial factor, the connective tissue between all versions of the antimodern rule of faith, is the assumption of orthodoxy that shapes how white Christians have, in the cases mentioned above, infused their versions of cultural Christianity with notions of purity, authority, and supremacy. In other words, it is not the culture in question that is the problem so much as the authoritarian and exclusionary account of Christianity that violently expels any impure mixtures. To chart a better way forward, we need to address the problem of orthodoxy itself.

THE PARADOX OF ORTHODOXY AND THE POLITICS OF ANTILIBERALISM

In *Silencing the Past*, Michel-Rolph Trouillot (1949–2012) examines the way Western historiography actively silences aspects of the past that it finds uncomfortable or unthinkable, usually through the "direct erasure of facts or their relevance" or through the more subtle banalization of their significance by piling up minor details.[61] Such strategies are the operation of power working in and through the production of history itself, and they appear whenever occurrences – in Trouillot's case, the Haitian revolution – disturb the sensibilities of those in positions of supremacy or conflict with the story people in those positions want to tell about others.

There is, however, another way power silences the past, and that is through the strategy of *normativization*.[62] When the past is valorized as normative, the past can longer be the past; it must now become present. But it must become present *as* the past – as the authoritative image of the past that the present demands. This necessarily leads to another kind of erasure, and we see this erasure in every antimodern account of historic Christian identity. The conservative quests for the rule of faith ultimately end up evading and distorting history, despite their appeals to Christian tradition. The paradox of Christian orthodoxy, and arguably any orthodoxy, is that the more it asserts the normativity of the past, the more it loses touch with the past. Orthodoxy requires continuity across both time and place, a unified community from Jesus to Nicaea to today.[63] And that is precisely what history cannot provide. To return to Fredriksen, if "theology" – meaning the norms of orthodoxy – "inscribes identity," then "history unsettles it."[64] The rule of faith in modernity has thus become a way to silence history (along with any other discourse that elevates the descriptive over the normative), even as it claims to ground the true faith in the past, and it does so by making the present-day community, the one wielding the *regula*, the exclusive embodiment and arbiter of that authoritative, normative history.

The concept of orthodoxy is a multivalent, context-dependent, and contested term, but in virtually every Christian context "orthodoxy is equated with theological truth," that is, with being a faithful extension of one's tradition. Staf Hellemans has argued that "claiming orthodoxy" can have five layers of meaning, not all of which are present at any given time. Orthodoxy, he says, means claiming to possess a doctrine and practice defined by (1) being true, (2) upholding the tradition, (3) being in unchanged continuity with the past, (4) having a strict mindset, and (5) submitting to authority.[65] As Hellemans points out, the first layer on its own is claimed by most liberals as well, so that alone is not distinctive of orthodoxy, and the rigidity of the fourth layer is something that only arose in modernity in reaction to liberalism. We can simplify matters by recognizing that the first, second, and fourth layers of meaning are functions of the third and fifth, and thus we can restate the definition as follows: orthodoxy claims to have doctrine and practice that are true and uphold the tradition *because they maintain the past in a strictly unchanged way by deferring to authority whenever there are disputes.* To be sure, like every orthodoxy, Christian orthodoxy only emerged *after* the "heresies" that it retroactively constructed as the foil for its supposedly pristine truth.[66] And as Newman and others have demonstrated, orthodoxy itself changes over time, always adapting itself to new situations, even if those who view themselves as orthodox do not recognize these changes. But the act of *claiming* orthodoxy involves insisting that, in essence, one is continuing to go on in the same way as those before and that this "going on in the same way" confirms that one is in the truth.

Orthodoxy, in other words, is fundamentally a matter of identity, and like every identity, it needs to maintain continuity over time. But not every identity is made equal. Unlike identities rooted in some visible or inherent characteristic – such as race, gender, sexuality, and class – religious identities are highly unnatural and require extensive catechesis and ritual maintenance. Strange and demanding rules, beliefs, and performances constitute religious identity precisely *because* they are strange and demanding; they work to set adherents apart from others.[67] Traditional Christian orthodoxy, especially within Western Christianity, has notoriously demanding beliefs about others (e.g., that all will be eternally tormented in hell unless they repent and join the church), which it reinforces with additional beliefs (e.g., all are condemned because of original sin). Identities defined by such beliefs are inherently fragile, prone to dissolution as a result of confronting the complexity of lived experience. An evangelical Christian who is taught that no one outside their specific church network can live morally good lives will likely experience severe dissonance when confronted by their neighbors, classmates, and future coworkers. It is no wonder that communities with more rigidly defined orthodoxies tend toward separatist subcultures where such dissonance will be kept to a minimum. Some, like Reformed Protestants, achieve a mental separatism by developing beliefs like the doctrine of predestination that deny the validity of personal experience. On the one hand, this doctrine assures believers that, no matter how sinful they may be, their ultimate salvation is secure; on the other hand, the same doctrine assures believers that, no matter how good their neighbors may seem, their ultimate condemnation is likewise secure. Such theology teaches followers not to trust their instincts.[68] American evangelical Christians developed their own ways to limit alternative sources of knowledge, such as by casting doubt on all knowledge promoted by "secular" institutions of higher education or anything broadcast on "liberal" mainstream media. These are all strategies at identity maintenance. By limiting access to alternative perspectives, including historical research, that might unsettle the dominant orthodoxy, they serve to buttress the community's religious identity.

In addition to various strategies of (anti)intellectual separatism, orthodoxy also resorts to sheer assertion. Perhaps the most common instance of this is the use of Vincent of Lérins's maxim that the rule of faith is what has been held "everywhere, always, and by all" (*semper et ubique et ab omnibus*). The line was particularly important to Newman and the Tractarians (see Chapter 2), and it remains the linchpin of many arguments today regarding matters such as marriage and sexuality. Darrin Snyder Belousek's 2021 work, *Marriage, Scripture, and the Church*, is a case in point. He opens his discussion with the statement: "The traditional doctrine that marriage is man-woman monogamy meets the classic criteria of catholic doctrine: it has been believed everywhere (universality), always (antiquity), and by all Christians (consensus)." He says that this doctrine of marriage "has greater claim to catholicity than some dogmas defined by the ecumenical councils."[69] Such a claim is doubly ironic. First, Belousek is himself a Mennonite, meaning he belongs to a church that is not only noncreedal (which, to be clear, does not mean anticreedal or nonconfessional) but also holds views, like believer's baptism and pacifism, that do not meet these supposedly catholic criteria. Second, Vincent of Lérins was himself writing *against* Augustine, and even if I might applaud almost any critique of the Bishop of Hippo, the fact that for many today Augustine is no longer the new, heterodox theologian but now belongs to the Great Tradition only underscores the point that Vincent's maxim is entirely a matter of perspective and involves – no matter when or where it is used – a great deal of erasure and silencing.[70] Ironies aside, the real problem lies with the Vincentian canon itself. Writing against Newman, Thomas Croskery argued that the maxim "has no justification. From the *ubique* we must leave out the lands where heresy is dominant; from the *omnibus*, we must exclude the heretics themselves; from the *semper*, the period prior to the full development of the system for which this sanction is claimed."[71] Vincent's canon, in other words, has never been true and could never be true. Its claims about universality and consensus necessarily erase the countless people of faith throughout history – indeed, entire traditions – who have not subscribed to every (or even any) tenet of orthodoxy. Such universalizing claims about the past end up turning the virtually infinite complexity of history into a reflection of the one making the claims. Christian orthodoxy thus serves as a magic mirror that shows the past as people want to see it.

One does not need to survey the complexities of the past to face this problem; the present is complex enough on its own. Even within ostensibly orthodox communities, the actual diversity of beliefs and practices can vary dramatically, as any local church pastor can attest. Two people might say the same creed together but take it to mean two very different things. In most ecclesial contexts today, such differences are either ignored entirely or taken for granted as part of the inherent goodness of human diversity. Insofar as this is the case, orthodoxy has ceased to matter at the practical level. Those who work at institutions that require employees to sign a statement of faith can confirm that, on a day-to-day level, those statements typically have no significance whatsoever. But there are moments when suddenly the statements matter a great deal and the need to maintain orthodoxy becomes paramount. In those instances, the deep truth about orthodoxy becomes apparent – namely, the truth that, given the manifest multiplicity of beliefs and practices that characterize even the smallest of local communities, orthodoxy is only possible through the coercion of an imagined conformity. Orthodox religious identity operates, in other words, under the threat of violence.

For most of the church's history, this violence was physical and involved exile, torture, and death. More recently, the violence tends to be economic and professional, resulting in the termination of employment, tenure, or ordination. To illustrate this problem at the heart of orthodoxy, I need to take a slight detour through evangelical higher education.

Take the example of Wheaton College in Illinois, which I know well as an alumnus. There are any number of instances of occupational violence to use here, from the termination of a prospective hire for believing scripture is ambiguous about the status of monogamous same-sex relationships (Christina Van Dyke, 1999), to termination of a professor for rejecting creationism (Alex Bolyanatz, 2001), to termination for getting a divorce and refusing to justify it to the college administration (Kent Gramm, 2008), to termination for wearing a hijab and declaring that Christians and Muslims worship the "same God" (Larycia Hawkins, 2016).[72]

In order to understand the logic behind these cases, we must turn to Duane Litfin, who was president of Wheaton College during the first three instances (from 1993 to 2010). Litfin published a book in 2004 on *Conceiving the Christian College*, in which he distinguished between two models of religious colleges: the "umbrella" model and the "systemic" model. Umbrella institutions provide a "canopy" for a diverse range of religious views that share the "broad educational mission of the school." By contrast, institutions that follow the systemic model "seek to make Christian thinking systemic throughout the institution, root, branch, and leaf," and they do so from the perspective of the school's "sponsoring Christian tradition," which could be as broad as the Apostles' Creed or as narrow as a specific denomination.[73] Wheaton, he said, follows the latter model. But as Andrew Chignell, a graduate of Wheaton who is now professor of religion and philosophy at Princeton University, pointed out in a retrospective on Litfin's presidency, the systemic model is theoretically compatible with a range of possible applications. On the one end is what he calls the "wiggle-room" approach, in which "a certain amount of space is allowed for differing – albeit still *reasonable* – interpretations of the propositions constituting the systemic core." On the other end is the "magisterial" approach, in which "a select group of academic administrators specifies which interpretations of the core doctrines and codes are to be propagated throughout the system."[74]

Despite being, or perhaps *because* it is, a Protestant evangelical institution, Wheaton represents the magisterial approach. As Chignell noted, one of the first moves Litfin made was to eliminate as much wiggle-room as possible with respect to the question of human origins. The college's statement of faith to this day says that "God directly created Adam and Eve, the historical parents of the entire human race," a relic of the fundamentalist disputes in the early twentieth century.[75] Litfin decided to enforce the boundaries of Wheaton's orthodoxy on this issue, though he was ultimately compelled by the Board of Trustees to relax enough to allow people to be "unsure" on the matter. It would have been hard to hire, much less retain, anyone for a serious science department under his desired conditions, which only highlights the inherent tension between the norms of orthodoxy and the norms of academic inquiry – the latter requiring the freedom to follow wherever the evidence leads. Bolyanatz, unfortunately, ran afoul of the norms of orthodoxy when he told students that creationism was not a legitimate option and lost his job as a result. Three years later another situation arose, one that exemplifies the magisterial model.

In my first semester at Wheaton in the fall of 2001 (immediately following Bolyanatz's termination), I took the introductory-level philosophy course from Joshua Hochschild. Today Hochschild is remembered as the professor who attended – and subsequently defended – the "Save America" rally on January 6, 2021, that became the violent storming of the Capitol.[76] But two decades earlier he was a new and exciting professor of philosophy at a flagship evangelical college. All that changed in 2004, however, when Hochschild expressed his intention to be received into the Roman Catholic Church. He assured the administration that he remained committed to the college's Statement of Faith, there being nothing in it that a Catholic could not agree to in principle, including the claim that the scriptures are "of supreme and final authority in all they say." Litfin, however, disagreed on the grounds that, as Alan Jacobs put it, the Statement of Faith "is *intended* to imply clear dissent from the Catholic position that Scripture is co-equal with Holy Tradition."[77] While Litfin conceded that the statement does not actually make this claim, it did not matter, in his view, what the statement said; what mattered was how *he* understood it. Ironically, as Chignell pointed out, Litfin set himself up as "both arbiter and mouthpiece" of what he regarded as the orthodox interpretation of the statement, thereby "laying claim to magisterial interpretive authority" as an evangelical Protestant administrator at a traditionally Protestant institution.[78]

The Hochschild affair is by no means the most egregious termination at Wheaton, but it best illustrates one of the central paradoxes of Christian orthodoxy. On the one hand, the typical statement of Christian faith has the goal of bringing the greatest number of people into the fold, and for this reason is written in as broad and inclusive a way as possible. At the same time, the typical statement of faith has the competing goal of shutting out those not welcome in the community, and for this reason is written in as narrow and exclusive a way as possible. The irresolvable tension between these two goals often means that statements of what a community considers orthodoxy vacillate between one goal and the other, and the deciding factor regarding who is included or excluded is not based on anything explicit in the community's dogma but is instead an arbitrary exercise of pure will – the magisterial will of the one granted the authority to decide, in the moment, what the community's orthodoxy will be. The paradox of orthodoxy thus leads to authoritarianism. Newman was therefore right to say that a Christianity defined by the rule of faith depends on obedience to an external authority whose infallibility is presumed from the outset.[79] A "wiggle-room" approach will never be a live option for a community committed to an identity defined by orthodoxy, since that places authority in the hands of the individual to decide if their theology fits within the mission of the organization. At best, the figure of authority will sovereignly *allow* people to deviate from the rule of faith, but that permission may be retracted at any time.

Wheaton's statement about human origins is a clear instance where the goal of exclusion prevailed over inclusion, and yet it is rarely enforced. The faculty, especially those in the science department, rely on the college's implicit agreement to operate in practice according to the goal of inclusion. While this seems generous, it actually means the faculty exists in a state of constant uncertainty about whether and when the college administration will exercise its power to enforce the goal of exclusion. Human origins is only the most obvious instance of this. As the Hochschild affair illustrates, any part of the statement can become the weapon of authoritarian power. And as the Hawkins affair illustrates, the stated reason (e.g., violation of the Statement of Faith) often masks the underlying reason (e.g., parents and donors threatening to withdraw students and donations).[80] Faculty thus try to get ahead of this by sending their manuscripts to the administration for approval before publication, but the cause for termination is seldom one's scholarship.[81] At the end of the day, the Statement of Faith functions as a "parchment barrier" – to borrow James Madison's term for the Constitution – for the professor seeking protection against termination, since agreement with it is no guarantee you will not find yourself on the outside of its boundaries. At the same time, the Statement of Faith functions as a "blank check" for the administration seeking to terminate someone, since those in leadership can declare arbitrarily and magisterially the one right interpretation of its articles.

None of this is necessarily unique to Wheaton College, and this discussion of its recent history should not be taken as a criticism of Wheaton in particular. There are good reasons why religious institutions – and why institutions in general – might want to protect a specific identity and branding, especially when so much (money, reputation, etc.) is at stake.[82] And ever since the Supreme Court adopted the "ministerial exception" to laws governing employment in its 2012 decision in *Hosanna-Tabor Evangelical Lutheran Church and School v. EEOC* – further reinforced in *Our Lady of Guadalupe School v. Morrissey-Berru* (2020) – institutions like Wheaton are legally protected against antidiscrimination laws.[83] The financially precarious world of higher education only compounds the problem, leading administrators to be especially risk-averse. When you infuse this fear with a global Christian identity defined by persecution, it is little wonder that conservative Christian institutions "are hunkering down in a reactionary posture," opting to sacrifice individuals in an effort to preserve their future interests.[84] Wheaton is an especially high-profile case, but it is not basically any different from other religious organizations in this regard.

The case of Wheaton College illustrates a number of important issues: the self-protecting nature of institutions, the increasing antagonism between faculty and administration within neoliberal higher education, and the culture of fear that characterizes white American society and American evangelicalism in particular. When seen in a wider historical perspective, it also highlights the way that conservative identities are often internally inconsistent and shaped by the politics of those endowed with magisterial authority. The same institution that excluded a faculty member for joining the Catholic Church in 2004 later partnered with the Catholic University of America in a 2012 lawsuit against President Obama's contraception mandate. Wheaton College president Philip Ryken, who replaced Litfin in 2010, called the Catholic groups "co-belligerents in our fight."[85] At the explicit, textual level, this alliance made little sense, based as it was on Ryken's erroneous claim that Plan B is an "abortion-inducing drug," something he either knew was false or could have learned from a little research. But like every effort to defend what someone claims to be orthodoxy, the actions made sense at an implicit level – in this case, the implicit goal of coalition formation. Partnering with Catholic institutions was politically advantageous in a time of apocalyptic anxiety over the changes in culture related to gender, sexuality, and religious affiliation. The lawsuit institutionalized the conservative discourse coalition on religious liberty.

For my purposes here, the Wheaton case is notable for illustrating the paradoxical workings of orthodoxy itself. Two of these paradoxes I discussed above. I first pointed out that *orthodoxy silences the complexity of the past*, requiring those who wish to participate in the community to accept a normativized account of the community's history – paradoxically distancing the community from the past at the same time that they seek to place themselves in continuity with it. Another word for this kind of erasure is "whitewashing." Even if the history is not explicitly racialized – as in the case of Euro-American Christianity silencing the contributions of majority world Christians – the power dynamic of normativization is one that has been shaped by white identity formation, most visibly in the "Lost Cause" monuments erected to valorize an alternative history of the Civil War and an alternative identity for those who fought for the Confederacy.[86] Next I observed that *orthodoxy erases the complexity of the present*, requiring communities to accept the fiction that everyone is in exact agreement with the list of doctrines that ostensibly define the community's religious identity. Here we see the paradox of orthodox doctrines that simultaneously seek to include as many as possible while excluding as many as necessary. Given the polysemy that characterizes human language, it is impossible for any doctrinal statement to demarcate precisely who is "in" and who is "out." A multiplicity of interpretations and understandings characterizes the people in a single organization, and even more so in a global network of communities. For this reason, orthodoxy tends toward authoritarianism, requiring a leader to remove interpretive ambiguity by assuming the responsibility of magisterial authority. The orthodoxy of the leader, in principle, cannot be questioned and indeed forms the tacitly assumed foundation for all subsequent evaluations of orthodoxy or heresy.[87] Orthodoxy's silencing of the past leads to the silencing of those in the present who deviate from the implicit, authorized norms, as well as those who question the norms themselves.

If the statement of orthodox doctrines is not in itself the determination of who belongs and instead requires the authoritative leader to define the community's identity in the magisterial act of declaring who is excluded, then this leads to the third paradox of orthodoxy: *the community constructs orthodoxy by policing heterodoxy*, which means orthodoxy cannot exist without heterodoxy. This is not a feature unique to religion. Economics professor John B. Davis observes the same dynamic in his own field, where the labels of orthodoxy and heterodoxy function much the way they do in religion, with the former referring to the mainstream economics that receives institutional legitimacy and the latter referring to the marginalized views of those who challenge the dominant program (e.g., evolutionary, Marxist, or neo-Ricardian economics). Davis argues that "the orthodoxy–heterodoxy distinction allows economics to claim economics is scientific by dismissing heterodoxy as unscientific." By rejecting marginal programs as heterodox and thus unscientific, mainstream economists are able to give assurances to an anxious public concerned about their financial future that the orthodox program is indeed scientific and so trustworthy. This arrangement therefore incentivizes the use of "visible discriminatory practices against heterodoxy" as a way to calm people's anxieties, but the institutions wielding this exclusionary power also must not eliminate heterodoxy entirely, or else risk losing the very basis for identifying orthodoxy as scientific. Davis concludes that, ironically, "eliminating heterodoxy eliminates orthodoxy."[88]

Virtually every aspect of what Davis describes is replicated, *mutatis mutandis*, in Christianity. The orthodoxy-heterodoxy distinction allows Christian churches and theologians to claim that their theology is truthful – that is, biblical, historically grounded, morally sound, or whatever prescriptive norm is held by one's community – by dismissing heterodoxy as untruthful. Christian organizations engage in visible discriminatory practices against religious heterodoxy (e.g., the termination of pastors and professors) as a way to calm the anxieties of a public concerned about their spiritual future. People who are worried that churches, colleges, or other institutions might deviate from their "historic" norms want the assurance that these communities and leaders are in line with the truth. Publicly excluding what these communities denounce as heterodoxy thus reinforces their own orthodoxy, thereby granting the desired assurance. But this relationship between orthodoxy and heterodoxy means that those in positions of magisterial power must continually engage in exclusion (or at least the threat of exclusion) in order to strengthen the sense of security for those on the inside. By abolishing the need for a boundary, the elimination of heterodoxy would eliminate orthodoxy itself.

Orthodoxy – understood as the enforcement of the norms that construct historic Christian identity – therefore functions like patriarchy. Kate Manne argues that misogyny is "the 'law enforcement' branch of a patriarchal order," meaning that misogyny is less about the hostility that individual men feel toward women and more about the institutionalized practices that police and enforce gender norms in order to buttress a patriarchal social order. Patriarchy thus needs women it can police if it is to maintain its framework of social dominance.[89] Similarly, within Christianity, the punishment and exclusion of heterodoxy is the "law enforcement" branch of an orthodox religious order, which is less about hostility toward any individual "heretic" and more about the policing and enforcing of the community's prescriptive norms. It is hardly a surprise that Christian orthodoxy's "law and order" approach toward heterodoxy might manifest, within American evangelicalism, as a "law and order" approach toward crime.[90] It also clarifies why the idea of universal salvation is the paradigmatic heresy, since universalism is the ultimate eradication of all boundaries and hierarchies. Proponents of universalism strike at the heart of orthodoxy's entire authority structure and are thus often the ones most quickly excluded from the circle of true faith. Even those Christians who are uncomfortable with a "law and order" Christianity have difficulty letting go of the assumption that a "law and order" god still awaits us after death.

To summarize, then, the implicit structure of Christian orthodoxy involves the whitewashing of history and the policing of a community's prescriptive norms, all under the assumption of obedience to a magisterial authority. Orthodoxy, as I have defined it here, is thus implicitly (and often explicitly) an authoritarian program of *making Christianity great again.* It is not hard to see why communities formed by this program might find themselves attracted to the politics of Make America Great Again, but there is no necessary relationship between MCGA and MAGA. To be sure, the conservative quests for the rule of faith have tended strongly in the direction of the white conservative politics of resentment and nostalgia that characterize the Trump-era Republican Party. But what distinguishes MCGA politically is not Trumpism so much as what Stephen Holmes calls antiliberalism: the intellectual tradition and political culture defined by opposition to modern ideas and attitudes – such as individualism, humanitarianism, and universalism – that advocates of antiliberalism consider to be "the prime symptoms of cultural decay and moral disintegration in the modern world."[91] Such antiliberalism can be "either politically anodyne or politically calamitous depending on contingent historical circumstances," and it happens to be the case that today's anxious, polarized, apocalyptic conditions have created an environment ripe for the weaponization of antiliberalism.[92] While the politics of Christian antiliberalism ranges from common good traditionalism to integralism, the resurgence of the latter since 2016 can be traced to Christian thinkers who, as part of the global persecution discourse coalition, view the church "as being under a uniquely hostile and more aggressive attack" and are willing to propose even more aggressive countermeasures.[93] The phenomenon of Trumpism is but one manifestation of antiliberalism, though a particularly belligerent one. The conservative quest for true Christianity that produces the politics of MCGA long predated the rise of Trump and will live beyond him in other forms. We will not solve the issue by merely changing the historical conditions. The problem rests with the logic of orthodoxy that compels the conservative quest in the first place.[94]

BEGINNING AGAIN – BEYOND ORTHODOXY

Christian orthodoxy has embedded within itself a mythical storyline, one that is widely accepted by both proponents and detractors. According to this storyline, orthodoxy pays no attention to historical circumstances and cultural changes; it is rigorously consistent in holding fast to the apostolic tradition, "the faith that was once and for all handed on to the saints" (Jude 3, NRSVUE). The storyline has obvious advantages. For those who view themselves as orthodox, it reassures them that their faith is true and right. For an older generation of liberals convinced of their own story of progress, this storyline reassures them that orthodoxy is stuck in the past, doomed to an ineluctable demise because of its inability to adapt.

Both are wrong, however, because the storyline itself is flawed. It is not simply that church authorities codify new doctrines as orthodoxy in response to new theological crises; that much can be described as the development or clarification of the same orthodox rule of faith, as Newman himself did. It is rather the case that orthodoxy itself, as a strategy for religious identify formation and social cohesion, has changed over the centuries, adapting with success to new historical conditions. "Orthodoxy should not be seen as an unchanged relic from earlier times," as Hellemans observes, "but as an identity-enhancing strategy, aiming at and resulting in religious change."[95] Orthodoxy has gone through numerous cycles of reform and reification, creative change and conservative institutionalization. Instead of speaking about orthodoxy as a singular entity, we should instead speak of "orthodox strategies" that are "always new and risky ventures in the face of ever changing reality." These strategies are "creative inventions," both theologically and practically. In the same way that there are only Christianities in the plural, so too "there are only orthodoxies in the plural, each constituting a different attempt at orthodoxy."[96] One goal of this book has been to illustrate this point, showing the range of efforts to construct an anti-modern orthodoxy within modernity.

Orthodoxy changes because the world changes, but the different strategies share certain features. Rather than assume that orthodoxy is something fixed and then evaluating whether it is true or false, the question to ask of orthodoxy is instead what its strategies reveal about how those who promote orthodoxy understand the norms of Christian faith. Put another way, what does the quest for the rule of faith imply about Christianity in the modern world? Why is adhering to an orthodox norm a prescription for authentic Christian faith? How has this norm been constructed? And to whose authority am I required to submit? The evasive or simplistic answers I have received to such questions suggest that orthodox strategies are often efforts to suppress critical inquiry by enforcing authoritarian power, while masking its operation through the pieties of religious community. As I have argued in this book, the strategies around historic Christian doctrine, normative Christian culture, and truly Christian politics end up distorting the past, creating the conditions for cultural imperialism, and generating political discourse coalitions premised on an us/them binary that not only violently suppress difference but also lead to warfare, both rhetorical and real. These strategies have been and continue to be remarkably successful, and their capacity to adapt to new circumstances suggests that the quest for the rule of faith will have a long future. The question is whether it is a future in which we will want, or even be able, to live.

None of this should be taken to suggest that those who propound orthodoxy are necessarily engaged in promoting authoritarian religion.

On the contrary, I have encountered many Christians who fervently embrace orthodoxy and would recoil at the examples I have surveyed in this work. But individual instances of what we might oxymoronically call "liberal orthodoxy" do not address two central problems. First, participation in orthodoxy contributes to a discourse coalition that legitimates and empowers the dangerous and deadly strategies that I have explored (as well as many others I did not have space to discuss). Second, participation in orthodoxy still trades on the assumptions about the nature of normative, prescriptive Christianity that I have examined here – assumptions that imply authoritarianism, even if they are never brought to conscious reflection. The problem of orthodoxy, like that of policing in general, is not a case of a few "bad apples." As in every instance, the problem is systemic – and the solution must be equally systemic.

This brings us back to liberalism and the essence of Christianity where this study began. While the conservative quest may have been a reaction to the liberal quest, this does not necessarily mean the solution lies in a recovery of the latter. That, too, can become yet another form of restorative nostalgia. The liberal Christianities I surveyed were specific to their time and place, and there is no returning to that world, even if we wanted to. Moreover, the liberal essences that theologians proposed were often as exclusionary as the orthodox alternative.

Karl Barth is the clearest example of this. He and the other dialectical theologians were fond of criticizing both orthodoxy and liberalism, viewing them both as failures to speak truly of God.[97] Orthodoxy – what Barth frequently called "dead orthodoxy" – fails because it seeks to objectify God in doctrinal propositions, while liberalism fails because it seeks to objectify God in human experience.[98] This oversimplification on both sides served their rhetorical purposes. The dialectical theologians had a tendency at times to imply that their alternative was the one authentic means by which to speak of God. Even if this was clearly not their intention, it was certainly how many read and used their work. Barth was at his most radical when he claimed that dogma – meaning orthodox theology – is an "eschatological concept" and thus something that only exists on the other side of eternity.[99] Consequently, no theology can claim to be orthodox and those that do run the risk of being idolatrous. Every theology is, at best, an effort to make sense of what God means today, and since "today" is always new, "the theologian cannot be content with establishing and communicating the results obtained by some classical period. ... For this reason, serious theological work is forced, again and again, to begin from the beginning."[100]

Barth did not always live up to this ideal, and those who adopted his program at times seemed flatly to reject it, insisting that theology follow Barth's precise method in order to be truly faithful to the gospel. But it remains a worthy compass pointing us in the right direction. Following where the compass leads today will involve listening again to the liberal voices that Barth himself disparaged, as well as the many others who were never included in – and indeed were actively excluded from – the quest from the beginning, because of the magisterial Protestant, Eurocentric, patriarchal, and heteronormative blinders that have characterized the Western Christian tradition. The purpose of this work is not to follow the compass; that is for another time and place, and others have already done so. But there is still a need for guidelines on how best to read it, and that is what I will provide in the Conclusion.

Conclusion

The Many Rules of Christianity

ANYONE WHO SPENDS TIME following the Christian discourse on social media will invariably come across statements like, "You cannot proclaim Jesus is Lord and be a nationalist," or "You cannot be a true Christian and support Trump," or "You cannot follow Jesus and support murdering babies."[1] Such statements are by no means a recent phenomenon. Frederick Douglass in 1845 similarly wrote, in effect: "You cannot follow Christ and participate in slaveholding religion."[2] By and large, those who make such claims and those who read them both intuitively understand that these are not meant to be taken as descriptive fact. Not only would it be impossible to evaluate the authenticity of each individual's Christian identity, but in most cases, setting any of these up as a descriptive criterion would conflict with the average person's views about what actually makes a person a "Christian" (e.g., baptism, personal confession of faith, etc.). We understand instead that such statements are meant to be taken as prescriptive ideals. It *ought* not to be the case, according to this person on social media, that someone proclaims Jesus is Lord on Sunday and joins a nationalist rally on Monday. Things *should* be otherwise.

There are, however, two problems with these claims, which concern descriptivism and prescriptivism respectively. I began this book by explaining the descriptivist problem, articulated most forcefully by Chrissy Stroop. By stating that such people *cannot* be Christian and thus, implicitly, *are* not, such statements are descriptively false and construct idealized versions of Christianity that conveniently omit those whom the speaker would like to exclude from the ranks. Both progressive and conservative Christians who engage in this rhetoric create an

271

oversimplified account of Christianity in which – like the "no true Scotsman" fallacy – "no true Christian" has a position that differs from their own, and thus genuine Christianity is always innocent of whatever they view as immoral or anathema. The result is the constant gerrymandering of Christianity to fit the definition of the moment. This leads us to the prescriptivist problem with these statements I raised at the end of the book, namely, that they reinforce an account of Christian orthodoxy that refuses to make space for difference and wishes to exercise magisterial authority to exclude anyone who violates the prescribed norms. I say "wishes to" because these statements are typically written by people who have no institutional power to exclude anyone, but they suggest that, were such power in their hands, they would not hesitate to employ it. There are, of course, some differences we rightly refuse to make space for, but the use of prescriptive orthodoxy as the mechanism for such refusal opens the door for weaponized forms of exclusion that only compound the problem.

It is tempting, in the face of these problems, to give up on norms altogether and opt for the most neutral version of descriptivism: Christianity is simply whatever people who call themselves Christian do. There is an important grain of truth in this to which I will return. Defining Christianity in such a detached way, however, would only work for journalists and academics seeking to analyze Christianity as an object. For those who view Christianity subjectively, as being in some sense normative for their own lives, a purely descriptivist attitude is impossible. But is it possible to conceive of a prescriptivism that does not repeat the errors of orthodoxy and Christian supremacy? That is what I hope to accomplish in the rest of this conclusion.

I have argued in this book that to be Christian in modernity is to be on a quest – a quest for the essence of Christianity. Conservatives no less than liberals are questing Christians, seeking to find a credible faith for the modern world. Not only are conservative questers reacting to liberalism, but they have constructed an antimodern essence that is defined in opposition to the liberal quest. Each aspect of the liberal quest – doctrine, culture, and politics, or believing, belonging, and behaving – has a corollary in the conservative quest, where antimodern antiliberals have doubled down on the boundaries of Christian identity in an effort to relieve the anxieties of modern society by pursuing the illusion of historic Christianity, the imperialism of Christian culture, and the martial politics of white cisheteronormative supremacy. The compulsion to construct a world without these anxieties is a many-headed hydra that will only breed more extreme efforts, with each failure only confirming their own sense of persecution and each success only revealing ever new anxieties that need to be suppressed. A clear example is the way, in the wake of *Roe v. Wade*'s overturning, conservative activists pushed harder for a nation-wide ban on abortion, restrictions on contraception, the end to same-gender marriage, and bans on transgender rights. It is inadequate to suggest that those who hold such views take the separatist route of forming intentional communities that abandon the rest of society to what they view as its heretical liberalism. The alternative to (Christo)fascism is not separatism but pluralism. Separatism maintains the logic of orthodoxy that divides the world into a pure, holy "us" in opposition to an impure, sinful "them." Dismantling the logic of orthodoxy itself is the task that lies ahead for Christianity in the twenty-first century.

The cliché conservative rejoinder is that this is just a new us-vs.-them, with the "us" being the liberals against the conservative "them." This is only superficially accurate. Conservatives like to play "gotcha" with liberals when it comes to tolerance, arguing that liberals are just as intolerant of conservatives as the conservatives are of liberals. Insofar as the divide is framed simply in terms of liberalism and conservatism, they have a valid point. Indeed, as I have argued in previous chapters, certain schools of liberal theology showed a tendency at times to be as prone to the logic of orthodoxy as the orthodox theologians. But the real division is *not* between conservatism and liberalism at all, but rather between fascism and pluralism – that is to say, between a vision of religion and society that seeks to exclude difference and dissent and a vision that encourages and even empowers multiple expressions of faith and multiple essences of Christianity. The problem with the conservative quest for the rule of faith is that it was self-consciously *not* a quest for an essence of Christianity, precisely because conservatives saw themselves as retrieving and inhabiting the only valid version of Christian identity to the exclusion of all heterodox alternatives. Dismantling orthodoxy does not necessarily mean uplifting liberal Christianity, but rather allowing for a plurality of Christianities to coexist, each recognizing the autonomy of the others and supporting their right to construct a faith that is meaningful to them.

The assumption by most is that this pluralist vision is only possible if we abandon norms and normativity entirely, as an older era of liberal theologians seemed to suggest was necessary. I want to propose instead that there is at least one way of retaining a normative, prescriptive Christianity that fosters pluralism, not only interreligious pluralism but also *intrareligious* pluralism – a pluralism internal to Christianity itself. To help articulate this, I turn to a resource from Reform Judaism, from which Christians have much to learn.

POLYDOXY: RELIGION AND THEOLOGY IN A PLURALISTIC AGE

The American Reform rabbi and philosopher of religion Alvin J. Reines (1926–2004) recognized that his community had a dilemma. While Reform Judaism clearly existed, it was not clear what kind of religion it actually was. Against those who claim that all Jews share a single religion – either Orthodox Judaism or a similar variation, which he calls the "Orthodox Jewish Cognate Complex" – Reines argues that there are multiple Jewish religions, one of which is Reform Judaism.[3] But with such ambiguity over what distinguishes the Reform Jewish community, the risk remained that the community would be unable "to attain a coherent religious identity."[4] Reines wrote his 1987 work *Polydoxy: Explorations in a Philosophy of Liberal Religion* to address this need.

Reines argues that the implicit defining characteristic of Reform Judaism is not a covenant with any divine power but instead what he calls the Freedom Covenant.[5] According to the Freedom Covenant, "every member possesses an ultimate right to religious self-authority, but, at the same time, has the duty to limit her or his exercise of freedom within the boundary set by the freedom of other members." The covenant thus establishes individual religious autonomy as well as the conditions for a community in which members enter into a relationship defined by this mutual recognition of religious autonomy. Another name for the Freedom Covenant is "polydoxy," which is a term that applies to any religious community that abides by the commitment to religious autonomy. Reines calls religions that accept this covenant as their norm "Freedom Covenant religions" or "polydox religions," while the communities that profess the covenant are "Freedom Covenant religious communities" or "polydox communities."[6] The Freedom Covenant is the one "essence" of polydoxy, the sole norm of those religions that embrace religious autonomy. Polydox religions that share this essence are essentially the same religion even if they differ from one another nonessentially, due to the use of different names, symbols, liturgies, and other nonessential beliefs and practices.[7] Religions that are "latent polydoxies" subscribe to beliefs that imply polydoxy, while "de facto polydox communities" are religious communities whose members behave as if they were polydoxies without explicitly claiming the label.[8]

Polydoxy stands against every form of orthodoxy and authoritarianism. Reines distinguishes between these terms with respect to religion, associating orthodoxy with beliefs about God and revelation and associating authoritarianism with beliefs about how religious communities are structured. Orthodox religions, according to Reines, are those that believe "there exists an entity ... who not only possesses absolute authority but who has also laid down dogmas and practices that the adherents of the religion must follow." Orthodoxy typically involves a belief in verbal revelation, with the assumption that such revelation is permanently binding on all adherents. Historically, orthodox religions have also been authoritarian, meaning they subscribe to what Reines calls the "absolute authority principle," which says that "the right exists in a religious community for a member or group of members to exercise absolute religious authority over the other members of the community."[9] These members act as the authoritative interpreters of revelation and the representatives of the entity that gave the revelation.

Polydoxy also stands in contrast to liberal religion. Reines categorizes liberal religions under the broad umbrella of orthodoxy (though halfway between orthodoxy and polydoxy), because they "limit the creedal freedom of their adherents, and impose dogmas beyond that which is logically or organizationally necessary for a maximum freedom liberal religious community."[10] He subdivides liberal religions into two categories: supernatural liberal religions and natural liberal religions. The former includes Liberal Judaism, Liberal Catholicism, and Liberal Protestantism, while the latter includes groups like the Unitarian Universalists and Ethical Humanists. The supernatural liberal religions affirm greater intellectual liberty but still mandate certain dogmas, such as the existence of a theistic God, the special status of the Bible, and in the case of Christianity, the divinity of Jesus. While the supernatural liberal religions are liberal in contrast to their traditional, orthodox versions, there remain dogmas and practices that are mandatory for members to remain in good standing. Reines is more critical of the natural liberal religions, which, in his judgment, have orthodoxies as extensive as traditional supernatural orthodoxies, but are still called "liberal" because of the assumption that norms regarding rationalism, empiricism, and antitheism are not dogmas.[11] For Reines, anything that is compulsory for participation in a community is a dogma. In contrast to traditional orthodoxy and the orthodox liberal religions, polydox religions have only "the one dogma of the Freedom Covenant" – a religious norm that liberates members from any obligatory beliefs and encourages the creative exploration of beliefs and practices, both old and new, that a person finds meaningful and fulfilling.[12]

Reines examines religious autonomy primarily in terms of doctrines and practices that relate to God, such as theism, (super)naturalism, providence, and revelation. He largely sidesteps whether this autonomy extends to sociocultural norms – often codified as doctrine – regarding how society should be structured and the way human beings are supposed to live. Because of the importance of such norms to the rule of faith today, especially within the context of American Christianity, it is necessary to reflect more directly on how the Freedom Covenant pertains to these norms. I have in mind patriarchy, cisheteronormativity, and religious nationalism as examples of such norms. In the context of describing Orthodox Judaism, Reines mentions its patriarchal rules regarding marriage and divorce that "clearly have calamitous consequences for the women they affect."[13] Reines does not say so, but he implies that polydox religion would not have such rules. I argue we can make this boundary explicit in a way that does not contradict the commitment to autonomy. While polydoxy does not place doctrinal restrictions around beliefs and practices pertaining to God, the Freedom

Covenant *does* place restrictions around beliefs and practices pertaining to human beings precisely in order to ensure each person's religious autonomy. Beliefs and practices regarding, for example, women's subordination, the rejection of LGBTQ persons, and the supremacy of a single nation over others infringe on the autonomy of those who do not conform to these norms and thus have no place in a polydox community. To be sure, polydoxy respects the right of individuals to hold such views in isolation from others, but it equally protects the community from positions that would undermine the community's very existence and raison d'être. It is irrelevant for the purposes of prohibition whether these social doctrines are justified on theological grounds rooted in God, but since the very enforcement of these norms requires appealing to some exclusive, hierarchical revelation – such as an infallible scripture – such theological grounding would already be in violation of polydoxy's foundational commitments. Once again, this is not the creation of a new orthodoxy but rather the conditions for a pluralistic community and society.

Reines does not articulate the basis for an alternative religion but rather provides a vocabulary and framework for thinking about religion as such. While he describes a concrete instance of polydoxy in the form of what he calls polydox Judaism, this is meant to show one possible example of what polydoxy looks like in practice. A virtually infinite variety of forms are theoretically possible. His work is a formal description of the normative parameters necessary for any religion that wishes to break free of orthodoxy – and thus the rule of faith – altogether. Following Reines's lead, my proposal in this conclusion is to develop a polydox Christianity, or rather polydox Christianities, that embrace the "many beliefs" or "many rules" of polydoxy.[14] What those beliefs or rules might be can only be decided by each individual exercising their religious autonomy, constructing a Christianity normative for no one beyond those who have freely embraced it for themselves. Whatever this Christianity looks like, it will not have a set of "right beliefs" but only the freedom to construct, explore, and hold many possible beliefs. Polydox Christianity will provide no basis for continuity or identity in the traditional senses of those terms. If there is continuity, it is only at the descriptive level of people self-identifying as Christian. Unlike the descriptivism of the journalist, polydox Christianity does not abandon prescriptivism entirely, but its prescribed norm is the polydox norm of religious autonomy – what Marcella Althaus-Reid calls "polyfidelity" – which provides a normative grounding for the messy pluralism of religious descriptivism.[15]

The proposal here is to democratize the quest for the essence of Christianity by relocating the quest from the work of academic and ecclesiastical professionals to the everyday lived religion of those who are now responsible for their own religious beliefs and practices. We need *more* quests for the Christian essence – though, in contrast to liberalism, it will not be *the* essence in the old sense of being the single, timeless point of continuity throughout the ages of history. Instead, each person will be on a quest for the essence as they understand it for themselves. Religious autonomy thus means that each person has the right to quest for their own essence, so long as they also respect everyone else's right to engage in their quests. Polydoxy is a quest not for continuity or communal identity but for a meaningful existence in the modern world.

While polydox religions have only one norm (the Freedom Covenant), polydox theologies may have any number of norms – so long as those norms do not reproduce the authoritarian dynamic of orthodoxy.[16] Any concrete polydox religion that makes space for multiple *doxa* will need polydox theologies that reflect on and generate multiple *doxa*. The distinction between polydox religion and polydox theology is particularly important with respect to the question of orthodoxy. Polydoxy in the sense of polydox religion is set in mutually exclusive contrast to orthodoxy, since these two terms refer to competing formal structures of authority: orthodoxy refers to the establishment of boundaries that are arbitrarily set by a magisterial authority that requires obedience, whereas polydoxy refers to the establishment of religious autonomy and thus the elimination of doctrinal boundaries. The formal distinction between orthodoxy and polydoxy is equivalent to the distinction between fascism and pluralism. Polydoxy in the sense of polydox theology, however, is not necessarily set in contrast to orthodox theology, because in this context the terms refer to material norms (e.g., incarnation, redemption, sacramentality, etc.) that are complex and already always open to multiple meanings and a plurality of embodied forms. Polydox theology – meaning a theology that supports the formation of polydox religious communities – can draw on the whole history of orthodox Christianity, so long as these theological concepts are differentiated from the boundary-making aspect of orthodoxy.[17] The purpose of this conclusion is not to develop a polydox theology but simply to begin thinking through the conditions for such theologies within the discursive field of Christianity.

Therapist and pastoral theologian Gary Pence made an initial attempt at polydox Christianity in a 2001 article, where he argued for embracing the changes in religious consciousness and commitment that were unfolding at the time. Rather than responding to a post-Christian North American society with a posture of anxiety, Pence argued instead for adopting Reines's model of polydox religion. The result would be an "open Christianity" that "repositions itself as a vital, curious, non-anxious community." The new forms of spirituality emerging among young adults are "not phenomena to be feared, but windows into transformations of Christian faith and practice."[18] While this is an important insight, Pence was on less sure footing when it came to the theological framework for Christian identity that would support his polydox vision, relying on the postliberal resources of Robert Jenson. For a better theoretical framework, we need to turn to the work on polydoxy developed at Drew University.

In 2009, the ninth annual Transdisciplinary Theological Colloquium at Drew University focused on the topic of polydoxy, resulting in the 2011 volume, *Polydoxy: Theology of Multiplicity and Relation*, edited by Catherine Keller and Laurel C. Schneider, as well as a 2014 special issue of *Modern Theology* with articles responding to the book. Despite sharing the title of Reines's book, the work of this colloquium represents an exercise in polydox theology, not polydox religion. Reines is not mentioned by any of the contributors, nor is he referenced in any of the ten essays in the special issue. This does not mean there are no points of overlap, but the meaning of polydoxy is decidedly different in each case. Whereas Reines articulates a practical philosophy of religion that describes in formal terms how a polydox religion should structure itself, the contributors and respondents to the Keller and Schneider volume explore a distinctively Christian process theology of multiplicity, uncertainty, and apophatic unknowing. Polydoxy for Reines refers to a structure that encourages multiple religions and beliefs, while polydoxy for Keller and Schneider refers to a theology that originates in multiplicity (e.g., divine multiplicity, multiple sacred texts, and multiple religions) and explores the ambiguity internal to theology.[19] Reines would likely classify the latter as "orthodox liberal" because of the way ideas like materialism and process philosophy – as well as even the triune nature of God – are held up as implicitly normative values, and it is notable that Keller pits polydoxy not against trinitarian orthodoxy but against monotheistic "monodoxy."[20] Nevertheless, I want to suggest that aspects of Keller and Schneider's account of polydoxy can help guide the quest to develop concretely Christian polydoxies (in Reines's sense).

When it comes to polydox *theology*, the closest Reines himself comes is to articulate the kinds of theology suitable for polydoxy. Any theology based on authoritative revelation is inappropriate, including those that combine revelation with natural knowledge, such as the medieval synthesis of Thomas Aquinas. This leaves theology based on "subjective evidence" (e.g., prophetic vision, mystical union, personal experience, etc.) and theology based on public, naturally accessible, and empirically verifiable "objective evidence" (e.g., scientific data, historical records, universal human experience, etc.), so long as any such theology renounces claims to authority.[21] This is as far as Reines takes us. He intentionally leaves his readers with the space to figure out what beliefs and practices fit with the evidence as they encounter and understand it.

In that light, I read Keller and Schneider's *Polydoxy* as a series of reflections on a Christian polydox theology that derives primarily from the evidence of the ambiguity and indeterminacy that characterize human existence. Keller, in her chapter, draws on the work of the seventeenth-century English philosopher, Anne Conway (1631–1679), whose single work of Platonist metaphysics develops what Keller calls a "cosmotheology of the multiple" rooted in the observation that each creature is a multiplicity because "we do not exist, let alone grow and thrive, without the help of the others and therefore of God."[22] Keller connects this empirical multiplicity with the apophatic insight into God's uncontrollability, grounded not in the private mystical experience of the divine but the public experience of life's complex multiplicity and relationality. The uncontrollable character of creaturely existence and divine becoming makes it impossible for any theology to become a discourse of mastery. Indeed, "negative theology *doctrinally* protects that uncontrollability," thereby preventing the establishment of new theological and religious authorities.[23]

The details of Keller's apophatic panentheism are not important here, as interesting as they may be. What is instead relevant are the two implicit norms that structure her chapter – and, by extension, most of the other work associated with the colloquium. The first norm focuses on publicly accessible, and typically empirical, evidence as the basis for understanding human existence and thus divine existence. The work associated with the "new materialist" turn in theology illustrates this norm in the way it embraces the empirical data of modern science to both exemplify and reconstruct theological claims.[24] Whitney Bauman, in an article reflecting on polydoxy and ecotheology, suggests a "phenomenological approach to epistemology" in which "we can only see, hear, taste, smell, touch and think so far into the past and future before our knowing shades off into mystery."[25] This norm prevents theologians from making appeals to unverifiable revelation as a source for exclusive knowledge and exclusionary authority. The second norm, which is the obverse of the first, is the uncontrollability of the divine. Whatever else a polydox theologian might want to say about the word "God," the idea of the divine refers to something that cannot be possessed or controlled in such a way that might give the theologian divine status or authority. Negative theology is merely one way to protect this uncontrollability. Many of the liberal theologies surveyed in Chapter 1 offer other resources to accomplish this, such as dialectical theology's emphasis on the eschatological event. Without the second norm, the first norm could lead to a natural theology in which the divine is objectified as part of the world, being available to empirical observation and analysis. The process theologians seek to obviate this concern by emphasizing the open-ended multiplicity of the world, but they also stress apophatic unknowing of the divine as a way to preclude any objectification. Both of these norms together make polydox theology functionally agnostic, not as a way of shutting off inquiry but instead keeping inquiry aware of its inherent limits and open toward new possibilities.

Another way to frame these norms is by returning to the distinction between intellectualism and voluntarism I introduced in Chapter 2 to help explain the rise of orthodoxy. Some of the earliest Christian theology was intellectualist, in the sense that theologians like Justin Martyr did not claim fundamentally new knowledge but rather related the person of Christ to Greek philosophical ideas that were understood to be available to any rational creature. It was precisely the connection of Jesus to this prior, publicly available knowledge that made the Christian story compelling. As time progressed, however, it was increasingly in the church's interest to confine saving knowledge to the beliefs and practices taught by the church authorities, which led to the abandonment of intellectualism in favor of theological voluntarism: whatever the church says was deemed the orthodox truth. Liberal theology, I argued, was a quest for a modern intellectualism, rooted no longer in Greek philosophy but in the moral law, human experience, political action, and the like. Theological intellectualism thus implies at least the first norm for polydox theology noted above – namely, the *public accessibility* of theological sources. But to prevent efforts at confining and controlling the divine within the limits of one's social, cultural, or political context, it is necessary to combine this first norm with the second regarding the *public inaccessibility* of the divine. In the interest of developing future theologies that achieve both, Keller and Schneider's polydoxy provides a useful model and resource.[26]

Ultimately, though, the development of a polydox Christianity (in Reines's sense of polydoxy) requires the subordination of all theological norms to the right of individuals to refuse beliefs and practices that do not align with their own sense of what is true, just, or spiritually meaningful. For this reason, in addition to the norms regarding accessibility of evidence and inaccessibility of the divine, we must add the norm of the *violability* – not just reformability – of all religion and theology. To better understand what this means, we must turn to the example of the United States Constitution and the question of constitutional disobedience.

THEOLOGICAL DISOBEDIENCE: TOWARD A
TRANSGRESSIVE CHRISTIANITY

The civil religion associated with the United States Constitution is as prescriptive as any traditional orthodox religion, complete with normative founders, a normative text, a normative interpretive method (Robert Bork's "orthodoxy" of originalism), a hierarchy endowed with magisterial authority over how to interpret and apply the text, and a civil theology of constitutional nationalism that purports to define the relation between this text and the identity of the people who are obedient to it. The disputes over constitutionalism thus provide a useful analog for similar disputes over Christian norms. Just as the dominant tension within Christian theology is between conservatives who seek to recover a traditional rule of faith and liberals who opt for an essence of Christianity that seeks to retain some level of continuity with the past, so too the dominant tension in constitutionalism is between originalists who advocate restricting the Constitution's meaning to the time when it was ratified and living constitutionalists who argue that the essence of the Constitution endures even if the application changes over time.[27] And just as polydoxy represents a contrast to both conservative and liberal Christianity, so too there is a contrast to both originalism and living constitutionalism – what Louis Michael Seidman calls constitutional disobedience.

Seidman's *On Constitutional Disobedience* is a concise but powerful argument that asks: Why should we obey a text written down over two hundred years ago? If "one thinks that, all-things-considered, the right thing to do is X, but the Constitution tells us to do not-X," on what grounds should we abandon our practical judgment simply because a group of men in the late eighteenth century said so?[28] While Seidman's argument is specific to the political system of the United States and there is no need to rehearse all of his points here, certain features of the constitutional debate are relevant to the relationship between present-day Christians and the tradition of the rule of faith. Seidman points out, for instance, how "vague and sweeping" the claims in the Constitution are, such that in most cases it is possible for each side of the political spectrum "to read [the Constitution] in a fashion that embodies its own contestable political programs while delegitimating the programs of its adversaries."[29] A much more pressing version of the same problem applies to the Bible and the creeds, for whom the distance of time and the complications of genre and audience compound already ambiguous texts. The problem of time raises the issue of who consented to these rules in the first place. Constitutionalism bases its obedience on the claim that "we the people" chose to be bound by this document, but as Seidman points out, "no one alive today had anything to do with the ratification process."[30] One generation cannot consent on behalf of a future generation. For this reason, Thomas Jefferson wrote in a letter to James Madison that "no society can make a perpetual constitution," for "every constitution then, and every law, naturally expires at the end of 19 years. If it be enforced longer, it is an act of force, and not of right."[31] There is no equivalent proposal with respect to the rule of faith for the simple reason that, traditionally at least, such doctrines were thought to derive from divine revelation and were thus timelessly valid.

Once we strip away these assumptions and examine the situation historically, we see that Christianity and constitutionalism face the same problem – namely, how to justify obedience over time. In both cases, it is a matter of identity, as I have been arguing throughout this book. Seidman observes that the argument for such obedience ultimately rests on the assumption that "the myth of connection over time is essential to national identity," and the same is true for religious identity. Defenders of tradition in both communities "rely on [their] connection to a shared, if invented, past if [they] are to be an authentic community," both assuming that the goal of their respective prescriptivisms is to establish a stable, authentic, transhistorical identity.[32] Seidman has an answer for what this connection over time might be, to which I will return, but it is important to face the reality that the idea of authentic group identity over time is nothing more than a myth – what Seidman, borrowing from the lawyer Felix Cohen, calls "transcendental nonsense."[33] This supposedly transhistorical constant is a convenient abstraction from the messy, constantly fluctuating reality of lived experience, in which virtually the only reason such an identity exists is that people say it does. The fact that communities continue to claim obedience to the same text over time cannot obscure the reality that this purported obedience is often anything but, as individuals and factions mold the tradition in the direction of what they believe is right. Appealing to the same texts guarantees nothing in terms of what the community believes and practices, much to the chagrin of those in authority. So why claim obedience at all?

This brings us back to the central question posed by every traditionalism, whether constitutional, biblical, creedal, or otherwise: Why should we disregard our current knowledge or experience in favor of what people said centuries ago? Within the context of Christianity, there are typically two main arguments in response. The hierarchical argument, the one that goes back to early Christianity's shift to theological voluntarism, simply says: "Because we, the church authorities who speak for God, say so." This position believes even asking such questions is an affront to the leaders of the church and thus, in practice, a denial of God. Since this approach is increasingly unpopular and nonsensical to those raised with a healthy skepticism of authority, the more common defense of the tradition – the one most similar to the constitutional defense – opts for the populist argument, most famously expressed by G. K. Chesterton: "Tradition means giving votes to the most obscure of all classes, our ancestors. It is the democracy of the dead. Tradition refuses to submit to the small and arrogant oligarchy of those who merely happen to be walking about."[34] As compelling as this sounds, "the dead" are in fact not obscure at all but rather a class that infinitely exceeds those who are living, growing at a rate that the living will never match. Giving votes to the dead means, in effect, permanently nullifying the views of those alive today and never making our ancestors answer for their crimes. If we held to this view in other domains, we would never abolish the injustices – colonialism, enslavement, patriarchy, racial oppression, and the like – that characterized large swaths of human history. Tradition in this sense is not the "democracy of the dead" but rather, as Seidman puts it, "intergenerational imperialism."[35]

Appealing to the democracy of the dead relinquishes our responsibility for making our community better and only makes sense for those privileged few who believe that reform is never warranted. We need to take a lesson from the environmental movement, in which a key refrain is that future generations have rights we are obligated to respect.[36] If we reframe tradition from this perspective, our concern should not be the democracy of the dead but the democracy of those-to-come – the democracy of the future, rather than the past. And since future generations have not yet had a chance to decide for themselves what kind of world or community they want, it is incumbent on those alive now, those who belong to the future's past, to create the best possible conditions for their existence. We need to replace "intergenerational imperialism" with "intergenerational justice." The democracy of the dead is simply the tyranny of the past, whereas the democracy of the future is the liberation of the present. The maxim that "the earth belongs to the living" – and to those not yet living – is as true for the church as it is for the nation.[37]

Jefferson's notion that constitutions expire after nineteen years should apply to religious rules of faith as much as it should to political rules of society. Ernst Troeltsch sought to do theology in light of the fact that humankind's time "upon earth amounts to several hundred thousand years or more" and humanity's "future may come to still more." It is therefore extremely difficult to identify a single doctrine, rule, or tradition as the exclusive norm for all. To say that all theology should be "Christocentric," meaning centered around a specific conception of Christ, "looks far too much like the absolutizing of our own contingent area of life. That is in religion what geocentrism and anthropocentrism are in cosmology and metaphysics."[38] No theological perspective is permanently valid. Because "each age interprets [Jesus] really quite differently" and claims him for their own account of the essence, Christianity throughout history has had "many Christs," to use Sarah Coakley's term, and there will be many more Christs to come.[39] For Troeltsch this is not something to lament but simply a fact of history. When Troeltsch stated that "the essence of Christianity differs in different epochs," this was meant as a statement of descriptive fact.[40] But polydox Christianity turns this description into a programmatic norm: the essence of Christianity *must* change in different epochs, even in different generations and different cultural situations. There ought to be many rules of faith, many essences, many Christs. Rudolf Bultmann similarly argued that every articulation of the Christian community's prescriptive norms is an act of historical translation from a previous generation to the present-day community. Contrary to those who claim that a previous creed or confession should stand for all time, he instead claims, like Jefferson, that "even the most accurate translation needs to be translated again in the next generation." Every articulation of the Christian essence is "formulated for today, and only for today."[41] The quest never arrives at its destination but is a constant *questing*.

Here we find, with Seidman's aid, a way to think about what constitutes the Christian community's connection – perhaps even identity, in a loose sense – over time. Seidman argues that the key to constitutional disobedience is not the rejection of past or present political structures, but rather the recognition that "these categories are constructed" and thus "we have an ongoing choice between structures." Within the context of political community, the choice means we could stick with a traditional constitution or opt instead for something entirely different.

> Once we see that we have a choice, the possibility emerges that the people alive at any one time will make different choices. In other words, it becomes plain that constitutionalism is a site for struggle and contestation rather than for settlement. ... On this view, the defining characteristic of our political order is precisely that the political order is never finally defined. ... On this view, constitutional disobedience is not only permissible; it is built into the fabric of our country.[42]

We can apply this directly to Christianity. A polydox Christianity, as I am defining it, would be a religion in which the defining characteristic is that its religious and theological order is never finally defined. Christian prescriptivism would be a site for struggle and dialogue over the essence or rule of faith, a constant contest over the structures and norms of Christian community. The possibility would be always open for people to choose what norms are more appropriate to the given moment. Theological disobedience would be built into the very fabric of the religion. Indeed, it already is. Christian faith harbors "an impulse toward total and defiant faithlessness" within itself, as David Bentley Hart observes. "Christianity is filled with an indomitable and subversive ferment, an inner force of dissolution that refuses to crystallize into something inert or stable," always oriented instead toward the future. It is this "ungovernable and seditious" element that polydoxy recognizes as normative.[43] A questing, polydox Christianity is a *transgressive* Christianity. Rather than frame Christianity as a binary tension between normativity and transgression, polydoxy constructs a Christianity whose normativity *is* transgression – an ongoing violation of past rules in search of new theological norms and structural forms.

Theological disobedience is a mode of religious practice that willingly disregards scripture, creeds, and confessions when they fail to suit the needs of the moment. Inculcating a blind obedience to the texts of the past on the assumption that what is ancient or original is thereby normative leads, as I have argued, to authoritarianism and warfare, since the only way to enforce arbitrary standards that do not actually serve the needs of the moment is to impose them by force. Instead of justifying religious norms based on their continuity with the past, we ought to base them instead on their continuity with the future, and since the future is inherently open-ended, the norms we articulate in the present must remain open as well to alternative possibilities.

Put another way, the pursuit of polydox Christianity means that everyone must embrace heresy.[44] The word "heresy" derives from the Greek word *hairesis*, meaning "choice" or "choosing," and can refer, depending on context, either to a chosen opinion (i.e., heresy) or to a group that follows their chosen opinions (i.e., sect or faction).[45] The assumption embedded in this term is that if an opinion is chosen, it must not be true and therefore cannot be orthodox. The idea of orthodoxy originated in the belief that truth is given, not chosen – discovered, not constructed. According to the Acts of the Apostles, the followers of Jesus are called a *hairesis*, a sect, because of their choice to follow a different authority from the available orthodoxies of the time (Acts 24:5), whereas in Paul's first letter to the Corinthians, he criticizes the church there for having "heresies among you" (1 Cor 11:19). The effort to police the boundaries of orthodoxy appears already in Paul but becomes especially pronounced in the later catholic epistles, where there are warnings about "false teachers" bringing in "destructive heresies" (2 Pet 2:1). The road to the orthodox rule of faith had an early start, which makes it all the more difficult to uproot from our theological imaginations. Peter Berger famously observed in 1979 that, by forcing everyone to choose their faith, modernity created heretics of us all.[46] Since then postliberals and antimoderns of all stripes have sought to suppress or reverse the "heretical imperative" of modernity, a pursuit that can only

lead to new religious wars. The proposal here is to embrace the imperative, not as a foreign imposition from modernity but as the essence of
Christianity itself.

Theological disobedience does not mean religious anarchy, any more
than constitutional disobedience entails political anarchy. Even though
"we should give up on the pernicious myth that we are bound in conscience to obey the commands of people who died several hundred years
ago," this does not relieve people of the responsibility of showing why
their positions – political or religious – warrant people's attention and
deserve their respect. "Rather than insisting on tendentious interpretations of the Constitution designed to force the defeat of our adversaries," Seidman writes, "we ought to talk about the merits of their proposals
and ours."[47] Embracing this idea will require abandoning the binary
logic that assumes a doctrine is either right or wrong, either inside the
bounds of authentic faith or outside. Rather than judge an idea or
doctrine based on whether it agrees with some magisterial authority,
such as an ancient text or present-day leader, the proposal here, again
following Seidman, is to examine in detail each theology or religious
system and evaluate it based on more practical and relevant criteria, such
as the emancipatory potential it contains, the quality of life it promotes,
and the intellectual rigor it evinces.

Crucially, these criteria are *not* means of evaluating whether a particular theology is "truly Christian," much less "biblical" or "faithful to the
gospel." Any theology that aims to say something about Christianity is
Christian, but that does not mean it is something worth saying, much less
worth hearing. Theologies, like public policies, are not right or wrong,
biblical or unbiblical, constitutional or unconstitutional – or at the very
least, this is the wrong question.[48] The logic of orthodoxy has taught
Christians to ask boundary questions that examine foundations when
they should be asking practical questions that examine consequences.
Theologies may not be right or wrong, but they may be better or worse.
Orthodox prescriptivism has to give way to *comparative* prescriptivism.

The picture I have sketched here of a polydox Christianity defined
primarily by religious autonomy and the right to exercise theological
disobedience may seem destructive of religious community, but this is

because we are conditioned to assume that community is only sustainable by means of one's ideally free but often coerced obedience to magisterial authority. Polydoxy is in fact the condition for community – at least a healthy one. A polydox Christianity, as I envision it, would encourage the formation of pluralistic religious communities in which each person freely consents to the values and norms of their chosen community. Such norms would likely need to be kept to a minimum, and none could contradict the Freedom Covenant, but the point is that a group identity would still be possible. The community would be held together by mutual consent and respect for each person's autonomy, not by threats of exclusion or claims of being vested with special divine authority. Polydox Christianity would be, in the words of Steven Nemes, a Christianity "without anathemas."[49] When members propose new theologies and religious policies, they would not justify them on the grounds that these beliefs or policies alone follow from the biblical text or any other purported source of authority. Their justification instead would come solely from the group's collective agreement that adopting these positions reflects the kind of community they all want. Most importantly, the right of each person to demur would remain sacrosanct, and obedience would never be expected as a condition for ongoing participation.

Polydox Christian communities would be characterized by what John J. Thatamanil calls "relational pluralism," referring to an entangled, polydox pluralism in which each person's understanding of God and religion is bound up in complex ways with their neighbors, both within and outside of their communities. The logic of orthodoxy encourages thinking of traditions as hermetically sealed spaces and discourses whose norms ideally remain unaffected by supposedly "external" conditions. Postliberalism was merely the most extreme version of this way of thinking, but it is basic to the concept of orthodoxy as such and finds expression in the language of the *regula fidei* with its mathematically precise rules. A polydox relational pluralism recognizes, by contrast, that all traditions – all religious essences and the individuals and communities who embody them – "grow as they learn from each other." Every tradition is a syncretistic, hybrid construction. A polydox Christianity informed by this understanding of pluralism "refuses to arrest processes of mutual transformation by which our traditions came to be in the first place."[50] Multiplicity and difference are essential to the human condition, and our religious communities ought to reflect this – both theologically and structurally.

The goal of polydox Christianity, in short, is a detoxified form of Christian community. Given just how toxic most forms of institutional religion have been and continue to be, the possibility of genuine polydoxy remains a question of religious imagination.

WHO IS A CHRISTIAN?

In his 1949 essay on the protest novels *Uncle Tom's Cabin* and *Native Son*, James Baldwin chastises the authors for their implicit theologies. The protest novelists, like "those alabaster missionaries to Africa," seek to save society from some obvious evil, while assuring those on the right side of their own salvation. *Uncle Tom's Cabin*, he says, "is activated by what might be called a theological terror, the terror of damnation." The novel breathes a self-righteous panic that "is not different from that spirit of medieval times which sought to exorcize evil by burning witches; and is not different from that terror which activates a lynch mob."[51] Similarly, the tragedy of Bigger Thomas's character is that "he has accepted a theology that denies him life," believing that his humanity is something he must prove.

Whether or not one agrees with Baldwin's judgment on the novels themselves, his essay is important for the way he diagnoses the failure of the protest novel as a *theological* failure. It promotes a theology, he says, marked by the "rejection of life, the human being, the denial of his beauty."[52] What makes the protest novel theological is not God-talk but rather the way it generates anxiety about salvation. By filling readers with panic about the evils that threaten them, the novel also gives them the "thrill of virtue" by assuring them they are within the circle of the redeemed.[53] The theological error here is the logic of orthodoxy itself. Orthodoxy is not the belief that one's views are correct; that is merely conviction, and we would be lost without it. Orthodoxy is instead the belief that everyone else's views are wrong unless they come to share one's own exact perspective. Until they conform to the supposedly true perspective, they are excluded from the identity of the true Christian –

that is, from salvation. The result is theological terror, because once the stakes are raised to the level of eternity, any action, no matter how violent, becomes justified in the mission to rescue the lost from damnation.

In castigating the protest novel's life-denying theology of orthodoxy, however, Baldwin suggests an alternative logic. Rather than setting orthodoxy up as the goal, and thus justifying whatever actions are needed to attain it, Baldwin alludes to the possibility of making the beauty of human existence itself, in all its complexity and multiplicity, the goal of our endeavors. The prescriptive goal for Christian theology would not be whether it is orthodox – the criteria for which are arbitrary and authoritarian – but rather whether it is *life-promoting*, whether it embraces the human condition in its pluriformity. The rule of such a faith would be difference rather than sameness, polydoxy rather than orthodoxy. Life rather than death.

The anxiety over group identities and religious boundaries leads us time and again to ask life-denying questions to determine whether someone or something is Christian or not. In response to the bewildering array of claims in our Internet Age, it may seem natural to ask, "Who is a Christian, and how can I tell?" I am suggesting that this is the wrong question, and we should cease trying to answer it. The more important questions are always the more difficult: How does this person understand Christianity? What sources and norms does their understanding presuppose? How does their understanding of Christianity compare to previous accounts and to my own? What implications does their understanding have for the common good and the flourishing of society? What implications does their understanding have for the future of religion and humanity? How does their understanding promote life rather than death?

Asking these questions will not tell us who is truly a Christian, but they might help construct a Christianity worth believing.

Notes

Preface

1 Michael Gryboski, "John MacArthur Says 'True Believers' Will Vote for Trump, Can't Affirm Abortion and Trans Activism," *Christian Post*, September 2, 2020.

2 I use the terms "traditionalist" and "conservative" interchangeably. The political overtones that come with the term "conservative Christian" are intentional, and the story I am telling seeks to show how doctrinal and cultural conservatism have been bound up with the political conservatism that characterizes so much talk of tradition today.

3 Michael Kammen, *Mystic Chords of Memory: The Transformation of Tradition in American Culture* (New York: Knopf, 1991), 6.

4 David W. Congdon, *The Mission of Demythologizing: Rudolf Bultmann's Dialectical Theology* (Minneapolis: Fortress, 2015); David W. Congdon, *Rudolf Bultmann: A Companion to His Theology* (Eugene: Cascade Books, 2015).

5 John G. Flett, *Apostolicity: The Ecumenical Question in World Christian Perspective* (Downers Grove: IVP Academic, 2016).

6 David Bentley Hart, *Tradition and Apocalypse: An Essay on the Future of Christian Belief* (Grand Rapids: Baker Academic, 2022).

7 The term "exvangelical" (referring to those who identify as ex-evangelical) was popularized by Blake Chastain, creator and host of the podcast of the same name.

8 Wheaton College, "Community Covenant," www.wheaton.edu/about-wheaton/community-covenan/t.

9 "Standards of Conduct," *InForm: Bulletin of Wheaton College* 57, no. 4 (1980): 17–19.

10 See Randall Balmer, *Bad Faith: Race and the Rise of the Religious Right* (Grand Rapids: Eerdmans, 2021).

Introduction

1 Franklin Graham, "Shame, shame on the ten Republicans," Facebook, January 14, 2021, www.facebook.com/FranklinGraham/posts/4048702435185907.

2 Russell D. Moore, "The Capitol Attack Signaled a Post-Christian Church, Not Merely a Post-Christian Culture," *Christianity Today*, January 5, 2022, www.christianitytoday.com/ct/2022/january-web-only/january-6-attack-russell-moore-post-christian-church.html.

3 Russell D. Moore, "Why the Church Should Neither Cave nor Panic about the Decision on Gay Marriage," *Washington Post*, June 26, 2015.

4 R. R. Reno, "Say 'No' to Death's Dominion," *First Things*, March 23, 2020, www.firstthings.com/web-exclusives/2020/03/say-no-to-deaths-dominion; Jason E. Vickers, "The Last Christians in America? R. R. Reno and the Bitter Remnant Mindset of *First Things*," *Providence*, April 7, 2020, https://providencemag.com/2020/04/last-christians-america-r-r-reno-bitter-remnant-mindset-first-things/.

5 PatriotTakes (@patriottakes), "Lauren Boebert claims the devil used the pandemic to trick people," Twitter, June 12, 2022, 7:15 p.m., https://twitter.com/patriottakes/status/1536140176006819844.

6 Avner Greif, *Institutions and the Path to the Modern Economy: Lessons from Medieval Trade* (Cambridge: Cambridge University Press, 2006), 30.

7 Harvey Whitehouse's theory of the ritual stance provides another way of understanding this from the perspective of social anthropology. According to Whitehouse, there are two ways to imitate another's behavior: the "instrumental stance" assumes that the behavior – such as that of a teacher or parent – ought to be causally transparent, meaning the action clearly achieves a desired end, and thus one imitates that behavior for the purpose of finding the best and most efficient way to achieve the goal; the "ritual stance" assumes that the behavior is "causally opaque," meaning it is "a random normative convention" that must be reproduced exactly in every detail. The instrumental stance encourages experimentation, while the ritual stance requires conformity: "Whereas the instrumental stance is a way of learning and improving useful technical skills via goal-directed imitation of both causally transparent and (theoretically resolvable) causally opaque behaviour, the ritual stance is a way of preserving cultural traditions via imitation of irremediably causally opaque behaviour." Causal opacity thus explains why rituals become essential to defining group identity. Whitehouse's theory might also explain why, in a time of rapid cultural change, religious groups would respond by ratcheting up the demand for obedience and creating new rituals and doctrines that have no function other than to demarcate who is "in" and who is "out." See Harvey Whitehouse, *The Ritual Animal: Imitation and Cohesion in the Evolution of Social Complexity* (Oxford: Oxford University Press, 2021), 25–28.

8 Michael J. Monahan, *The Creolizing Subject: Race, Reason, and the Politics of Purity* (New York: Fordham University Press, 2011), 71.

9 The term "to think whitely" comes from Jacob Alan Cook, who uses it to understand Bill Pannell's insight that, despite being a Black evangelical, he was culturally and theologically white. Whiteness thus operates transparently in the guise of cultural and theological norms. Jacob Alan Cook, *Worldview Theory, Whiteness, and the Future of Evangelical Faith* (Lanham: Lexington Books/Fortress Academic, 2021), 157–58, 176–79. Cook is also drawing on Willie James Jennings's idea of the "white gaze" and the social and theological imaginary of whiteness. See Willie James Jennings, *The Christian Imagination: Theology and the Origins of Race* (New Haven: Yale University Press, 2010), 103.

10 See John G. Gager, *The Origins of Anti-Semitism: Attitudes toward Judaism in Pagan and Christian Antiquity* (New York: Oxford University Press, 1983); J. Kameron Carter, *Race: A Theological Account* (New York: Oxford University Press, 2008); Jonathan Boyarin, *The Unconverted Self: Jews, Indians, and the Identity of Christian Europe* (Chicago: University of Chicago Press, 2009); Magda Teter, *Christian Supremacy: Reckoning with the Roots of Antisemitism and Racism* (Princeton: Princeton University Press, 2023). I think it best to avoid getting entangled in the question of whether the logic of orthodoxy or the logic of whiteness came first. Insofar as race is an invention of the Middle Ages, as Geraldine Heng argues, orthodoxy precedes it. But Benjamin Isaac points to protoracist ideas in classical antiquity, and the construction of Christian orthodoxy begins around the same time that the gentile church moved to exclude Jewish people – that is to say, in the early second century. So arguably Christian orthodoxy and racism were formed together from the same basic impulse to exclude difference and otherness. See Geraldine Heng, *The Invention of Race in the European Middle Ages* (New York: Cambridge University Press, 2018); Benjamin H. Isaac, *The Invention of Racism in Classical Antiquity* (Princeton: Princeton University Press, 2004).

11 See John Colman, *Everyone Orthodox to Themselves: John Locke and His American Students on Religion and Liberal Society* (Lawrence: University Press of Kansas, 2023).

12 Ernst Troeltsch, "What Does 'Essence of Christianity' Mean? [1903]," in *Writings on Theology and Religion*, ed. Robert Morgan and Michael Pye (Atlanta: John Knox Press, 1977), 124–81, at 152, 157. Harnack's lectures were published in English as Adolf von Harnack, *What Is Christianity? Sixteen Lectures Delivered in the University of Berlin during the Winter-Term 1899–1900*, trans. Thomas Bailey Saunders (London: Williams & Norgate, 1901).

13 Hans Wagenhammer, *Das Wesen des Christentums: Eine begriffsgeschichtliche Untersuchung* (Mainz: Matthias-Grünewald-Verlag, 1973); Stephen Sykes, *The Identity of Christianity: Theologians and the Essence of Christianity from Schleiermacher to Barth* (Philadelphia: Fortress Press, 1984).

14 Gerald Izenberg, *Identity: The Necessity of a Modern Idea* (Philadelphia: University of Pennsylvania Press, 2016).

15 Saba Mahmood, *Religious Difference in a Secular Age: A Minority Report* (Princeton: Princeton University Press, 2016), 8; Talal Asad, *Formations of the Secular: Christianity, Islam, Modernity* (Stanford: Stanford University Press, 2003); Gil Anidjar, *Blood: A Critique of Christianity* (New York: Columbia University Press, 2014).

16 Jocelyne Cesari, *We God's People: Christianity, Islam and Hinduism in the World of Nations* (Cambridge: Cambridge University Press, 2021).

17 See Alasdair C. MacIntyre, *After Virtue: A Study in Moral Theory* (Notre Dame: University of Notre Dame Press, 1981); John Milbank, *Theology and Social Theory: Beyond Secular Reason* (Oxford: Blackwell, 1991); Brad S. Gregory, *The Unintended Reformation: How a Religious Revolution Secularized Society* (Cambridge, MA: Belknap Press, 2012).

18 Charles Taylor, *Sources of the Self: The Making of the Modern Identity* (Cambridge, MA: Harvard University Press, 1989); Charles Taylor, *A Secular Age* (Cambridge, MA: Belknap Press of Harvard University Press, 2007), 539–44.

19 Ethan H. Shagan, *The Birth of Modern Belief: Faith and Judgment from the Middle Ages to the Enlightenment* (Princeton: Princeton University Press, 2018), 136.

20 Eric C. Miller, "Who Defines Evangelicalism? An Interview with Mark Noll," *Religion & Politics*, April 28, 2020, https://religionandpolitics.org/2020/04/28/who-defines-evangel icalism-an-interview-with-mark-noll/. See Mark A. Noll, David Bebbington, and George M. Marsden, eds., *Evangelicals: Who They Have Been, Are Now, and Could Be* (Grand Rapids: Eerdmans, 2019). For an early critique of the new evangelical historiography on this point, see Leonard I. Sweet, "Wise as Serpents, Innocent as Doves: The New Evangelical Historiography," *Journal of the American Academy of Religion* 56, no. 3 (1988): 397–416.

21 The traditional account of evangelicalism is associated with David Bebbington, Thomas Kidd, Timothy Larsen, and Mark Noll. The revisionist approach that sees evangelicalism as a cultural and political, rather than theological, entity is associated with Darren Dochuk, Kristin Kobes Du Mez, Timothy Gloege, Marie Griffiths, Kevin Kruse, Daniel Silliman, Matthew Avery Sutton, Lauren Frances Turek, and Molly Worthen. On the apocalyptic aspect of modern American evangelicalism, see especially Matthew Avery Sutton, *American Apocalypse: A History of Modern Evangelicalism* (Cambridge, MA: Harvard University Press, 2014).

22 I use the terms mainline, ecumenical, and liberal Protestants to refer to the same group: generally speaking, those Christians, organizations, and denominations who were affiliated with the National Council of Churches and World Council of Churches. Key scholars include Elesha Coffman, David A. Hollinger, and Gene Zubovich. Mark Thomas Edwards is relatively alone in making the argument that a group of mainline Protestants, the neoorthodox "Christian Realists," were the religious right of their day. See Mark Thomas Edwards, *The Right of the Protestant Left: God's Totalitarianism* (New York: Palgrave Macmillan, 2012).

23 David A. Hollinger, *Christianity's American Fate: How Religion Became More Conservative and Society More Secular* (Princeton: Princeton University Press, 2022), 4, 133. On the Christian Right as originally a reaction to mainline, ecumenical Protestantism more than a response to political liberalism, see Neil J. Young, *We Gather Together: The Religious Right and the Problem of Interfaith Politics* (New York: Oxford University Press, 2016), 4–7. Regarding the term "ecumenicals," Zubovich also prefers "ecumenical Protestantism" to move away from the categories of "mainline" and "liberal" Protestantism. See Gene Zubovich, *Before the Religious Right: Liberal Protestants, Human Rights, and the Polarization of the United States* (Philadelphia: University of Pennsylvania Press, 2022), 313n3. No label is wholly satisfactory; the problem with "ecumenical" is that evangelicals had their own global, ecumenical networks. While Young points out that these interfaith and ecumenical partnerships began already in the mid-twentieth century, evangelicals became increasingly ecumenical in the late twentieth century as they formed deeper alliances with Catholic and Orthodox groups.

24 I use the term "Christian Right" in a descriptive sense to refer to those on the political right who self-describe as Christian and advocate for their right-wing version of Christianity. I use "Christian Right" and "Religious Right" interchangeably, though the former helps to connect their politics to their distinctively Christian claims.

25 Diana Butler Bass, "Militant Nostalgia," *The Cottage*, June 8, 2022, https://dianabutlerbass.substack.com/p/militant-nostalgia.

26 Melani McAlister, "A Kind of Homelessness: Evangelicals of Color in the Trump Era," *Religion and Politics*, August 7, 2018, https://religionandpolitics.org/2018/08/07/a-kind-of-homelessness-evangelicals-of-color-in-the-trump-era/.

27 See Jessica Martínez and Gregory A. Smith, "How the Faithful Voted: A Preliminary 2016 Analysis," *Pew Research Center*, November 9, 2016, www.pewresearch.org/fact-tank/2016/11/09/how-the-faithful-voted-a-preliminary-2016-analysis/. For the 2020 election, the 81 percent figure comes from the AP VoteCast survey. See NPR Staff, "Understanding The 2020 Electorate: AP VoteCast Survey," *NPR*, November 3, 2020, www.npr.org/2020/11/03/929478378/understanding-the-2020-electorate-ap-votecast-survey. Other surveys and exit polls showed "between 76 and 81% of white evangelical and 'born again' voters supporting Trump." Tom Gjelten, "2020 Faith Vote Reflects 2016 Patterns," *NPR*, November 8, 2020, www.npr.org/2020/11/08/932263516/2020-faith-vote-reflects-2016-patterns.

28 "Religion and the Presidential Vote," *Pew Research Center*, December 6, 2004, www.pewresearch.org/politics/2004/12/06/religion-and-the-presidential-vote/.

29 See Chrissy Stroop, "About Those Trump Voters for God? Stop Calling Them 'Fake Christians,'" *Not Your Mission Field*, May 3, 2017, https://cstroop.com/2017/05/03/about-those-trump-voters-for-god-stop-calling-them-fake-christians/.

30 Bob Smietana, "Many Who Call Themselves Evangelical Don't Actually Hold Evangelical Beliefs," *Lifeway Research*, December 6, 2017, https://lifewayresearch.com/2017/12/06/many-evangelicals-dont-hold-evangelical-beliefs/. See also Jeremy Weber, "Evangelical vs. Born Again: A Survey of What Americans Say and Believe Beyond Politics," *Christianity Today*, December 6, 2017, www.christianitytoday.com/news/2017/december/you-must-be-born-again-evangelical-beliefs-politics-survey.html.

31 Gregory A. Smith, "Among White Evangelicals, Regular Churchgoers Are the Most Supportive of Trump," *Pew Research Center*, April 26 2017, www.pewresearch.org/fact-tank/2017/04/26/among-white-evangelicals-regular-churchgoers-are-the-most-supportive-of-trump/. See also Paul A. Djupe and Ryan P. Burge, "Regular Churchgoing Doesn't Make Trump Voters More Moderate. It Makes Them More Enthusiastic for Trump," *Washington Post*, October 9, 2018.

32 Thomas S. Kidd, *Who Is an Evangelical? The History of a Movement in Crisis* (New Haven: Yale University Press, 2019), 3.

33 Kidd, *Who Is an Evangelical?*, 154.

34 Kidd, *Who Is an Evangelical?*, 4. His definition in full: "Evangelicals are born-again Protestants who cherish the Bible as the Word of God and who emphasize a personal relationship with Jesus Christ through the Holy Spirit."

35 See David W. Bebbington, *Evangelicalism in Modern Britain: A History from the 1730s to the 1980s* (London: Unwin Hyman, 1989).

36 See "What Is an Evangelical?," www.nae.net/what-is-an-evangelical/. The LifeWay Research reduces activism to evangelism ("it is very important for me personally to encourage non-Christians to trust Jesus Christ as their Savior").

37 Alan Jacobs, "*Evangelical* Has Lost Its Meaning," *The Atlantic*, September 22, 2019. Larsen's definition is far more restrictive: "(1) an orthodox Protestant (2) who stands in the tradition of the global Christian networks arising from the eighteenth-century revival movements associated with John Wesley and George Whitefield; (3) who has a preeminent place for the Bible in her or his Christian life as the divinely inspired, final authority in matters of faith and practice; (4) who stresses reconciliation with God through the atoning work of Jesus Christ on the cross; (5) and who stresses the work of the Holy Spirit in the life of an individual to bring about conversion and an ongoing life of fellowship with God and service to God and others, including the duty of all believers to participate in the task of proclaiming the gospel to all people." See Timothy Larsen, "Defining and Locating Evangelicalism," in *The Cambridge Companion to Evangelical Theology*, ed. Timothy Larsen and Daniel J. Treier (Cambridge: Cambridge University Press, 2007), 1–14, at 1.

38 Daniel Silliman points out that this is how the word "evangelical" has been used throughout its modern American history. In the eighteenth century, the word "came to connote 'true Christian,'" and "by the early 1900s" the word was used "to make an argument about who was or was not really Protestant." Daniel Silliman, "An Evangelical Is Anyone Who Likes Billy Graham: Defining Evangelicalism with Carl Henry and Networks of Trust," *Church History* 90 (2021): 621–43, at 625–26.

39 Silliman, "An Evangelical Is Anyone Who Likes Billy Graham," 627.

40 Alvin Plantinga, *Warranted Christian Belief* (New York: Oxford University Press, 2000), 245.

41 Timothy Gloege, "#ItsNotUs: Being Evangelical Means Never Having to Say You're Sorry," *Religion Dispatches*, January 3, 2018, https://religiondispatches.org/itsnotus-being-evangelical-means-never-having-to-say-youre-sorry/.

42 Kristin Kobes Du Mez, "Defining Evangelicalism and the Problem of Whiteness," *Anxious Bench*, March 22, 2018, www.patheos.com/blogs/anxiousbench/2018/03/defin ing-evangelicalism-and-the-problem-of-whiteness.

43 Gloege, "#ItsNotUs."

44 Bob Smietana, "What Is an Evangelical? Four Questions Offer New Definition," *Christianity Today*, November 19, 2015, www.christianitytoday.com/news/2015/novem ber/what-is-evangelical-new-definition-nae-lifeway-research.html; Kristin Kobes Du Mez, *Jesus and John Wayne: How White Evangelicals Corrupted a Faith and Fractured a Nation* (New York: Liveright, 2020), 6.

45 Chrissy Stroop, "Stop Trying to Save Jesus: 'Fandamentalism' Reinforces the Problem of Christian Supremacism," *Religion Dispatches*, January 29, 2021, https:// religiondispatches.org/stop-trying-to-save-jesus-fandamentalism-reinforces-the-problem-of-christian-supremacism/.

46 Stroop, "About Those Trump Voters for God?"

47 Stroop, "Stop Trying to Save Jesus."

48 Timothy Gloege, "The Crisis of Corporate Evangelicalism (Part 2 – Defining Evangelicalism)," *Anxious Bench*, July 14, 2016, www.patheos.com/blogs/anxious bench/2016/07/the-crisis-of-corporate-evangelicalism-part-2-defining-evangelicalism/.

49 Larsen, "Defining and Locating Evangelicalism," 1.

50 Gloege, "The Crisis of Corporate Evangelicalism." In itself, this definition is incomplete, because liberal theology was also the application of Enlightenment ideas to Protestantism, as I will discuss in Chapter 1. In order to distinguish between American liberalism and American evangelicalism, we therefore need to qualify Gloege's definition. Liberalism is the application of Enlightenment ideas to Protestantism for the purpose of accommodating modern society, while evangelicalism is the application of Enlightenment ideas to Protestantism for the purpose of opposing modern society.

51 Du Mez, *Jesus and John Wayne*, 298.

52 Silliman, "An Evangelical Is Anyone Who Likes Billy Graham," 642.

53 Anthea D. Butler, *White Evangelical Racism: The Politics of Morality in America* (Chapel Hill: University of North Carolina Press, 2021), 139.

54 Henry Hitchings, *The Language Wars: A History of Proper English* (New York: Farrar, Straus and Giroux, 2011), 23.

55 David Foster Wallace, "Authority and American Usage," in *Consider the Lobster and Other Essays* (New York: Little, Brown, 2005), 66–127, at 72–73. Wallace's alternative title is: "(or, 'Politics and the English Language' Is Redundant)."

56 Paula Fredriksen, "No, Seriously: How Jewish Is God? Response to Eric Barreto," *Syndicate*, June 16, 2020, https://syndicate.network/symposia/theology/paul-the-pagans-apostle/.

57 Kevin W. Hector, *Theology without Metaphysics: God, Language, and the Spirit of Recognition* (Cambridge: Cambridge University Press, 2011), 56–62. See Robert Brandom, *Making It Explicit: Reasoning, Representing, and Discursive Commitment* (Cambridge, MA: Harvard University Press, 1994).

58 Brandom, *Making It Explicit*, 28–29, 36.

59 Bruce Lincoln, "Theses on Method," *Method & Theory in the Study of Religion* 8, no. 3 (1996): 225–27, at 227 (thesis 13).

60 Gloege, "#ItsNotUs."

61 On the damage characteristic to Christian practice, see Lauren F. Winner, *The Dangers of Christian Practice: On Wayward Gifts, Characteristic Damage, and Sin* (New Haven: Yale University Press, 2018).

62 Susan Harding, "A We Like Any Other," *Hot Spots*, January 18, 2017, https://culanth .org/fieldsights/a-we-like-any-other. The critique of the concept of religion as inherently biased and prescriptivist is a long-standing academic conversation. See, e.g., Jonathan Z. Smith, *Imagining Religion: From Babylon to Jonestown* (Chicago: University of Chicago Press, 1982); Tomoko Masuzawa, *The Invention of World Religions, or, How European Universalism Was Preserved in the Language of Pluralism* (Chicago: University of Chicago Press, 2005); Brent Nongbri, *Before Religion: A History of a Modern Concept* (New Haven: Yale University Press, 2013); Russell T. McCutcheon, *Fabricating Religion: Fanfare for the Common e.g.* (Berlin: De Gruyter, 2018). This body of literature stresses the point that the idea of religion as a specially demarcated sphere of life distinct from other, nonreligious spheres is an inherently modern idea, one that Western Christianity helped bring into existence.

63 L. Benjamin Rolsky, "Producing the Christian Right: Conservative Evangelicalism, Representation, and the Recent Religious Past," *Religions* 12, no. 3 (2021): 1–17, at 15.

64 An example of this occurred in July 2022 when CNN journalist John Blake quoted sociologist Samuel Perry's April 2020 claim that white Christian nationalism (WCN) is an "imposter Christianity." The statement received significant criticism on Twitter for policing the boundaries of "true Christianity" and ignoring the way that American Christianity has historically been deeply tied up with white nationalism. The problem could have been avoided had Perry framed his comment as prescriptive rather than descriptive. Perry, who has publicly acknowledged his own Christian faith, naturally has prescriptive views about WCN that he should be free to express. But when presented as a statement by a descriptive sociologist, such claims can lead to confusion and misunderstanding. See John Blake, "An 'Imposter Christianity' Is Threatening American Democracy," *CNN*, July 24, 2022, www.cnn.com/2022/07/24/us/white-christian-nation alism-blake-cec/index.html; Kristin Kobes Du Mez, "Is White Christian Nationalism 'Imposter Christianity'?," *Du Mez CONNECTIONS*, July 25, 2022, https://kristindumez .substack.com/p/is-white-christian-nationalism-imposter.

65 Frederick Douglass, *Autobiographies*, The Library of America 68 (New York: Library of America, 1994), 97.

66 W. H. Auden, *The Age of Anxiety: A Baroque Eclogue*, ed. Alan Jacobs, W. H. Auden: Critical Editions (Princeton: Princeton University Press, 2011), 3, 108.

67 W. H. Auden, *Collected Poems*, ed. Edward Mendelson (New York: Vintage International, 1991), 400.

68 Auden, *Collected Poems*, 371–73, 400.

69 Auden, *Collected Poems*, 639.

70 Richard Hofstadter, *Anti-intellectualism in American Life* (New York: Knopf, 1963), 117–41. On the five fundamentals of the Northern Presbyterians, see William Jennings Bryan, *Orthodox Christianity versus Modernism* (New York: F. H. Revell, 1923), 7–28. Hofstadter's inclusion of Bryan represents the way the latter's activism against evolution late in life came to overshadow his earlier commitment to socially progressive policies. While Bryan was theologically conservative in his commitment to biblical literalism, his liberal politics puts him at odds with the other fundamentalists. But that only highlights the way antimodern Christianity was not limited to the conservative evangelical camp.

71 Justine S. Murison, *The Politics of Anxiety in Nineteenth-Century American Literature* (Cambridge: Cambridge University Press, 2011), 2–3.

72 Archibald Alexander Hodge and Benjamin Breckinridge Warfield, "Inspiration," *Presbyterian Review* 2, no. 6 (1881): 225–60, at 235, 237.

73 Hodge and Warfield, "Inspiration," 239–40. Archibald Hodge is the son of Charles Hodge, who not only employed slave labor but was also a leader of the American Colonization Society. The ACS was still in force at Princeton during the time Archibald Hodge and Warfield published. See "Princeton Seminary and Slavery: A Journey of Confession and Repentance," https://slavery.ptsem.edu.

74 Upon his death in June 1890, Welch left behind funds to create what became the Welch Memorial Hall, which, along with the conjoining Willard Memorial Chapel, was

declared a National Historic Landmark in 2005 and is all that remains of the original Auburn Theological Seminary campus. The buildings feature the only remaining stained glass art of Louis Comfort Tiffany still in their original ecclesiastical setting.

75 R. B. Welch, "The Prevalent Confusion; and, the Attitude of Christian Faith," *Presbyterian Review* 2, no. 6 (1881): 261–83, at 261–62.

76 Welch, "The Prevalent Confusion," 263–64.

77 Welch, "The Prevalent Confusion," 279.

78 Welch, "The Prevalent Confusion," 280–83.

79 R. B. Welch, "Faith; Its Place and Prerogative: The Written and Living Word," *The Presbyterian Quarterly and Princeton Review* 8 (1873): 603–20, at 606.

80 Wallace Radcliffe, "Presbyterian Imperialism," *The Assembly Herald* 1, no. 7 (1899): 5–6. For a fuller exploration of white American imperialism and Christian missions, see Edward J. Blum, *Reforging the White Republic: Race, Religion, and American Nationalism, 1865–1898* (Baton Rouge: Louisiana State University Press, 2005).

81 "Rev. Dr. Radcliffe Dies in Washington," *New York Times*, June 9, 1930.

82 The postliberalism I explore here (and in more detail in Chapter 3) is primarily the school of thought associated with George Lindbeck, Hans Frei, and others in the so-called Yale School. For an accessible overview, see Ronald T. Michener, *Postliberal Theology: A Guide for the Perplexed* (London: Bloomsbury, 2013). But that is only the inner, theological circle of what is a much larger and more diffuse movement that is not limited to Christian theology or even to religion as such. The rise of theological postliberalism in the late twentieth century occurred at the same time as the rise of political postliberalism, and both have their roots in early twentieth-century conservative revolutions that emerged in the wake of the First World War. What unites both the theological and sociopolitical wings of postliberalism is their visceral rejection of modernity, with some reacting by trying to recover an idealized premodern past and others rejecting the past in favor of a previously inconceivable conservative future. For a nuanced account of political postliberalism, see Matthew Rose, *A World after Liberalism: Philosophers of the Radical Right* (New Haven: Yale University Press, 2021).

83 Hans-Werner Bartsch, ed., *Kerygma and Myth: A Theological Debate*, trans. Reginald H. Fuller, vol. 1 (London: SPCK, 1953); Hans Werner Bartsch, ed., *Kerygma and Myth: A Theological Debate*, trans. Reginald H. Fuller, vol. 2 (London: SPCK, 1962).

84 "An Existential Way of Reading the Bible," *Time*, May 22, 1964, 86.

85 Dietrich Bonhoeffer, *Prisoner for God: Letters and Papers from Prison*, ed. Eberhard Bethge, trans. Reginald H. Fuller (London: SCM Press, 1953); Gabriel Vahanian, *The Death of God: The Culture of Our Post-Christian Era* (New York: G. Braziller, 1961); Paul M. van Buren, *The Secular Meaning of the Gospel: Based on an Analysis of Its Language* (New York: Macmillan, 1963); John A. T. Robinson, *Honest to God* (London: SCM Press, 1963); Harvey Cox, *The Secular City: Secularization and Urbanization in Theological Perspective* (New York: Macmillan, 1965); Thomas J. J. Altizer and William Hamilton, *Radical Theology and the Death of God* (Indianapolis: Bobbs-Merrill, 1966); Thomas J. J. Altizer, *The Gospel of Christian Atheism* (Philadelphia: Westminster Press, 1966).

86 Harold Lindsell, *The Battle for the Bible* (Grand Rapids: Zondervan, 1976).

87 Hans W. Frei, *The Eclipse of Biblical Narrative: A Study in Eighteenth and Nineteenth Century Hermeneutics* (New Haven: Yale University Press, 1974); David H. Kelsey, *The Uses of Scripture in Recent Theology* (Philadelphia: Fortress, 1975).

88 I will have much more to say about postliberalism later, especially in Chapter 3.

89 George A. Lindbeck, *The Nature of Doctrine: Religion and Theology in a Postliberal Age* (Philadelphia: Westminster Press, 1984).

90 George A. Lindbeck, "The Gospel's Uniqueness: Election and Untranslatability," *Modern Theology* 13, no. 4 (1997): 423–50, at 429–31.

91 George A. Lindbeck, "Confession and Community: An Israel-like View of the Church," *Christian Century* 107, no. 16 (1990): 492–96, at 492.

92 Lindbeck, "Confession and Community," 495. He adds that talk of "Christian America" and "Christian Europe" makes him "uncomfortable," but witnessing "a number of totally unexpected improbabilities come to pass," such as "communism's collapse," means that he "cannot rule these out as impossible" (Lindbeck, "Confession and Community," 495). What Lindbeck seems to be saying is that "Christian America" and "Christian Europe" are desirable but unlikely. What makes him uncomfortable is not the thought of Christian society as such but rather something else, such as the conviction that these lands are already Christian, or the hasty attempt to make them Christian as soon as possible.

93 The annual Wheaton Theology Conference began in 1992 and ended in 2021.

94 George A. Lindbeck, "Atonement and the Hermeneutics of Intratextual Social Embodiment," in *The Nature of Confession: Evangelicals and Postliberals in Conversation*, ed. Timothy R. Phillips and Dennis L. Okholm (Downers Grove: InterVarsity, 1996), 221–40, at 227.

95 Lindbeck, "Atonement and the Hermeneutics of Intratextual Social Embodiment," 226. Lindbeck's logic here is a gloss on his earlier claim that "it is the text, so to speak, which absorbs the world, rather than the world the text" (Lindbeck, *Nature of Doctrine*, 118).

96 George A. Lindbeck, "The Sectarian Future of the Church," in *The God Experience: Essays in Hope*, ed. Joseph P. Whelan (New York: Newman, 1971), 226–43, at 230.

97 A point made well in Adam Kotsko, "The Evangelical Mind," *n+1*, Issue 35, Fall 2019.

98 Donald Dayton made this point in his review of Lindsell's *The Battle for the Bible*, published in *Christian Century* in 1976: "Evangelicals are beginning to understand that the real questions about appropriating the Scriptures are not so much matters of *doctrine* as they are of *hermeneutics*." Donald W. Dayton, "The Battle for the Bible: Renewing the Inerrancy Debate," *Christian Century*, November 10, 1976, 976–80.

99 David F. Wells, *The Courage to Be Protestant: Truth-Lovers, Marketers, and Emergents in the Postmodern World* (Grand Rapids: Eerdmans, 2008), 10.

100 George A. Lindbeck et al., "A Panel Discussion," in *The Nature of Confession: Evangelicals and Postliberals in Conversation*, ed. Timothy R. Phillips and Dennis L. Okholm (Downers Grove: InterVarsity Press, 1996), 246–53, at 252–53.

101 Kevin J. Vanhoozer and Daniel J. Treier, *Theology and the Mirror of Scripture: A Mere Evangelical Account* (Downers Grove: IVP Academic, 2015), 40, 117.

102 "The Chicago Call of 1977," www.ancientfuturefaithnetwork.org/wp-content/ uploads/2013/12/TheChicagoCall-1977.pdf. See Chapter 4 for more on this document.

103 Writing in 2002, Robert Webber said, "there was no room in the evangelical subculture for this kind of witness to historic Christianity" and thus "The Chicago Call" was "largely ignored by the evangelical establishment." But as Webber's book pointed out, times had changed. Webber pointed to the work of Lindbeck and other post-liberals as a key part of that shift. Robert Webber, *The Younger Evangelicals: Facing the Challenges of the New World* (Grand Rapids: Baker Books, 2002), 35, 99–100, 113–14.

104 Chris Armstrong, "The Future Lies in the Past," *Christianity Today*, February 8, 2008, 22–29.

105 R. R. Reno, "End-Times Anxiety," *First Things*, March 2018, issue 281, www.firstthings .com/article/2018/03/end-times-anxiety. It is all the more appropriate that Reno published these reflections on Lindbeck in a piece on "end-times anxiety" that begins with a reflection on the political moment: "An atmosphere of crisis envelops us. . . . Our present cultural moment is one of suspicion, anxiety, and worries about vulner-ability." Reno claims that "the anxiety baffles me," but the anxiety he primarily has in mind concerns leftwing charges of "patriarchy, racism, heteronormativity," though he also acknowledges religious believers who "see themselves under assault." Nevertheless, he traces the source of this anxiety to the liberal elites "in the upper reaches of society," contributing to the rightwing anxiety narrative that cultural elites and government leaders are the problem. He goes on to claim that "charges of racism, anti-Semitism, and bigotry . . . function these days in the same way assassinations did during the 1930s," which hardly seems free of anxiety. Reno, who was also a vocal Trump supporter, developed the ideas in this column in his subsequent book: R. R. Reno, *Return of the Strong Gods: Nationalism, Populism, and the Future of the West* (Washington: Regnery Gateway, 2019).

106 R. R. Reno, "Series Preface," in Jaroslav Pelikan, *Acts* (Grand Rapids: Brazos Press, 2005), 11–16, at 14.

107 Armstrong, "The Future Lies in the Past."

108 The culture wars are a multifaceted, polycentric religious and political development that, depending on how one defines it, began either in the late 1980s or in the early twentieth century – or, as I suggest here, arguably has roots back in the early modern period. For much of this history, however, the conflict was not viewed in cultural terms. Postliberals and other postwar theorists introduced cultural discourse into religious, and specifically Christian, self-understanding. The result was a refinement of what we can in retrospect understand as the right-wing culture war on modern society – a refinement that expanded the movement beyond a narrow band of radical right activists and Christian fundamentalists to include those who considered themselves moderate and even liberal in certain respects. A social and intellectual "war" waged on behalf of one culture against another did not have to involve subscription to specific doctrines or religious practices. Such a war could cross denominational lines that were previously seen as inviolable and could even include agnostics and atheists who were

willing to be cobelligerents with Christians on behalf of a shared cultural cause. It is worth noting that, while some sociologists have questioned whether the term "culture war" accurately describes the polarized political situation, it is certainly the case that those leading the effort view it in those terms, and that is the focus of my work here.

109 For an insightful examination of white Christian supremacy throughout US history, see Khyati Y. Joshi, *White Christian Privilege: The Illusion of Religious Equality in America* (New York: New York University Press, 2020), esp. 62–125.

110 Lisa Isherwood and Dirk von der Horst, "Normativity and Transgression," in *Contemporary Theological Approaches to Sexuality*, ed. Lisa Isherwood and Dirk von der Horst (London: Routledge, 2017), 3–21, at 3.

111 In my earlier work I described this as "orthoheterodoxy," which sees heterodoxy as internal to orthodoxy. True orthodoxy generates heterodox theological claims, not as something antithetical to orthodoxy but as the proper expression of orthodoxy, precisely because the normative (ortho) and the different (hetero) are not in competition with each other. "Indeed, we can even say that difference is *internal* to the norm of the gospel; the norm generates its own diversity." See David W. Congdon, *The God Who Saves: A Dogmatic Sketch* (Eugene: Cascade Books, 2016), 57.

112 Alvin J. Reines, *Polydoxy: Explorations in a Philosophy of Liberal Religion* (Buffalo: Prometheus Books, 1987); Catherine Keller and Laurel C. Schneider, eds., *Polydoxy: Theology of Multiplicity and Relation* (New York: Routledge, 2011).

113 Ernst Troeltsch, "The Dogmatics of the 'Religionsgeschichtliche Schule,'" *The American Journal of Theology* 17, no. 1 (1913): 1–21, at 12–13.

Chapter 1

1 Andrew F. Walls, *The Missionary Movement in Christian History: Studies in the Transmission of Faith* (Maryknoll: Orbis, 1996), 3–7.

2 Staf Hellemans, "Religious Orthodoxy as a Modality of 'Adaptation,'" in *Orthodoxy, Liberalism, and Adaptation: Essays on Ways of Worldmaking in Times of Change from Biblical, Historical and Systematic Perspectives*, ed. Bob Becking (Leiden: Brill, 2011), 9–32, at 23.

3 Hellemans, "Religious Orthodoxy," 25.

4 Hellemans, "Religious Orthodoxy," 26.

5 Hellemans, "Religious Orthodoxy," 28.

6 Hellemans, "Religious Orthodoxy," 26.

7 Peter Harrison, *"Religion" and the Religions in the English Enlightenment* (Cambridge: Cambridge University Press, 1990), 63.

8 Francis Bacon, *The Essays of Lord Bacon*, ed. John Hunter (London: Longmans, Green, and Co., 1873), 12–13.

9 Walls, *Missionary Movement in Christian History*, 6–7.

10 See Stephen Sykes, *The Identity of Christianity: Theologians and the Essence of Christianity from Schleiermacher to Barth* (Philadelphia: Fortress Press, 1984).

11 Rolf Schäfer, "Welchen Sinn hat es, nach einem Wesen des Christentums zu suchen?," *Zeitschrift für Theologie und Kirche* 65, no. 3 (1968): 329–47, at 330.

12 Hellemans, "Religious Orthodoxy as a Modality," 23.

13 Evan Kuehn, "Liberalism's Interest in Theology," *Marginalia*, December 17, 2021, https://themarginaliareview.com/liberalisms-interest-in-theology/.

14 Samuel Loncar, "Are Evangelicals the New Liberals?," *Marginalia*, December 9, 2014, https://marginalia.lareviewofbooks.org/evangelicals-new-liberals/.

15 Winnifred Fallers Sullivan, *The Impossibility of Religious Freedom* (Princeton: Princeton University Press, 2005), 7–8.

16 Carl Ullmann, *Reformers before the Reformation: Principally in Germany and the Netherlands*, trans. Robert Menzies, 2 vols. (Edinburgh: T & T Clark, 1855).

17 See Christine Helmer, *How Luther Became the Reformer* (Louisville: Westminster John Knox Press, 2019). Helmer points out that German liberal theologians, especially those associated with the Luther renaissance (about which I will have more to say in Chapter 3), were invested in portraying Luther as the original modern theologian as a way to claim him for their German nationalist project. By contrast, Helmer follows Heiko Oberman in seeing Luther as a thoroughly medieval figure. See Heiko A. Oberman, *The Harvest of Medieval Theology: Gabriel Biel and Late Medieval Nominalism* (Grand Rapids: Eerdmans, 1967). I think the answer lies somewhere in the middle. Luther the reformer was certainly a man of the medieval period, but some of Luther's ideas anticipated and lay the groundwork for developments that flourished in modernity.

18 Hans Wagenhammer, *Das Wesen des Christentums: Eine begriffsgeschichtliche Untersuchung* (Mainz: Matthias-Grünewald-Verlag, 1973).

19 Thomas Aquinas, *Scriptum super libros Sententiarum*, II.12.2.

20 Wagenhammer, *Das Wesen des Christentums*, 104, 34–38.

21 Martin Luther, *Martin Luthers Werke: Kritische Gesamtausgabe*, 73 vols. (Weimar: H. Böhlau, 1883–2009), 1:354.19–20. Hereafter cited as WA.

22 WA 2:145–46.

23 WA 40/3:352.3.

24 WA 18:614.15–18.

25 Martin Luther, *Die deutsche Bibel*, 12 vols., Martin Luthers Werke, Kritische Gesamtausgabe (Weimar: H. Böhlaus Nachfolger, 1906–1961), 7:384.27–30.

26 WA 7:97.21–23.

27 WA 3:11.33–34.

28 Ethan H. Shagan, *The Birth of Modern Belief: Faith and Judgment from the Middle Ages to the Enlightenment* (Princeton: Princeton University Press, 2018), 291.

29 John Locke, *John Locke: Writings on Religion*, ed. Victor Nuovo (New York: Oxford University Press, 2002), 81.

30 John Locke, *An Essay Concerning Human Understanding*, ed. Peter H. Nidditch, The Clarendon Edition of the Works of John Locke (Oxford: Clarendon Press, 1975), 2.28.8.

31 Locke, *An Essay Concerning Human Understanding*, 4.16.14.

32 Locke, *An Essay Concerning Human Understanding*, 4.19.14.

33 John Locke, *The Reasonableness of Christianity: As Delivered in the Scriptures*, ed. John C. Higgins-Biddle, The Clarendon Edition of the Works of John Locke (Oxford:

Clarendon Press, 1999), 5. The tradition of American liberal theology has its origins here, as well as in the later, more speculative philosophy of religion of Samuel Clarke (1675–1729). Clarke's work on *The Scripture Doctrine of the Trinity* (1712) stirred up controversy over his heterodox views. As Gary Dorrien points out in the first volume of his history of American liberal theology, the New England Arminians who planted the seeds of American theological liberalism "took their concept of reasonable religion from the leading English rationalists of the previous half-century, philosophers John Locke . . . and Samuel Clarke." Gary J. Dorrien, *The Making of American Liberal Theology*, 3 vols. (Louisville: Westminster John Knox Press, 2001–2006), 1:2.

34 John Edwards, *Socinianism Unmask'd* (London: J. Robinson, 1696), 1, 21.

35 Richard Hooker, *Of the Laws of Ecclesiastical Polity: A Critical Edition with Modern Spelling*, ed. Arthur Stephen McGrade (Oxford: Oxford University Press, 2013), 1:139 (3.1.4).

36 Wagenhammer, *Das Wesen des Christentums*, 105–9.

37 Johann Salomo Semler, *Abhandlung von freier untersuchung des Canon* (Halle: Carl Hermann Hemmerde, 1771), 579; Johann Salomo Semler, *Beantwortung der Fragmente eines Ungenanten* (Halle: Verlag des Erziehungsinstituts, 1779), 350.

38 Friedrich Schleiermacher, *On Religion: Speeches to Its Cultured Despisers* (Cambridge: Cambridge University Press, 1996), 22.

39 Schleiermacher, *On Religion*, 22.

40 Schleiermacher, *On Religion*, 23.

41 Friedrich Schleiermacher, *Christian Faith: A New Translation and Critical Edition*, trans. Terrence N. Tice, Catherine L. Kelsey, and Edwina G. Lawler (Louisville: Westminster John Knox, 2016), §3, 8; §4, 24.

42 Schleiermacher, *Christian Faith*, §13, 100–1.

43 Some historians date the origins of historical consciousness earlier, in the sixteenth century. As Constantin Fasolt points out, the early proponents of history were primarily engaged in a political dispute with medieval universalism – the notion that the world ought to be governed by "the Roman emperor and the Roman pope." By the time of Giambattista Vico (1668–1744), however, we see the rise of historicism, which views "the pursuit of historical knowledge for its own sake" as a worthy goal and interprets all things through the lens of this knowledge. Constantin Fasolt, *The Limits of History* (Chicago: University of Chicago Press, 2004), 17, 30.

44 In his letters to the theologian G. C. F. Lücke, Schleiermacher proposed an "eternal covenant between the living Christian faith, and completely free, independent, scientific inquiry, so that faith does not hinder science and science does not exclude faith." Friedrich Schleiermacher, *On the Glaubenslehre: Two Letters to Dr. Lücke*, trans. James Duke and Francis Fiorenza (Chico: Scholars Press, 1981), 64. See Daniel James Pedersen, *The Eternal Covenant: Schleiermacher on God and Natural Science* (Boston: Walter de Gruyter, 2017). Hegel explored the concept of reconciliation throughout his work in various ways – as the reconciliation of faith and knowledge (see *Faith and Knowledge*, 1802), the reconciliation of spirit with itself (*Phenomenology of Spirit*, 1807), and the reconciliation of God and the world (*Lectures of the Philosophy of Religion*, 1824–1831), all of which are also ways of speaking about the reconciliation of the self

and modern society. See Thomas A. Lewis, "Religion, Reconciliation, and Modern Society: The Shifting Conclusions of Hegel's *Lectures on the Philosophy of Religion*," *Harvard Theological Review* 106, no. 1 (2013): 37–60.

45 Ludwig Feuerbach, *The Essence of Christianity*, trans. Marian Evans (London: John Chapman, 1854), 2–3.

46 See Martin Bauspiess, "The Essence of Early Christianity: On Ferdinand Christian Baur's View of the Synoptic Gospels," in *Ferdinand Christian Baur and the History of Early Christianity*, ed. Martin Bauspiess, Christof Landmesser, and David Lincicum (Oxford: Oxford University Press, 2017), 177–205, esp. 204–5.

47 Albrecht Ritschl, *The Christian Doctrine of Justification and Reconciliation*, ed. H. R. Mackintosh and A. B. Macaulay, vol. 3 (Edinburgh: T & T Clark, 1900), 540, 538–39.

48 Ritschl, *The Christian Doctrine of Justification and Reconciliation*, 282.

49 Ritschl, *The Christian Doctrine of Justification and Reconciliation*, 284–85. Emphasis mine.

50 Karl Barth made the following observation: "The year 1900 brought the 19th century to its chronological end and marked at the same time a climax in the history of its theology: the publication of Harnack's *What Is Christianity?* Due to this achievement, 19th-century theology continued to live for some time with force and dignity almost unbroken, in spite of signs of dissolution." Karl Barth, "Evangelical Theology in the 19th Century [1957]," in *The Humanity of God* (Richmond: John Knox Press, 1960), 11–33, at 14.

51 Adolf von Harnack, *What Is Christianity?*, trans. Thomas Bailey Saunders (New York: Harper, 1957; reprint, 1986), 6. At the time of giving the lectures, he was known as Adolf Harnack, since he did not receive the title of nobility until 1914.

52 Harnack, *What Is Christianity?*, 12.

53 Harnack, *What Is Christianity?*, 12.

54 Harnack, *What Is Christianity?*, 13–14.

55 Troeltsch, "The Dogmatics of the 'Religionsgeschichtliche Schule,'" 1–21, at 12–13.

56 Harnack, *What Is Christianity?*, 13.

57 Harnack, *What Is Christianity?*, 51.

58 Harnack, *What Is Christianity?*, 52.

59 Harnack, *What Is Christianity?*, 24.

60 Harnack, *What Is Christianity?*, 62, 26.

61 See Johannes Weiss, *Jesus' Proclamation of the Kingdom of God*, ed. Richard Hyde Hiers and David Larrimore Holland (Philadelphia: Fortress, 1971).

62 Karl Barth, *The Epistle to the Romans*, trans. Edwyn C. Hoskyns (London: Oxford University Press, 1933; reprint, 1968), 314; translation revised.

63 Rudolf Bultmann, *Primitive Christianity in Its Contemporary Setting*, trans. R. H. Fuller (Cleveland: World, 1956), 198.

64 Rudolf Bultmann, *History and Eschatology: The Gifford Lectures 1955* (Edinburgh: Edinburgh University Press, 1957), 37.

65 Friedrich Gogarten, *Was ist Christentum?* (Göttingen: Vandenhoeck & Ruprecht, 1956), 79.

66 Rudolf Bultmann, "Das Befremdliche des christlichen Glaubens [1958]," in *Glauben und Verstehen: Gesammelte Aufsätze*, 4 vols. (Tübingen: Mohr, 1933–1965), 3:197–212, at 199, 207.

67 In the Göttingen dogmatics, Barth says: "The *Deus dixit* is revelation, not revealedness."
   And in the later Münster dogmatics, *Die christliche Dogmatik im Entwurf* (Christian
   dogmatics in outline), he says: "Revealed*ness* is not revelation." See Karl Barth, *The
   Göttingen Dogmatics: Instruction in the Christian Religion*, ed. Hannelotte Reiffen, trans.
   Geoffrey W. Bromiley, vol. 1 (Grand Rapids: Eerdmans, 1991), 59; Karl Barth, *Die
   christliche Dogmatik im Entwurf*, ed. Gerhard Sauter, Gesamtausgabe 2.14 (Zürich:
   Theologischer Verlag, 1982), 469.

68 While often translated as capitalized "Word of God," the German is ambiguous, since all
   nouns are capitalized. The German *Wort* encompasses both the lowercase "word"
   (referring to the divine message of the gospel) and the uppercase "Word" (referring
   to the second mode of God's being). I have chosen to use "word" except when referring
   explicitly to the eternal divine being of Christ.

69 Barth, *Göttingen Dogmatics*, 58–63.

70 Karl Barth, *Church Dogmatics*, ed. G. W. Bromiley and T. F. Torrance, 4 vols. (Edinburgh:
   T & T Clark, 1956–1975), 1.2:856; hereafter cited as *CD*. See also *CD* 1.2:815.

71 *CD* 1.2:862.

72 *CD* 1.2:866.

73 *CD* 1.2:867.

74 *CD* 1.2:866.

75 Sykes, *The Identity of Christianity*, 215.

76 Johann Salomo Semler, *Versuch einer freiern theologischen Lehrart* (Halle: Carl Hermann
   Hemmerde, 1777), §3, 5.

77 Adolf von Harnack, *History of Dogma*, trans. Neil Buchanan, 7 vols. (London: Williams &
   Norgate, 1894), 1:159.

78 Martin Dibelius, *From Tradition to Gospel*, trans. Bertram Lee Woolf (London: James
   Clarke, 1971), 17.

79 Karl Barth, *The Resurrection of the Dead*, trans. H. J. Stenning (New York: Fleming
   H. Revell, 1933; reprint, 2003 by Wipf and Stock), 155; Rudolf Bultmann, "Karl Barth,
   The Resurrection of the Dead [1926]," in *Faith and Understanding*, ed. Robert W. Funk
   (Philadelphia: Fortress, 1987), 66–94, at 82–83.

80 Rudolf Bultmann, *Theology of the New Testament*, trans. Kendrick Grobel, 2 vols. (New
   York: Charles Scribner's Sons, 1951–1955), 2:239–40.

81 Charles G. Finney, *Lectures on Revivals of Religion*, 2nd ed. (New York: Leavitt, Lord & Co.,
   1835), 372.

82 Finney, *Lectures on Revivals of Religion*, 184.

83 Walter Rauschenbusch, *Christianity and the Social Crisis* (New York: Macmillan,
   1907), 178.

84 Rauschenbusch, *Christianity and the Social Crisis*, 179–80.

85 Rauschenbusch, *Christianity and the Social Crisis*, 198.

86 Walter Rauschenbusch, *Christianizing the Social Order* (New York: Macmillan, 1912), 397.

87 See David R. Berman, *Socialist Mayors in the United States: Governing in an Era of Municipal
   Reform, 1900–1920* (Lawrence: University Press of Kansas, 2022).

88 Rauschenbusch, *Christianizing the Social Order*, 403.

89 James H. Cone, *God of the Oppressed* (New York: Seabury Press, 1975), 202.

90 Cone, *God of the Oppressed*, 200.

91 James H. Cone, *Black Theology and Black Power* (New York: Seabury Press, 1969), 34.

92 James H. Cone, *A Black Theology of Liberation* (Philadelphia: Lippincott, 1970), 197.

93 Cone, *A Black Theology of Liberation*, 120, 203; Cone, *God of the Oppressed*, 136.

94 Gustavo Gutiérrez, *A Theology of Liberation: History, Politics, and Salvation* (Maryknoll: Orbis Books, 1973), 9–15.

95 Juan Luis Segundo, *Liberation of Theology* (Maryknoll: Orbis Books, 1976), 73–74, 81, 94–95.

96 Segundo, *Liberation of Theology*, 94.

97 To take but one example among many, Brad East criticizes theologian Andrew Root for asserting, "without justification, that modernity is not to be resisted, revised, or overturned." Instead, East writes: "Thanks, but no thanks. Modernity is both an epoch and an ideology. We have to live in the epoch; we don't have to accept the ideology, even for a moment. . . . If it is false – and it is false – we don't have to give it the time of day. Not only should we rebel against it, we should try to topple it as a widely shared presupposition." Brad East, "The Church in the Immanent Frame," *First Things*, July 14, 2022, www .firstthings.com/web-exclusives/2022/07/the-church-in-the-immanent-frame.

98 Jocelyne Cesari, *We God's People: Christianity, Islam and Hinduism in the World of Nations* (Cambridge: Cambridge University Press, 2021), 19–20.

99 Thandeka, *The Embodied Self: Friedrich Schleiermacher's Solution to Kant's Problem of the Empirical Self* (Albany: State University of New York Press, 1995), 95.

Chapter 2

1 Theodore Parker, *Experience as a Minister, with Some Account of His Early Life, and Education for the Ministry* (Boston: Rufus Leighton Jr., 1859), 69.

2 Theodore Parker, *A Discourse on the Transient and Permanent in Christianity* (Boston: Freeman and Bolles, 1841), 11.

3 Parker, *A Discourse on the Transient and Permanent in Christianity*, 8–9.

4 Parker, *Experience as a Minister*, 70–71.

5 Parker, *Experience as a Minister*, 77.

6 Henry W. Bellows, *The Suspense of Faith* (New York: C. S. Francis & Co., 1859), 15.

7 Bellows, *The Suspense of Faith*, 22. Bellows asked: "Who can believe, or who . . . desires to believe, that the nineteenth century, however important in its place, is to be indefinitely continued?" (26).

8 Bellows, *The Suspense of Faith*, 45.

9 Henry W. Bellows, *A Sequel to "The Suspense of Faith"* (New York: D. Appleton and Company, 1859), 22.

10 Bellows, *A Sequel*, 23–24.

11 John Cotton Smith, "The Suspense and Restoration of Faith," *The Protestant Episcopal Quarterly Review* 6, no. 4 (1859): 525–49, at 530. The essay was reprinted in John Cotton Smith, *Miscellanies, Old and New* (New York: T. Whittaker, 1876), 57–107.

12 Smith, "The Suspense and Restoration of Faith," 533.

13 Smith, "The Suspense and Restoration of Faith," 537, 542–43.

14 An example of this approach is the Stone-Campbell tradition that gave birth to the Churches of Christ and Disciples of Christ.

15 A full account of this story would need to give more attention to J. Gresham Machen, whose *Christianity and Liberalism* played an important role in setting the terms for antimodern Protestantism in the twentieth century. His work also exemplifies the doctrinal version of the rule of faith. Christianity, he says, is based on facts, and doctrines convey the meaning of those facts. For this reason, "Christian doctrine lies at the very roots of faith. It must be admitted, then, that if we are to have a non-doctrinal religion, or a doctrinal religion founded merely on general truth, we must give up not only Paul, not only the primitive Jerusalem Church, but also Jesus Himself." Machen also stresses the importance of the creeds and the "great historic presentations of Biblical teaching" over the centuries, which showed a sensitivity to the history of Christian theology that was not present among the more biblicist fundamentalists. See J. Gresham Machen, *Christianity and Liberalism* (New York: Macmillan, 1923), 44–46. Machen's role in this story is more well known, and others have discussed it already. While his aggressive antiliberalism is the driving spirit within modern evangelicalism, his rigidly Calvinist theology was not the form that antimodern Christianity took outside of a narrow Presbyterian orbit. What interests me is the way Machen's opponents were themselves engaged in their own version of antimodernism, and it is this version, more cultural and political than doctrinal, that ultimately rose to dominance.

16 The cultural turn, of course, involves not only Protestants but also Roman Catholics and even some Eastern Orthodox Christians (though mostly converts to Orthodoxy). My focus is on Protestants because it highlights the contention over the essence of Christian faith and theology (e.g., biblical authority, creedal doctrines, cultural norms, etc.).

17 Lorraine Daston, *Rules: A Short History of What We Live By* (Princeton: Princeton University Press, 2022), 13, 23–26, 29.

18 Daston, *Rules*, 27, 33–40.

19 Daston, *Rules*, 28.

20 *Acts of Justin* 2, Recension B, quoted in Everett Ferguson, *The Rule of Faith: A Guide* (Eugene: Cascade Books, 2015), 3.

21 *Against Heresies* 1.10.1; Ferguson, 4.

22 *On the Prescription of Heretics* 13; Ferguson, *The Rule of Faith*, 6.

23 *On the Veiling of Virgins* 1.3–4; Ferguson, *The Rule of Faith*, 7.

24 *Against Heresies* 3.15.1; Ferguson, *The Rule of Faith*, 18.

25 *First Apology* 46, rev; Justin Martyr, *Writings of Saint Justin Martyr*, trans. Thomas B. Falls, The Fathers of the Church (Washington: The Catholic University of America Press, 1948), 83.

26 *First Apology* 5; Justin Martyr, *Writings*, 38.

27 Everett Ferguson, "*Paradosis* and *Traditio*: A Word Study," in *Tradition and the Rule of Faith in the Early Church: Essays in Honor of Joseph T. Lienhard, S.J.*, ed. Ronnie J. Rombs and

Alexander Y. Hwang (Washington: Catholic University of America Press, 2011), 3–29, at 11.

28 Ferguson, "*Paradosis* and *Traditio*," 13.

29 H. A. Drake, *Constantine and the Bishops: The Politics of Intolerance* (Baltimore: Johns Hopkins University Press, 2000), 438; Paula Fredriksen, "Lambs into Lions," *The New Republic*, June 18, 2001, 35–39, at 37.

30 Drake, *Constantine and the Bishops*, 408.

31 Some traditionalists, as we will see, sought to unify, or rather conflate, intellectualism and voluntarism – arguing that the church's apostolic tradition represents the highest fulfillment of common rationality.

32 Of course, those who subscribe to the latter understand it as identical with the former, either because what the church says is continuous with what scripture says (the *Anglo*-Catholic or Protestant approach) or because the voice of the church *is* the voice of God (the Anglo-*Catholic* approach).

33 Otto Pfleiderer, *The Development of Theology in Germany since Kant, and Its Progress in Great Britain since 1825*, trans. J. Frederick Smith (London: Swan Sonnenschein, 1890), 307.

34 Pfleiderer, *The Development of Theology in Germany since Kant*, 317.

35 Thomas Erskine, *Remarks on the Internal Evidence for the Truth of Revealed Religion* (Edinburgh: Waugh & Innes, 1820), 16, 36. Quoted in John Henry Newman, "On the Introduction of Rationalistic Principles into Revealed Religion," in *Essays, Critical and Historical*, 2 vols. (London: B. M. Pickering, 1871), 1:30–99, at 53–54. Newman italicizes both "leading idea" and "direct and natural."

36 Stephen Sykes, *The Identity of Christianity: Theologians and the Essence of Christianity from Schleiermacher to Barth* (Philadelphia: Fortress Press, 1984), 105.

37 Newman, "On the Introduction of Rationalistic Principles," 41. This language, as well as Newman's argument against systematization, foreshadows Karl Barth's work. Like Newman, Barth opposed the systematic construction of theology according to a rational principle, as I discussed in Chapter 1. Barth also spoke of revelation being *veiled* in human language, though Barth used this point to argue that the language could be changed.

38 One is reminded here of Dietrich Bonhoeffer's notion of the "positivism of revelation" in Barth's theology: "Barth was the first theologian – to his great and lasting credit – to begin the critique of religion, but he then put in its place a positivist doctrine of revelation that says, in effect, 'like it or lump it.' Whether it's the virgin birth, the Trinity, or anything else, all are equally significant and necessary parts of the whole, which must be swallowed whole or not at all." Dietrich Bonhoeffer, *Letters and Papers from Prison*, ed. John W. De Gruchy, trans. Isabel Best et al., Dietrich Bonhoeffer Works 8 (Minneapolis: Fortress, 2010), 373.

39 John Henry Newman, *Lectures on the Prophetical Office of the Church: Viewed Relatively to Romanism and Popular Protestantism* (London: J. G. & F. Rivington, 1837), 53.

40 Newman, *Lectures on the Prophetical Office of the Church*, 50–51. The branch theory of the Tractarians held that Anglicanism was one of the three branches of the original apostolic tradition, alongside Roman Catholicism and Eastern Orthodoxy.

41 The classic Protestant argument that scripture is self-authenticating is superficial, on Newman's reasoning. The canon of scripture did not just fall from the heavens fully formed. We only have the canon we do because of decisions made by church authorities. Protestants are only able to claim that scripture authenticates itself by ignoring the material realities of the text.

42 Newman, *Lectures on the Prophetical Office of the Church*, 34.

43 Newman, *Lectures on the Prophetical Office of the Church*, 326–27.

44 John Henry Newman, *The Via Media of the Anglican Church: Illustrated in Lectures, Letters, and Tracts Written between 1830 and 1841*, 2 vols. (London: Basil Montagu Pickering, 1877), 2:253–54.

45 Newman, 2:268–69. Here Newman is quoting his own 1836 article in the *British Critic* on Nicholas Wiseman's *Lectures on the Principal Doctrines and Practices of the Catholic Church*.

46 He began the work while still an Anglican, but in the course of printing Newman "recognised in himself a conviction of the truth of the conclusion to which the discussion leads," and so added a postscript to the work. John Henry Newman, *An Essay on the Development of Christian Doctrine* (London: James Toovey, 1845), x.

47 Avery Dulles, *John Henry Newman*, Outstanding Christian Thinkers (London: Continuum, 2002), 7.

48 Newman, *Essay* (1845), 28.

49 Bruno Forte, "'Historia Veritatis': On Newman's *Essay on the Development of Christian Doctrine*," in *Newman and Faith*, ed. Ian Ker and Terrence Merrigan (Louvain: Peeters Press, 2004), 75–92, at 76.

50 Newman, *Essay* (1845), 1–2.

51 Newman, *Essay* (1845), 5.

52 John Henry Newman, *An Essay on the Development of Christian Doctrine*, New ed. (London: B. M. Pickering, 1878), 8.

53 Lucas Laborde, "'Continuity of Principles' in John Henry Newman's *An Essay on the Development of Christian Doctrine*," *Newman Studies Journal* 10, no. 2 (2013): 59–73, at 60.

54 The seven tests in 1845 are: (1) preservation of type or idea, (2) continuity of principles, (3) power of assimilation, (4) early anticipation, (5) logical sequence, (6) preservative additions, and (7) chronic continuance. In 1878 they are: (1) preservation of its type, (2) continuity of its principles, (3) its power of assimilation, (4) its logical sequence, (5) anticipation of its future, (6) conservative action upon its past, and (7) its chronic vigor.

55 David Bentley Hart, *Tradition and Apocalypse: An Essay on the Future of Christian Belief* (Grand Rapids: Baker Academic, 2022), 31.

56 Hart, *Tradition and Apocalypse*, 45.

57 Newman, *Essay* (1878), 1.1.2, 34.

58 Newman, *Essay* (1878), 1.1.2, 34–35.

59 Newman, *Essay* (1878), 1.1.3, 36.

60 Newman, *Essay* (1878), 5.2.1, 178–79.

61 John Henry Newman, *An Essay in Aid of a Grammar of Assent* (London: Burns, Oates, & Co., 1870), 426.

62 Newman, *Essay* (1878), 7.1.4–5, 325–26.

63 Newman, *Essay* (1878), 7.1.2, 324.

64 Hart, *Tradition and Apocalypse*, 47.

65 Newman, *Essay* (1878), 6.1.30, 246.

66 Newman, *Essay* (1878), 6.0, 208.

67 Newman, *Essay* (1845), 117; Newman, *Essay* (1878), 2.2.4, 78.

68 Newman, *Essay* (1878), 2.2.11, 86. Emphasis mine. Only the phrase "of necessity" is lacking in the 1845 version. See Newman, *Essay* (1845), 124.

69 Newman, *Essay* (1878), 2.2.4, 78.

70 Thomas Croskery, "Conversions to Romanism," *The Presbyterian Review* 6, no. 22 (1885): 201–25, at 208–10.

71 It may be more accurate to describe neoorthodoxy as an Anglo-American movement, particularly if one includes the likes of John and Donald Baillie within its orbit.

72 Dennis N. Voskuil, "American Protestant Neo-Orthodoxy and Its Search for Realism (1925–1939)," *Ultimate Reality and Meaning* 8, no. 4 (1985): 277–87, at 281–82.

73 William Silva, "The Expression of Neo-orthodoxy in American Protestantism, 1939–1960" (PhD diss., Yale University, 1988), 19.

74 Gustav Krüger, "The 'Theology of Crisis': Remarks on a Recent Movement in German Theology," *The Harvard Theological Review* 19, no. 3 (1926): 227–58.

75 Karl Barth, "The Inward Man," *The Student World* 21, no. 3 (1928): 298–308; Karl Barth, *The Word of God and the Word of Man*, trans. Douglas Horton (London: Hodder and Stoughton, 1928). The original German sermon from June 13, 1920, "Der innere Mensch," is available in the Karl Barth Gesamtausgabe 42:211–23.

76 Emil Brunner, *The Theology of Crisis* (New York: C. Scribner's Sons, 1929).

77 John McConnachie, *The Significance of Karl Barth* (London: Hodder and Stoughton, 1931); Wilhelm Pauck, *Karl Barth, Prophet of a New Christianity?* (New York: Harper & Brothers, 1931).

78 Karl Barth, *The Epistle to the Romans*, trans. Edwyn C. Hoskyns (London: Oxford University Press, 1933; reprint, 1968).

79 See Heather A. Warren, "The Theological Discussion Group and Its Impact on American and Ecumenical Theology, 1920–1945," *Church History* 62, no. 4 (1993): 528–43, esp. 531–33.

80 Henry P. Van Dusen, "The Sickness of Liberal Religion," *World Tomorrow* 14 (1931): 256–59.

81 Gaius Glenn Atkins, "Whither Liberalism?," *Religion in Life* 3, no. 3 (1934): 335–39; Wilhelm Pauck, "What Is Wrong with Liberalism?," *The Journal of Religion* 15, no. 2 (1935): 146–60; Harry Emerson Fosdick, "The Church Must Go Beyond Modernism," *Christian Century*, December 4, 1935, 1549–52. See Voskuil, "American Protestant Neo-Orthodoxy," 279.

82 Pauck, "What Is Wrong with Liberalism?," 148–49.

83 Pauck, "What Is Wrong with Liberalism?," 152.

84 Pauck, "What Is Wrong with Liberalism?," 154.

85 Pauck, "What Is Wrong with Liberalism?," 156.

86 Elesha J. Coffman, *The Christian Century and the Rise of the Protestant Mainline* (New York: Oxford University Press, 2013), 123–25.

87 Charles Clayton Morrison, "How Their Minds Have Changed," *Christian Century*, October 4, 1939, 1194–98, at 1194; Elesha J. Coffman, "Constituting the Protestant Mainline: *The Christian Century*, 1908–1947" (PhD diss., Duke University, 2008), 219.

88 John A. Mackay, "The Restoration of Theology," *Princeton Seminary Bulletin* 31, no. 1 (1937): 7–18, at 8.

89 Mackay, "The Restoration of Theology," 9.

90 Mackay, "The Restoration of Theology," 11, 13.

91 Kevin J. Vanhoozer, *Remythologizing Theology: Divine Action, Passion, and Authorship* (Cambridge: Cambridge University Press, 2010), 81. See Karl Adam, "Die Theologie der Krisis," *Hochland* 23, no. 2 (1926): 271–86.

92 Vanhoozer, *Remythologizing Theology*, 105.

93 Peter Heltzel and Christian Collins Winn open their essay on Barth and the triune God with the acknowledgment that "it has become commonplace to attribute the twentieth-century recovery of the doctrine of the Trinity to the Swiss theologian Karl Barth." Peter Goodwin Heltzel and Christian T. Collins Winn, "Karl Barth, Reconciliation, and the Triune God," in *The Cambridge Companion to the Trinity*, ed. Peter C. Phan (Cambridge: Cambridge University Press, 2011), 173–91, at 173.

94 *CD* 1.1:xiii.

95 *CD* 1.1:295–96.

96 *CD* 1.2:866.

97 George M. Marsden, *Reforming Fundamentalism: Fuller Seminary and the New Evangelicalism* (Grand Rapids: Eerdmans, 1987), 100–101.

98 Marsden, *Reforming Fundamentalism*, 111.

99 Paul Lehmann, "Orthodoxy Appraises Neo-Orthodoxy," *Christendom* 11, no. 4 (1946): 528–30, at 528.

100 Lehmann, "Orthodoxy Appraises Neo-Orthodoxy," 529–30.

101 Rudolf Bultmann, "Bericht über unsere Amerika-Reise 1951," in *Bultmann–Bornkamm Briefwechsel 1926–1976*, ed. Werner Zager (Tübingen: Mohr Siebeck, 2014), 222–55, at 244–45.

102 *CD* 1.2:866.

103 *CD* 1.2:860, 862.

104 C. S. Lewis, *Mere Christianity* (New York: HarperCollins, 2001; 1952), 52. Hereafter future references will be parenthetical.

105 C. S. Lewis, *God in the Dock: Essays on Theology and Ethics* (Grand Rapids: Eerdmans, 1970), 201. See George M. Marsden, *C. S. Lewis's Mere Christianity: A Biography* (Princeton: Princeton University Press, 2016), 91–92.

106 This is not an isolated claim. Earlier in the book he writes: "That is one of the reasons I believe Christianity. It is a religion you could not have guessed. . . . It is not the sort of thing anyone would have made up" (41–42). Lewis here shows no grasp of the way religions and other cultural scripts are never made up out of whole cloth all at once, but like all historical forms are the product of gradual development over long periods of time.

107 Lewis, *God in the Dock*, 66–67.

108 Lewis repeats this point in order to make it especially clear: "It is the whole of Christianity. Christianity offers nothing else at all" (195).

109 Lewis, *God in the Dock*, 129, 131.

110 Lewis, *God in the Dock*, 132.

111 Lewis, *God in the Dock*, 44–45.

112 Newman, *Essay* (1878), 5.1.1, 172; Lewis, *God in the Dock*, 45.

113 William R. Hutchison, "Preface: From Protestant to Pluralist America," in *Between the Times: The Travail of the Protestant Establishment in America, 1900–1960*, ed. William R. Hutchison (Cambridge: Cambridge University Press, 1989), vii–xv, at vii.

114 Thomas C. Oden, *Agenda for Theology: Recovering Christian Roots* (San Francisco: Harper & Row, 1979), 157–58.

115 Thomas C. Oden, *A Change of Heart: A Personal and Theological Memoir* (Downers Grove: IVP Academic, 2014), 161.

116 Bernard L. Ramm, *After Fundamentalism: The Future of Evangelical Theology* (San Francisco: Harper & Row, 1983), 11, 28.

117 Ramm, *After Fundamentalism*, 37.

118 Marsden, *C. S. Lewis's Mere Christianity*, 73.

119 Quoted in Marsden, *C. S. Lewis's Mere Christianity*, 77.

120 Clyde Kilby, "C. S. Lewis and His Critics," *Christianity Today*, December 8, 1958, 13–15.

121 Marsden, *C. S. Lewis's Mere Christianity*, 112.

122 Marsden, *C. S. Lewis's Mere Christianity*, 76, 113–14.

123 "C. S. Lewis and InterVarsity," *InterVarsity.org*, December 7, 2005, https://intervarsity.org/news/c-s-lewis-and-intervarsity.

Chapter 3

1 Martin E. Marty, *Dietrich Bonhoeffer's Letters and Papers from Prison: A Biography* (Princeton: Princeton University Press, 2011), 113.

2 John A. T. Robinson, *Honest to God* (London: SCM Press, 1963), 25. See Sherwood Eliot Wirt, "The Final Interview of C. S. Lewis," *Christian Broadcasting Network*, 1963, https://www.cbn.com/special/Narnia/articles/ans_LewisLastInterviewA.aspx; Bultmann, "Ist der Glaube an Gott erledigt? [1963]," 4:107–12; Rudolf Bultmann, "The Idea of God and Modern Man [1963]," in *World Come of Age: A Symposium on Dietrich Bonhoeffer*, ed. Ronald Gregor Smith (London: Collins, 1967), 256–73.

3 Robinson, *Honest to God*, 29–39.

4 William Hamilton, *The New Essence of Christianity*, rev. ed. (New York: Association Press, 1966).

5 I will avoid giving a precise definition of culture largely because there is no consistent definition operative among the theologians and scholars who participated in the twentieth-century cultural turn. While George Lindbeck referred to the work of anthropologist Clifford Geertz, ultimately the term "culture" for Lindbeck was interchangeable with "language" and referred to the inner logic or grammar of a community underlying its doctrines and practices. Put another way, culture refers to whatever

"shapes the entirety of life and thought." George A. Lindbeck, *The Nature of Doctrine: Religion and Theology in a Postliberal Age* (Philadelphia: Westminster Press, 1984), 33. Kathryn Tanner has done the most to analyze the concept of culture in recent theology, particularly in relation to postliberalism. See Kathryn Tanner, *Theories of Culture: A New Agenda for Theology* (Minneapolis: Fortress, 1997). The amorphous character of the concept is precisely what made it so attractive to theologians. One could smuggle additional norms into one's account of Christianity by describing them as integral to Christian culture, even if they had no place in any traditional doctrine or practice.

6 See Heiko Schulz, "A Modest Head Start: The German Reception of Kierkegaard," in *Kierkegaard's International Reception, Tome I: Northern and Western Europe*, ed. Jon Stewart, Kierkegaard Research: Sources, Reception and Resources 8 (Farnham: Ashgate, 2009), 307–420, at 336. Schulz points out that the dialectical theologians were not Kierkegaard scholars by any means, but they "exerted a profound influence on generations of students and extra-academic circles alike, and this also and in particular as multiplicators of (their particular reading of) Kierkegaard's thought" (335). But as Schulz also points out, Barth was by no means the first to initiate the rediscovery of Kierkegaard among German speakers. Much of that credit belongs to Theodor Haecker (1879–1945), who translated both Kierkegaard and John Henry Newman into German and was one of the first to publish on Kierkegaard in 1913. See also Charlie Cahill, "Rescuing the Individual: The Kierkegaard Renaissance in Weimar Germany" (PhD diss., University of Wisconsin-Madison, 2016), 40–55. Cahill also points to an even earlier influence in Albert Bärthold (1843–1918), who highlighted "Kierkegaard's distinction between true Christianity and Christendom," thus paving the way for the dialectical theologians (30). Bärthold was a student of Johann Tobias Beck (1804–1878), who had taught Barth's father and grandfather.

7 Samuel Moyn, "Transcendence, Morality, and History: Emmanuel Levinas and the Discovery of Søren Kierkeggard in France," *Yale French Studies*, no. 104 (2004): 22–54, at 25.

8 Karl Barth to Eduard Thurneysen, June 23, 1925, in Karl Barth and Eduard Thurneysen, *Briefwechsel, Band II: 1921–1930*, ed. Eduard Thurneysen, Gesamtausgabe 4 (Zürich: TVZ, 1974), 344.

9 For a study of Bultmann's reception of Kierkegaard, see Cora Bartels, *Kierkegaard Receptus: Die Theologiegeschichtliche Bedeutung der Kierkegaard-Rezeption Rudolf Bultmanns*, 2 vols. (Göttingen: V & R Unipress, 2008).

10 Karl Barth's newsletter to friends, November 26, 1924, in Barth and Thurneysen, *Briefwechsel, Band II*, 294. Geismar gained an international reputation that led to his invitation to give the 1936 Stone Lectures at Princeton Theological Seminary. Princeton president John Mackay, due to his interest in both Barth and Emil Brunner, saw Kierkegaard as an important part of his plan to renew American theology and culture.

11 Schulz, "A Modest Head Start," 344–47.

12 For the most extensive study of the Luther Renaissance, see Heinrich Assel, *Der andere Aufbruch: Die Lutherrenaissance – Ursprünge, Aporien und Wege* (Göttingen: Vandenhoeck & Ruprecht, 1994). For an accessible account in English, see James M. Stayer, *Martin*

Luther, German Saviour: German Evangelical Theological Factions and the Interpretation of Luther, 1917–1933 (Montreal: McGill-Queen's University Press, 2000). See also the essays in Christine Helmer and Bo Kristian Holm, eds., *Lutherrenaissance Past and Present* (Göttingen: Vandenhoeck & Ruprecht, 2015).

13 Charlie Cahill points out the irony of "how communists and fascists used Kierkegaard" and explores how these groups that subordinate the individual engaged Kierkegaard's existential thought as a way of shaping their understandings of authentic existence (Cahill, "Rescuing the Individual," v).

14 See Christine Helmer, *How Luther Became the Reformer* (Louisville: Westminster John Knox Press, 2019), 8–14, 26–29. Holl delivered his lecture, "What Did Luther Understand by Religion?" on October 31, 1917. It was published later that year and then expanded for the publication of his collected writings on Luther in 1921. See Karl Holl, *Gesammelte Aufsätze zur Kirchengeschichte*, 3 vols., Band 1: *Luther* (Tübingen: J. C. B. Mohr, 1921), 1–110; Karl Holl, *What Did Luther Understand by Religion?* (Philadelphia: Fortress, 1977). The fact that Holl's volume was published the same year as the second edition of Barth's *Epistle to the Romans* meant that the Luther Renaissance and dialectical theology developed side-by-side as rival efforts at reforming theology. See Heinrich Assel, "Introduction: Luther Renaissance and Dialectical Theology – A tour d'horizon 1906–1935," in *Luther, Barth, and Movements of Theological Renewal (1918–1933)*, ed. Heinrich Assel and Bruce McCormack (Boston: De Gruyter, 2020), 1–16.

15 Helmer, *How Luther Became the Reformer*, 80–81.

16 While the Luther Renaissance had strong connections to the Nazi *Deutsche Christen*, the movement was not uniformly on the side of extreme German nationalism. Holl's work, and the Luther Renaissance more broadly, also inspired key figures in the Confessing Church, including Hans Joachim Iwand and Dietrich Bonhoeffer. See Heinrich Assel, "Die *Lutherrenaissance* in Deutschland von 1900 bis 1960: Herausforderung und Inspiration," in *Lutherrenaissance Past and Present*, ed. Christine Helmer and Bo Kristian Holm (Göttingen: Vandenhoeck & Ruprecht, 2015), 23–53.

17 The story is told well in Sarah Shortall, *Soldiers of God in a Secular World: Catholic Theology and Twentieth-Century French Politics* (Cambridge, MA: Harvard University Press, 2021).

18 Jürgen Mettepenningen, "Nouvelle Théologie: Four Historical Stages of Theological Reform Towards Ressourcement (1935–1965)," in *Ressourcement: A Movement for Renewal in Twentieth-Century Catholic Theology*, ed. Gabriel Flynn and Paul D. Murray (Oxford: Oxford University Press, 2012), 172–84.

19 Patricia Kelly, "Introduction," in *Ressourcement Theology: A Sourcebook*, ed. Patricia Kelly (London: T&T Clark, 2020), 1–9, at 3.

20 Kelly, "Introduction," 4.

21 Scottish Presbyterians at T&T Clark in Edinburgh published the *Ante-Nicene Christian Library* between 1867 and 1873 in response to the Anglo-Catholic series.

22 Keith F. Pecklers, "Ressourcement and the Renewal of Catholic Liturgy: On Celebrating the New Rite," in *Ressourcement: A Movement for Renewal in Twentieth-Century Catholic Theology*, ed. Gabriel Flynn and Paul D. Murray (Oxford: Oxford University Press, 2012), 318–32, at 319.

23 Pecklers, "Ressourcement and the Renewal of Catholic Liturgy," 321–24.

24 Kelly, "Introduction," 4.

25 Frank C. Senn, "What Has Become of the Liturgical Movement? Its Origins, Current Situation and Future Prospects," *Pro Ecclesia* 6, no. 3 (1997): 319–32, at 320–321.

26 Senn, "What Has Become of the Liturgical Movement?," 324–26.

27 At the 1952 meeting of the IMC in Willigen, the Protestant council agreed that the mission of the church is grounded in the trinity, represented by the term *missio Dei* (mission of God). In *Ad gentes*, the Roman Catholic Church declared that "the pilgrim Church is missionary by her very nature" and provided a trinitarian basis for missionary activity. Both councils thus supported a broad, ecumenical consensus that mission, in an expansive sense of the term, is essential to the Christian faith – essential both to God and to the church commissioned by God. This new sense of Christian mission did not occur in a vacuum. There was widespread anxiety on all sides about the cultural changes and political instability occurring throughout the world at the time, as well growing secularism in Europe, North America, and Australasia. This concern was reinforced especially in the Catholic Church's next statement on mission, *Evangelii nuntiandi* (1975), which states: "This faith is nearly always today exposed to secularism, even to militant atheism. ... One is forced to note in the very heart of this contemporary world the phenomenon which is becoming almost its most striking characteristic: secularism."

28 The Lutheran World Federation and the Roman Catholic Church, *Joint Declaration on the Doctrine of Justification* (Grand Rapids: Eerdmans, 2000).

29 Westminster Confession of Faith, 1.2, 1.5, 1.9.

30 Second Helvetic Confession, 2.1.

31 Harry Emerson Fosdick, *The Modern Use of the Bible* (New York: Macmillan, 1924), 102–3.

32 Gaius Glenn Atkins, *Religion in Our Times* (New York: Round Table Press, 1932), 86.

33 I use "post-liberal" to refer to theological ideas that are critical of liberalism, especially German liberal theology; I use "postliberal" to refer to the school of postliberalism that developed especially in the United States in the late twentieth century.

34 W. Eugene Marsh, "'Biblical Theology,' Authority and the Presbyterians," *Journal of Presbyterian History* 59, no. 2 (1981): 113–30, at 118; Brevard S. Childs, *Biblical Theology in Crisis* (Philadelphia: Westminster Press, 1970), 18–21. Childs rightly observes that "the Biblical Theology Movement in America was clearly dependent on this European revival," but it was nevertheless "so distinctive as to demand a separate characterization" (18).

35 Childs, *Biblical Theology in Crisis*, 14.

36 Otto A. Piper, "Discovering the Bible," *Christian Century*, February 27, 1946, 266–68, at 267.

37 Otto A. Piper, "How I Study My Bible," *Christian Century*, March 6, 1946, 299–301, at 299–300.

38 Otto A. Piper, "The Bible as 'Holy History,'" *Christian Century*, March 20, 1946, 362–64, at 363–64.

39 John A. Mackay, "Our Aims, and the Present Number," *Theology Today* 1, no. 1 (1944): 3–15, at 4.

40 John A. Mackay, "God Has Spoken," *Theology Today* 3, no. 2 (1946): 145–50, at 145.

41 Mackay, "Our Aims," 7–8.

42 Mackay, "Our Aims," 10.

43 Mackay, "Our Aims," 7, 5–6.

44 Mackay, "Our Aims," 15.

45 Paul S. Minear, "Wanted: A Biblical Theology," *Theology Today* 1, no. 1 (1944): 47–58; Holmes Rolston, "A Theological Watershed: Barth's *Römerbrief*: A Digest with Notes," *Theology Today* 1, no. 1 (1944): 103–20; F. W. Dillistone, "The Re-Discovery of the Gospel," *Theology Today* 1, no. 1 (1944): 59–77, at 60, 71.

46 Joseph L. Hromádka, "Civilization's Doom and Resurrection," *Theology Today* 1, no. 1 (1944): 18–33, at 22, 32.

47 Emil Brunner, *Christianity and Civilisation*, 2 vols., Gifford Lectures 1947–1948 (New York: C. Scribner's Sons, 1948), 1:1.

48 Edwards, *The Right of the Protestant Left*, 92.

49 Editors, "Whose Word? An Editorial," *Interpretation* 1, no. 3 (1947): 360–62, at 360.

50 Editors, "The House of the Interpreter: An Editorial," *Interpretation* 1, no. 1 (1947): 49–51, at 49–50.

51 This anxious, postwar energy was hardly limited to the Presbyterians. The same year that *Interpretation* released its first issue, Fuller Theological Seminary was founded.

52 Harold Henry Rowley, "The Relevance of Biblical Interpretation," *Interpretation* 1, no. 1 (1947): 3–19, at 3.

53 Editors, "'A' Bible or 'the' Bible? An Editorial," *Interpretation* 1, no. 4 (1947): 466–70, at 466.

54 To appreciate just how confusing the conversation over demythologizing was, it helps to compare the German and English editions of *Kerygma and Myth*. Compared to the 1948 volume in German, the first English volume inexplicably leaves out the essay and letter by Bultmann's friend and supporter Götz Harbsmeier, as well as essays by Hermann Sauter and Paul Olivier. It adds an essay from Austin Farrer that is unique to the English books. It also includes Bultmann's important 1952 essay clarifying his program of demythologizing that was published originally in volume 2 of *Kerygma und Mythos* – but crucially, it only includes part of the essay. The second *Kerygma and Myth* volume contains none (!) of the essays in the second *Kerygma und Mythos* book, including the two important essays by Christian Hartlich and Walter Sachs that Bultmann thought were particularly helpful explanations of his thought. Instead it features three essays from the third *Kerygma und Mythos* and some additional writings published elsewhere, most notably Karl Barth's long essay on Bultmann.

55 Rudolf Bultmann, "New Testament and Mythology: The Problem of Demythologizing the New Testament Proclamation [1941]," in *New Testament and Mythology and Other Basic Writings*, ed. Schubert M. Ogden (Philadelphia: Fortress, 1984), 1–43, at 3.

56 Hans Asmussen to Ernst Wolf, March 21, 1942, in Rudolf Bultmann, *Briefwechsel mit Götz Harbsmeier und Ernst Wolf, 1933–1976*, ed. Werner Zager (Tübingen: Mohr Siebeck, 2017), 474.

57 Dietrich Bonhoeffer to Ernst Wolf, March 24, 1942, in Dietrich Bonhoeffer, *Conspiracy and Imprisonment: 1940–1945*, ed. Mark S. Brocker, Dietrich Bonhoeffer Works 16

(Minneapolis: Fortress, 2006), 260–61; Bultmann, *Briefwechsel mit Götz Harbsmeier und Ernst Wolf, 1933–1976*, 475.

58 Childs, *Biblical Theology in Crisis*, 34.

59 Joseph Haroutunian, "Recent Theology and the Biblical Mind," *Journal of Bible and Religion* 8, no. 1 (1940): 18–23, at 20.

60 According to Bultmann, "the biblical writings … speak in a strange language, in concepts of a faraway time, of a world picture that is alien to us. Simply put, they must be *translated*, and translation is the work of the science of history." Rudolf Bultmann, "Is Exegesis without Presuppositions Possible? [1957]," in *New Testament and Mythology and Other Basic Writings*, ed. Schubert M. Ogden (Philadelphia: Fortress, 1984), 145–53, at 148.

61 James Barr, *The Semantics of Biblical Language* (London: Oxford University Press, 1961).

62 Childs, *Biblical Theology in Crisis*, 63.

63 "Bultmann: Stone of Stumbling," *The Christian Century*, March 20, 1963, 383.

64 Krister Stendahl, "Biblical Theology, Contemporary," in *The Interpreter's Dictionary of the Bible*, ed. George A. Buttrick (Nashville: Abingdon, 1962), 1:418–32.

65 Gustaf Wingren, *Theology in Conflict: Nygren, Barth, Bultmann* (Philadelphia: Muhlenberg Press, 1958), ix.

66 Wingren, *Theology in Conflict*, 163.

67 Robert Clyde Johnson, *Authority in Protestant Theology* (Philadelphia: Westminster Press, 1959), 13.

68 Johnson, *Authority in Protestant Theology*, 189.

69 Johnson, *Authority in Protestant Theology*, 190.

70 Johnson, *Authority in Protestant Theology*, 192.

71 Robert H. Bryant, *The Bible's Authority Today* (Minneapolis: Augsburg, 1968), 13.

72 J. Christiaan Beker, "Reflections on Biblical Theology," *Interpretation* 24, no. 3 (1970): 303–20, at 303–4.

73 James D. Smart, *The Strange Silence of the Bible in the Church: A Study in Hermeneutics* (Philadelphia: Westminster Press, 1970), 16–17.

74 James Barr, "Old Testament and the New Crisis of Biblical Authority," *Interpretation* 25, no. 1 (1971): 24–40, at 25, 37.

75 David H. Kelsey, *The Uses of Scripture in Recent Theology* (Philadelphia: Fortress, 1975), 8.

76 Gabriel Vahanian, *The Death of God: The Culture of Our Post-Christian Era* (New York: G. Braziller, 1961); Harvey Cox, *The Secular City: Secularization and Urbanization in Theological Perspective* (New York: Macmillan, 1965); Ronald Gregor Smith, *Secular Christianity* (New York: Harper & Row, 1966); Thomas J. J. Altizer and William Hamilton, *Radical Theology and the Death of God* (Indianapolis: Bobbs-Merrill, 1966).

77 Mary Daly, *The Church and the Second Sex* (New York: Harper & Row, 1968); James H. Cone, *Black Theology and Black Power* (New York: Seabury Press, 1969).

78 See Elizabeth Hinton, *America on Fire: The Untold History of Police Violence and Black Rebellion since the 1960s* (New York: Liveright Publishing, 2021).

79 "The Chicago Statement on Biblical Inerrancy," Article 12.

80 Harold Lindsell, *The Battle for the Bible* (Grand Rapids: Zondervan, 1976), 10.

81 Lindsell, *The Battle for the Bible*, 166.

82 Lindsell, *The Battle for the Bible*, 39.

83 Lindsell, *The Battle for the Bible*, 82.

84 Lindsell, *The Battle for the Bible*, 25.

85 The Evangelical Theological Society (ETS) adopted the Chicago Statement on Biblical Inerrancy in 2005 in response to the vote by members of ETS in 2003 *not* to revoke the membership of Clark Pinnock and John Sanders for their belief in open theism. The 2003 vote led Norman Geisler to resign from ETS in protest, claiming that it had lost its way. While ETS leaders thought that the adoption of the Chicago Statement might be a way to ensure the removal of Pinnock and Sanders, both theologians claimed they could affirm the statement – only reinforcing the ambiguity of biblical authority. A decade later, in 2013, ETS held its annual meeting on the topic, "Evangelicalism, Inerrancy, and ETS," on the grounds that, according to ETS program chair Thomas Schreiner, "Today there are new challenges and questions to Scripture's authority." The issue now was LGBTQ inclusion and "same-sex marriage." See Jeff Robinson, "Evangelical Theological Society Adopts Inerrancy Statement," *Baptist Press*, November 20, 2006, www.baptistpress .com/resource-library/news/evangelical-theological-society-adopts-inerrancy-state ment/; Greg Strand, "Evangelicalism, Inerrancy, and ETS," *EFCA Blog*, November 18, 2013, https://go.efca.org/blog/understanding-scripture/evangelicalism-inerrancy-and-ets; Richard Rice, *The Future of Open Theism: From Antecedents to Opportunities* (Downers Grove: IVP Academic, 2020), 52–58.

86 Mainline postliberal Protestants were not the only group evangelicals allied themselves with and intellectually pilfered; they did both with the Roman Catholics as well, by entering ecumenical partnerships like Evangelicals and Catholics Together and borrowing theological concepts like Thomistic natural law. That side of the story is relevant to but beyond the scope of this study. The common point of connection is the strategic shift that elite evangelicals made away from scripture toward other normative categories – whether culture, in the case of postliberalism (as I explore in this chapter), or natural law, in the case of Catholics. Both strategies were related to the larger evangelical goal of accommodating their activist and apologetic agenda to a rapidly changing social context. For a study of how this shift has played out in the pages of *Christianity Today* with respect to the issue of homosexuality, see Jeremy N. Thomas and Daniel V. A. Olson, "Evangelical Elites' Changing Responses to Homosexuality 1960–2009," *Sociology of Religion* 73, no. 3 (2012): 239–72.

87 Hans W. Frei, "Remarks in Connection with a Theological Proposal [1967]," in *Theology and Narrative: Selected Essays*, ed. George Hunsinger and William C. Placher (New York: Oxford University Press, 1993), 26–44, at 31.

88 Frei, "Remarks in Connection with a Theological Proposal [1967]," 32.

89 Hans W. Frei, *The Eclipse of Biblical Narrative: A Study in Eighteenth and Nineteenth Century Hermeneutics* (New Haven: Yale University Press, 1974), 24.

90 Frei, *The Eclipse of Biblical Narrative*, 2, 8.

91 Hans W. Frei, "The Doctrine of Revelation in the Thought of Karl Barth, 1909 to 1922: The Nature of Barth's Break with Liberalism" (PhD diss., Yale University, 1956), 150–51.

92 Jason A. Springs, *Toward a Generous Orthodoxy: Prospects for Hans Frei's Postliberal Theology* (Oxford: Oxford University Press, 2010), 8. See William C. Placher, *Unapologetic Theology: A Christian Voice in a Pluralistic Conversation* (Louisville: Westminster/John Knox Press, 1989).

93 Karl Barth, *Barth in Conversation: Volume 3, 1964–1968*, ed. Eberhard Busch, trans. Translation Fellows of the Center for Barth Studies (Louisville: Westminster John Knox Press, 2019), 113. See Carl F. H. Henry, "Basic Issues in Modern Theology: Revelation in History," *Christianity Today*, December 4, 1964, 13.

94 Karl Barth, *Barth in Conversation: Volume 1, 1959–1962*, ed. Eberhard Busch, trans. Translation Fellows of the Center for Barth Studies (Louisville: Westminster John Knox Press, 2017), 222.

95 Carl F. H. Henry, "Narrative Theology: An Evangelical Appraisal," *Trinity Journal* 8, no. 1 (1987): 3–19, at 3. For the best account of the exchange between Henry and Frei, see George Hunsinger, "What Can Evangelicals and Postliberals Learn from Each Other? The Carl Henry/Hans Frei Exchange Reconsidered (1995)," in *Disruptive Grace: Studies in the Theology of Karl Barth* (Grand Rapids: Eerdmans, 2000), 338–60.

96 Henry, "Narrative Theology," 5, 8–9.

97 Henry, "Narrative Theology," 19.

98 Hans W. Frei, "Response to 'Narrative Theology: An Evangelical Appraisal,'" *Trinity Journal* 8, no. 1 (1987): 21–24, at 21.

99 Frei, "Response to 'Narrative Theology,'" 24.

100 Hunsinger even uses this term to describe Henry's position, stating that Frei's position does not "conform to Henry's canons of 'objectivity' in the nonperspectival or value-neutral sense that seems so important to him" (Hunsinger, "What Can Evangelicals and Postliberals Learn from Each Other?," 343).

101 Frei, "Remarks in Connection with a Theological Proposal," 31. Emphasis mine.

102 In addition to the work of Jason Springs, for a nuanced reading of Frei's theology, see Paul J. DeHart, *The Trial of the Witnesses: The Rise and Decline of Postliberal Theology* (Oxford: Blackwell, 2006).

103 Frei, "The Doctrine of Revelation in the Thought of Karl Barth," 488, 492.

104 Lindbeck, *Nature of Doctrine*, 33.

105 Lindbeck, *Nature of Doctrine*, 49.

106 To be clear, Lindbeck was in no way lessening the importance of doctrine but rather redefined it, moving away from the traditional propositional account toward a regulative understanding of doctrine as a grammatical rule for the cultural-linguistic religious community. Instead of representing the content a person was required to believe for salvation, doctrine now represented the basis for one's cultural identity as a Christian. Doctrine is whatever is "unconditionally and permanently necessary to mainstream Christian identity"; it is any characteristic "considered essential to the identity or welfare of the group in question" (Lindbeck, *Nature of Doctrine*, 96, 74). The emphasis on identity here is notable and reflects the period in which he was writing. Ed Watson describes this as the "constitutive function" of doctrine in Lindbeck's work. Lindbeck, according to Watson, "presents doctrines as constitutive of essential Christian identity

across time." While this shift to identity was politically useful to the postliberals in their ecumenical and society-transforming project, it also opened Lindbeck's postliberalism up to later critique, especially in the work of Kathryn Tanner. See Ed Watson, "Another Nature of Doctrine: George Lindbeck, Kathryn Tanner and Christian Identities," *Scottish Journal of Theology* 74 (2021): 262–73, at 264–65.

107 Gerald Izenberg traces the idea of collective identity to the 1960s, when sociologists, historians, and theorists began applying Erik Erikson's concept of individual identity to groups in light of the civil rights movement, decolonization, and second-wave feminism. See Gerald Izenberg, *Identity: The Necessity of a Modern Idea* (Philadelphia: University of Pennsylvania Press, 2016), 172–86.

108 On the untranslatability of the Christian norms, see George A. Lindbeck, "The Gospel's Uniqueness: Election and Untranslatability," *Modern Theology* 13, no. 4 (1997): 423–50.

109 Hans Frei, "The 'Literal Reading' of Biblical Narrative in the Christian Tradition: Does It Stretch or Will It Break? [1983]," in *Theology and Narrative*, 117–152, at 122.

110 Robert L. Wilken, "The Church as Culture," *First Things* 142 (2004): 31–36, at 35; Robert L. Wilken, "The Church's Way of Speaking," *First Things* 155 (2005): 27–31, at 30.

111 Stephen L. Young, "Protective Strategies and the Prestige of the 'Academic': A Religious Studies and Practice Theory Redescription of Evangelical Inerrantist Scholarship," *Biblical Interpretation* 23 (2015): 1–35, at 18.

112 See Rod Dreher, *The Benedict Option: A Strategy for Christians in a Post-Christian Nation* (New York: Sentinel, 2017); Various, "Against the Dead Consensus," *First Things*, March 21, 2019, www.firstthings.com/web-exclusives/2019/03/against-the-dead-consensus.

113 Lindbeck, *Nature of Doctrine*, 118.

114 George A. Lindbeck, "Atonement and the Hermeneutics of Intratextual Social Embodiment," in *The Nature of Confession: Evangelicals and Postliberals in Conversation*, ed. Timothy R. Phillips and Dennis L. Okholm (Downers Grove: InterVarsity, 1996), 226; George A. Lindbeck, "Confession and Community: An Israel-like View of the Church," *Christian Century* 107, no. 16 (1990): 495.

115 Frei, "The 'Literal Reading' of Biblical Narrative in the Christian Tradition," 149.

116 See Brian D. McLaren, *A Generous Orthodoxy: Why I Am a Missional, Evangelical, Post/Protestant, Liberal/Conservative, Mystical/Poetic, Biblical, Charismatic/Contemplative, Fundamentalist/Calvinist, Anabaptist/Anglican, Methodist, Catholic, Green, Incarnational, Depressed-Yet-Hopeful, Emergent, Unfinished Christian* (Grand Rapids: Zondervan, 2004).

117 See Young, "Protective Strategies," 17–29. Put another way, whereas evangelicals located their protectionism in the supposed inerrancy of the text, postliberals located it in the untranslatability of cultural discourse.

118 See Lindbeck, "Atonement and the Hermeneutics of Intratextual Social Embodiment," 221–40; George A. Lindbeck et al., "A Panel Discussion," in *The Nature of Confession: Evangelicals and Postliberals in Conversation*, ed. Timothy R. Phillips and Dennis L. Okholm (Downers Grove: InterVarsity Press, 1996), 252–53.

119 Lindbeck, "Gospel's Uniqueness," 429.

120 Lindbeck, "Gospel's Uniqueness," 430, 433.

121 See James Orr, *The Christian View of God and the World as Centring in the Incarnation: Being the First Series of Kerr Lectures* (New York: Anson D. F. Randolph, 1893); Abraham Kuyper, *Calvinism: Six Stone-Lectures* (Amsterdam-Pretoria: Höveker & Wormser, 1899).

122 David K. Naugle, *Worldview: The History of a Concept* (Grand Rapids: Eerdmans, 2002), 13.

123 See Gordon H. Clark, *A Christian View of Men and Things: The Payton Lectures Delivered in Condensed Form at the Fuller Theological Seminary, Pasadena, 1951* (Grand Rapids: Eerdmans, 1952); Arthur F. Holmes, *Contours of a World View* (Grand Rapids: Eerdmans, 1983); James W. Sire, *The Universe Next Door: A Basic World View Catalog* (Downers Grove: InterVarsity Press, 1976).

124 Carl F. H. Henry, *God, Revelation and Authority*, 6 vols. (Waco: Word Books, 1976), 1:31, 17.

125 Molly Worthen, *Apostles of Reason: The Crisis of Authority in American Evangelicalism* (New York: Oxford University Press, 2014), 27.

126 Worthen points out that conservative Catholics had adopted the word as well, viewing Thomism as a *Weltanschauung* and joining forces with libertarians to create the *National Review* in 1955 in order to oppose the liberal *Weltanschauung* (Worthen, *Apostles of Reason*, 28–29). The story of consensus conservatism will become more important in Chapter 4 when we turn to politics.

127 Orr, *The Christian View of God and the World*, 4–5.

128 It is no accident that postliberalism peaked in the mid-1990s at the same time that Samuel Huntington published his notorious book, *The Clash of Civilizations and the Remaking of World Order*. According to Huntington, "cultural identity is what is most meaningful to most people. ... The central theme of this book is that culture and cultural identities, which at the broadest level are civilization identities, are shaping the patterns of cohesion, disintegration, and conflict in the post-Cold War world." See Samuel P. Huntington, *The Clash of Civilizations and the Remaking of World Order* (New York: Simon & Schuster, 1996), 20. The postliberals could and did say much the same with respect to religious identities and conflicts. And just as Huntington's book went on to inspire right-wing political movements, so too postliberalism contributed to right-wing religious movements.

129 Lindbeck, "Gospel's Uniqueness," 430–31.

130 Stanley E. Porter, "Was James Barr Wrong? Assessing His Critics on Biblical Theology," in *James Barr Assessed: Evaluating His Legacy over the Last Sixty Years*, ed. Stanley E. Porter (Leiden: Brill, 2021), 257–77, at 257.

131 Daniel J. Treier, *Introducing Theological Interpretation of Scripture: Recovering a Christian Practice* (Grand Rapids: Baker Academic, 2008), 14, 17.

132 Craig G. Bartholomew and Heath A. Thomas, eds., *A Manifesto for Theological Interpretation* (Grand Rapids: Baker Academic, 2016), 1.

133 D. Christopher Spinks, "Catching up on a Conversation: Recent Voices on Theological Interpretation of Scripture," *Anglican Theological Review* 99, no. 4 (2017): 769–86, at 772.

134 This can be seen from the way proponents of TIS generally do not view the writings of Rudolf Bultmann as an inspiration, despite the fact he was equally involved in the work of theological interpretation in the Weimar era, as indicated by his 1925 essay on "The Problem of a Theological Exegesis of the New Testament" and his commentary on the Gospel of John. See Rudolf Bultmann, "The Problem of a Theological Exegesis of the New Testament [1925]," in *The Beginnings of Dialectic Theology*, ed. James M. Robinson (Richmond: John Knox Press, 1968), 236–56; Rudolf Bultmann, *The Gospel of John: A Commentary*, trans. G. R. Beasley-Murray, R. W. N. Hoare, and J. K. Riches (Philadelphia: Westminster Press, 1971).

135 David C. Steinmetz, "The Superiority of Pre-Critical Exegesis," *Theology Today* 37, no. 1 (1980): 27–38. The essay was included as the second chapter in Stephen E. Fowl, ed., *The Theological Interpretation of Scripture: Classic and Contemporary Readings*, Blackwell Readings in Modern Theology (Malden: Blackwell, 1997), 26–38. It was also included in Darren Sarisky, *Theology, History, and Biblical Interpretation: Modern Readings* (London: Bloomsbury, 2015), 267–78.

136 Klyne Snodgrass, "Introduction," *Ex Auditu* 30 (2014): vii–ix, at viii.

137 George A. Lindbeck, "The Story-Shaped Church: Critical Exegesis and Theological Interpretation," in *Scriptural Authority and Narrative Interpretation*, ed. Garrett Green (Philadelphia: Fortress, 1987), 161–78. It has been anthologized in Fowl, ed., *Theological Interpretation of Scripture*, 39–52.

138 While Jack Rogers was the first evangelical to use the term "postconservative" in 1973, Roger Olson first used the term in 1995 as the label for a group of evangelical theologians – most notably, Stanley Grenz, Clark Pinnock, and John Sanders – who had embraced some of the lessons from the postmodern and postliberal thinkers. Bernard Ramm, George Ladd, and Donald Bloesch would also broadly fall under the postconservative umbrella. The term largely identifies anyone who rejects the Old Princeton doctrine of inerrancy, opposes the rationalist propositionalism of fundamentalism and early neoevangelicalism, and is open to metaphysical creativity with respect to the doctrine of God. See Jack Rogers, "Confessions of a Post-Conservative Evangelical," *Reformed Journal* 23, no. 2 (1973): 10–13; Roger E. Olson, "Postconservative Evangelicals Greet the Postmodern Age," *Christian Century*, May 3, 1995, 480. John Franke said that the term postconservative "high-lights the similarity between developments in liberal theology and the advent of postliberalism and those in the conservative community and is thus suggestive of . . . the possibilities for genuine convergence." See John R. Franke, *The Character of Theology: An Introduction to Its Nature, Task, and Purpose* (Grand Rapids: Baker Academic, 2005), 38. In an effort to defend the older evangelical "consensus," Russell Moore has painted the postconservative evangelicals as repristinating elements from fundamentalist dispensationalism as a way of distancing neoevangelicalism from both fundamentalism and postconservatism. See Russell D. Moore, "Leftward to Scofield: The Eclipse of the Kingdom in Post-Conservative Evangelical Theology," *Journal of the Evangelical Theological Society* 47, no. 3 (2004): 423–40.

139 Roger E. Olson, "What Is a Postconservative Evangelical?," *Roger E. Olson: My Evangelical Arminian Theological Musings*, October 22, 2018, www.patheos.com/blogs/rogereolson/2018/10/what-is-a-postconservative-evangelical/.

140 Spinks, "Catching up on a Conversation," 772–73. See Kevin J. Vanhoozer, *Is There a Meaning in This Text?: The Bible, the Reader, and the Morality of Literary Knowledge* (Grand Rapids: Zondervan, 1998); Craig G. Bartholomew, Colin J. D. Greene, and Karl Möller, eds., *Renewing Biblical Interpretation*, Scripture and Hermeneutics Series 1 (Grand Rapids: Zondervan, 2000); Kevin J. Vanhoozer et al., eds., *Dictionary for Theological Interpretation of the Bible* (Grand Rapids: Baker Academic, 2005).

141 Joel B. Green, "The (Re-)Turn to Theology," *Journal of Theological Interpretation* 1, no. 1 (2007): 1–3, at 1.

142 Richard B. Hays, "Reading the Bible with Eyes of Faith: The Practice of Theological Exegesis," *Journal of Theological Interpretation* 1, no. 1 (2007): 5–21, at 11; Joel B. Green, *Practicing Theological Interpretation: Engaging Biblical Texts for Faith and Formation* (Grand Rapids: Baker Academic, 2011), 2; Bartholomew and Thomas, eds., *A Manifesto for Theological Interpretation*, ix (original emphasis removed).

143 Karl Barth, *The Epistle to the Romans*, trans. Edwyn C. Hoskyns (London: Oxford University Press, 1933; reprint, 1968), 332–33.

144 Bernhard W. Anderson, "The Bible in the Church Today," *Theology Today* 37, no. 1 (1980): 1–6, at 3. In discussing Barr, Anderson slips in a reference to John A. T. Robinson: "Many sensitive Christians, who want to be honest to God in the life of faith, would agree with James Barr."

145 Steinmetz, "The Superiority of Pre-Critical Exegesis," 38.

146 Peter Stuhlmacher, "Ex Auditu and the Theological Interpretation of Holy Scripture," *Ex Auditu* 2 (1986): 1–6, at 6.

147 David S. Yeago, "The New Testament and the Nicene Dogma: A Contribution to the Recovery of Theological Exegesis," *Pro Ecclesia* 3, no. 2 (1994): 152–64, at 153.

148 Brevard S. Childs, "Toward Recovering Theological Exegesis," *Pro Ecclesia* 6, no. 1 (1997): 16–26, at 16–17. This article was reprinted in *Ex Auditu* in 2000.

149 Green, *Practicing Theological Interpretation*, 74.

150 Daniel J. Treier, *Virtue and the Voice of God: Toward Theology as Wisdom* (Grand Rapids: Eerdmans, 2006), 162. Treier, like his teacher Vanhoozer, represents an evangelical variation on postliberalism. Vanhoozer's most well-known work, *The Drama of Doctrine*, advocated a "canonical-linguistic," rather than "cultural-linguistic," approach to theology, a move that illustrates his more classically Protestant conviction about biblical authority. But this was less a protest against the postliberals than it was against fellow evangelicals who had become too culturally modern: "Many Evangelicals have unknowingly made the cultural-linguistic turn already, though the cultures they have appropriated have not been altogether holy." Vanhoozer argues instead for what he calls "catholic-evangelical orthodoxy." See Kevin J. Vanhoozer, *The Drama of Doctrine: A Canonical-Linguistic Approach to Christian Theology* (Louisville: Westminster John Knox Press, 2005), 26–27. The canonical-linguistic model is thus a cultural-linguistic theology that attempts to provide a stronger account of ecclesial and doctrinal

authority. In their more recent coauthored work, Treier and Vanhoozer go so far as to argue that "the church too is part of the content of the gospel, and the pattern of theological authority," and thus they seek to move beyond older evangelical authority by advocating "interpretation of Scripture in the church." Kevin J. Vanhoozer and Daniel J. Treier, *Theology and the Mirror of Scripture: A Mere Evangelical Account* (Downers Grove: IVP Academic, 2015), 13. The distance between evangelicalism and postliberalism at this point has vanished.

151 R. W. L. Moberly, "Biblical Criticism and Religious Belief," *Journal of Theological Interpretation* 2, no. 1 (2008): 71–100, at 84.

152 Hays, "Reading the Bible with Eyes of Faith," 14.

153 R. R. Reno, "Series Preface," in Jaroslav Pelikan, *Acts* (Grand Rapids: Brazos Press, 2005), 12–14. Emphasis mine.

154 It is hardly coincidental that one of the leading proponents of TIS, Craig Bartholomew, is also one of the leading proponents of Kuyper's Dutch Reformed worldview theology. See Craig G. Bartholomew, *Contours of the Kuyperian Tradition: A Systematic Introduction* (Downers Grove: IVP Academic, 2017); Bob Goudzwaard and Craig G. Bartholomew, *Beyond the Modern Age: An Archaeology of Contemporary Culture* (Downers Grove: IVP Academic, 2017); Bruce Riley Ashford and Craig G. Bartholomew, *The Doctrine of Creation: A Constructive Kuyperian Approach* (Downers Grove: IVP Academic, 2020). In the interest of full disclosure, I acquired all three of these books for InterVarsity Press. Kuyper's theology has played an outsized role in the evangelical adoption of culture language – as seen, for example, in Andy Crouch's *Culture Making*. See Andy Crouch, *Culture Making: Recovering our Creative Calling* (Downers Grove: IVP Books, 2008), 11.

155 Jacob Alan Cook, *Worldview Theory, Whiteness, and the Future of Evangelical Faith* (Lanham: Lexington Books/Fortress Academic, 2021), 177. Cook here draws on the work of Willie James Jennings, *The Christian Imagination: Theology and the Origins of Race* (New Haven: Yale University Press, 2010), 15–64. In his 2017 SBL paper, J. R. Daniel Kirk argued that "TIS is designed to eliminate diversity in favor of a ruled reading" and thereby contributes to the maintenance of white hegemony. See J. R. Daniel Kirk, "Theological Interpretation and White Hegemony in the Biblical Studies Academy" (paper presented at the Society of Biblical Literature, Boston, MA, November 18, 2017). Drawing on the field of whiteness studies, David Horrell argues that the colonizing project of whiteness pervades the field of New Testament studies. See David G. Horrell, *Ethnicity and Inclusion: Religion, Race, and Whiteness in Constructions of Jewish and Christian Identities* (Grand Rapids: Eerdmans, 2020), 310–41.

156 On the protectionism of mainstream New Testament scholarship, see Stephen L. Young, "'Let's Take the Text Seriously': The Protectionist *Doxa* of Mainstream New Testament Studies," *Method and Theory in the Study of Religion* 32 (2020): 328–63.

157 Hays, "Reading the Bible with Eyes of Faith," 12.

158 John L. Thompson, "Scripture, Tradition, and the Formation of Christian Culture: The Theological and Pastoral Function of the History of Interpretation," *Ex Auditu* 19 (2003): 22–41, at 23–24.

159 Stephen E. Fowl, *Theological Interpretation of Scripture* (Eugene: Cascade Books, 2009), 21–22.

160 Hays, "Reading the Bible with Eyes of Faith," 8–9.

161 Hays, "Reading the Bible with Eyes of Faith," 9–10; Robert W. Jenson, "Scripture's Authority in the Church," in *The Art of Reading Scripture*, ed. Ellen F. Davis and Richard B. Hays (Grand Rapids: Eerdmans, 2003), 27–37, at 27.

162 H. Richard Niebuhr, *Christ and Culture*, 50th Anniversary ed. (New York: HarperOne, 2001), 11.

163 Niebuhr, *Christ and Culture*, 12, 14.

164 See Robert W. Jenson, "Christ as Culture 1: Christ as Polity," *International Journal of Systematic Theology* 5, no. 3 (2003): 323–29; Robert W. Jenson, "Christ as Culture 2: Christ as Art," *International Journal of Systematic Theology* 6, no. 1 (2004): 69–76; Robert W. Jenson, "Christ as Culture 3: Christ as Drama," *International Journal of Systematic Theology* 6, no. 2 (2004): 194–200.

165 See Izenberg, *Identity*, 105–86.

Chapter 4

1 Donald J. Trump, "Remarks by President Trump at the National Day of Prayer Service," *Trump White House National Archives*, May 2, 2019, https://trumpwhitehouse.archives .gov/briefings-statements/remarks-president-trump-national-day-prayer-service/.

2 Salvador Rizzo, "President Trump's Shifting Claim that 'We Got Rid' of the Johnson Amendment," *Washington Post*, May 9, 2019; I.R.C. §501(c)(3).

3 Tom Gjelten, "Another Effort To Get Rid Of The 'Johnson Amendment' Fails," *NPR*, March 22, 2018, www.npr.org/2018/03/22/596158332/another-effort-to-get-rid-of-the-johnson-amendment-fails; Erik Eckholm, "Legal Alliance Gains Host of Court Victories for Conservative Christian Movement," *New York Times*, May 12, 2014, A10.

4 Elizabeth Landers, "Trump: I Will 'Destroy' Johnson Amendment," *CNN*, February 2, 2017. On the Fellowship and the National Prayer Breakfast, see Jeff Sharlet, *The Family: The Secret Fundamentalism at the Heart of American Power* (New York: HarperCollins, 2008).

5 Kate Shellnutt, "Johnson Amendment Repeal Removed from Final GOP Tax Bill," *Christianity Today*, December 15, 2017, www.christianitytoday.com/news/2017/decem ber/johnson-amendment-repeal-blocked-final-gop-tax-bill-byrd.html. Evangelicals had been unhappy even with Trump's executive order, since it lacked exemptions for religious groups wanting the freedom to discriminate against LGBTQ persons without legal ramifications. Kate Shellnutt, "Trump's Religious Liberty Order Doesn't Answer Most Evangelicals' Prayers," *Christianity Today*, May 4, 2017, www.christianitytoday.com/ news/2017/november/tax-reform-unborn-529s-adoption-johnson-amendment.html.

6 Jacqueline Thomsen, "House Passes Measure Blocking IRS from Revoking Churches' Tax-Exempt Status over Political Activity," *The Hill*, July 19, 2018, https://thehill.com/ policy/finance/domestic-taxes/397996-house-passes-measure-blocking-irs-from-revok ing-churches-tax; Nanette Byrnes, "As Churches Get Political, IRS Stays Quiet," *Reuters*, June 21, 2012.

7 98 Cong. Rec. H771 (February 4, 1952).

8 98 Cong. Rec. S976–977 (February 14, 1952) (statement of Sen. Robertson).

9 S. Res. 276, 82d Cong., 98 Cong. Rec. 977, 66 Stat. 64.

10 Jared A. Goldstein, *Real Americans: National Identity, Violence, and the Constitution* (Lawrence: University Press of Kansas, 2021), 76. For the full story of how political elites crafted the civil religion underpinning today's Christian nationalism, see Andrew R. Polk, *Faith in Freedom: Propaganda, Presidential Politics, and the Making of an American Religion* (Ithaca: Cornell University Press, 2021).

11 Jonathan P. Herzog, *The Spiritual-Industrial Complex: America's Religious Battle against Communism in the Early Cold War* (New York: Oxford University Press, 2011), 91, 6.

12 Herzog, *The Spiritual-Industrial Complex*, 92, 99.

13 Goldstein, *Real Americans*, 92–93.

14 Will Herberg, *Protestant, Catholic, Jew: An Essay in American Religious Sociology* (Garden City: Doubleday, 1955), 265.

15 Goldstein, *Real Americans*, 3.

16 Goldstein, *Real Americans*, 6.

17 Goldstein, *Real Americans*, 11. Philip S. Gorski and Samuel L. Perry, in their analysis of the specific mythology of "white Christian nationalism," call this account of true Americanism a "deep story," drawing on the work of Arlie Russell Hochschild. See Philip S. Gorski and Samuel L. Perry, *The Flag and the Cross: White Christian Nationalism and the Threat to American Democracy* (New York: Oxford University Press, 2022), 3–6.

18 I use "historical-theological biblicism" as a catch-all for three different approaches to the Bible that mirror the role of originalism with respect to the Constitution – namely, to enforce an orthodox interpretation of the text that bolsters the prescriptive account of communal identity, whether national or ecclesial. The old evangelical approach of inerrantist hermeneutics goes by the name of grammatical-historical exegesis and claims to find the true meaning of the text in the words themselves understood as the supernaturally inspired revelation of God. The newer evangelical approach of redemptive-historical exegesis places more emphasis on historical research and finds the meaning of the text in the canonical narrative of salvation history. The postliberal approach of theological interpretation of scripture eschews historical research and emphasizes the canonical narrative of scripture understood in terms of the rule of faith.

19 See Clyde Wilcox, *God's Warriors: The Christian Right in Twentieth-Century America* (Baltimore: Johns Hopkins University Press, 1992); Daniel K. Williams, *God's Own Party: The Making of the Christian Right* (Oxford: Oxford University Press, 2010); and Darren Dochuk, *From Bible Belt to Sunbelt: Plain-Folk Religion, Grassroots Politics, and the Rise of Evangelical Conservatism* (New York: W. W. Norton, 2011). Chelsea Ebin refers more specifically to the "New Religious Right" or "New Christian Right" to highlight the coalition composed of the Protestant evangelical Religious Right, led by the likes of Pat Robertson and Jerry Falwell, and the New Right movement orchestrated by Paul Weyrich and Richard Viguerie. See Chelsea Ebin, "A New Religious Right: Conservative Catholic and Protestant Coalition Building, 1971–1981" (PhD diss., The New School for Social Research, 2018). For more on the Catholic religious roots of Weyrich's activism,

see Chelsea Ebin, "Paul Weyrich: The Religious Roots of a New Right Radical," *American Catholic Studies* 131, no. 3 (2020): 29–56. Following Mark Massa's work, Ebin points out that, in the 1960s, Roman Catholics had to wrestle – much like the Protestants of an earlier generation – with historical consciousness and the meaning of tradition in the midst of cultural change, thus making it possible to be both "traditionalist" and "radical" at the same time. See Mark S. Massa, *The American Catholic Revolution: How the Sixties Changed the Church Forever* (New York: Oxford University Press, 2010).

20 Ernst Troeltsch, *Protestantism and Progress: The Significance of Protestantism for the Rise of the Modern World* (Philadelphia: Fortress Press, 1986), 21–23 (translation revised).

21 Aristotle, *Politics*, 1.1253a.

22 Winnifred Fallers Sullivan, *The Impossibility of Religious Freedom* (Princeton: Princeton University Press, 2005), 7.

23 The terms "liberal" and "conservative" are notoriously slippery and have widely different meanings in politics, philosophy, and theology. As we have already seen, the so-called liberals who secured a public victory over the fundamentalists in the early twentieth century were sometimes proponents of conservative political positions. A religious conservative should technically refer to someone who maintains the received tradition, but part of the problem I am exploring in this chapter is that the tradition itself became associated with conservative politics. To be sure, there are many theologically conservative Christians who have left-wing politics (particularly in the Catholic and Anglican traditions). While this is a minority population overall, the phenomenon is related to the larger story I am telling regarding the rise of the *regula fidei* as normative for Christian identity, especially since some of those in this category are evangelicals who support racial justice and economic equality but remain opposed to LGBTQ inclusion.

24 William Wilberforce, *A Practical View of the Prevailing Religious System of Professed Christians, in the Higher and Middle Classes in This Country, Contrasted with Real Christianity* (London: T. Cadell and W. Davies, 1797), 398–99.

25 Wilberforce, *A Practical View of the Prevailing Religious System*, 380. We can see why a proponent of the Religious Right like Eric Metaxas would find so much to admire about Wilberforce. While Wilberforce's opposition to slavery is inspiring, he is also a model representative of Christian nationalism. The way to end slavery, in his view, is to fully Christianize society, converting people to "real Christianity" and thereby eliminating the selfishness and greed that supports the slave trade. Wilberforce's binary, moralizing perspective – dividing the world into real and nominal (or fake) Christians, connected to their moral behavior – is easily applied to different social and political situations. See Eric Metaxas, *Amazing Grace: William Wilberforce and the Heroic Campaign to End Slavery* (New York: HarperSanFrancisco, 2007).

26 Wilberforce, *A Practical View of the Prevailing Religious System*, 449–51.

27 On what follows, see the discussion of John Locke, Benjamin Franklin, James Madison, and Thomas Jefferson in John Colman, *Everyone Orthodox to Themselves: John Locke and His American Students on Religion and Liberal Society* (Lawrence: University Press of Kansas, 2023).

28 Thomas Jefferson to Mathew Carey, November 11, 1816, in Thomas Jefferson, *The Papers of Thomas Jefferson: Retirement Series*, ed. J. Jefferson Looney, 16 vols. (Princeton: Princeton University Press, 2004–2020), 10:518–19.

29 John Adams to Thomas Jefferson, January 23, 1825, *Founders Online*, National Archives, https://founders.archives.gov/documents/Adams/99-02-02-7940.

30 John Jay, *The Selected Papers of John Jay*, ed. Elizabeth M. Nuxoll, 6 vols. (Charlottesville: University of Virginia Press, 2010–2020), 1:480.

31 John Jay to John Murray, October 12, 1816, in William Jay, *The Life of John Jay: With Selections from His Correspondence and Miscellaneous Papers*, 2 vols. (New York: J. & J. Harper, 1833), 2:376.

32 John Adams to John Quincy Adams, March 28, 1816, *Founders Online*, National Archives, https://founders.archives.gov/documents/Adams/99-03-02-3016.

33 Adams to Jefferson, January 23, 1825, *Founders Online*, National Archives, https://founders.archives.gov/documents/Adams/99-03-02-3016.

34 Troeltsch, *Protestantism and Progress*, 22 (translation revised).

35 Aaron Hill to Thomas Jefferson, May 24, 1810, in Jefferson, *The Papers of Thomas Jefferson: Retirement Series*, 2:411.

36 George Washington to the Convention of the Universal Church, August 9, 1790, in George Washington, *The Papers of George Washington: Presidential Series*, ed. Dorothy Twohig et al., 21 vols. (Charlottesville: University Press of Virginia, 1987–2020), 6:223–25.

37 Paul Finkelman, *Slavery and the Founders: Race and Liberty in the Age of Jefferson*, 3rd ed. (Armonk: M. E. Sharpe, 2014), x.

38 Mark A. Noll, *The Civil War as a Theological Crisis* (Chapel Hill: University of North Carolina Press, 2006).

39 Katharine Gerbner, *Christian Slavery: Conversion and Race in the Protestant Atlantic World* (Philadelphia: University of Pennsylvania Press, 2018), 2–3. See also Khyati Y. Joshi, *White Christian Privilege: The Illusion of Religious Equality in America* (New York: New York University Press, 2020), 64–82.

40 Gerbner, *Christian Slavery*, 42.

41 Gerbner, *Christian Slavery*, 31. On the way "heathen" has been racialized in Christian history, see Kathryn Gin Lum, *Heathen: Religion and Race in American History* (Cambridge, MA: Harvard University Press, 2022).

42 Gerbner, *Christian Slavery*, 83–86.

43 Gerbner, *Christian Slavery*, 3.

44 George B. Cheever, *God against Slavery: And the Freedom and Duty of the Pulpit to Rebuke It, as a Sin against God* (New York: Joseph H. Ladd, 1857), iv.

45 Cheever, *God against Slavery*, 51.

46 It is worth noting, by way of anticipation, that the opposite is the case with a situation like abortion today, where enshrining it as legal and national hardly gave it a tabernacle of protection, much less that sermons supporting abortion were treated as gospel conservatism or that speech against it was branded as political preaching.

47 James Henley Thornwell, *The Collected Writings of James Henley Thornwell*, ed. John B. Adger, 4 vols. (Richmond: Presbyterian Committee of Publication, 1871–1873), 4:473, 405.

48 Marcus J. McArthur, "Treason in the Pulpit: Disloyal Clergy in Civil War Missouri" (PhD diss., Saint Louis University, 2012), 1n1. McArthur builds on the prior work of Preston Graham. See Preston D. Graham, *A Kingdom Not of This World: Stuart Robinson's Struggle to Distinguish the Sacred from the Secular during the Civil War* (Macon: Mercer University Press, 2002).

49 Luke E. Harlow, *Religion, Race, and the Making of Confederate Kentucky, 1830–1880* (New York: Cambridge University Press, 2014), 138.

50 McArthur, "Treason in the Pulpit," 4.

51 McArthur, "Treason in the Pulpit," 58.

52 Jack P. Maddex, "From Theocracy to Spirituality: The Southern Presbyterian Reversal on Church and State," *Journal of Presbyterian History* 54, no. 4 (1976): 438–57, at 438.

53 William R. Black, in his study of the Cumberland Presbyterians, argues that the Cumberland church was able to avoid taking a side on slavery only because they already had a "shared commitment to the project of the Christian nation, in which white people were to be the primary actors." In other words, they could hold to a supposedly "neutral" stand on slavery because they were committed to Christian nationalism, hardly a neutral or apolitical position. See William Robert Black, "No Northern or Southern Religion: Cumberland Presbyterians and the Christian Nation, 1800–1877" (PhD diss., Rice University, 2018), 90.

54 Maddex, "From Theocracy to Spirituality," 446–47; Aaron Astor, *Rebels on the Border: Civil War, Emancipation, and the Reconstruction of Kentucky and Missouri* (Baton Rouge: Louisiana State University Press, 2012), 34.

55 Maddex, "From Theocracy to Spirituality," 448.

56 See "The Spirituality of the Church: The Doctrine of the Presbyterian Church, North. Declaration of Principles," *Christian Observer*, March 21, 1906, 2.

57 Some Northerners, like the Black minister Francis James Grimké (1850–1937), who graduated from Princeton Seminary in 1878, sought to combine the spirituality of the church with a concern for racial justice, seen for example in his opposition to reunion with Cumberland. He was able to combine these views by promoting the moralistic and classist racial uplift ideology, which placed responsibility on individuals, especially Black elites (e.g., W. E. B. Du Bois's "talented tenth"), to improve conditions for Black Americans, rather than on systemic, political changes. See Mark A. Noll, "Theology, Presbyterian History, and the Civil War," *Journal of Presbyterian History* 89, no. 1 (2011): 4–15.

58 Joe L. Coker, "The Sinnott Case of 1910: The Changing Views of Southern Presbyterians on Temperance, Prohibition, and the Spirituality of the Church," *Journal of Presbyterian History* 77, no. 4 (1999): 247–62, at 251.

59 Mark Lawrence Schrad, *Smashing the Liquor Machine: A Global History of Prohibition* (New York: Oxford University Press, 2021), xiii.

60 Coker, "The Sinnott Case of 1910," 254–56.

61 As Marthame E. Sanders notes, one observer pointed out that it was "the only national body other than the American Nazi Party to do so." See Marthame E. Sanders, "'A Fellowship of Concern' and the Declining Doctrine of the Spirituality of the

Church in the Presbyterian Church in the United States," *Journal of Presbyterian History* 75, no. 3 (1997): 179–95, at 181.

62 "A Fellowship of Concern," *Presbyterian Outlook*, January 6, 1964, 1; Sanders, "A Fellowship of Concern," 182.

63 Sanders, "A Fellowship of Concern," 192.

64 David VanDrunen, *Living in God's Two Kingdoms: A Biblical Vision for Christianity and Culture* (Wheaton: Crossway, 2010), 15. See also David VanDrunen, *Natural Law and the Two Kingdoms: A Study in the Development of Reformed Social Thought* (Grand Rapids: Eerdmans, 2010).

65 Marcus J. McArthur, "5 Civil War Lessons for the Church," September 7, 2015, www .thegospelcoalition.org/article/5-civil-war-lessons-for-the-church/. McArthur's dissertation can be read as an effort to defend the "apolitical theology" of border state conservatives. He stresses that apolitical theology "well predated the nineteenth century" and that its increased use in the border states and the South was a response to "the rising tide of abolitionist attacks" on slavery and "the widespread practice of political preaching" by those in the North. Much of his study looks at the loyalty oaths that were imposed upon border-state ministers (ruled unconstitutional in the 1867 Supreme Court decision of *Cummings v. Missouri*), which suggests that they were a marginalized group denied their religious freedom. See McArthur, "Treason in the Pulpit," 68–69.

66 Abraham Kuyper's famous line at the opening of the Free University in 1880 – "There's not a square inch in the whole domain of our human existence over which Christ, who is Sovereign over *all*, does not cry, 'Mine!'" – has become "something of a mantra among culturally engaged evangelicals." James Bratt, "Why I'm Sick of 'Every Square Inch,'" October 12, 2013, https://blog.reformedjournal.com/2013/10/12/why-im-sick-of-every-square-inch/. In his Stone Lectures, Kuyper says similarly: "If everything that is, exists for the sake of God, then it follows that the whole creation must give glory to God." Abraham Kuyper, *Calvinism: Six Stone-Lectures* (Amsterdam-Pretoria: Höveker & Wormser, 1899), 61. Andy Crouch and Makoto Fujimura, among many others, represent this position in evangelicalism today. See Andy Crouch, *Culture Making: Recovering our Creative Calling* (Downers Grove: IVP Books, 2008); Makoto Fujimura, *Culture Care: Reconnecting with Beauty for Our Common Life* (Downers Grove: IVP Books, 2017). On the importance of Schaeffer, see Barry Hankins, *Francis Schaeffer and the Shaping of Evangelical America* (Grand Rapids: Eerdmans, 2008).

67 Michael McVicar documents not only the influence of Kuyper on Cornelius Van Til, the longtime professor of apologetics at Westminster Seminary in Philadelphia, but also the significant impact of Van Til's work on Rushdoony. See Michael J. McVicar, *Christian Reconstruction: R. J. Rushdoony and American Religious Conservatism* (Chapel Hill: The University of North Carolina Press, 2015), 18–45.

68 See Lilliana Mason, *Uncivil Agreement: How Politics Became Our Identity* (Chicago: University of Chicago Press, 2018).

69 As an example, WSC professor Michael Horton has written about the similarity between Radical Orthodoxy and Kuyperian neo-Calvinism: "Radical Orthodoxy and neo-Kuyperianism offer remarkably similar critiques of secular culture and thought, namely,

autonomous philosophy as atheistic and therefore nihilistic; the criticism of all forms of dualism (although Kuyperians typically target rather than celebrate Plato in this regard); and insistence upon seeing all human thinking and action in relation to God. Both display a determination to 'take every thought captive to obey Christ.'" Michael S. Horton, "Participation and Covenant," in *Radical Orthodoxy and the Reformed Tradition: Creation, Covenant, and Participation*, ed. James K. A. Smith and James H. Olthuis (Grand Rapids: Baker Academic, 2005), 107–32, at 107.

70 Kathleen M. Sands, *America's Religious Wars: The Embattled Heart of Our Public Life* (New Haven: Yale University Press, 2019), 9.

71 William M. Leftwich, *Martyrdom in Missouri: A History of Religious Proscription, the Seizure of Churches, and the Persecution of Ministers of the Gospel, in the State of Missouri during the Late Civil War, and Under the "Test Oath" of the New Constitution*, 2 vols. (Saint Louis: S. W. Book & Publishing Co., 1870), 1:3–4.

72 Mary Anna Randolph Custis Lee to Letitia McCreery Burwell, November 15, 1870, in Lee Family Digital Archive, https://leefamilyarchive.org/9-family-papers/110-mary-anna-randolph-custis-lee-to-letitia-mccreery-burwell-1870-november-15. Tertullian's actual statement is *semen est sanguis Christianorum*, "the blood of the Christians is seed." Bryan M. Litfin, *Early Christian Martyr Stories: An Evangelical Introduction with New Translations* (Grand Rapids: Baker Academic, 2014), 121. Without questioning the value of Litfin's work, it is worth pondering why there is an audience for a specifically "evangelical introduction" to early Christian martyr narratives. The editor, Bryan Litfin, is also the son of A. Duane Litfin, former president of Wheaton College, the flagship school of American evangelicalism. I discuss the elder Litfin in more detail in Chapter 5.

73 Quoted in W. Stuart Towns, *Enduring Legacy: Rhetoric and Ritual of the Lost Cause* (Tuscaloosa: University of Alabama Press, 2012), 84.

74 Daniel W. Stowell, *Rebuilding Zion: The Religious Reconstruction of the South, 1863–1877* (New York: Oxford University Press, 1998), 42; Charles Reagan Wilson, *Baptized in Blood: The Religion of the Lost Cause, 1865–1920*, new ed. (Athens: University of Georgia Press, 2009), 51; Towns, *Enduring Legacy*, 32.

75 Jason Bruner and Ryan Linde, "Eusebius and the Global War on Christians," *Sacred Matters*, June 2, 2014, https://sacredmattersmagazine.com/eusebius-and-the-global-war-on-christians/. See Candida R. Moss, *The Myth of Persecution: How Early Christians Invented a Story of Martyrdom* (New York: HarperOne, 2013).

76 Jason Bruner, *Imagining Persecution: Why American Christians Believe There Is a Global War against Their Faith* (New Brunswick: Rutgers University Press, 2021), 40–41.

77 Christopher Clark and Michael Ledger-Lomas, "The Protestant International," in *Religious Internationals in the Modern World: Globalization and Faith Communities since 1750*, ed. Abigail Green and Vincent Viaene (Basingstoke: Palgrave Macmillan, 2012), 23–52, at 23.

78 Ian R. Tyrrell, *Reforming the World: The Creation of America's Moral Empire* (Princeton: Princeton University Press, 2010), 3.

79 Tyrrell, *Reforming the World*, 4.

80 Bruner, *Imagining Persecution*, 73.

81 Bruner, *Imagining Persecution*, 74.

82 Bruner, *Imagining Persecution*, 75.

83 This is primarily the postwar period that Larry Ceplair calls "institutional anticommunism." See Larry Ceplair, *Anti-Communism in Twentieth-Century America: A Critical History* (Santa Barbara: Praeger, 2011), 113–30.

84 David A. Hollinger, *Protestants Abroad: How Missionaries Tried to Change the World but Changed America* (Princeton: Princeton University Press, 2017), 94.

85 Hollinger, *Protestants Abroad*, 105.

86 Matthew Bowman, *Christian: The Politics of a Word in America* (Cambridge, MA: Harvard University Press, 2018), 111; David Stoll, *Is Latin America Turning Protestant? The Politics of Evangelical Growth* (Berkeley: University of California Press, 1990), 71; Andrew Preston, "Evangelical Internationalism: A Conservative Worldview for the Age of Globalization," in *The Right Side of the Sixties: Reexamining Conservatism's Decade of Transformation*, ed. Laura Jane Gifford and Daniel K. Williams (New York: Palgrave Macmillan, 2012), 221–41.

87 Lauren Frances Turek, *To Bring the Good News to All Nations: Evangelical Influence on Human Rights and U.S. Foreign Relations* (Ithaca: Cornell University Press, 2020), 72.

88 See Hubert Villeneuve, *Teaching Anticommunism: Fred Schwarz and American Postwar Conservatism* (Montreal: McGill-Queen's University Press, 2020).

89 Turek, *To Bring the Good News to All Nations*, 10.

90 While the Cold War–era language of "underground church" is most associated with the Chinese Catholic churches who were cut off from the Vatican in the People's Republic of China, the terminology is often used for any Christian community that existed under a regime of state atheism. See, for instance, Tomáš Halík, *From the Underground Church to Freedom*, trans. Gerald Turner (Notre Dame: University of Notre Dame Press, 2019).

91 Communist Exploitation of Religion: Hearing before the Subcommittee to Investigate the Administration of the Internal Security Act and Other Internal Security Laws of the Committee on the Judiciary, United States Senate, 89 Cong. 9 (1966) (Statement by Richard Wurmbrand).

92 Bruner, *Imagining Persecution*, 87.

93 Bruner, *Imagining Persecution*, 88.

94 The university started admitting Black students in 1971, but only if they were married. That changed in 1975, but the prohibition of interracial dating or marriage remained in force.

95 See Randall Balmer, *Bad Faith: Race and the Rise of the Religious Right* (Grand Rapids: Eerdmans, 2021). This book is an expansion of his earlier article: Randall Balmer, "The Real Origins of the Religious Right," *Politico*, May 27, 2014, www.politico.com/magazine/story/2014/05/religious-right-real-origins-107133/. For an alternative take on this history, however, see Gillian Frank and Neil J. Young, "What Everyone Gets Wrong about Evangelicals and Abortion," *Washington Post*, May 16, 2022. Frank and Young rightly point out that there were much earlier grassroots campaigns against abortion among Protestant evangelicals, in addition to long-standing Catholic antiabortion

efforts. Balmer's narrative is primarily helpful in pushing back against present-day claims that evangelicals were always and unanimously opposed to abortion.

96 Too many criticisms of Christian nationalism attempt to critique the idea of Christian America by comparing it to the supposedly "biblical" idea of the kingdom of God, seeing the former as violent and imperialistic (which it often is) and the latter as a realm of peace and justice. For an example, see Richard T. Hughes, *Christian America and the Kingdom of God* (Urbana: University of Illinois Press, 2009). While it is highly questionable, given the violent eschatological vision in John's Apocalypse, to paint the kingdom of God as a peaceful concept on strictly scriptural grounds, the problem with this argument lies rather in the attempt to use the Bible to discern the single, normative vision of Christianity. Part of what I am suggesting in this book, which subsequent chapters will unfold in more detail, is that the quest for a pure essence of Christianity that is both immune to critique and set over against alternative accounts, which are viewed as heretical, is constitutive of the violent imperialism that Hughes and others are nobly trying to reject.

97 Little wonder then that originalists have been the greatest allies of the Religious Right on the bench of the Supreme Court.

98 Patrick J. St G. Johnstone, *Operation World: A Brief Survey of Some of the Prayer Needs of Each Country of the World* (Pretoria, South Africa: Dorothea Mission, 1974).

99 Patrick Johnstone, "*Operation World* – A Tool for Missions," *Missiology* 27, no. 1 (1999): 21–26, at 22.

100 Editors, "The Top 50 Books That Have Shaped Evangelicals," *Christianity Today*, October 6, 2006, 51–55.

101 Gina A. Zurlo, "'A Miracle from Nairobi': David B. Barrett and the Quantification of World Christianity, 1957–1982" (PhD diss., Boston University, 2017), 215–16.

102 See Jan Jongeneel, "David Barrett's World Christian Encyclopedia," *Exchange* 30, no. 4 (2001): 372–76; Mark A. Noll, "Review of *World Christian Encyclopedia: A Comparative Survey of Churches and Religions in the Modern World*," *Church History* 71, no. 2 (2002): 448–54.

103 Gina A. Zurlo, "More than Numbers: David B. Barrett and the Twentieth-Century Historiography of World Christianity," *Journal of World Christianity* 8, no. 2 (2018): 89–108, at 100.

104 As Noll points out in his review, the 2001 *WCE* lists the number of Great Commission Christians in the United States as 98.7 million. According to the 2001 American Religious Identification Survey, there were 159 million Christians in the United States at that time. Noll, following Gallup and other pollsters, places the number of regular churchgoers at 110–120 million. See Barry A. Kosmin, Egon Mayer, and Ariela Keysar, "American Religious Identification Survey, 2001" (New York: The Graduate Center of the City University of New York, 2001), www.gc.cuny.edu/cuny_gc/media/cuny-graduate-center/pdf/aris/aris-pdf-version.pdf; Noll, "Review of *World Christian Encyclopedia*," 451.

105 Bruner, *Imagining Persecution*, 116.

106 Todd M. Johnson and Gina A. Zurlo, "Christian Martyrdom as a Pervasive Phenomenon," *Society* 51, no. 6 (2014): 679–85, at 679–80; Bruner, *Imagining Persecution*, 116–17.

107 Johnson and Zurlo, "Christian Martyrdom as a Pervasive Phenomenon," 681. There is a great need for more scholarly scrutiny of the work associated with Barrett and the CSGC. Zurlo's 2017 dissertation on Barrett is full of helpful information, but Johnson was a second reader on her thesis. Zurlo has since become the codirector of the CSGC and coauthor of the *WCE*. As good as her work may be, she is hardly a neutral voice and disinclined to scrutinize the methods or conclusions of the institute where she now works.

108 Bruner, *Imagining Persecution*, 117–18.

109 Bruner, *Imagining Persecution*, 132.

110 Paul A. Marshall, *Their Blood Cries Out: The Untold Story of Persecution against Christians in the Modern World* (Dallas: Word, 1997), 248, 246.

111 Marshall, *Their Blood Cries Out*, 258. Whereas *Their Blood Cries Out* criticizes American Christians for their lack of action, Marshall's 2013 book, *Persecuted*, speaks to an audience that he knows is mobilized for action. After relating a story about a Ugandan man who was persecuted for converting from Islam to Christianity, Marshall and his coauthors make a direct appeal to the reader: "We, as citizens living in freedom, are not powerless. Sometimes within our given circumstances we are able to take steps on our own to help. ... One of the most effective means is to use our rights as citizens to influence the foreign policy of our own government." Paul A. Marshall, Lela Gilbert, and Nina Shea, *Persecuted: The Global Assault on Christians* (Nashville: Thomas Nelson, 2013), 301.

112 Turek, *To Bring the Good News to All Nations*, 27.

113 Stella Nyanzi, "Dismantling Reified African Culture through Localised Homosexualities in Uganda," *Culture, Health & Sexuality* 15, no. 8 (2013): 952–67, at 953.

114 "President Assents to Anti-Homosexuality Act," Parliament of the Republic of Uganda, May 30, 2023, www.parliament.go.ug/news/6737/president-assents-anti-homosexuality-act.

115 Kapya Kaoma, *Globalizing the Culture Wars: U.S. Conservatives, African Churches, and Homophobia* (Somerville: Political Research Associates, 2009), 3; Steven M. Tipton, *Public Pulpits: Methodists and Mainline Churches in the Moral Argument of Public Life* (Chicago: University of Chicago Press, 2007), 146–85. See also Kapya Kaoma, "Exporting the Anti-Gay Movement," *American Prospect*, April 24, 2012, 44–49; Kapya Kaoma, "How US Clergy Brought Hate to Uganda," *The Gay & Lesbian Review* 17, no. 3 (2010): 20–23.

116 Nyanzi, "Dismantling Reified African Culture," 956–62; Kaoma, *Globalizing the Culture Wars*, 13. On the question of whether homosexuality is "foreign to Africa," see also Kapya Kaoma, "The Paradox and Tension of Moral Claims: Evangelical Christianity, the Politicization and Globalization of Sexual Politics in Sub-Saharan Africa," *Critical Research on Religion* 2, no. 3 (2014): 227–45, at 230–32; Kapya Kaoma, "An African or Un-African Sexual Identity? Religion, Globalisation and Sexual Politics in Sub-Saharan Africa," in *Public Religion and the Politics of Homosexuality in Africa*, ed. Klinken Adriaan van and Chitando Ezra (London: Routledge, 2016), 113–29.

117 Marshall, Gilbert, and Shea, *Persecuted*, viii.

118 Former members of IRD's Board of Directors include Carl F. H. Henry and Thomas Oden.

119 Ted Reinert, "'To Destroy the Liberal World Order': Trump, Putin, and the Imperiled Trans-Atlantic Alliance," *Order from Chaos: Foreign Policy in a Troubled World*, July 20, 2018, www.brookings.edu/blog/order-from-chaos/2018/07/20/to-destroy-the-liberal-world-order-trump-putin-and-the-imperiled-trans-atlantic-alliance/; Steve Benen, "'We're All Victims': Trump Pushes Persecution Complex to Supporters," *MSNBC: Maddowblog*, December 7, 2020, www.msnbc.com/rachel-maddow-show/we-re-all-victims-trump-pushes-persecution-complex-supporters-n1250206.

120 On Russia's conservative turn, see Chrissy Stroop, "Bad Ecumenism: The American Culture Wars and Russia's Hard Right Turn," *The Wheel* 6 (2016): 20–24; Kristina Stoeckl, "The Russian Orthodox Church's Conservative Crusade," *Current History* 116, no. 792 (2017): 271–76. On the change of location, see Billy Hallowell, "World Summit to Defend Persecuted Christians Pulls Out of Russia Following New Religion Law," *Deseret News*, August 6, 2016, www.deseret.com/2016/8/7/20593400/world-summit-to-defend-persecuted-christians-pulls-out-of-russia-following-new-religion-law.

121 Mike Pence, "Speech at the World Summit in Defense of Persecuted Christians," *American Rhetoric*, May 11, 2017, www.americanrhetoric.com/speeches/mikepence persecutedchristianssummit.htm.

122 Kate Shellnutt, "Sam Brownback Finally Confirmed as America's Religious Freedom Ambassador," *Christianity Today*, January 24, 2018, www.christianitytoday.com/news/2018/january/sam-brownback-is-ambassador-international-religious-freedom.html; Chelsen Vicari, "Global Christian Persecution Summit: Why Don't Christians Care about Christians?," *Juicy Ecumenism: The Institute on Religion & Democracy's Blog*, April 17, 2018, https://juicyecumenism.com/2018/04/17/global-christian-persecution-summit-dont-christians-care-christians/.

123 Bruner, *Imagining Persecution*, 145.

124 Sam Brownback, "Ambassador Sam Brownback Delivers Opening Remarks at IRD's Global Religious Freedom Summit," May 18, 2018, *YouTube*, produced by the IRD, www.youtube.com/watch?v=zwGRBphUg1c.

125 Clifford Bob, *The Global Right Wing and the Clash of World Politics* (New York: Cambridge University Press, 2012).

126 Andrey Shishkov, "Two Ecumenisms: Conservative Christian Alliances as a New Form of Ecumenical Cooperation," *State, Religion and Church* 4, no. 2 (2017): 58–87, at 72–73; Stroop, "Bad Ecumenism," 20–24.

127 Kristina Stoeckl, "The Rise of the Russian Christian Right: The Case of the World Congress of Families," *Religion, State & Society* 48, no. 4 (2020): 223–38, at 223–25.

128 See Human Rights Campaign, "The World Congress of Families: An American Organization Exporting Hate (June 2015 Update)" (Washington, 2015), 18.

129 Stroop, "Bad Ecumenism," 24.

130 Hélène Barthélemy, "How the World Congress of Families Serves Russian Orthodox Political Interests," *Southern Poverty Law Center Hatewatch*, May 16, 2018, www.splcenter

.org/hatewatch/2018/05/16/how-world-congress-families-serves-russian-orthodox-pol
itical-interests; Bethany Moreton, "The U.S. Christians Who Pray for Putin," *Boston
Review*, March 11, 2022, https://bostonreview.net/articles/the-u-s-christians-who-pray-
for-putin/.

131 Daniel Bennett, *Defending Faith: The Politics of the Christian Conservative Legal Movement*
(Lawrence: University Press of Kansas, 2017), 129.

132 Kaleigh Rogers, "Jan. 6 Has Given the Right Hundreds of New Martyrs," September 22,
2021, https://fivethirtyeight.com/features/jan-6-has-given-the-right-hundreds-of-new-
martyrs/.

133 See the database at www.canceledpeople.com/cancelations.

134 Brooke Gladstone, "Reputation," December 31, 2021, *On the Media*, produced by Katya
Rogers, www.wnycstudios.org/podcasts/otm/episodes/on-the-media-reputation.

135 David Remnick, "Is Alexandria Ocasio-Cortez an Insider Now?," *New Yorker*, February
14, 2022, www.newyorker.com/culture/the-new-yorker-interview/is-alexandria-ocasio-
cortez-an-insider-now.

136 See Robert Webber and Phil Kenyon, "A Call to an Ancient Evangelical
Future," https://iws.edu/wp-content/uploads/2012/07/Call-to-An-Ancient-Evangelical-
Future.pdf.

137 In addition to Webber, the committee consisted of: Richard Holt, Donald G. Bloesch, Jan
P. Dennis, Lane T. Dennis, Gerald D. Erickson, Peter E. Gillquist, Thomas Howard and
Victor Oliver. The group met nine times in December 1976 and January 1977. See Records
of the Chicago Call, Billy Graham Center (BGC) Archives, CN 033, Wheaton College.

138 Packet of Materials Given to Each Participant, Records of the Chicago Call, BGC
Archives, CN 033, Box 1, Folder 6. Elesha Coffman says that she "couldn't find …
any textual evidence that the Chicago Call conference actively referred to Hartford,"
but the Chicago Call papers at Wheaton College provide that evidence. Elesha
J. Coffman, "The Chicago Call and Responses," in *Evangelicals and the Early Church:
Recovery, Reform, Renewal*, ed. George Kalantzis and Andrew Tooley (Eugene: Cascade
Books, 2012), 108–24, at 116.

139 David R. Swartz, *Moral Minority: The Evangelical Left in an Age of Conservatism*
(Philadelphia: University of Pennsylvania Press, 2012), 178–83. Signers included
Donald Dayton, Samuel Escobar, Carl F. H. Henry, Carl T. McIntire (son of the famous
fundamentalist), John Perkins, Bernard Ramm, Jim Wallis, and Robert Webber.

140 Shishkov, "Two Ecumenisms," 70.

141 Mouw and Smedes also signed the Chicago Declaration.

142 Signers of the Appeal, "An Appeal for Theological Affirmation: The Hartford
Statement," *Worldview* 18, no. 4 (1975): 39–41.

143 Harvey Cox et al., "The Hartford Appeal: A Symposium," *Worldview* 18, no. 5 (1975):
22–27, at 22–23.

144 Cox et al., "The Hartford Appeal," 26–27.

145 Boston Industrial Mission Task Force, "The Boston Affirmations," *Worldview* 19, no. 3
(1976): 45–47. See Kenneth A. Briggs, "Theologians Plead for Social Activism," *New
York Times*, January 6, 1976, A1, 21.

146 Robert Webber, "Behind the Scenes: A Personal Account," in *The Orthodox Evangelicals: Who They Are and What They Are Saying*, ed. Robert E. Webber and Donald G. Bloesch (Nashville: Thomas Nelson, 1978), 19–39, at 25; Donald G. Bloesch, "A Call to Spirituality," in *The Orthodox Evangelicals: Who They Are and What They Are Saying*, ed. Robert E. Webber and Donald G. Bloesch (Nashville: Thomas Nelson, 1978), 146–65, at 162.

147 Elesha Coffman organizes the sociopolitical contexts of the Chicago Call in three categories: cultural, ecumenical, and evangelical. The cultural context includes reference to civil rights, postcolonialism, and the environmental movement, along with vague references to religious and political scandals in leadership (e.g., Richard Nixon). The ecumenical context refers to Vatican II and the Hartford Appeal, as Protestants and Catholics began working together to address social and ecclesial concerns. And the evangelical context refers to the rapidly growing evangelical movement that had become socially prominent thanks to the election of Jimmy Carter and *Newsweek*'s designation of 1976 as the "Year of the Evangelical." See Coffman, "The Chicago Call and Responses," 113–18.

148 Webber, "Behind the Scenes," 36–37.

149 "A Call to Servanthood and Stewardship," Records of the Chicago Call, BGC Archives, CN 033, Box 1, Folder 6.

150 "Prologue," Records of the Chicago Call, BGC Archives, CN 033, Box 1, Folder 6.

151 "The Chicago Call: An Appeal to Evangelicals," in *The Orthodox Evangelicals: Who They Are and What They Are Saying*, ed. Robert E. Webber and Donald G. Bloesch (Nashville: Thomas Nelson, 1978), 11–18, at 13.

152 Morris Inch, "A Call to Creedal Identity," in *The Orthodox Evangelicals: Who They Are and What They Are Saying*, ed. Robert E. Webber and Donald G. Bloesch (Nashville: Thomas Nelson, 1978), 77–93, at 84–87.

153 Inch, "A Call to Creedal Identity," 81.

154 Timothy E. W. Gloege, *Guaranteed Pure: The Moody Bible Institute, Business, and the Making of Modern Evangelicalism* (Chapel Hill: University of North Carolina Press, 2015), 10.

155 Peter L. Berger, "The Desecularization of the World: A Global Overview," in *The Desecularization of the World: Resurgent Religion and World Politics*, ed. Peter L. Berger (Grand Rapids: Eerdmans, 1999), 1–18, at 2. See also Peter L. Berger, "Secularization Falsified," *First Things*, February 2008, 23–27.

156 Webber and Kenyon, "A Call to an Ancient Evangelical Future."

157 The increasing use of "gnosticism" as a descriptor of contemporary ideologies has coincided with the scholarly consensus that "gnosticism" as a unitary religious system in the ancient world simply did not exist. Perhaps this is not an accident. The more the term is decoupled from any historical referent, the more easily it is applied to any person or group one wishes to tarnish with the brush of heresy. For the definitive scholarly criticism of the modern category of gnosticism, see Michael A. Williams, *Rethinking "Gnosticism": An Argument for Dismantling a Dubious Category* (Princeton: Princeton University Press, 1996). For the best historical accounts of how and why this category was formed, see Karen L. King, *What Is Gnosticism?* (Cambridge, MA: Belknap

Press of Harvard University Press, 2003); David G. Robertson, *Gnosticism and the History of Religions* (New York: Bloomsbury Academic, 2021).

158 Edmund Fawcett, *Conservatism: The Fight for a Tradition* (Princeton: Princeton University Press, 2020), 306.

159 Eric Voegelin, *The New Science of Politics: An Introduction* (Chicago: University of Chicago Press, 1952), 126.

160 Voegelin, *The New Science of Politics*, 132. Voegelin differentiates the varieties of gnosticism "according to the faculty which predominates in the operation of getting this grip on God" (the secure grip on God being the definition of gnostic experience): an intellectual gnosticism would involve the "speculative penetration of the mystery of creation"; emotional gnosticism would lead to sectarian leaders; volitional gnosticism would involve the "activist redemption" of society (124).

161 Fawcett, *Conservatism*, 311.

162 J. I. Packer, "Review of Rudolf Bultmann, *History and Eschatology*," *The Evangelical Quarterly* 31, no. 4 (1959): 225–27, at 225.

163 N. T. Wright, *Paul and the Faithfulness of God* (Minneapolis: Fortress, 2013), 458.

164 Philip J. Lee, *Against the Protestant Gnostics* (New York: Oxford University Press, 1987), xii.

165 Lee, *Against the Protestant Gnostics*, 189.

166 Lee, *Against the Protestant Gnostics*, 81.

167 Lee, *Against the Protestant Gnostics*, 129–39.

168 Oliver O'Donovan, "Transsexualism and Christian Marriage," *The Journal of Religious Ethics* 11, no. 1 (1983): 135–62, at 155–56. The 1983 article is an expanded version of the 1982 pamphlet published by Grove Books.

169 O'Donovan, "Transsexualism and Christian Marriage," 147. O'Donovan at least acknowledges that "transsexuals do not retreat from their bodies into a Gnostic spirituality; if anything, they are preoccupied with them" (147). This leads him to support reassignment surgery and the social acceptance of transgender persons according to the gender with which they identify. But according to O'Donovan, such surgery, while helpful to the individual, cannot achieve the change in sexual identity and thus they must be excluded from "Christian marriage."

170 A Working Party of the House of Bishops, *Some Issues in Human Sexuality: A Guide to the Debate* (London: Church House, 2003), 230 (7.3.10); Fraser Watts, "Transsexualism and the Church," *Theology & Sexuality* 9, no. 1 (2002): 63–85, at 73.

171 Robert Song, *Human Genetics: Fabricating the Future* (Cleveland: Pilgrim Press, 2002), 68.

172 Christina Beardsley, "Taking Issue: The Transsexual Hiatus in *Some Issues in Human Sexuality*," *Theology* 108, no. 845 (2005): 338–46, at 342–43. Beardsley also points out that the bishops and O'Donovan are simply wrong since transgender persons are not "trapped in the wrong body" but "trapped in the wrong gender." They are not rejecting the body but seeking "a fuller embodiment of the person" (343).

173 Kevin J. Vanhoozer, "A Drama-of-Redemption Model," in *Four Views on Moving beyond the Bible to Theology*, ed. Gary T. Meadors, Counterpoints (Grand Rapids: Zondervan, 2009), 151–99, at 195.

174 N. T. Wright, "Gender-Fluid World; Letters to the Editor," *The Times of London*, August 3, 2017.

175 Peter J. Leithart, "Invasive Gnosticism," *Leithart*, February 26, 2016, www.patheos.com/ blogs/leithart/2016/02/invasive-gnosticism/.

176 Robert Barron, "Bruce Jenner, the 'Shadow Council,' and St. Irenaeus," *Word on Fire*, June 9, 2015, www.wordonfire.org/articles/barron/bruce-jenner-the-shadow-council-and-st-irenaeus/; Anna Magdalena Patti, "Are Transgender People Gnostic? An Answer to Robert Barron," *CatholicTrans*, February 12, 2016, https://catholictrans .wordpress.com/2016/02/12/are-transgender-people-gnostic/.

177 Robert P. George, "Gnostic Liberalism," *First Things*, December 2016, 33–38.

178 R. R. Reno, "Gnostic Politics," *First Things*, April 2021, 59–68.

179 Helen Pluckrose and James A. Lindsay, *Cynical Theories: How Activist Scholarship Made Everything about Race, Gender, and Identity – and Why This Harms Everybody* (Durham: Pitchstone, 2020), 17. On the grievance studies hoax, see Zack Beauchamp, "The Controversy around Hoax Studies in Critical Theory, Explained," *Vox*, October 15, 2018, www.vox.com/2018/10/15/17951492/grievance-studies-sokal-squared-hoax.

180 Bob Smietana, "Why Grievance Studies Hoaxer and Atheist James Lindsay Wants to Save Southern Baptists," *Religion News Service*, May 18, 2021, https://religionnews.com/ 2021/05/18/james-lindsay-southern-baptists-crt-al-mohler-hoax-new-discourses-beth-moorerace-ofallon/.

181 Pluckrose and Lindsay, *Cynical Theories*, 209, 32–35, 16–17.

182 James Lindsay (@ConceptualJames), "Blatantly Queer Marxism. Blatantly Queer Gnosticism," Twitter, June 17, 2022, 9:04 p.m., https://twitter.com/ ConceptualJames/status/1537979450054148096.

183 James Lindsay (@ConceptualJames), "Drag queens in the presence of children is an initiation rite into the cult of Queer Gnosticism," Twitter, December 29, 2022, 10:55 a. m., https://twitter.com/ConceptualJames/status/1608507091869896704; James Lindsay (@ConceptualJames), "Also, that's not 'secular liberal.' That's Queer Gnosticism," Twitter, January 2, 2023, 4:14 p.m., https://twitter.com/ConceptualJames/status/ 1610036952916434945.

184 Brian S. Barnett, Ariana E. Nesbit, and Renée M. Sorrentino, "The Transgender Bathroom Debate at the Intersection of Politics, Law, Ethics, and Science," *Journal of the American Academy of Psychiatry and Law* 46, no. 2 (2018): 232–41, at 232.

185 Nico Lang, "2022 Was the Worst Year Ever for Anti-Trans Bills. How Did We Get Here?," *Them*, December 29, 2022, www.them.us/story/2022-anti-trans-bills-history-explained.

186 Chris Geidner, "The Anti-Trans Legislative Wave Isn't Stopping," *Law Dork*, March 17, 2023, www.lawdork.com/p/anti-trans-bills-arkansas-laws-and-more.

187 Act of March 8, 2023, No. 237, sec. 16 (codified at Ark. Code Ann. § 6-16-156); Protecting Minors from Medical Malpractice Act of 2023, No. 274, sec. 1 (codifed at Ark. Code Ann. § 16-114-402).

188 Phillip M. Bailey, "2022 Could Be Most Anti-Trans Legislative Years in History, Report Says," *USA Today*, January 20, 2022; Anne Branigin, "An Idaho Bill Would Criminalize

Medical Treatments for Trans Youths. It Echoes Abortion Bans," *Washington Post*, March 11, 2022.

189 Genital Mutilation of a Child, H.B. 675, 66th Leg., Reg. Sess. (Ida. 2022); Child Protection Act, H.B. 71, 67th Leg., Reg. Sess. (Ida. 2023).

190 Education, S.B. 1071, 67th Leg., Reg. Sess. (Ida. 2023).

191 Betsy Russell, "Governor Signs Both HB 500 and HB 509, the Anti-Transgender Bills," *Idaho Press*, March 30, 2020, www.idahopress.com/eyeonboise/governor-signs-both-hb-500-and-hb-509-the-anti-transgender-bills/article_5daaf33d-4dcb-5457-a160-fb8f34f124fb.html.

192 Moreton, "The U.S. Christians Who Pray for Putin."

193 Hadley Malcolm, "More than 700,000 Pledge to Boycott Target over Transgender Bathroom Policy," *USA Today*, April 25, 2016, www.usatoday.com/story/money/2016/04/25/conservative-christian-group-boycotting-target-transgender-bathroom-policy/83491396/.

194 Imara Jones, "It's Not Really About Sports," June 14, 2021, *The Anti-Trans Hate Machine: A Plot Against Equality*, produced by TransLash Media, https://translash.org/antitranshatemachine/.

195 See Bruce D. Skaug et al., "Memorandum in Support of Motion to Intervene," *Hecox v. Little*, May 26, 2020, www.aclu.org/cases/hecox-v-little?document=Alliance-Defending-Freedom-Motion-to-Intervene; Nathan Brown, "Group That Helped Craft Trans Sports Ban Seeks to Join Court Case," *Idaho Press*, May 26, 2020, www.idahopress.com/news/local/group-that-helped-craft-trans-sports-ban-seeks-to-join-court-case/article_7d077cc4-59b7-5838-82f8-bc9714de53f1.html. Skaug also partnered with the ADF in the 2009 case *Cordova v. Laliberte*, arguing that discriminatory Christian student groups should receive student funding like other groups. The Supreme Court ruled against Christian student groups in *Christian Legal Society v. Martinez* (2010), a decision that was opposed at the time by justices Alito, Roberts, Scalia, and Thomas.

196 Allan C. Carlson, *Conjugal America: On the Public Purposes of Marriage* (New Brunswick: Transaction, 2007), 2.

197 Carlson, *Conjugal America*, 9, 12.

198 Carlson, *Conjugal America*, 17, 15.

199 Voddie T. Baucham, *Fault Lines: The Social Justice Movement and Evangelicalism's Looming Catastrophe* (Washington: Salem Books, 2021), 92.

200 Judith N. Shklar, *After Utopia: The Decline of Political Faith*, New ed. (Princeton: Princeton University Press, 2020; original ed., 1957), 65.

201 Christopher Dawson, *Religion and the Modern State* (London: Sheed & Ward, 1935), 58; Shklar, *After Utopia*, 207–8.

202 Shklar, *After Utopia*, 210.

203 Shklar, *After Utopia*, 210, 207.

204 Shklar, *After Utopia*, 176.

205 Shklar, *After Utopia*, 211.

206 See Sohrab Ahmari, *The Unbroken Thread: Discovering the Wisdom of Tradition in an Age of Chaos* (New York: Convergent, 2021), esp. 227–45. Ahmari has an extended discussion

of Hans Jonas, who studied gnosticism as a student of Martin Heidegger and Rudolf Bultmann.

207 Shklar, *After Utopia*, 212.

208 Emil Edenborg, "Anti-Gender Politics as Discourse Coalitions: Russia's Domestic and International Promotion of 'Traditional Values,'" *Problems of Post-Communism* (2021): 1–10, at 2.

209 Maarten Hajer, "Doing Discourse Analysis: Coalitions, Practices, Meanings," in *Words Matter in Policy and Planning: Discourse Theory and Method in the Social Sciences*, ed. Margo van den Brink and Tamara Metze (Utrecht: Netherlands Graduate School of Urban and Regional Research, 2006), 65–74, at 70.

210 Edenborg, "Anti-Gender Politics as Discourse Coalitions," 3–4.

211 Maarten Hajer, "Discourse Coalitions and the Institutionalization of Practice: The Case of Acid Rain in Great Britain," in *The Argumentative Turn in Policy Analysis and Planning*, ed. Frank Fischer and John Forester (Durham: Duke University Press, 1993), 51–84, at 56.

212 There are many such pieces, including Ethan Richardson, "The New Gnosticism of the Transhumanists," *Mockingbird*, June 13, 2017, https://mbird.com/religion/the-new-gnosticism-of-the-transhumanists/; Paul Tyson, "Virtual Gnosticism and the Church – Some Disturbing Thoughts about Covid19," *Theopolis*, June 16, 2020, https://theopolisinstitute.com/virtual-gnosticism-and-the-church-some-disturbing-thoughts-about-covid19/.

213 Sohrab Ahmari, "Against David French-ism," *First Things*, May 29, 2019, www.firstthings.com/web-exclusives/2019/05/against-david-french-ism.

214 Stroop, "Bad Ecumenism," 20.

Chapter 5

1 Samuel Loncar, "Are Evangelicals the New Liberals?," *Marginalia*, December 9, 2014, https://marginalia.lareviewofbooks.org/evangelicals-new-liberals/. The two books reviewed by Loncar were: David A. Hollinger, *After Cloven Tongues of Fire: Protestant Liberalism in Modern American History* (Princeton: Princeton University Press, 2013); Molly Worthen, *Apostles of Reason: The Crisis of Authority in American Evangelicalism* (New York: Oxford University Press, 2014).

2 See Diana Butler Bass, "New Old-Time Religion," *The Cottage*, April 7, 2022, https://dianabutlerbass.substack.com/p/new-old-time-religion.

3 My thanks to James F. Kay for highlighting this point in conversation with me.

4 Anthea Butler touches on this when she points out that "evangelicals live in silos to keep themselves pure," though I would add that purity does not have to be separatist. It can also take an imperialist form, in which one seeks to *purify* the society. This is what has happened as evangelicals, or their allies, have assumed positions of political power, as seen since George W. Bush took office and in a more aggressive way since Donald Trump. See Anthea D. Butler, *White Evangelical Racism: The Politics of Morality in America* (Chapel Hill: University of North Carolina Press, 2021), 144.

5 A lesson that evangelical critics of Kristin Kobes Du Mez seem not to have learned.

6 Robert G. Flood, *America: God Shed His Grace on Thee* (Chicago: Moody Press, 1975), 6.

7 Mark A. Noll, Nathan O. Hatch, and George M. Marsden, *The Search for Christian America* (Westchester: Crossway Books, 1983), 13, 15.

8 David Bentley Hart, *Tradition and Apocalypse: An Essay on the Future of Christian Belief* (Grand Rapids: Baker Academic, 2022), 3.

9 Exec. Order No. 13958, 3 C.F.R. 471 (2020). Subsequent EO quotes refer to this source.

10 See Nikole Hannah-Jones et al., eds., *The 1619 Project: A New Origin Story* (New York: One World, 2021).

11 Jared A. Goldstein, *Real Americans: National Identity, Violence, and the Constitution* (Lawrence: University Press of Kansas, 2021), 3.

12 In Lincoln's case, that is more complicated, since he was until late in his life still committed to white supremacy in the sense that he was unconvinced free white and Black Americans could live together. Moreover, he waged war not to combat white supremacy but to combat white treason and maintain the Union. Nevertheless, the war was a threat to key institutions of white supremacy, namely, slavery and states' rights.

13 Individual Freedom Act, Fla. CS for HB 7 (2022), 7; Fla. Stat. § 760.10 (1992), amended by Act effective July 1, 2022, ch. 2022-72.

14 Required Instruction Planning and Reporting, Fla. Admin. Code R. 6A-1.094124 (2021).

15 *Dobbs v. Jackson Women's Health Organization*, 597 U.S. ___ (2022), at 25.

16 *Dobbs v. Jackson Women's Health Organization*, at 17.

17 Lauren MacIvor Thompson points out the hypocrisy of Justice Alito using history as an authority while simultaneously dismissing the work of actual historians. She highlights the legal practice of only using whatever evidence supports your argument and ignoring opposing evidence, a practice that is normative in law but anathema in historical research. See Lauren MacIvor Thompson, "Held: Legal Authority and the Abuse of History," *Perspectives on History*, March 16, 2023, www.historians.org/research-and-publications/perspectives-on-history/april-2023/held-legal-authority-and-the-abuse-of-history.

18 Svetlana Boym, *The Future of Nostalgia* (New York: Basic Books, 2001), 41.

19 Judith Lieu, *Christian Identity in the Jewish and Graeco-Roman World* (Oxford: Oxford University Press, 2004), 62, 299.

20 David S. Yeago, "The New Testament and the Nicene Dogma: A Contribution to the Recovery of Theological Exegesis," *Pro Ecclesia* 3, no. 2 (1994): 152–64, at 160.

21 Yeago, "The New Testament and the Nicene Dogma." 159.

22 Jordan P. Barrett, "Biblical Judgments and Theological Concepts: Toward a Defence of Imputed Righteousness," *Scottish Bulletin of Evangelical Theology* 32, no. 2 (2014): 152–69, at 164–67.

23 Kevin J. Vanhoozer, "Augustinian Inerrancy: Literary Meaning, Literal Truth, and Literate Interpretation in the Economy of Biblical Discourse," in *Five Views on Biblical Inerrancy*, ed. J. Merrick and Stephen M. Garrett (Grand Rapids: Zondervan, 2013), 199–235, at 212–13. See also Kevin J. Vanhoozer, *The Drama of Doctrine: A Canonical-Linguistic Approach to Christian Theology* (Louisville: Westminster John Knox Press, 2005), 344.

24 Paula Fredriksen, "How High Can Early High Christology Be?," in *Monotheism and Christology in Greco-Roman Antiquity*, ed. Matthew V. Novenson (Leiden: Brill, 2020), 293–319, at 303–4.

25 Paula Fredriksen, "Philo, Herod, Paul, and the Many Gods of Ancient Jewish 'Monotheism,'" *Harvard Theological Review* 115, no. 1 (2022): 23–45, at 29.

26 Fredriksen, "How High Can Early High Christology Be?," 294–95.

27 Fredriksen, "How High Can Early High Christology Be?," 316.

28 Hart, *Tradition and Apocalypse*, 134.

29 J. R. Daniel Kirk, *A Man Attested by God: The Human Jesus of the Synoptic Gospels* (Grand Rapids: Eerdmans, 2016), 4.

30 Fredriksen, "How High Can Early High Christology Be?," 317. On Christologies in the second century, see James L. Papandrea, *The Earliest Christologies: Five Images of Christ in the Postapostolic Age* (Downers Grove: IVP Academic, 2016).

31 Hart, *Tradition and Apocalypse*, 31.

32 Robert W. Jenson, *Unbaptized God: The Basic Flaw in Ecumenical Theology* (Minneapolis: Fortress Press, 1992), 138. See the analysis in John G. Flett, *Apostolicity: The Ecumenical Question in World Christian Perspective* (Downers Grove: IVP Academic, 2016), 103–37.

33 N. T. Wright, *History and Eschatology: Jesus and the Promise of Natural Theology* (Waco, Texas: Baylor University Press, 2019), 74–75, 100.

34 Fredriksen, "How High Can Early High Christology Be?," 318.

35 For an incisive critique of the racist white social imaginary embedded in talk of the "Christian worldview," see Jacob Alan Cook, *Worldview Theory, Whiteness, and the Future of Evangelical Faith* (Lanham: Lexington Books/Fortress Academic, 2021).

36 David S. Yeago, "Modern but Not Liberal," *First Things*, June 2012, 25–30.

37 Terry Eagleton, *The Idea of Culture* (Oxford: Blackwell, 2000), 34.

38 Kathryn Tanner, *Theories of Culture: A New Agenda for Theology* (Minneapolis: Fortress, 1997), 114.

39 Tanner, *Theories of Culture*, 152.

40 See R. W. L. Moberly, "Theological Interpretation, Presuppositions, and the Role of the Church: Bultmann and Augustine Revisited," *Journal of Theological Interpretation* 6, no. 1 (2012): 1–22; David W. Congdon, "Kerygma and Community: A Response to R. W. L. Moberly's Revisiting of Bultmann," *Journal of Theological Interpretation* 8, no. 1 (2014): 1–21; R. W. L. Moberly, "Bible and Church, Bultmann and Augustine: A Response to David Congdon," *Journal of Theological Interpretation* 9, no. 1 (2015): 39–48; David W. Congdon, "The Nature of the Church in Theological Interpretation: Culture, *Volk*, and Mission," *Journal of Theological Interpretation* 11, no. 1 (2017): 101–17; R. W. L. Moberly, "The Significance of the Church for Theological Interpretation: A Response to David Congdon," *Journal of Theological Interpretation* 12, no. 2 (2018): 274–86.

41 *Answer to the Letter of Mani Known as The Foundation*, 5.6, in Augustine, *The Manichean Debate*, The Works of Saint Augustine I/19 (Hyde Park: New City Press, 2005), 236–37.

42 My earlier analysis lacked clarity, which led to some confusion on Moberly's part. In his summary of my argument, he writes: "The church as norm is the problem. This is the

notion that the church is to be identified as a 'distinct culture.'" On the contrary, there is nothing inherently problematic about the church being a norm, because it all depends on what we mean by the church – which was the point of my 2017 article. Understanding the church as a culture is one of three norms I described in that piece: culture, *Volk*, and eschatological community. Evidently, Moberly wishes to have his position associated with the church-as-context idea, claiming that the church "gives content to" scripture merely by showing "what faith and faithfulness look like in practice." He asks "why does church-as-plausibility-structure become church-as-norm?" See Moberly, "Significance of the Church," 278–80. I want to give Moberly a charitable reading here, and based on his further responses it seems that his position comes down to something like this: *People interpret and use the Bible because they have been socially formed by the church, therefore theologians ought to make the church's role in the practice of biblical interpretation explicit.* The first part of the sentence expresses the idea of the church as context. It is not entirely unproblematic, but for the sake of argument I accept that Moberly and I agree on this. I will admit the second half is not stated as such, but it is strongly implied. He criticizes Bultmann for not giving the church an explicit and central place in his hermeneutics. In the conclusion to his 2012 article, he says that Bultmann's "unconcern [about the church] should surely no longer be an option when the frames of reference for life and thought have become both plural and sharply contested" (Moberly, "Theological Interpretation," 21). In other words, because of cultural pluralism, it is necessary for Christians to name the church's role in biblical interpretation. But Moberly's normative argument – as indicated by the "should" – goes well beyond this. He says that Bible and theology "need to be publicly embodied, and that embodiment must primarily be in and through the life of the church in its many forms." He further says that studying the Bible at a "secular university" is only appropriate if "the church plays a significant public role within the wider society where the university is located" (Moberly, "Theological Interpretation," 21–22). Moberly not only advocates making the church normative in interpretation; he wants the church to be normative in society as well. Moberly calls my reading "infelicitous," but his position, read charitably, seems to me even more problematic than I previously made it out to be.

43 Moberly, "Significance of the Church," 279.

44 On plausibility structure, see Peter L. Berger and Thomas Luckmann, *The Social Construction of Reality: A Treatise in the Sociology of Knowledge* (Garden City: Doubleday, 1966). On "cultural world," see Peter L. Berger, *The Sacred Canopy: Elements of a Sociological Theory of Religion* (Garden City: Doubleday, 1967), 10, 45. For social imaginary, see Charles Taylor, *Modern Social Imaginaries* (Durham: Duke University Press, 2004).

45 Berger and Luckmann, *Social Construction of Reality,* 158.

46 Moberly recognizes the importance of mission to my analysis ("Congdon's own concern explicitly and repeatedly relates to mission and the church's missionary calling"), but he seems to think that by "mission" I am referring to the evangelistic activity of the church, as evidenced by the fact that in his final response to me he contrasts mission (which he views as a practical matter) with epistemology, which he says is his main concern.

He fails to recognize that mission as I understand it encompasses epistemology and pertains to the very practice of interpretation itself. Further compounding the problem, Moberly points to his use of the missiologist Lesslie Newbigin – "an on-the-ground practitioner of Christian mission" – as proof that his approach is fruitful for mission and wonders why I avoid engaging him. My respect for Newbigin does not necessarily mean I agree with him, and in this case, I do not. I chose not to engage Moberly's use of Newbigin because it was a distraction from the central problem (viz., how we understand norms). See Moberly, "Significance of the Church," 281.

47 Elana Schor, "Christianity on Display at Capitol Riot Sparks New Debate," *Associated Press*, January 28, 2021. See Luke Winkie, "What Those Animal Pelts Tell Us About the Future of the Far Right," *The Atlantic*, January 12, 2021, www.theatlantic.com/culture/archive/2021/01/why-capitol-rioters-wore-animal-pelts/617639/; Luke Mogelson, "A Reporter's Footage from Inside the Capitol Siege," *The New Yorker*, January 17, 2021, https://youtu.be/270F8s5TEKY; Jack Jenkins, "How Christian Nationalism Paved the Way for Jan. 6," *Religion News Service*, June 9, 2022, https://religionnews.com/2022/06/09/how-christian-nationalism-paved-the-way-for-january-6/; Jack Jenkins, "The Insurrectionists' Senate Floor Prayer Highlights a Curious Trumpian Ecumenism," *Religion News Service*, February 25, 2021, https://religionnews.com/2021/02/25/the-insurrectionists-senate-floor-prayer-highlights-a-curious-trumpian-ecumenism/.

48 Katelyn Beaty, "QAnon: The Alternative Religion That's Coming to Your Church," *Religion News Service*, August 17, 2020, https://religionnews.com/2020/08/17/qanon-the-alternative-religion-thats-coming-to-your-church/; Jack Jenkins, "More Than a Quarter of White Evangelicals Believe Core QAnon Conspiracy Theory," *Religion News Service*, February 11, 2021, https://religionnews.com/2021/02/11/survey-more-than-a-quarter-of-white-evangelicals-believe-core-qanon-conspiracy-theory/; Jack Jenkins, "QAnon Draws from Several Faith Groups, Numbers More than 40 Million," *Religion News Service*, February 24, 2022, https://religionnews.com/2022/02/24/study-qanon-draws-from-several-faith-groups-numbers-more-than-40-million/.

49 Philip S. Gorski and Samuel Perry, "Practices of Relation: Gorski and Perry," *The Immanent Frame*, April 2, 2020, https://tif.ssrc.org/2020/04/02/gorski-and-perry/; John Blake, "An 'Imposter Christianity' Is Threatening American Democracy," *CNN*, July 24, 2022, www.cnn.com/2022/07/24/us/white-christian-nationalism-blake-cec/index.html; Kristin Kobes Du Mez, "Is White Christian Nationalism 'Imposter Christianity'?," *Du Mez CONNECTIONS*, July 25, 2022, https://kristindumez.substack.com/p/is-white-christian-nationalism-imposter; Annika Brockschmidt (@ardenthistorian), "Happy to see CNN discovering White Christian nationalism," Twitter, July 24, 2022, 4:35 p.m., https://twitter.com/ardenthistorian/status/1551320070961434626.

50 Chrissy Stroop, "About Those Trump Voters for God? Stop Calling them 'Fake Christians,'" *Not Your Mission Field*, May 3, 2017, https://cstroop.com/2017/05/03/about-those-trump-voters-for-god-stop-calling-them-fake-christians/.

51 For a more complete version of this argument, see Congdon, "Nature of the Church in Theological Interpretation," 101–17. In my earlier work, I compared the postliberal church-as-culture with the German Christian church-as-*Volk* by arguing that both

conflate theological norm and cultural context but in different directions: the postliberals impose their norm on their context (assimilating elements from other cultures into the church), while the German Christians impose their context on their norm (turning the church into an extension of German culture). While there is some truth to this, I am unsatisfied with this account because it suggests that the postliberal norm (i.e., their concept of church tradition) is not already culturally shaped by racial, national, and political factors. The postliberal concept of church is thoroughly Euro-American and should be analyzed as such.

52 As stated in the original 1920 National Socialist Party platform: "Das 25-Punkte-Programm der Nationalsozialistischen Deutschen Arbeiterpartei," Feburary 24, 1920, no. 4.

53 Robert L. Wilken, "The Church as Culture," *First Things* 142 (2004): 31–36.

54 R. R. Reno, "Series Preface," in Jaroslav Pelikan, *Acts* (Grand Rapids: Brazos Press, 2005), 14.

55 Robert W. Jenson, "Christ as Culture 1: Christ as Polity," *International Journal of Systematic Theology* 5, no. 3 (2003): 323–29, at 323–24, 328. On his antiabortion position, see Robert W. Jenson, "A Theological Autobiography, to Date," *Dialog: A Journal of Theology* 46, no. 1 (2007): 46–54.

56 In the case of Jenson's argument that "Christian culture" is actually "Jewish culture," it is even worse than colorblind: it is a supersessionist version of Christian history that openly appropriates Jewish identity (including Jewish suffering and marginalization) for the purpose of bolstering a whitewashed Eurocentric Christianity.

57 Among the many writings on this topic, see Barbara J. Flagg, *Was Blind, But Now I See: White Race Consciousness and the Law* (New York: New York University Press, 1998). Peggy McIntosh's 1989 article, "White Privilege: Unpacking the Invisible Knapsack," is often credited with being one of the first articulations of this phenomenon.

58 R. R. Reno, *Return of the Strong Gods: Nationalism, Populism, and the Future of the West* (Washington: Regnery Gateway, 2019).

59 Vanhoozer, *Drama of Doctrine*, 26.

60 On the way theological interpretation of scripture maintains white supremacy in biblical and theological studies, see J. R. Daniel Kirk, "Theological Interpretation and White Hegemony in the Biblical Studies Academy" (paper presented at the Society of Biblical Literature, Boston, November 18, 2017). On Christofascism, see Dorothee Sölle, "Christofascism," in *The Window of Vulnerability: A Political Spirituality* (Minneapolis: Fortress Press, 1990), 133–41. Given the way traditionalist, antimodern Christianity has so thoroughly defined "true Christianity" in terms of opposition to modernity, it is probable that adherents will see any movement that claims also to oppose modernity in the name of Christ, even if it is openly racist and nationalist, as compatible with Christian faith.

61 Michel-Rolph Trouillot, *Silencing the Past: Power and the Production of History* (Boston: Beacon Press, 1995), 96–97.

62 Readers may notice some parallels here between normativization and Michel Foucault's concept of normalization, which refers to the way modern disciplinary society uses

tactics of control to impose greater homogeneity upon a population. One could argue that normativization, as I have defined it, is an exercise of power over the past that parallels the exercise of biopower over bodies in the present that Foucault describes as normalization. See Michel Foucault, *Discipline and Punish: The Birth of the Prison* (New York: Pantheon Books, 1977). Mark G. E. Kelly argues for Foucault's "non-normative" position against other theorists who retain some account of normative theory. My own work here falls somewhere between Foucault and what Kelly describes as Deleuze's "denormativization as norm." See Mark G. E. Kelly, *For Foucault: Against Normative Political Theory* (Albany: State University of New York Press, 2017).

63 This is the difference between prescriptivism and orthodoxy. Prescriptivism merely affirms the need for norms to guide one's beliefs and actions. Orthodoxy declares that one set of norms are binding for all people of a particular identity across all times and places. This is why orthodoxy is not just a set of "right beliefs"; it is the notion that there is a set of beliefs that places a person in the present in continuity with the original Christian community.

64 Fredriksen, "How High Can Early High Christology Be?," 319.

65 Staf Hellemans, "Religious Orthodoxy as a Modality of 'Adaptation,'" in *Orthodoxy, Liberalism, and Adaptation: Essays on Ways of Worldmaking in Times of Change from Biblical, Historical and Systematic Perspectives*, ed. Bob Becking (Leiden: Brill, 2011), 9–32, at 12.

66 The dominant historical paradigm remains the classic work by Walter Bauer, *Orthodoxy and Heresy in Earliest Christianity*, ed. Robert A. Kraft and Gerhard Krodel (Philadelphia: Fortress Press, 1971; German original, 1934), though the historical details have since been revised by subsequent scholarship. As Virginia Burrus points out, Bauer successfully challenged the Eusebian storyline, but his reconstruction of Christian history failed "to escape the constraints of the very categories he so astutely criticized." Virginia Burrus, "History, Theology, Orthodoxy, Polydoxy," *Modern Theology* 30, no. 3 (2014): 7–16, at 7.

67 Harvey Whitehouse refers to this as the "causal opacity" of ritual. The lack of instrumental function (i.e., their mysteriousness and strangeness) is precisely what makes them so effective at defining group identity. When ritual becomes institutionalized and standardized, it leads to what Whitehouse calls the "doctrinal mode" of religiosity. See Harvey Whitehouse, *The Ritual Animal: Imitation and Cohesion in the Evolution of Social Complexity* (Oxford: Oxford University Press, 2021), 28–36, 40–46, 55–58.

68 This was further reinforced by the doctrine of total depravity and the resulting belief in the epistemic effects of sin: the notion that our minds are inescapably clouded by sin, and thus we cannot trust our natural observations and intuitive perceptions.

69 Darrin W. Snyder Belousek, *Marriage, Scripture, and the Church: Theological Discernment on the Question of Same-Sex Union* (Grand Rapids: Baker Academic, 2021), 13.

70 J. B. Heard observes with respect to Vincent's rule: "Tried by these three tests of constancy, ubiquity, universality, in all three directions Augustine was the innovator, and Pelagius of the two was the one who, in the opinion of the whole East, stood in the old ways." John Bickford Heard, *Alexandrian and Carthaginian Theology Contrasted* (Edinburgh: T. & T. Clark, 1893), 122.

71 Thomas Croskery, "Conversions to Romanism," *The Presbyterian Review* 6, no. 22 (1885): 201–25, at 210.

72 Andrew Chignell, "Whither Wheaton?," *SoMA*, January 13, 2010; Beth McMurtrie, "Do Professors Lose Academic Freedom by Signing Statements of Faith?," *Chronicle of Higher Education*, May 24, 2002, www.chronicle.com/article/do-professors-lose-academic-free dom-by-signing-statements-of-faith/; Catrin Einhorn, "At College, a High Standard on Divorce," *New York Times*, May 4, 2008, A26; Ruth Graham, "Acts of Faith," *New York Times Magazine*, October 16, 2016, 48–53, 60–61. Peter Enns points out that the Hawkins affair is also connected to evolution, and one of the explicit points raised against her by Wheaton's provost concerned her understanding of human origins. Peter Enns, "Wheaton College vs. Larycia Hawkins: Maybe It's About Evolution (It's ALWAYS Evolution)," *Pete Enns*, January 18, 2016, https://peteenns.com/wheaton-college-vs-lar ycia-hawkins-maybe-its-about-evolution-its-always-evolution/.

73 A. Duane Litfin, *Conceiving the Christian College* (Grand Rapids: Eerdmans, 2004), 14–15, 18.

74 Chignell, "Whither Wheaton?"

75 Wheaton College, "Statement of Faith," *Wheaton.edu*, www.wheaton.edu/about-whea ton/statement-of-faith-and-educational-purpose/.

76 Joshua Hochschild, "Once Upon a Presidency," *The American Mind*, February 19, 2021, https://americanmind.org/salvo/once-upon-a-presidency/. Subsequently, there was a petition among students at Mount St. Mary's University calling for him to resign. Bruce Leshan, "Students Call on Mt. St. Mary's University Professor to Resign After He Wrote about Attending Protest that Led to Uprising at Capitol," *WUSA9*, February 25, 2021, www.wusa9.com/article/news/national/capitol-riots/students-at-mt-st-marys-uni versity-want-joshua-hochschild-resign-over-capitol-uprising-rally/65-51388010-2e5b-4456-a037-9660f3de6b2b.

77 Alan Jacobs, "To Be a Christian College," *First Things*, April 2006, 17–20.

78 Chignell, "Whither Wheaton?"

79 John Henry Newman, *An Essay on the Development of Christian Doctrine* (London: James Toovey, 1845), 117. See the discussion of this in Chapter 2.

80 Ruth Graham reported: "One home-schooling mother of seven left an indignant message for [Leah] Anderson, Hawkins's department chairwoman, saying the family made great sacrifices to send their daughter to Wheaton, and they expected her to receive a Christian worldview there. December is a month in which many donors make significant end-of-year gifts and when high-school seniors are making their final deci sions about where to apply to college. Jones would later describe the response from prospective students' parents as a 'tidal wave'; at the time the post appeared, he characterized the financial threat as one that would imperil 15 to 20 faculty jobs" (Graham, "Acts of Faith," 53).

81 I know this from experience as the former acquisitions editor for several books written by Wheaton College faculty.

82 As Chignell pointed out in a letter to me, "I know that they [i.e., Wheaton College], like many small colleges and regional universities, are struggling to recruit enough students

to keep their budgets intact, and are even downsizing departments and releasing tenured faculty. . . . I suppose that given the financial situation, the College might feel the need to shore up its image among serious evangelicals so that they will continue to send their kids to the school. That could reduce ideological diversity even as they have become appropriately concerned over the past decade to increase the racial and class diversity of the faculty and student body." Andrew Chignell, email message to author, March 20, 2023.

83 *Hosanna-Tabor Evangelical Lutheran Church and School v. EEOC*, 565 U.S. 171 (2012); *Our Lady of Guadalupe School v. Morrissey-Berru*, 591 U.S. ___ (2020).

84 David Gushee, "What the Larycia Hawkins Case Means for Evangelical Colleges," *Religion News Service*, January 8, 2016, https://religionnews.com/2016/01/08/what-the-larycia-hawkins-case-means-for-evangelical-colleges-commentary/.

85 David Gibson, "Evangelical Wheaton College Joins Suits against Obama Contraception Mandate," *Religion News Service*, July 18, 2012, https://religionnews.com/2012/07/18/evangelical-wheaton-college-joins-suits-against-obama-contraception-mandate/.

86 See Adam H. Domby, *The False Cause: Fraud, Fabrication, and White Supremacy in Confederate Memory* (Charlottesville: University of Virginia Press, 2020).

87 Steven Nemes points out that "judgments of heresy presuppose a commitment to a prior orthodoxy." Put another way, "an idea is 'orthodox' or 'heretical' only relative to other ideas the 'orthodoxy' or 'canonicity' of which is taken for granted." Steven Nemes, *Orthodoxy and Heresy*, Elements in the Problems of God (Cambridge: Cambridge University Press, 2022), 7, 50.

88 John B. Davis, "The Turn in Recent Economics and Return of Orthodoxy," *Cambridge Journal of Economics* 32, no. 3 (2007): 349–66, at 352.

89 Kate Manne, *Down Girl: The Logic of Misogyny* (New York: Oxford University Press, 2018), 63.

90 See Aaron Griffith, "'Policing Is a Profession of the Heart': Evangelicalism and Modern American Policing," *Religions* 12, no. 3 (2021): 1–18.

91 Stephen Holmes, *The Anatomy of Antiliberalism* (Cambridge: Harvard University Press, 1993), 5.

92 Stephen Holmes, "The Antiliberal Idea," in *Routledge Handbook of Illiberalism*, ed. András Sajó, Renáta Uitz, and Stephen Holmes (New York: Routledge, 2022), 3–15, at 3.

93 Gladden Pappin, "Contemporary Christian Criticism of Liberalism," in *Routledge Handbook of Illiberalism*, ed. András Sajó, Renáta Uitz, and Stephen Holmes (New York: Routledge, 2022), 43–59, at 56–57.

94 It is no accident that Robert Bork (1927–2012), the conservative jurist who popularized the theory of originalism, argued that originalism or "original understanding" of the Constitution is "the American orthodoxy," which is "anathema to a liberal culture" that "hate[s] the American orthodoxy" and embraces the "heresy" of a living constitutionalism that allows judges to depart from original understanding. Robert H. Bork, *The Tempting of America: The Political Seduction of the Law* (New York: Simon & Schuster, 1991), 6–7.

95 Hellemans, "Religious Orthodoxy as a Modality," 10.

96 Hellemans, "Religious Orthodoxy as a Modality," 16.

97 Barth does this in each of his efforts at dogmatic (or systematic) theology, but especially in Karl Barth, *The Göttingen Dogmatics: Instruction in the Christian Religion*, ed. Hannelotte Reiffen, trans. Geoffrey W. Bromiley, vol. 1 (Grand Rapids: Eerdmans, 1991), §11, 273–74. Bultmann makes this argument in his posthumously published lectures in theology, translated as Rudolf Bultmann, *What Is Theology?*, trans. Roy A. Harrisville (Minneapolis: Fortress, 1997), §6, 45–49.

98 See, e.g., *CD* 1.2:239; 4.3:655.

99 *CD* 1.1:309.

100 Karl Barth, *Protestant Theology in the Nineteenth Century: Its Background and History*, trans. Brian Cozens and John Bowden (Grand Rapids: Eerdmans, 2002), 2–3.

Conclusion

1 These are all real examples I saw on Twitter.

2 "Between the Christianity of this land, and the Christianity of Christ, I recognize the widest possible difference – so wide, that to receive the one as good, pure, and holy, is of necessity to reject the other as bad, corrupt, and wicked. . . . Indeed, I can see no reason, but the most deceitful one, for calling the religion of this land Christianity." Frederick Douglass, *Autobiographies*, The Library of America 68 (New York: Library of America, 1994), 97.

3 Alvin J. Reines, *Polydoxy: Explorations in a Philosophy of Liberal Religion* (Buffalo: Prometheus Books, 1987), 81. Reines identifies Orthodox Judaism as the version of Judaism that was dominant before the nineteenth century. On this point, more recent historical scholarship has nuanced that picture. Adam S. Ferziger argues that Orthodox Judaism is as much a product of the Jewish Enlightenment and the nineteenth century as Reform Judaism. See Adam S. Ferziger, *Exclusion and Hierarchy: Orthodoxy, Nonobservance, and the Emergence of Modern Jewish Identity* (Philadelphia: University of Pennsylvania Press, 2005). Though there are some important differences, Ferziger's argument is similar to the one I am making in this book with respect to conservative, traditionalist Christianity.

4 Reines, *Polydoxy*, 13.

5 Reines, *Polydoxy*, 121.

6 Reines, *Polydoxy*, 25.

7 Reines, *Polydoxy*, 42.

8 Reines, *Polydoxy*, 26.

9 Reines, *Polydoxy*, 23–24.

10 Reines, *Polydoxy*, 34.

11 Reines, *Polydoxy*, 35–40. Reines is more dismissive of natural liberal religions than I think is warranted. While it is certainly true that some of those communities are exclusive of more traditional religious beliefs, on the whole I think they tend to be de facto polydoxies. The same is true for many liberal Protestant communities, but only

on a local case-by-case basis. I belonged for several years to an Episcopal church that was and is a de facto polydoxy, but there were other Episcopal churches nearby that functioned instead with a strong orthodoxy.

12 Reines, *Polydoxy*, 41. It makes more sense to me to define as "dogma" any belief that infringes on one's religious autonomy, and for this reason I would not call the belief in religious autonomy itself a dogma but rather a norm.

13 Reines, *Polydoxy*, 108.

14 In my earlier work I proposed the idea of "orthoheterodoxy," which is a paradoxical concept that unites orthodoxy and heterodoxy and means "thinking differently in the right way." The proposal was to encourage a creative plurality of theological views. In an effort to preserve both normativity and difference, I suggested "that difference is *internal* to the norm of the gospel." I still think this concept is quite valuable. Polydoxy captures everything that orthoheterodoxy was trying to articulate but without the confusion that potentially arose from keeping the "ortho" (i.e., thinking "in the right way"). Communities that are looking to transition out of orthodoxy but are not yet ready for polydoxy might find the idea of orthoheterodoxy more useful. See David W. Congdon, *The God Who Saves: A Dogmatic Sketch* (Eugene: Cascade Books, 2016), 57.

15 Marcella Althaus-Reid, *The Queer God* (London: Routledge, 2003), 128–29. Linn Tonstad calls "polyfidelity" the "theological method of polydoxy." Linn Marie Tonstad, "The Logic of Origin and the Paradoxes of Language: A Theological Experiment," *Modern Theology* 30, no. 3 (2014): 50–73, at 54n6.

16 Peter Berger distinguishes between "intrinsic packages" and "extrinsic packages." The former "is one that cannot be taken apart if a particular action is to succeed," while the latter "is one that can be taken apart and re-assembled in a different way, without the action failing." So the norm of the Freedom Covenant is the intrinsic package for polydoxy, while the norms of various polydox theologies are extrinsic packages. Peter L. Berger, *The Many Altars of Modernity: Toward a Paradigm for Religion in a Pluralist Age* (Boston: De Gruyter, 2014), 73–74.

17 Virginia Burrus, writing in response to the Catherine Keller and Laurel C. Schneider volume on *Polydoxy* (see below), raises the question whether "polydoxy's advocates may find themselves … having not so much deconstructed the discourse of orthodoxy as inverted it, thereby making a heresy of orthodoxy and instating polydoxy as … well, yet another orthodoxy announcing the triumph over false belief – or rather, in this case, the triumph over the falseness of belief as such." Virginia Burrus, "History, Theology, Orthodoxy, Polydoxy," *Modern Theology* 30, no. 3 (2014): 7–16, at 15. Burrus's point only applies if orthodoxy and polydoxy are distinct theological categories with a stable set of norms, principles, doctrines, and practices. In that case, replacing one with the other would maintain the same logic of orthodoxy, merely infused with new content. This is why any polydox theology has to occur within the formal framework set by polydox religion, which does not set up a new orthodoxy because pluralism does not police doctrinal boundaries and thus allows people to retain the doctrines associated with traditional orthodoxy.

18 Gary Pence, "Constructing a Christian Polydoxy," *Dialog: A Journal of Theology* 40, no. 4 (2001): 264–69, at 268.

19 The shift in the meaning of polydoxy explains why Reines's structural polydoxy is clearly set in contrast to orthodoxy, both terms referring to modes of authority and power dynamics, whereas polydoxy in the Keller and Schneider volume is not set in contrast to orthodoxy – or at least only in an ambiguous way. Shannon Craigo-Snell examines this issue in detail, arguing that "orthodoxy – even repressive, normative, Christian boundary-making – is also multiple," and thus multiplicity cannot serve as a means of distinguishing polydoxy from orthodoxy. See Shannon Craigo-Snell, "Tradition on Fire: Polydoxy, Orthodoxy, and Theological Epistemology," *Modern Theology* 30, no. 3 (2014): 17–33, at 30. This is why theological polydoxy must be linked with structural polydoxy.

20 Catherine Keller, "Be a Multiplicity: Ancestral Anticipations," in *Polydoxy: Theology of Multiplicity and Relation*, ed. Catherine Keller and Laurel C. Schneider (New York: Routledge, 2011), 81–101, at 94. Burrus's essay, referenced above, questions whether the volume sets up polydoxy as a new orthodoxy, which points to the need for placing polydox theology within the context of polydox religion. Linn Tonstad points out (the irony?) that "in a polydox Christian theology that values multiplicity, the God of whom theology speaks takes trinitarian form." Tonstad, "Logic of Origin and the Paradoxes of Language," 54. The introduction to the 2011 volume opens by saying that "a discernible movement within theology has emerged around a triune intuition," suggesting that polydoxy is rooted in the concept of God as triune. Catherine Keller's chapter grounds polydoxy "in a surprisingly orthodox origin," in the "trinitarian logic" of divine relationality. John Thatamanil's chapter even speaks of "trinitarian polydoxy." To be sure, as Colleen Hartung points out, "theology does not have to assume a God or divinity to be theological," so the use of trinitarian language is rooted less in confirming orthodoxy than in finding the concept of trinity to be socially and politically useful, something Tonstad critiques as continuing unwittingly "to serve hierarchies of gender and sexuality" (55). See Catherine Keller and Laurel C. Schneider, "Introduction," in *Polydoxy: Theology of Multiplicity and Relation*, ed. Catherine Keller and Laurel C. Schneider (New York: Routledge, 2011), 1–15, at 1; John J. Thatamanil, "God as Ground, Contingency, and Relation: Trinitarian Polydoxy and Religious Diversity," in *Polydoxy: Theology of Multiplicity and Relation*, ed. Catherine Keller and Laurel C. Schneider (New York: Routledge, 2011), 238–57; Colleen Hartung, "Faith and Polydoxy in the Whirlwind," in *Polydoxy: Theology of Multiplicity and Relation*, ed. Catherine Keller and Laurel C. Schneider (New York: Routledge, 2011), 151–64, at 153.

21 Reines, *Polydoxy*, 161–63.

22 Keller, "Be a Multiplicity," 82, 87.

23 Keller, "Be a Multiplicity," 95.

24 This first norm naturally encourages a close dialogue between religion and science. Catherine Keller and Mary-Jane Rubenstein coedited a volume on this topic based on another Transdisciplinary Theological Colloquium. See Catherine Keller and Mary-Jane Rubenstein, eds., *Entangled Worlds: Religion, Science, and New Materialisms* (New York: Fordham University Press, 2017). The chapters in this volume reflect the new materialist presupposition not only that public, empirical data provide the source material for (re)thinking the theological, but also that the empirical world is itself a messy

multiplicity always already entangled with the metaphysical and the political. Rubenstein furthers this approach to theology in her recent work on the multiverse, which conceptually bridges scientific speculations about quantum mechanics and theological investigations into multiplicity. See Mary-Jane Rubenstein, *Worlds without End: The Many Lives of the Multiverse* (New York: Columbia University Press, 2014). The work of others from the colloquium, especially Karen Barad, Beatrice Marovich, and Theodore Walker Jr., is relevant to the kind of polydox theology I am sketching here.

25 Whitney Bauman, "Theological Topographies: Multiple Methods for Planetary Theologies," *Theology* 116, no. 1 (2013): 18–22, at 20.

26 The literature associated with polydox theology in the constructive sense of the term that Keller and Schneider develop – along with others connected to the colloquium, such as Marion Grau, Mayra Rivera, Mary-Jane Rubenstein, and John J. Thatamanil – is of course much broader and richer than I am able to examine here. It is also beyond the scope of my inquiry. Polydoxy as I define it, drawing primarily on Reines, is first and foremost a formal, institutional account of religion that articulates the framework within which theologies can develop and flourish. These theologies do not need to be polydox theologies in the Keller and Schneider sense of the term, so long as they respect each person's religious autonomy, but their approach to polydox theology is an account that has much to commend itself and offers one of the most viable ways forward for theology beyond orthodoxy.

27 On the relation between theological and constitutional conservatism, scholars have observed the similarities and differences between originalism and biblical literalism, though much of this literature is written by legal experts who are not well-versed in the intricacies of biblical interpretation. The most important text on this topic is the law review article by Peter J. Smith and Robert W. Tuttle, "Biblical Literalism and Constitutional Originalism," *Notre Dame Law Review* 86, no. 2 (2011): 693–763. Smith and Tuttle point out a number of the obvious similarities, but their attempt to describe the differences falls flat. For instance, they claim that literalism stems from the belief that the Bible is the word of God, whereas originalism "naturally follows" whenever "the authority of the text is assumed," which could be any document (761). But the distinction between a supposedly divine origin and a human origin is banal and irrelevant; the issue is precisely the assumption of authority and how we are supposed to interpret authoritative texts. Smith and Tuttle also argue that biblical literalism assumes the text is morally good and right, whereas "originalism requires fidelity to the text regardless of – indeed, at times even in spite of – the moral character of its provisions." This, too, is only a superficial distinction. Many biblical literalists similarly believe we should read the Bible literally regardless of whether we morally agree with the provisions. Smith and Tuttle's analysis only works with a very rough understanding of how the Bible is read and understood. In the end, the comparison with biblical literalism is largely unhelpful. It would be more fruitful to compare it with the broader category of biblicism, or even the historical-grammatical method. In an apologetic piece, Elizabeth-Jane McGuire and Steven F. McGuire argue that originalism is more like the latter method, which they call "authentic biblical interpretation," an indication of both the bias and lack of hermeneutical sophistication that pervades this conversation. Elizabeth-Jane McGuire and

Steven F. McGuire, "Originalism Isn't the Judicial Version of Biblical Fundamentalism," *Church Life Journal*, October 12, 2020, https://churchlifejournal.nd.edu/articles/origin alism-isnt-the-judicial-version-of-biblical-fundamentalism/.

28 Even if they were a group of saintly exemplars of the human race, it would change nothing about the argument, but it surely does not help that the Constitution was composed by a group of white settler colonialists who enslaved Africans and supported Indigenous genocide.

29 Louis Michael Seidman, *On Constitutional Disobedience* (Oxford: Oxford University Press, 2012), 26, 7.

30 Seidman, *On Constitutional Disobedience*, 7.

31 Thomas Jefferson to James Madison, September 6, 1789, in Thomas Jefferson, *The Papers of Thomas Jefferson*, ed. Julian P. Boyd et al., 44 vols. (Princeton: Princeton University Press, 1950–2019), 15:396. For an extended reflection on Jefferson's idea, see Beau Breslin, *A Constitution for the Living: Imagining How Five Generations of Americans Would Rewrite the Nation's Fundamental Law* (Stanford: Stanford University Press, 2021).

32 Seidman, *On Constitutional Disobedience*, 30.

33 Seidman, *On Constitutional Disobedience*, 58–59.

34 G. K. Chesterton, *Orthodoxy* (New York: Dodd, Mead and Co., 1908), 85.

35 Seidman, *On Constitutional Disobedience*, 57.

36 See Terence Ball, "'The Earth Belongs to the Living': Thomas Jefferson and the Problem of Intergenerational Relations," *Environmental Politics* 9, no. 2 (2000): 61–77.

37 David Bentley Hart argues that tradition ought to be defined by the eschatological future – its final cause – rather than the past, and for that reason we have to remain open to any doctrinal possibility: "If Christian tradition is truly a living thing, it is a spiritual reality, and the Spirit breathes where it will." David Bentley Hart, *Tradition and Apocalypse: An Essay on the Future of Christian Belief* (Grand Rapids: Baker Academic, 2022), 130.

38 Ernst Troeltsch, "The Significance of the Historical Existence of Jesus for Faith (1911)," in *Writings on Theology and Religion*, ed. Robert Morgan and Michael Pye (Atlanta: John Knox Press, 1977), 182–207, at 189. Translation slightly revised.

39 Ernst Troeltsch, "What Does 'Essence of Christianity' Mean? [1903]," in *Writings on Theology and Religion*, ed. Robert Morgan and Michael Pye (Atlanta: John Knox Press, 1977), 124–81, at 147. See Sarah Coakley, *Christ Without Absolutes: A Study of the Christology of Ernst Troeltsch* (Oxford, NY: Oxford University Press, 1988), 164–87.

40 Ernst Troeltsch, "The Dogmatics of the 'Religionsgeschichtliche Schule,'" *The American Journal of Theology* 17, no. 1 (1913): 1–21, at 12–13.

41 Rudolf Bultmann, "Theology as Science [1941]," in *New Testament and Mythology and Other Basic Writings*, ed. and trans. Schubert M. Ogden (Philadelphia: Fortress, 1984), 45–67, at 59–60; translation revised.

42 Seidman, *On Constitutional Disobedience*, 60–61.

43 Hart, *Tradition and Apocalypse*, 137.

44 Clayton Crockett coined the term "polyhairesis" to refer to the heretical nature of polydoxy. See Clayton Crockett, "Polyhairesis: On Postmodern and Chinese Folds," *Modern Theology* 30, no. 3 (2014): 34–49.

45 According to Steven Nemes, *hairesis* "refers to a collection of persons who have chosen for themselves a particular way of living and of thinking about things." Steven Nemes, *Orthodoxy and Heresy*, Elements in the Problems of God (Cambridge: Cambridge University Press, 2022), 2.

46 Peter L. Berger, *The Heretical Imperative: Contemporary Possibilities of Religious Affirmation* (Garden City: Anchor Press, 1979). Berger uses Karl Barth, Rudolf Bultmann, and Friedrich Schleiermacher to chart three possible responses to modernity. His reading of these figures, especially Barth and Bultmann, reflects the distorted way they were received in Anglo-American theological studies. He associates Barth with neoorthodoxy's reaffirmation of the tradition and Bultmann with an excessively reductionistic capitulation to modernity, neither of which is an accurate reading of those theologians, though they represent the way postliberals in the late twentieth century framed the theological options.

47 Seidman, *On Constitutional Disobedience*, 9.

48 It is the wrong question in multiple senses. While it is beyond the scope of this book, Christian theology should follow Seidman also in viewing the Bible and the creeds more like works of art that give us an inspiring vocabulary for describing faith today: "It makes sense to talk about obeying the law, but no sense to talk about obeying a symphony or a painting" (Seidman, *On Constitutional Disobedience*, 8).

49 Nemes, *Orthodoxy and Heresy*, 54–57. My own project goes beyond what Nemes proposes in his vision of "theology without anathemas," but our projects share a common critique of the "catholic" tradition, with its appeals to "inaccessible" truth that justifies "creating a privileged class of interpreters" (50–52).

50 John J. Thatamanil, *Circling the Elephant: A Comparative Theology of Religious Diversity* (New York: Fordham University Press, 2020), 254. Thatamanil takes the term "relational pluralism" from the work of Roland Faber and Catherine Keller. See Roland Faber and Catherine Keller, "A Taste for Multiplicity: The Skillfull Means of Religious Pluralism," in *Religions in the Making: Whitehead and the Wisdom Traditions of the World*, ed. John B. Cobb (Eugene: Cascade Books, 2012), 180–207. I demur from Thatamanil only in the process trinitarian argument he advances as a way of grounding different traditions in a single metaphysical or ultimate reality, albeit one marked by divine multiplicity. I remain agnostic on the metaphysical question and generally favor the apophatic approach of Faber and Keller, though I deeply appreciate Thatamanil's ethical, interreligious, and comparative approach to the topic.

51 James Baldwin, "Everybody's Protest Novel," in *The Price of the Ticket: Collected Nonfiction, 1948–1985* (Boston: Beacon Press, 2021), 38–45, at 41–42.

52 Baldwin, "Everybody's Protest Novel," 44–45.

53 Baldwin, "Everybody's Protest Novel," 42.

Select Bibliography

Althaus-Reid, Marcella. *The Queer God.* London: Routledge, 2003.

Assel, Heinrich. *Der andere Aufbruch: Die Lutherrenaissance – Ursprünge, Aporien und Wege.* Göttingen: Vandenhoeck & Ruprecht, 1994.

Barr, James. *The Semantics of Biblical Language.* London: Oxford University Press, 1961.

Barth, Karl. *The Epistle to the Romans.* Translated by Edwyn C. Hoskyns. London: Oxford University Press, 1933. Reprint, 1968.

    The Göttingen Dogmatics: Instruction in the Christian Religion. Vol. 1. Edited by Hannelotte Reiffen. Translated by Geoffrey W. Bromiley. Grand Rapids: Eerdmans, 1991.

    The Word of God and the Word of Man. Translated by Douglas Horton. London: Hodder and Stoughton, 1928.

Barth, Karl, and Eduard Thurneysen. *Briefwechsel, Band II: 1921–1930.* Edited by Eduard Thurneysen. Gesamtausgabe 4. Zürich: TVZ, 1974.

Bauer, Walter. *Orthodoxy and Heresy in Earliest Christianity.* Edited by Robert A. Kraft and Gerhard Krodel. Philadelphia: Fortress Press, 1971. German original, 1934.

Beardsley, Christina. "Taking Issue: The Transsexual Hiatus in *Some Issues in Human Sexuality.*" *Theology* 108, no. 845 (2005): 338–46.

Bebbington, David W. *Evangelicalism in Modern Britain: A History from the 1730s to the 1980s.* London: Unwin Hyman, 1989.

Bennett, Daniel. *Defending Faith: The Politics of the Christian Conservative Legal Movement.* Lawrence: University Press of Kansas, 2017.

Berger, Peter L. "The Desecularization of the World: A Global Overview." In *The Desecularization of the World: Resurgent Religion and World Politics,* edited by Peter L. Berger, 1–18. Grand Rapids: Eerdmans, 1999.

    The Heretical Imperative: Contemporary Possibilities of Religious Affirmation. Garden City: Anchor Press, 1979.

The Sacred Canopy: Elements of a Sociological Theory of Religion. Garden City: Doubleday, 1967.

Berger, Peter L., and Thomas Luckmann. *The Social Construction of Reality: A Treatise in the Sociology of Knowledge*. Garden City: Doubleday, 1966.

Bork, Robert H. *The Tempting of America: The Political Seduction of the Law*. New York: Simon & Schuster, 1991.

Boston Industrial Mission Task Force. "The Boston Affirmations." *Worldview* 19, no. 3 (1976): 45–47.

Bowman, Matthew. *Christian: The Politics of a Word in America*. Cambridge, MA: Harvard University Press, 2018.

Boym, Svetlana. *The Future of Nostalgia*. New York: Basic Books, 2001.

Bruner, Jason. *Imagining Persecution: Why American Christians Believe There Is a Global War against Their Faith*. New Brunswick: Rutgers University Press, 2021.

Bultmann, Rudolf. "Bericht über unsere Amerika-Reise 1951." In *Bultmann–Bornkamm Briefwechsel 1926–1976*, edited by Werner Zager, 222–55. Tübingen: Mohr Siebeck, 2014.

Briefwechsel mit Götz Harbsmeier und Ernst Wolf, 1933–1976. Edited by Werner Zager. Tübingen: Mohr Siebeck, 2017.

History and Eschatology: The Gifford Lectures 1955. Edinburgh: Edinburgh University Press, 1957.

New Testament and Mythology and Other Basic Writings. Edited by Schubert M. Ogden. Philadelphia: Fortress, 1984.

"The Problem of a Theological Exegesis of the New Testament [1925]." In *The Beginnings of Dialectic Theology*, edited by James M. Robinson, 236–56. Richmond: John Knox Press, 1968.

Theology of the New Testament. Translated by Kendrick Grobel. 2 vols. New York: Charles Scribner's Sons, 1951–55.

Burrus, Virginia. "History, Theology, Orthodoxy, Polydoxy." *Modern Theology* 30, no. 3 (2014): 7–16.

Butler, Anthea D. *White Evangelical Racism: The Politics of Morality in America*. Chapel Hill: University of North Carolina Press, 2021.

Cesari, Jocelyne. *We God's People: Christianity, Islam and Hinduism in the World of Nations*. Cambridge: Cambridge University Press, 2021.

Chignell, Andrew. "Whither Wheaton?" *SoMA*, January 13, 2010.

Coakley, Sarah. *Christ without Absolutes: A Study of the Christology of Ernst Troeltsch*. Oxford, NY: Oxford University Press, 1988.

Coffman, Elesha J. "The Chicago Call and Responses." In *Evangelicals and the Early Church: Recovery, Reform, Renewal*, edited by George Kalantzis and Andrew Tooley, 108–24. Eugene: Cascade Books, 2012.

The Christian Century and the Rise of the Protestant Mainline. New York: Oxford University Press, 2013.

Cook, Jacob Alan. *Worldview Theory, Whiteness, and the Future of Evangelical Faith.* Lanham: Lexington Books/Fortress Academic, 2021.

Cox, Harvey, John C. Bennett, Gabriel Moran, and Gregory Baum. "The Hartford Appeal: A Symposium." *Worldview* 18, no. 5 (1975): 22–27.

Crockett, Clayton. "Polyhairesis: On Postmodern and Chinese Folds." *Modern Theology* 30, no. 3 (2014): 34–49.

Daston, Lorraine. *Rules: A Short History of What We Live By.* Princeton: Princeton University Press, 2022.

Drake, H. A. *Constantine and the Bishops: The Politics of Intolerance.* Baltimore: Johns Hopkins University Press, 2000.

Du Mez, Kristin Kobes. *Jesus and John Wayne: How White Evangelicals Corrupted a Faith and Fractured a Nation.* New York: Liveright, 2020.

Eagleton, Terry. *The Idea of Culture.* Oxford: Blackwell, 2000.

Edwards, Mark Thomas. *The Right of the Protestant Left: God's Totalitarianism.* New York: Palgrave Macmillan, 2012.

Fasolt, Constantin. *The Limits of History.* Chicago: University of Chicago Press, 2004.

Fawcett, Edmund. *Conservatism: The Fight for a Tradition.* Princeton: Princeton University Press, 2020.

Ferguson, Everett. *The Rule of Faith: A Guide.* Eugene: Cascade Books, 2015.

Fredriksen, Paula. "How High Can Early High Christology Be?" In *Monotheism and Christology in Greco-Roman Antiquity*, edited by Matthew V. Novenson, 293–319. Leiden: Brill, 2020.

Frei, Hans W. "The Doctrine of Revelation in the Thought of Karl Barth, 1909 to 1922: The Nature of Barth's Break with Liberalism." PhD diss., Yale University, 1956.

   The Eclipse of Biblical Narrative: A Study in Eighteenth and Nineteenth Century Hermeneutics. New Haven: Yale University Press, 1974.

   "Response to 'Narrative Theology: An Evangelical Appraisal.'" *Trinity Journal* 8, no. 1 (1987): 21–24.

   Theology and Narrative: Selected Essays, edited by George Hunsinger and William C. Placher. New York: Oxford University Press, 1993.

Gerbner, Katharine. *Christian Slavery: Conversion and Race in the Protestant Atlantic World.* Philadelphia: University of Pennsylvania Press, 2018.

Gin Lum, Kathryn. *Heathen: Religion and Race in American History.* Cambridge, MA: Harvard University Press, 2022.

Gloege, Timothy. *Guaranteed Pure: The Moody Bible Institute, Business, and the Making of Modern Evangelicalism.* Chapel Hill: University of North Carolina Press, 2015.

"#ItsNotUs: Being Evangelical Means Never Having to Say You're Sorry." *Religion Dispatches*, January 3, 2018, https://religiondispatches.org/itsnotus-being-evangelical-means-never-having-to-say-youre-sorry/.

Goldstein, Jared A. *Real Americans: National Identity, Violence, and the Constitution.* Lawrence: University Press of Kansas, 2021.

Gorski, Philip S., and Samuel L. Perry. *The Flag and the Cross: White Christian Nationalism and the Threat to American Democracy.* New York: Oxford University Press, 2022.

Greif, Avner. *Institutions and the Path to the Modern Economy: Lessons from Medieval Trade.* Cambridge: Cambridge University Press, 2006.

Hajer, Maarten. "Discourse Coalitions and the Institutionalization of Practice: The Case of Acid Rain in Great Britain." In *The Argumentative Turn in Policy Analysis and Planning,* edited by Frank Fischer and John Forester, 51–84. Durham: Duke University Press, 1993.

"Doing Discourse Analysis: Coalitions, Practices, Meanings." In *Words Matter in Policy and Planning: Discourse Theory and Method in the Social Sciences,* edited by Margo van den Brink and Tamara Metze, 65–74. Utrecht: Netherlands Graduate School of Urban and Regional Research, 2006.

Harlow, Luke E. *Religion, Race, and the Making of Confederate Kentucky, 1830–1880.* New York: Cambridge University Press, 2014.

Harrison, Peter. *"Religion" and the Religions in the English Enlightenment.* Cambridge: Cambridge University Press, 1990.

Hart, David Bentley. *Tradition and Apocalypse: An Essay on the Future of Christian Belief.* Grand Rapids: Baker Academic, 2022.

Hellemans, Staf. "Religious Orthodoxy as a Modality of 'Adaptation.'" In *Orthodoxy, Liberalism, and Adaptation: Essays on Ways of Worldmaking in Times of Change from Biblical, Historical and Systematic Perspectives,* edited by Bob Becking, 9–32. Leiden: Brill, 2011.

Helmer, Christine. *How Luther Became the Reformer.* Louisville: Westminster John Knox Press, 2019.

Helmer, Christine, and Bo Kristian Holm, eds. *Lutherrenaissance Past and Present.* Göttingen: Vandenhoeck & Ruprecht, 2015.

Herzog, Jonathan P. *The Spiritual-Industrial Complex: America's Religious Battle against Communism in the Early Cold War.* New York: Oxford University Press, 2011.

Hollinger, David A. *After Cloven Tongues of Fire: Protestant Liberalism in Modern American History.* Princeton: Princeton University Press, 2013.

Christianity's American Fate: How Religion Became More Conservative and Society More Secular. Princeton: Princeton University Press, 2022.

Protestants Abroad: How Missionaries Tried to Change the World but Changed America. Princeton: Princeton University Press, 2017.

Holmes, Stephen. *The Anatomy of Antiliberalism.* Cambridge, MA: Harvard University Press, 1993.

"The Antiliberal Idea." In *Routledge Handbook of Illiberalism*, edited by András Sajó, Renáta Uitz, and Stephen Holmes, 3–15. New York: Routledge, 2022.

Horrell, David G. *Ethnicity and Inclusion: Religion, Race, and Whiteness in Constructions of Jewish and Christian Identities.* Grand Rapids: Eerdmans, 2020.

Isherwood, Lisa, and Dirk von der Horst. "Normativity and Transgression." In *Contemporary Theological Approaches to Sexuality*, edited by Lisa Isherwood and Dirk von der Horst, 3–21. London: Routledge, 2017.

Izenberg, Gerald. *Identity: The Necessity of a Modern Idea.* Philadelphia: University of Pennsylvania Press, 2016.

Jennings, Willie James. *The Christian Imagination: Theology and the Origins of Race.* New Haven: Yale University Press, 2010.

Johnson, Robert Clyde. *Authority in Protestant Theology.* Philadelphia: Westminster Press, 1959.

Joshi, Khyati Y. *White Christian Privilege: The Illusion of Religious Equality in America.* New York: New York University Press, 2020.

Kaoma, Kapya. *Globalizing the Culture Wars: U.S. Conservatives, African Churches, and Homophobia.* Somerville: Political Research Associates, 2009.

Keller, Catherine, and Laurel C. Schneider, eds. *Polydoxy: Theology of Multiplicity and Relation.* New York: Routledge, 2011.

Keller, Catherine, and Mary-Jane Rubenstein, eds. *Entangled Worlds: Religion, Science, and New Materialisms.* New York: Fordham University Press, 2017.

Kelly, Patricia, ed. *Ressourcement Theology: A Sourcebook.* London: T&T Clark, 2020.

Kelsey, David H. *The Uses of Scripture in Recent Theology.* Philadelphia: Fortress, 1975.

Kidd, Thomas S. *Who Is an Evangelical? The History of a Movement in Crisis.* New Haven: Yale University Press, 2019.

King, Karen L. *What Is Gnosticism?* Cambridge, MA: Belknap Press of Harvard University Press, 2003.

Kirk, J. R. Daniel. *A Man Attested by God: The Human Jesus of the Synoptic Gospels.* Grand Rapids: Eerdmans, 2016.

"Theological Interpretation and White Hegemony in the Biblical Studies Academy." Paper presented at Society of Biblical Literature. Boston, November 18, 2017.

Kuehn, Evan. "Liberalism's Interest in Theology." *Marginalia*, December 17, 2021, https://themarginaliareview.com/liberalisms-interest-in-theology/.

Lee, Philip J. *Against the Protestant Gnostics*. New York: Oxford University Press, 1987.

Lieu, Judith. *Christian Identity in the Jewish and Graeco-Roman World*. Oxford: Oxford University Press, 2004.

Lincoln, Bruce. "Theses on Method." *Method & Theory in the Study of Religion* 8, no. 3 (1996): 225–27.

Lindbeck, George A. "Atonement and the Hermeneutics of Intratextual Social Embodiment." In *The Nature of Confession: Evangelicals and Postliberals in Conversation*, edited by Timothy R. Phillips and Dennis L. Okholm, 221–40. Downers Grove: InterVarsity, 1996.

  "The Gospel's Uniqueness: Election and Untranslatability." *Modern Theology* 13, no. 4 (1997): 423–50.

  The Nature of Doctrine: Religion and Theology in a Postliberal Age. Philadelphia: Westminster Press, 1984.

Locke, John. *An Essay Concerning Human Understanding*. Edited by Peter H. Nidditch. The Clarendon Edition of the Works of John Locke. Oxford: Clarendon Press, 1975.

  John Locke: Writings on Religion. Edited by Victor Nuovo. New York: Oxford University Press, 2002.

  The Reasonableness of Christianity: As Delivered in the Scriptures. Edited by John C. Higgins-Biddle. The Clarendon Edition of the Works of John Locke. Oxford: Clarendon Press, 1999.

Loncar, Samuel. "Are Evangelicals the New Liberals?" *Marginalia*, December 9, 2014, https://marginalia.lareviewofbooks.org/evangelicals-new-liberals/.

Manne, Kate. *Down Girl: The Logic of Misogyny*. New York: Oxford University Press, 2018.

Marsden, George M. *Reforming Fundamentalism: Fuller Seminary and the New Evangelicalism*. Grand Rapids: Eerdmans, 1987.

Marty, Martin E. *Dietrich Bonhoeffer's Letters and Papers from Prison: A Biography*. Princeton: Princeton University Press, 2011.

Mason, Lilliana. *Uncivil Agreement: How Politics Became Our Identity*. Chicago: University of Chicago Press, 2018.

McArthur, Marcus J. "Treason in the Pulpit: Disloyal Clergy in Civil War Missouri." PhD diss., Saint Louis University, 2012.

McVicar, Michael J. *Christian Reconstruction: R. J. Rushdoony and American Religious Conservatism*. Chapel Hill: The University of North Carolina Press, 2015.

Monahan, Michael J. *The Creolizing Subject: Race, Reason, and the Politics of Purity*. New York: Fordham University Press, 2011.

Moreton, Bethany. "The U.S. Christians Who Pray for Putin." *Boston Review*, March 11, 2022, https://bostonreview.net/articles/the-u-s-christians-who-pray-for-putin/.

Moss, Candida R. *The Myth of Persecution: How Early Christians Invented a Story of Martyrdom*. New York: HarperOne, 2013.

Murison, Justine S. *The Politics of Anxiety in Nineteenth-Century American Literature*. Cambridge: Cambridge University Press, 2011.

Naugle, David K. *Worldview: The History of a Concept*. Grand Rapids: Eerdmans, 2002.

Nemes, Steven. *Orthodoxy and Heresy*. Elements in the Problems of God. Cambridge: Cambridge University Press, 2022.

Newman, John Henry. *An Essay on the Development of Christian Doctrine*. New ed. London: B. M. Pickering, 1878. Orig. ed., London: James Toovey, 1845.

Niebuhr, H. Richard. *Christ and Culture*. 50th Anniversary ed. New York: HarperOne, 2001.

Noll, Mark A. *The Civil War as a Theological Crisis*. Chapel Hill: University of North Carolina Press, 2006.

Noll, Mark A., David Bebbington, and George M. Marsden, eds. *Evangelicals: Who They Have Been, Are Now, and Could Be*. Grand Rapids: Eerdmans, 2019.

Noll, Mark A., Nathan O. Hatch, and George M. Marsden. *The Search for Christian America*. Westchester: Crossway Books, 1983.

Pappin, Gladden. "Contemporary Christian Criticism of Liberalism." In *Routledge Handbook of Illiberalism*, edited by András Sajó, Renáta Uitz, and Stephen Holmes, 43–59. New York: Routledge, 2022.

Pence, Gary. "Constructing a Christian Polydoxy." *Dialog: A Journal of Theology* 40, no. 4 (2001): 264–69.

Polk, Andrew R. *Faith in Freedom: Propaganda, Presidential Politics, and the Making of an American Religion*. Ithaca: Cornell University Press, 2021.

Porter, Stanley E. "Was James Barr Wrong? Assessing His Critics on Biblical Theology." In *James Barr Assessed: Evaluating His Legacy over the Last Sixty Years*, edited by Stanley E. Porter, 257–77. Leiden: Brill, 2021.

Preston, Andrew. "Evangelical Internationalism: A Conservative Worldview for the Age of Globalization." In *The Right Side of the Sixties: Reexamining Conservatism's Decade of Transformation*, edited by Laura Jane Gifford and Daniel K. Williams, 221–41. New York: Palgrave Macmillan, 2012.

Reines, Alvin J. *Polydoxy: Explorations in a Philosophy of Liberal Religion*. Buffalo: Prometheus Books, 1987.

Robertson, David G. *Gnosticism and the History of Religions*. New York: Bloomsbury Academic, 2021.

Robinson, John A. T. *Honest to God.* London: SCM Press, 1963.

Rolsky, L. Benjamin. "Producing the Christian Right: Conservative Evangelicalism, Representation, and the Recent Religious Past." *Religions* 12, no. 3 (2021): 1–17.

Rose, Matthew. *A World after Liberalism: Philosophers of the Radical Right.* New Haven: Yale University Press, 2021.

Rubenstein, Mary-Jane. *Worlds without End: The Many Lives of the Multiverse.* New York: Columbia University Press, 2014.

Sands, Kathleen M. *America's Religious Wars: The Embattled Heart of Our Public Life.* New Haven: Yale University Press, 2019.

Schäfer, Rolf. "Welchen Sinn hat es, nach einem Wesen des Christentums zu suchen?" *Zeitschrift für Theologie und Kirche* 65, no. 3 (1968): 329–47.

Schleiermacher, Friedrich. *Christian Faith: A New Translation and Critical Edition.* Translated by Terrence N. Tice, Catherine L. Kelsey, and Edwina G. Lawler. Louisville: Westminster John Knox, 2016.

  On Religion: Speeches to Its Cultured Despisers. Cambridge: Cambridge University Press, 1996.

Seidman, Louis Michael. *On Constitutional Disobedience.* Oxford: Oxford University Press, 2012.

Shagan, Ethan H. *The Birth of Modern Belief: Faith and Judgment from the Middle Ages to the Enlightenment.* Princeton: Princeton University Press, 2018.

Shishkov, Andrey. "Two Ecumenisms: Conservative Christian Alliances as a New Form of Ecumenical Cooperation." *State, Religion and Church* 4, no. 2 (2017): 58–87.

Shklar, Judith N. *After Utopia: The Decline of Political Faith.* New ed. Princeton: Princeton University Press, 2020. Orig. ed., 1957.

Shortall, Sarah. *Soldiers of God in a Secular World: Catholic Theology and Twentieth-Century French Politics.* Cambridge, MA: Harvard University Press, 2021.

Silliman, Daniel. "An Evangelical Is Anyone Who Likes Billy Graham: Defining Evangelicalism with Carl Henry and Networks of Trust." *Church History* 90 (2021): 621–43.

Sölle, Dorothee. "Christofascism." In *The Window of Vulnerability: A Political Spirituality,* 133–41. Minneapolis: Fortress Press, 1990.

Springs, Jason A. *Toward a Generous Orthodoxy: Prospects for Hans Frei's Postliberal Theology.* Oxford: Oxford University Press, 2010.

Steinmetz, David C. "The Superiority of Pre-Critical Exegesis." *Theology Today* 37, no. 1 (1980): 27–38.

Stendahl, Krister. "Biblical Theology, Contemporary." In *The Interpreter's Dictionary of the Bible,* edited by George A. Buttrick, 1:418–32. Nashville: Abingdon, 1962.

Stoeckl, Kristina. "The Rise of the Russian Christian Right: The Case of the World Congress of Families." *Religion, State & Society* 48, no. 4 (2020): 223–38.

Stroop, Chrissy. "About Those Trump Voters for God? Stop Calling them 'Fake Christians.'" *Not Your Mission Field*, May 3, 2017, https://cstroop .com/2017/05/03/about-those-trump-voters-for-god-stop-calling-them-fake-christians/.

"Bad Ecumenism: The American Culture Wars and Russia's Hard Right Turn." *The Wheel* 6 (Summer 2016): 20–24.

"Stop Trying to Save Jesus: 'Fandamentalism' Reinforces the Problem of Christian Supremacism." *Religion Dispatches*, January 29, 2021, https:// religiondispatches.org/stop-trying-to-save-jesus-fandamentalism-reinforces-the-problem-of-christian-supremacism/.

Sullivan, Winnifred Fallers. *The Impossibility of Religious Freedom*. Princeton: Princeton University Press, 2005.

Sutton, Matthew Avery. *American Apocalypse: A History of Modern Evangelicalism*. Cambridge, MA: Harvard University Press, 2014.

Swartz, David R. *Moral Minority: The Evangelical Left in an Age of Conservatism*. Philadelphia: University of Pennsylvania Press, 2012.

Sweet, Leonard I. "Wise as Serpents, Innocent as Doves: The New Evangelical Historiography." *Journal of the American Academy of Religion* 56, no. 3 (1988): 397–416.

Sykes, Stephen. *The Identity of Christianity: Theologians and the Essence of Christianity from Schleiermacher to Barth*. Philadelphia: Fortress Press, 1984.

Tanner, Kathryn. *Theories of Culture: A New Agenda for Theology*. Minneapolis: Fortress, 1997.

Taylor, Charles. *Modern Social Imaginaries*. Durham: Duke University Press, 2004.

A Secular Age. Cambridge, MA: Belknap Press of Harvard University Press, 2007.

Sources of the Self: The Making of the Modern Identity. Cambridge, MA: Harvard University Press, 1989.

Teter, Magda. *Christian Supremacy: Reckoning with the Roots of Antisemitism and Racism*. Princeton: Princeton University Press, 2023.

Thandeka. *The Embodied Self: Friedrich Schleiermacher's Solution to Kant's Problem of the Empirical Self*. Albany: State University of New York Press, 1995.

Thatamanil, John J. *Circling the Elephant: A Comparative Theology of Religious Diversity*. New York: Fordham University Press, 2020.

"God as Ground, Contingency, and Relation: Trinitarian Polydoxy and Religious Diversity." In *Polydoxy: Theology of Multiplicity and Relation*, edited by Catherine Keller and Laurel C. Schneider, 238–57. New York: Routledge, 2011.

Tonstad, Linn Marie. "The Logic of Origin and the Paradoxes of Language: A Theological Experiment." *Modern Theology* 30, no. 3 (2014): 50–73.

Troeltsch, Ernst. "The Dogmatics of the 'Religionsgeschichtliche Schule.'" *The American Journal of Theology* 17, no. 1 (1913): 1–21.

Protestantism and Progress: The Significance of Protestantism for the Rise of the Modern World. Philadelphia: Fortress Press, 1986.

"What Does 'Essence of Christianity' Mean? [1903]." In *Writings on Theology and Religion*, edited by Robert Morgan and Michael Pye, 124–81. Atlanta: John Knox Press, 1977.

Trouillot, Michel-Rolph. *Silencing the Past: Power and the Production of History*. Boston: Beacon Press, 1995.

Turek, Lauren Frances. *To Bring the Good News to All Nations: Evangelical Influence on Human Rights and U.S. Foreign Relations*. Ithaca: Cornell University Press, 2020.

Tyrrell, Ian R. *Reforming the World: The Creation of America's Moral Empire*. Princeton: Princeton University Press, 2010.

Voskuil, Dennis N. "American Protestant Neo-Orthodoxy and Its Search for Realism (1925–1939)." *Ultimate Reality and Meaning* 8, no. 4 (1985): 277–87.

Wagenhammer, Hans. *Das Wesen des Christentums: Eine begriffsgeschichtliche Untersuchung*. Mainz: Matthias-Grünewald-Verlag, 1973.

Walls, Andrew F. *The Missionary Movement in Christian History: Studies in the Transmission of Faith*. Maryknoll: Orbis, 1996.

Webber, Robert, and Donald G. Bloesch, eds. *The Orthodox Evangelicals: Who They Are and What They Are Saying*. Nashville: Thomas Nelson, 1978.

Whitehouse, Harvey. *The Ritual Animal: Imitation and Cohesion in the Evolution of Social Complexity*. Oxford: Oxford University Press, 2021.

Wilcox, Clyde. *God's Warriors: The Christian Right in Twentieth-Century America*. Baltimore: Johns Hopkins University Press, 1992.

Williams, Daniel K. *God's Own Party: The Making of the Christian Right*. Oxford: Oxford University Press, 2010.

Williams, Michael A. *Rethinking "Gnosticism": An Argument for Dismantling a Dubious Category*. Princeton: Princeton University Press, 1996.

Wilson, Charles Reagan. *Baptized in Blood: The Religion of the Lost Cause, 1865–1920*. New ed. Athens: University of Georgia Press, 2009.

Worthen, Molly. *Apostles of Reason: The Crisis of Authority in American Evangelicalism*. New York: Oxford University Press, 2014.

Yeago, David S. "The New Testament and the Nicene Dogma: A Contribution to the Recovery of Theological Exegesis." *Pro Ecclesia* 3, no. 2 (1994): 152–64.

Young, Neil J. *We Gather Together: The Religious Right and the Problem of Interfaith Politics*. New York: Oxford University Press, 2016.

Young, Stephen L. "'Let's Take the Text Seriously': The Protectionist Doxa of Mainstream New Testament Studies." *Method and Theory in the Study of Religion* 32 (2020): 328–63.

"Protective Strategies and the Prestige of the 'Academic': A Religious Studies and Practice Theory Redescription of Evangelical Inerrantist Scholarship." *Biblical Interpretation* 23 (2015): 1–35.

Zubovich, Gene. *Before the Religious Right: Liberal Protestants, Human Rights, and the Polarization of the United States.* Philadelphia: University of Pennsylvania Press, 2022.

Zurlo, Gina A. "'A Miracle from Nairobi': David B. Barrett and the Quantification of World Christianity, 1957–1982." PhD diss., Boston University, 2017.

Index